HARVARD STUDIES IN EAST ASIAN LAW

1. *Law in Imperial China: Exemplified by 190 Ch'ing Dynasty Cases (translated from the* Hsing-an hui-lan) *with Historical, Social, and Juridical Commentaries.* By Derk Bodde and Clarence Morris. 1967

2. *The Criminal Process in the People's Republic of China, 1949-1963: An Introduction.* By Jerome Alan Cohen. 1968

3. *Agreements of the People's Republic of China, 1949-1967: A Calendar.* By Douglas M. Johnston and Hungdah Chiu. 1968

HARVARD STUDIES IN EAST ASIAN LAW, 3

Agreements of the People's Republic of China 1949-1967: A Calendar

Agreements of the People's Republic of China 1949-1967 A Calendar

by Douglas M. Johnston

and Hungdah Chiu

Harvard University Press

Cambridge, Massachusetts

1968

Distributed in Great Britain by Oxford University Press, London
Library of Congress Catalog Card Number 68-28694
Printed in the United States of America

Foreword

With the publication of this volume Harvard Studies in East Asian Law enters a new field. The first volume in the series, *Law in Imperial China,* by Derk Bodde and Clarence Morris, offered a comprehensive introduction to the judicial processes and case law of the Ch'ing dynasty. In the series' second volume, *The Criminal Process in the People's Republic of China, 1949-1963,* I sought to provide an overview of the administration of criminal justice as it has evolved under Chinese Communist rule. Professors Johnston and Chiu now open up a third area of study—that of China and international law.

Incredible as it may seem, despite the fact that almost two decades have passed since Mao Tse-tung swept to power over the entire mainland of China, the study of Chinese Communist attitudes and practices in the field of international law has only just begun. Yet the record available for study is substantial, for, unlike contemporary China's domestic law, which has virtually disappeared from sight in recent years, its international legal conduct cannot be insulated from foreign scrutiny. How substantial this record is has been suggested by the compilers of this Calendar, who, with admirable industry and scholarship, have catalogued some two thousand agreements made by the People's Republic since 1949. They have thereby greatly facilitated the tasks of specialists in Chinese affairs, in international politics, and in international law, who, one can confidently predict, will become increasingly interested in analyzing the treaty-making activities of the Peking regime.

This Calendar is only the first of a number of volumes relating to China and international law that will appear in this series during the next few years. Work on the Calendar was supported by funds provided to the Harvard Law School under a research contract with the Arms Control and Disarmament Agency of the United States Government, which has wisely seen the need to sponsor basic research in this field.

Jerome Alan Cohen

Preface

1. Scope of inquiry

The compilation of this calendar has been undertaken as part of the Harvard International Law Project on the People's Republic of China (PRC), which is concerned with a broad survey of that country's attitudes toward international law as evidenced in its practices and in its pronouncements and other writings. The comprehensiveness of the calendar owes much, therefore, to the breadth of inquiry which characterizes the whole Project. Yet, even as an independent task, the compilation of a state's treaties would be justified only insofar as it reflects a broad and vital conception of what constitutes an agreement.

The primacy of treaty obligations in the theory of international law has been virtually unchallenged, East and West, since the beginning of the twentieth century. Soviet commentators have always attached crucial significance to obligations incurred through the consensual acts of sovereign states. If nontreaty "sources" of international law have received increasing acceptance in Soviet theory of recent years, it remains true that treaty obligations have a kind of priority ranking, as they have in "bourgeois" theory.[1] In the People's Republic of China, though professional literature on the subject is thin, it seems clear that treaty dealings are regarded as the natural outgrowth of normal relations with other powers and that treaty obligations are subordinate only to certain ideological commitments, which may or may not result in consensual acts.[2]

Consistent with the emphasis laid on treaty obligations in their political and legal theory, the Communist states have made wide use of international agreements despite restrictions on their dealings with non-Communist states in their earlier years. Their consensual instruments, like those of other countries. have assumed a wide variety of forms and designations. It seems clear from state practice throughout the world that the use of different forms and designations is not intended to have legal significance internationally, though a pattern of consistency may be discernible in diplomatic usage.[3] It is also true that states differ in their conception of what constitutes a legally binding commitment, and legal regulation is by no means the most conspicuous consequence or function of every international agreement.[4]

1. J. F. Slusser and R. M. Triska, *The Theory, Law and Policy of Soviet Treaties* (Stanford, 1962), pp. 29-31.

2. H. Chiu, "The Theory and Practice of Communist China with Respect to the Conclusion of Treaties," *Col. J. Transn'l. L.* 5:1 (1966).

3. D. P. Myers, "The Name and Scope of Treaties," *Am. J. Int'l. L.* 51:574 (1957).

4. D. M. Johnston, "Treaty Analysis and Communist China: Preliminary Observations," *Proceedings of Am. Soc. Int'l. L.* (April 27-29, 1967), p. 126.

Accordingly, from every point of view, a treaty calendar for a state such as the PRC has to be contructed by canvassing the widest possible range of sources so as to secure sufficient evidence of the state's dealings with the outside world. In working through such a mass of material, we have concentrated our efforts on documenting *all official and semi-official exchanges of commitments involving the People's Republic of China* from its officially proclaimed establishment on October 1, 1949, to the close of its eighteenth year on September 30, 1967. In so doing, we have declined to adopt any definition of what constitutes a legally binding agreement or an agreement "governed by international law."[5]

2. *Principles of selection*

In determining what does or does not constitute an official or semiofficial exchange of commitments, we have felt it necessary to include all governmental exchanges which the parties themselves have seemed to regard as involving them in commitments. Accordingly, our calendar includes every entry in the PRC's official treaty series (TYC) and every PRC agreement listed in any other national treaty series available to us. On the other hand, we have gone far beyond official treaty listings: first, by including all unlisted examples of every class of document represented in the official treaty series of the PRC and its treaty partners; second, by introducing as completely as possible additional classes of documents which seem to meet the test of evidencing an official or semi-official exchange of commitments involving the PRC. Among other things, this test excludes commitments that are wholly unilateral in function, such as an offshore territorial claim by Declaration, but not those that are merely unilateral in form, such as a gift. This test also excludes commitments that involve only subnational entities, such as a province or a city.

In applying the test the chief difficulty lies in the problem of distinguishing between unofficial and official or semiofficial exchanges. For the purpose of inclusion in this calendar it has been assumed that where a meeting or correspondence is official or semiofficial, then so are commitments exchanged thereby. Normally, an agreement is regarded as official if signed or issued by an accredited representative of the branch of government responsible for that function. But in a country such as the PRC it is not always easy to know how treaty-making powers are allocated. Organs like the China Committee for the Promotion of International Trade, the China National Import and Export Company, the Chinese Red Cross Society, and the China Fishery Association have been permitted to transact in the name of the PRC within their field of

5. The Draft Articles on the Law of Treaties completed by the International Law Commission in 1966 relate to "international agreements concluded between states in written form and governed by international law, whether embodied in a single instrument or in two or more related instruments and whatever its particular designation."

interest. Sometimes representatives of these organs seem to have been given ad hoc powers to negotiate outside their special field of interest.

Special problems of inclusion are presented by "unorthodox" agreements, that is, those signed or issued in the name of countries which have not yet established, or have suspended, normal diplomatic relations. We have included these agreements where unofficial government approval on both sides can be read from the context of the unorthodox relationship, either in its presignatory or postsignatory phases.

When confronted with difficult problems of inclusion, we have taken solace in the thought that arbitrariness cannot be entirely eliminated. But it may be said, in summary, that in attempting to reduce the degree of sin, we have resorted to four kinds of considerations:

(a) official listing by the governments concerned;

(b) status and function of those who signed or issued the document and of the institutions they represent;

(c) government approval or acceptance of some responsibility before or after signing;

(d) predominant national governmental interest in the subject matter.

In the case of many doubtful entries we have supplied a note with information relevant to the problem of inclusion.

No effort has been made to seek out from private sources unreported treaties or clauses. This involves a special kind of research which we do not have the opportunity to undertake. To avoid unnecessary duplication we have excluded instruments for the ratification of an agreement which is already entered in the calendar at the date of signing. For the same reason we have also excluded some interim joint statements which merely report that negotiations are in progress. Strictly diplomatic agreements—such as agreements to establish diplomatic relations, to exchange ambassadors, and to raise missions to the status of embassies—have been omitted.

3. *Features of the calendar*

(a) *Sequence:* All entries, regardless of their nature, are listed chronologically by the date of signing or issue. Where the sources show a discrepancy in the reported date of signing, and it cannot be resolved by reference to the text, we have taken the way of convenience and accepted the date reported in the most authoritative source of information available. Since the references are cited in order of authoritativeness (see 3(h) infra), this means that we resolve discrepancies in reporting by following the version presented at the source cited first. To facilitate cross-reference within the calendar, we have numbered each entry according to the order of sequence for each calendar year. For example, the cross-reference number of the fifty-fourth entry listed for 1961 is 61-54.

(b) *Effective date:* The effective date, listed immediately after the date of signing or issue, is the date from which the agreement is reported to be effective. A dash in the text indicates that the effective date is not reported. In the absence of evidence to the contrary, the effective date and the date of entry into force are presumed to be the same. When the listed effective date is earlier than the listed date of signing, this means that the agreement has been made effective retroactively, as in the case of many trade agreements. In these cases it may be presumed that the retroactive agreement entered into force on the date of signing. In most cases where no effective date is listed, because no effective date is reported in the sources available, it may be presumed that both the date of entry into force and the effective date are the same as the date of signature. It can usually be presumed that the parties to quasi-agreements, such as joint communiqués, intend them to take effect from the date of signing or issue. Since these documents are never signed or issued subject to ratification, it may be argued that entry into force is automatic upon signature or issue.

(c) *Ratification:* It falls outside the scope of this calendar to describe the process of ratification for each agreement. Under the 1954 Constitution of the PRC the function of ratification is to be exercised jointly by the Standing Committee of the National People's Congress and the Chairman of the Government. Ratification is mandatory for treaties of peace, mutual non-aggression, friendship, alliance and assistance, and all other treaties which expressly provide for ratification. All other agreements may be submitted for approval by the State Council.

Where further explanation of the ratification procedure for a particular agreement seems desirable, it has been added in a note.

(d) *Place of signature or issue:* Where reported, the place of signature or issue has been entered immediately before the non-Chinese partner. In a few cases only, a dash has been inserted to indicate that the place is not known.

(e) *Multilateral agreements:* Two distinct kinds of agreements are described as "multilateral": "international" conventions and other agreements kept open universally for signature or accession, and "plurilateral" agreements with four or more parties. In the case of the latter we have listed the non-Chinese signatory states in a note, instead of in the column reserved for parties; in the case of the former we have not enumerated the signatory states. Trilateral agreements are listed in the same way as bilateral, with the two non-Chinese parties entered together in the appropriate column.

(f) *Nature of document:* Any public document that evidences an official or semiofficial exchange of commitments involving the PRC qualifies for inclusion, regardless of the form it takes. This calendar includes treaties, agreements, accords, protocols, statutes, contracts, arrangements, exchanges of letters, exchanges of notes, joint statements, joint communiqués and declarations, a few other bilateral forms, minutes, a few unilateral statements which are multilateral in function (for example, "recognition" of existing international conventions), and one "agreed announcement." Variations in the names of the documents follow the official Chinese terminology as reported in TYC, WCC, or JMJP. A dash indicates that the form of document used is not reported. A glossary of some Chinese characters used in these official listings, with the translations used in this calendar, is appended.

(g) *Subject matter:* In general, we have described the subject matter of each agreement in accordance with the official Chinese title of the document as given in TYC, WCC, or JMJP. In some cases we have abbreviated the title for economy of space; in others we have expanded the description for clarification. For the reader's convenience, we have summarized the contents of joint communiqués and in many cases have supplied additional information in a note, but our main purpose has been to direct the reader to accessible sources of information rather than to supply a full description of each entry.

(h) *Sources:* We have drawn upon over eighty different sources in more than a dozen languages for references and texts. Where translation services have not been available, we have provided our own translations. Most of these sources are cited in abbreviated form, by initials or short title. A table of abbreviations is provided at the end of this Preface.

The sources used are of different kinds. The most useful kind of source is, of course, the text of the agreement. Where the full text is available at the source, we have added an initial, in parentheses, indicating the language in which a version of the text is given. Languages used not more than once in this calendar are spelled out in full. It is necessary for the reader to refer to the text to discover whether or not the version given at the source is an official version. In other kinds of sources, the text is supplied in an abbreviated form (for example, G, abbrev.). We have also denoted those sources that supply a fairly detailed summary of the contents of an agreement (for example, E, sum.), especially in the case of SCMP, which is the most useful English language source generally available to readers of the calendar.

References not followed by an initial or the name of a language indicate that the information given at the source is limited. In many of these cases there is little to be learned by consulting the source over and above what is already provided in the calendar entry.

The citations to these sources have been arranged in order, more or less by the degree of authoritativeness of the source from the presumed point of view of the PRC. Accordingly, first place is given to untranslated official and semiofficial PRC sources (TYC, FKHP, FLHP, YHTY, WCC, JMJP, JMST); second place to official PRC sources translated (into English) by the PRC (NCNA[E], PR, PC); third place to official PRC sources translated (into English) outside the PRC (SCMP, CB, ECMM, SCMM, JPRS, CCD, FBIS); fourth place to the official international treaty series (UNTS) and to official and semiofficial sources other than those of the PRC (FTS[FFF], FTS[SAS], CTS, PakTS, NeTS, NoTS, YTS, UST, TIAS, DSB, PakDS, BFSP, ADTJ, ADFO, ND, BQ, URSS, Izv, Pr, ZD);

and last place to unofficial sources such as private collections, digests, newspapers, textbooks, and periodicals. Citations to all sources in the first place of priority are exhaustive. Virtually the same is true of citations to PR, PC, SCMP, CB, ECMM, CCD, UNTS, and to most of the non-Chinese official sources. References to NCNA(E), however, are intended to be supplementary only, since it covers the same original sources as SCMP. The JPRS materials were searched fairly thoroughly, but this source is so voluminous that exhaustive treatment was out of the question. The appropriate entries from most of the other sources have been completely incorporated. But the *Calendar of Soviet Treaties, 1917-1957* by R. M. Slusser and J. F. Triska and its annual supplements up to 1962, prepared mostly by G. Ginsburgs, were so complete in Russian references to Sino-Soviet agreements that we normally cite only their collections. In selected cases we incorporate the Pravda and Izvestia sources as cited by these compilers. The Slusser and Triska calendar and its annual supplements have served as an admirable model for us in many respects.

This book was prepared under a contract with the United States Arms Control and Disarmament Agency. The judgments expressed in this book are those of the editors and do not necessarily reflect the views of the United States Arms Control and Disarmament Agency or any other department or agency of the United States Government.

This study owes its existence to Professor Jerome A. Cohen, whose continuing example in the conduct and promotion of East Asian legal studies at Harvard Law School has encouraged many of us to labor in long neglected fields of scholarship. We are grateful to him for his contribution of the Foreword and for his advice in many matters.

The promptness in publishing this calendar is owing in large measure to the competent staff of the Harvard University Press. We are also grateful for the prompt release of this manuscript by the United States Arms Control and Disarmament Agency, under whose auspices our research was undertaken, and for the coordinating services of Miss Edith Brown, Agency Project Officer.

For sharing much of the tedium involved in this research, credit is due to John Evans, Nien-tsu Tzou, and Frank Snyder, who acted as diligent assistants in dusty places. On the distaff side, typing and proofreading duties were performed with dispatch by Kate Rachstein, Leslee King, Janet Johnson, and Ellen Tolstuk.

Professor Chiu wishes to thank Dr. Chien Ssu-liang, President of National Taiwan University and Dr. Yen Chen-hsing, Minister of Education of the Republic of China, for granting him two years' leave of absence to undertake research in the United States.

Cambridge, Massachusetts — Douglas M. Johnston
May 1968 — Hungdah Chiu

Contents

Abbreviations

Languages

A – Arabic	C – Chinese	E – English	F – Finnish
Fr – French	G – German	It – Italian	L – Laotian
N – Norwegian	P – Polish	R – Russian	S – Sinhala
S-C – Serbo-Croatian	Sp – Spanish	Sw – Swedish	

Note: Following a citation, the abbreviations above mean that the full text of the agreement is available in that source in the language indicated.

Sources

A/D	Ambekar, G. V., and V. D. Divekar (ed.), *Documents on China's Relations with South and South-East Asia (1949-1962)* (Bombay, 1964)
ADFO	Articles et documents: faits et opinions. *La Documentation française*
ADTJ	Articles et documents: textes du jour. *La Documentation française*
AfD	*Africa Diary* (New Delhi)
AGF	Archiv für Gesamtdeutsche Fragen, *Zusammenstellung der von der "Deutschen Demokratischen Republik" seit deren Gründung (7 October 1949) abgeschlossen internationalen Verträge und Vereinbarungen* (Bonn, 1965)
AfR	*African Recorder* (New Delhi)
AJIL	*American Journal of International Law* (Washington, D. C.)
AsR	*Asian Recorder* (New Delhi)
A/M/K	Abou-Fadel, H., J. Malha, and I. Kraidy (ed.), *Lebanon: Its Treaties and Agreements* (Beirut, 1967)
Beloff	*Beloff, M., Soviet Policy in Far East* (London, 1953)
BFSP	*British and Foreign State Papers* (London)
BQ	Bulletin quotidien de presse étrangère. *La Documentation francaise*
CB	*Current Background* (US Consulate, Hong Kong)
CCD	*Communist China Digest* (Joint Publications Research Service)
CDSP	*Current Digest of Soviet Press* (New York)
CTS	*Ceylon Treaty Series* (Colombo)
DAFR	*Documents on American Foreign Relations* (Boston)
DIA	*Documents on International Affairs* (Royal Institute of International Affairs, London)
Dok	*Dokumente zur Aussenpolitik der Deutschen Demokratischen Republik* (Deutsches Institut für Zeitgeschichte, Berlin)
DSB	*Department of State Bulletin* (Washington, D.C.)
ECMM	*Extracts China Mainland Magazines* (US Consulate, Hong Kong)
FBIS	*Foreign Broadcast Information Service* (Washington, D.C.)

FEER	*Far Eastern Economic Review* (Hong Kong)
FIYB	Federation of Industries of United Arab Republic, *Yearbook* (Cairo)
FKHP	*Chung-hua jen-min kung-ho-kuo fa-kuei hui-pien* (Collection of laws and regulations of the People's Republic of China; Peking, 1954-63)
FLHP	*Chung-yang jen-min cheng-fu fa-ling hui pien* (Collection of laws and decrees of the Central People's Government; Peking, 1949-54)
FTS(FFF)	*Finlands Författningssamlings Fordragsserie* (Finnish Statute-book and Treaty Series-in Swedish; Helsinki)
FTS(SAS)	*Suomen Asetuskokoelman Sopimussarja* (Finnish Statute-book and Treaty Series-in Finnish; Helsinki)
G60	Ginsburgs, G., "A Calendar of Soviet Treaties, January-December 1960," *Osteuropa-Recht* 9:120 (1963)
G61	Ginsburgs, G., "A Calendar of Soviet Treaties, January-December 1961," *Osteuropa-Recht* 10:116 (1964)
G62	Ginsburgs, G., "A Calendar of Soviet Treaties, January-December 1962," *Osteuropa-Recht* 11:129 (1965)
G/S	Ginsburgs, G., and R. M. Slusser, "A Calendar of Soviet Treaties, January-December 1959," *Osteuropa-Recht* 8:132 (1962)
H1 and H12	*Verträge der Volksrepublic China mit anderen Staaten* (Institut für Asienkunde, Hamburg) vol. 1 and vol. 12 (in 3 parts)
Horak	Horak, S., *Poland's International Affairs 1919-60* (Bloomington, Ind., 1964)
IA	*International Affairs* (Moscow)
ILM	*International Legal Materials* (American Society of International Law, Washington, D.C.)
Izv	*Izvestia* (Moscow)–as cited in S/T, S/G, G/S, G60, G61, and G62
JMJP	*Jen-min jih-pao* (People's daily; Peking)
JMST	*Jen-min shou-ts'e* (People's handbook; Hong Kong)
JPRS	*Joint Publications Research Service* (Washington, D.C.)
Maki	Maki, J. McG. (ed.), *Conflict and Tension in the Far East: Key Documents, 1894-1960* (Seattle, 1961)
Meissner	Meissner, B. (ed.), *Das Ostpakt-System* (Franfurt-am- Main, 1955)
NCNA(E)	*New China (Hsin-hua) News Agency* (English language service), Daily news release (Peking)
ND	Notes et études documentaires. *La Documentation française*
NeTS	*Tractatenblad van het Koninkrijk der Nederlanden* (Treaty Journal of the Kingdom of the Netherlands; The Hague)
NoTS	*Overenskomester med Fremmede Stater* (Agreements with Foreign States; Oslo)
NT	*New Times* (Moscow)
NYT	*New York Times*
OR	*Osteuropa-Recht* (Stuttgart)
PakDS	*Pakistan Document Series* (Pakistan Embassy, Washington, D.C.)
PakTS	*Pakistan Treaty Series* (Karachi)
PC	*People's China* (Peking)
PI(H)	*Politica Internacional* (Instituto de Politica Internacional, Ministero de Relaciones Exteriores, Havana)

PI(M)	*Politica Internacional* (Instituto de Estudios Politicos, Madrid)
PR	*Peking Review*
Pr	*Pravda* (Moscow)–as cited in S/T, S/G, G/S, G60, G61, and G62
RGDIP	*Revue générale du droit international public* (Paris)
RI	*Relazioni Internazionali* (Milan)
SCMM	*Survey China Mainland Magazines* (US Consulate, Hong Kong)
SCMP	*Survey China Mainland Press* (US Consulate, Hong Kong)
S/G	Slusser, R. M., and G. Ginsburgs, "A Calendar of Soviet Treaties, January-December 1958," *Osteuropa-Recht* 7:100 (1961
SIA	*Survey of International Affairs* (Royal Institute of International Affairs, London)
S/T	Slusser, R. M., and J. F. Triska, *A Calendar of Soviet Treaties, 1917-1957*
STS	Recueil des Accords Internationaux conclus par la Syrie depuis 1946 (Bureau des Documentations Syriennes et Arabes; Damascus, 4th ed.?)
TIAS	*Treaties and Other International Acts Series* (Washington, D.C.)
TYC	*Chung-hua jen-min kung-ho-kuo t'iao-yueh-chi* (Compilation of treaties of People's Republic of China; Peking, 1949-64)
UA	*United Asia* (Bombay)
UNTS	*United Nations Treaty Series*
URSS	Chroniques étrangères: URSS *La Documentation française*
UST	*United States Treaties and Other International Acts Series* (Washington, D.C.)
V-P(2)	Ronnefarth, H. K. G., and H. Euler (ed.), *Konferenzen und Verträge.* Vertrags-Ploetz, ein Handbuch geschichtlich bedeutsamer Zusammenkünfte und Vereinbarungen, vol. 2: Neueste Zeit, 1914-1959 (Würzburg, 1959)
WCC	*Chung-hua jen-min kung-ho-kuo tui-wai kuan-hsi wen-chien-chi* (Compilation of foreign relations documents of the People's Republic of China; Peking, 1949-63)
Wei	Wei, H., *China and Soviet Russia* (Princeton, N.J., 1956)
WGO	*Die Wichtigsten Gesetzgebungsakte in den Ländern Ost-, Südosteuropas und in den ostasiatischen Volksdemokratien* (Hamburg)
Wint	Wint, G. (ed.), *Asia: A Handbook* (New York, 1966)
YHTY	*Chung-hua jen-min kung-ho-kuo yu-hao t'iao-yueh hui-pien* (Collection of Frienship Treaties concluded by the People's Republic of China; Peking, 1965)
YTS	*Yougoslavija Sluzebni List: Medunarodni Ugovari i Drugi Sporazumi* (Yugoslav Official Journal: International Treaties and Other Agreements; Belgrade)
ZD	*Zbior Dokumentów* (Collection of Documents; Polski Instytut Spraw Miedzynarodowych, Warsaw)

Agreements of the People's Republic of China 1949-1967: A Calendar

1949

49-1 **12/25/49** 2/1/50 Peking **Korea (N)** Agreement
Postal services

TYC 1:150(C); JMJP 1/28/50(C); NCNA(E) 269:122 (1/27/50); CB 438:11

49-2 **12/25/49** – Peking **Korea (N)** Protocol
Amendments to 1949 Postal Agreement [49-1]

TYC 1:154(C)

49-3 **12/25/49** 2/1/50 Peking **Korea (N)** Agreement
Establishment of telecommunications

TYC 1:155(C); JMJP 1/28/50(C); NCNA(E) 269:122 (1/27/50); CB 438:11

49-4 **12/25/49** 2/1/50 Peking **Korea (N)** Agreement
Establishment of telephone services

TYC 1:160(C); JMJP 1/28/50(C); NCNA(E) 269:122 (1/27/50)

49-5 **12/25/49** – Peking **Korea (N)** Protocol
Amendments to 1949 Telecommunications and Telephone Agreements [49-3,4]

TYC 1:164(C)

1950

50-1 **2/7/50** 3/1/50 Moscow **USSR** Agreement
Telephone and telegraph communications

TYC 1:126(C); JMJP 3/1/50(C); NCNA(E) 296:121 (2/25/50); CB 438:1

50-2 **2/7/50** 3/1/50 Moscow **USSR** Agreement
Exchange of mails and parcels

TYC 1:110(C); JMJP 3/1/50(C); NCNA(E) 296:121(2/25/50); CB 438:1

50-3 **2/14/50** – Moscow **USSR** Joint Communiqué
Talks culminating in six agreements listed below

WCC 1:74(C); NCNA(E) 289:79 (2/16/50)(E); PC 1:5:25(E); CB 62:3(E); BQ 1505:1(Fr); Meissner, p. 166(G)

50-4 **2/14/50** 4/11/50 Moscow **USSR** Treaty
Friendship, alliance, and mutual assistance

The Treaty provides that it will come into effect "immediately upon its ratification." Both the USSR and the PRC ratified on 4/11/50, which is officially construed as effective date by both parties though instruments of ratification were not exchanged until 9/30/50. Registered by USSR with UN Secretariat 1/3/56.

TYC 1:1(C); YHTY 81(C,R); WCC 1:75(C); JMJP 2/15/50(C); JMST 1953, p. 916(C), 1955, p. 295(C); NCNA(E) 289:80(2/16/50)(E); PC 1:5:25(E); CB 62:4(E); UNTS 226:5 (R,C,E,Fr); BFSP 157:633(E); ND 1306:2, 2062:31(Fr); BQ 1505:2(Fr); DIA 1949-50, p. 541(E); RI 1950:8:107(It), 1959:7:270(It); S/T p. 269; V-P(2):384(G , sum.); Meissner, p. 166(G); Beloff, p. 343(E); Wei, p. 343(E); Wint, p. 770(E)

50-5 **2/14/50** 4/11/50 Moscow **USSR** Agreement
Joint administration (and future transfer to PRC) of Chinese Changchun Railway, Port Arthur, and Dairen

See note above.

TYC 1:3(C); WCC 1:77(C); JMJP 2/15/50(C); NCNA(E) 289:81 (2/16/50)(E); PC 1:5:26(E); CB 62:6(E); UNTS 226:33(R,C,E,Fr); BFSP 157:636(E); ND 1306:3, 2062:32(Fr); DIA 1949-50, p. 543(E); RI 1950:8:108(It), 1959:7:270(It); S/T p. 269; Wint, p. 771(E); Meissner, p. 167(G); Beloff, p. 262(E)

50-6 **2/14/50** 2/14/50 Moscow **USSR** Agreement
Soviet grant of credit to PRC over five-year period from 1/1/50

The Agreement provides that it will come into effect on date of signature. Both parties ratified on 4/11/50 and instruments of ratification were exchanged on 9/30/50. Registered by USSR with UN Secretariat 1/3/56.

TYC 1:45(C); WCC 1:79(C); JMJP 2/15/50(C); NCNA(E) 289:83 (2/16/50)(E); PC 1:5:28(E); CB 62:8(E); UNTS 226:22(R,C,E,Fr); BFSP 157:639(E); ND 1306:4(Fr); DIA 1949-50, p. 545(E); RI 1950:8:108(It), 1959:7:271(It); S/T p. 270; Meissner, p. 168(G); Beloff, p. 266(E)

50-7 **2/14/50** – Moscow **USSR** Exchange of Notes
Abrogation of the Sino-Soviet Treaty of Friendship and Alliance and of the Agreements on the Chinese Changchun Railway, Dairen, and Port Arthur, signed 8/14/45; and recognition of the independence of the Mongolian People's Republic

NCNA(E) 289:80 (2/16/50); UNTS 226:10(R,C,E,Fr); BFSP 157:641(E); S/T p. 269

50-8 **2/14/50** – Moscow **USSR** Exchange of Notes
Gratuitous transfer by USSR to PRC of property acquired by Soviet organizations from Japanese owners in Manchuria in 1945

Provides for establishment of Sino-Soviet joint committee for carrying out transfer of property within three months.

NCNA(E) 289:80 (2/16/50); S/T p.270

50-9 **2/14/50** Moscow **USSR** Exchange of Notes
Gratuitous transfer by USSR of all buildings of the Soviet military compound in Peking

NCNA(E) 289:80 (2/16/50); S/T p. 270

50-10 **2/15/50** 4/1/50 Peking **USSR** Protocol
Postal services

Supplements Sino-Soviet Agreement of 2/7/50 on exchange of mails and parcels.

TYC 1:122(C)

50-11 **3/1/50** – Peking **Poland** Agreement
Exchange of goods in 1950

JMJP 4/7/50; NCNA(E) 426:48 (7/6/50); CB 438:13

50-12 **3/1/50(?)** – Peking **Poland** Protocol
Exchange of goods in 1950

JMJP 4/17/50; CB 438:13

50-13 **3/27/50** – Moscow **USSR** Agreement
Establishment of Sino-Soviet Non-Ferrous and Rare Metals Joint Stock Company in Sinkiang

Ratified by PRC on 4/21/50 and USSR on 6/3/50. Instruments of ratification exchanged 9/30/50. Joint Communiqué also issued. Text at sources cited below; also ND 2062:35(Fr); Meissner, p. 181(G).

WCC 1:250; JMJP 3/29/50; NCNA(E) 329:129 (3/30/50);
CB 62:10

50-14 **3/27/50** – Moscow **USSR** Agreement
Establishment of Sino-Soviet Petroleum Joint Stock Company in Sinkiang

Ratified by PRC on 4/21/50 and USSR on 6/3/50. Instruments of ratification exchanged 9/30/50. Joint Communiqué also issued. (Text at sources cited below; also ND 2062:35(Fr); Meissner, p. 181(G)).

WCC 1:250; JMJP 3/29/50; NCNA(E) 329:129 (3/30/50); CB 62:10

50-15 **3/27/50** – Moscow **USSR** Agreement
Establishment of Sino-Soviet Civil Aviation Joint Stock Company

Joint Communiqué also issued. Text at sources cited below; also ND 2062:34(Fr); Meissner, p. 181(G).

WCC 1:250; JMJP 4/2/50; NCNA(E) 333:10 (4/3/50); CB 62:13

50-16 **3/27/50** – Moscow **USSR** Agreement
Working conditions for Soviet experts in PRC

CB 62:2; S/T p. 272; Meissner, p. 193

50-17 **4/19/50** 1/1/50 Moscow **USSR** Agreement
Trade

Ratifications exchanged 9/30/50.

TYC 1:47(C); JMJP 4/21/50; NCNA(E) 352:103(4/22/50); CB 62:11; S/T p. 273; Meissner, p. 194

50-18 **4/19/50** – Moscow **USSR** Protocol
Exchange of goods in 1950

Ratified by PRC on 5/12/50 and by USSR on 6/3/50. Instruments of ratification exchanged 9/30/50.

TYC 1:50(C); JMJP 4/21/50; NCNA(E) 352:103 (4/22/50); CB 62:11; S/T p. 273; Meissner, p. 194

50-19 **4/19/50** – Moscow **USSR** Protocol
General conditions for delivery of goods

TYC 1:51(C)

50-20 **4/19/50** – Moscow **USSR** Protocol
Supply by the USSR to PRC of industrial equipment and materials from 1950 to 1952

JMJP 4/21/50; NCNA(E) 352:103 (4/22/50); CB 62:11; S/T p.273; Meissner, p. 194(G)

50-21 **4/25/50** – Peking **USSR** Protocol
Organization of the Chinese Changchun Railway Company

NCNA(E) 357:135 (4/27/50); CB 62:14; S/T p. 273

50-22 **6/14/50** 6/14/50 Peking **Czechoslovakia** Agreement
Trade in 1950

TYC 1:71(C); JMJP 6/23/50; NCNA(E) 406:91 (6/16/50); CB 438:5

50-23 **7/20/50** – – **USSR** Protocol
Completion of transfer to PRC of all buildings of the Soviet military compound in Peking

S/T p. 276

50-24 **8/7/50** – Mukden **USSR** Protocol
Measures for free transfer to PRC of Japanese properties in Manchuria taken over by USSR in 1945

Signed at meeting of Sino-Soviet joint committee which began negotiations for transfer of property on 7/8/50 under Exchange of Notes of 2/14/50 [50-8].

SCMP 52:7; CB 62:16; S/T p. 276

50-25 **8/18/50** 8/18/50 Peking **Korea (N)** Agreement
Barter

TYC 1:84(C)

50-26 **8/28/50** – Mukden **USSR** Agreement
Completion of free transfer to PRC of Japanese properties in Manchuria taken over by USSR in 1945

Four subordinate agreements and two volumes of documentary evidence also signed. Completion of work by Sino-Soviet joint committee in 1950 announced in Soviet Statement of 1/18/51. CB 62:16; Pr 1/18/51(R); Meissner, p. 170(G). Meissner also refers (p. 194) to Final Protocol of 1/18/51.

SCMP 52:8; CB 62:16; S/T p. 277

50-27 **10/10/50** 10/10/50 Peking **Germany (E)** Agreement
Exchange of goods and payments in 1951

TYC 1:90(C); JMJP 10/11/50; NCNA(E) 517:89 (10/11/50);
SCMP 20:4; Dok 1:323

50-28 **10/25/50** – – **USSR** Agreement
Working conditions for Soviet experts in PRC

S/T p. 278

50-29 **11/4/50** – – **Germany (E)** Exchange of Notes
General conditions for delivery of goods

TYC 1:93(C)

50-30 **12/5/50** – Peking **Multilateral** Statement
"Acceptance" by PRC of Universal Postal Convention (1947) and various postal arrangements

JMJP 12/7/50; NCNA(E) 566:58 (12/7/50)(E); SCMP 24:5(E)

1951

51-1 **1/2/51** 1/2/51 Harbin **USSR** Agreeement
Navigation procedures and construction on border rivers Amur, Ussuri, Argun, and Sungacha and on Lake Hanka

TYC 1:6(C); S/T p.279

51-2 **1/16/51** – – **USSR** Agreement
Direct rail communication

Apparently superseded by agreement of 3/14/51 [51-11].
S/T p. 279

51-3 **1/22/51** 1/22/51 Peking **Hungary** Agreement
Exchange of goods and payments in 1951

TYC 1:35(C); SCMP 55:1

51-4 **1/29/51** 1/29/51 Peking **Poland** Agreement
Exchange of goods and payments in 1951

TYC 1:60(C); JMJP 2/7/51; SCMP 63:15; Horak, p. 89

51-5 **1/29/51** 1/1/51 Peking **Poland** Agreement
Telecommunications
TYC 1:131(C); JMJP 2/7/51; SCMP 63:15; Horak, p. 89

51-6 **1/29/51** 1/1/51 Peking **Poland** Agreement
Exchange of mail and parcels
TYC 1:138(C); JMJP 2/7/51; SCMP 63:15; Horak, p. 89

51-7 **1/29/51** – Peking **Poland** Agreement
Shipping and navigation
JMJP 2/7/51; SCMP 63:15; Horak, p. 89

51-8 **1/29/51** – Peking **Poland** Agreement
Air traffic
H1:17; Meissner, p. 195

51-9 **2/1/51** – Peking **Poland** Protocol
General conditions for delivery of goods in 1951
TYC 1:64(C)

51-10 **2/19/51** – Peking **Hungary** –
General conditions for delivery of goods
TYC 1:38(C)

51-11 **3/14/51** – Peking **USSR** Agreement
Through rail traffic
Apparently supersedes agreement of 1/16/51 [51-2].
JMJP 3/30/51; SCMP 89:9; S/T p. 280; Meissner, p. 194

51-12 **4/3/51** 1/25/52 Warsaw **Poland** Agreement
Cultural cooperation
Registered by Poland with UN Secretariat 7/1/58.
TYC 1:102(C); JMJP 4/4/51; SCMP 91:1; UNTS 304:189(C,P,R,E,Fr); Horak, p. 90

51-13 **4/25/51** – Peking **India** Contract
Delivery by PRC of rice to India
SCMP 99:2

51-14 **5/23/51** – – **India** Contract
Delivery by PRC of grain to India
NCNA(E) 705:95 (5/24/51); SCMP 107:36

51-15 **5/23/51** 5/23/51 Peking **Tibet** Agreement
"Peaceful liberation" of Tibet

Not regarded by PRC as international agreement but included here as legal basis of official commitment towards semiautonomous entity.

FLHP 1951, p. 6(C); PC 3:12 Supp.(E); CB 76:3(E); PI(M) 44:198(Sp); BFSP 158:731(E); ND 2562:5(Fr); DIA 1951, p. 577(E); RI 1959:7:277(It); V-P(2):403(G, sum.); Wint, p. 763(E); Meissner, p. 171(G); RGDIP 63:613(Fr)

51-16 **June** – – **Poland** Agreement
Establishment of Sino-Polish Shipping Joint Stock Company
SCMP 127:26

51-17 **6/15/51** – Moscow **USSR** Protocol
Exchange of goods in 1951
TYC 1:59(C); JMJP 6/22/51; SCMP 122:1; S/T p. 281

51-18 **6/15/51** – Moscow **USSR** Protocol
Supply of industrial equipment and materials by USSR to PRC in 1951
JMJP 6/22/51; SCMP 122:1; S/T p. 281

51-19 **6/21/51** 6/21/51 Peking **Czechoslovakia** Agreement
Exchange of goods and payments in 1951
TYC 1:74(C); JMJP 6/22/51; SCMP 122:4

51-20 **6/21/51** – Peking **Czechoslovakia** –
General conditions for delivery of goods
TYC 1:77(C)

51-21 **7/12/51** 12/22/51 Peking **Hungary** Agreement
Cultural cooperation
TYC 1:100(C); JMJP 10/19/51; NCNA(E) 749:61 (7/14/51); SCMP 134:5

51-22 **7/28/51** – Peking **USSR** Agreement
Establishment of Sino-Soviet Joint Stock Company for Ship Building and Repair
S/T p. 282

51-23 **10/9/51** 2/14/52 Peking **Germany (E)** Agreement
Cultural cooperation
TYC 1:107(C); JMJP 10/10/51; SCMP 192:3 AGF p. 49; Dok 4:71(G)

51-24 **10/12/51** 12/1/51 Peking **Germany (E)** Agreement
Postal services
TYC 1:176(C); JMJP 10/13/51; SCMP 193:5; AGF p. 49; Dok 4:73(G)

51-25 **10/21/51** 12/1/51 Peking **Germany (E)** Agreement
Telecommunications

TYC 1:173(C); SCMP 193:5; AGF p.49; Dok 4:81(G)

51-26 **12/6/51** – – **USSR** Agreement
Technical training for PRC specialists in USSR

Referred to in atomic energy agreement of 4/27/55 as basis for training of PRC atomic specialists in USSR.

S/T p. 283

51-27 **12/12/51** 6/23/52 Peking **Rumania** Agreement
Cultural cooperation

TYC 1:105(C); JMJP 12/13/51; SCMP 235:1

1952

52-1 **2/8/52** – Peking **Poland** –
1952 plan for cultural cooperation

SCMP 275:12

52-2 **3/29/52** – Moscow **USSR** Protocol
Amendment of 1950 Protocol on general conditions for delivery of goods [50-19]

TYC 2:40(C); S/T p. 285

52-3 **4/7/52** – Peking **Vietnam (N)** –
General conditions for delivery of goods

TYC 2:136(C)

52-4 **4/10/52** – Moscow **Germany (W)** Agreement
Trade

Signed at nongovernmental International Economic Conference held at Moscow April 3-12, 1952, attended by persons from forty-nine states. Never implemented, this agreement was apparently replaced by private Trade Agreement of 6/25/52 [52-27].

SCMP 373:6; H12(3):4

52-5 **4/12/52** – Moscow **USSR** Protocol
Exchange of goods in 1952

TYC 2:42(C); JMJP 4/17/52; SCMP 317:2; S/T p. 286

52-6 **4/12/52** – Moscow **USSR** Protocol
Supply by USSR to PRC of industrial equipment and materials in 1952

JMJP 4/17/52; SCMP 317:2; S/T p. 286

52-7 **4/12/52** – Moscow **UK** Agreement
Trade

This and the nine trade agreements listed below were signed at the nongovernmental International Economic Conference held at Moscow April 3-12, 1952, attended by persons from forty-nine states. Most of these agreements may be regarded as semiofficial. Communiqué also issued at end of Conference on 4/12/52. DIA 1952, p. 249(E). See also E. Luard, *Britain and China* 143-47 (1962).

JMJP 4/14/52; PC 1952:9:32; SCMP 315:2; SIA 1952, p. 344

52-8 **4/12/52(?)** – Moscow **Italy** Agreement
Trade

See note above.

JMJP 4/20/52; PC 1952:9:32; H1:52

52-9 **4/12/52(?)** – Moscow **Belgium** Agreement
Trade

See note above.

JMJP 4/20/52; PC 1952:9:32; H1:50

52-10 **4/12/52(?)** – Moscow **Pakistan** Agreement
Trade

See note above.

JMJP 4/20/52; PC 1952:9:32; H1:44

52-11 **4/12/52(?)** – Moscow **Indonesia** Agreement
Trade

See note above.

JMJP 4/20/52; PC 1952:9:32; H1:38

52-12 **4/12/52(?)** – Moscow **Finland** Agreement
Trade in 1952-53

See note above.

JMJP 4/20/52; PC 1952:9:32; H1:36

52-13 **4/14/52** – Moscow **France** Agreement
Trade

See note above.

JMJP 4/20/52; PC 1952:9:32; SCMP 315:2; H1:51

52-14 **4/14/52(?)** – Moscow **Switzerland** Agreement
Trade

See note above.

JMJP 4/20/52; PC 1952:9:32; SCMP 315:2; H1:45

52-15 **4/14/52(?)** – Moscow **Ceylon** Agreement
Trade

See note above.

JMJP 4/20/52; PC 1952:9:32; SCMP 315:2; H1:34

52-16 **4/14/52** – Moscow **Netherlands** Agreement
Trade

See note above.

JMJP 4/20/52; PC 1952:9:32; SCMP 317:2

52-17 **5/6/52** 7/1/52 Peking **Czechoslovakia** Agreement
Postal services

TYC 2:216(C); JMJP 5/7/52; SCMP 331:15

52-18 **5/6/52** 7/1/52 Peking **Czechoslovakia** Agreement
Telecommunications

TYC 2:225(C); SCMP 331:15

52-19 **5/6/52** 5/6/52 Peking **Czechoslovakia** Agreement
Scientific and technical cooperation

TYC 2:197(C); SCMP 331:15

52-20 **5/6/52** 9/18/52 Peking **Czechoslovakia** Agreement
Cultural cooperation

TYC 2:190(C); SCMP 331:15

52-21 **5/24/52** – – **Czechoslovakia** Agreement
Air traffic

Meissner, p. 195

52-22 **5/26/52** – Peking **India** Contract
Shipment of rice to India

Signed by PRC Minister of Trade and Indian Ambassador to PRC.

JMJP 6/8/52; SCMP 351:4

52-23 **5/28/52** 1/1/52 Berlin **Germany (E)** Agreement
Exchange of goods and payments in 1952

TYC 2:144(C); JMJP 6/1/52; H1:12; AGF p. 49; Dok 1:324

52-24 **5/28/52** 5/28/52 Berlin **Germany (E)** Protocol
General conditions for delivery of goods in 1952

TYC 2:148(C)

52-25 **5/31/52** 7/1/52 Peking **Korea (N)** Protocol
Amendments to 1949 Postal, Telephone and Telecommunications Agreements and Protocols [49-1,2,3,4,5]

TYC 1:167(C)

52-26 **6/1/52** – Peking **Japan** Accord
Trade in 1952

Signed by representatives of China Committee for Promotion of International Trade and of Japanese delegation to International Economic Conference, Japan-China Trade Promotion Association of Japan, and Japanese Diet Members' League for Promotion of Sino-Japanese Trade.

TYC 2:367(C); JMJP 6/2/52(C); PC 1952:12:10(E); SCMP 348:2(E, sum.); A/D p. 303(E)

52-27 **6/25/52** – Berlin **Germany (W)** Agreement
Trade

Signed on German side by private businessmen, apparently replacing Trade Agreement of 4/10/52 which was not implemented [52-4].

JMJP 7/12/52; SCMP 373:6; H1:51

52-28 **7/11/52** – Warsaw **Poland** Protocol
Extension of Agreement on Exchange of Goods and Payments in 1951 for another year[51-4]

TYC 2:45(C); SCMP 377:5; Horak, p. 89

52-29 **7/11/52** – Warsaw **Poland** Protocol
Extension of Protocol on General Conditions for Delivery of Goods in 1951 for another year [51-9]

TYC 2:46(C)

52-30 **7/13/52** – Peking **Multilateral** Statement
"Recognition" of accession "in name of China" on 8/7/29 of Protocol for the Prohibition of the Use in War of Asphyxiating, Poisonous, or Other Gases and of Bacteriological Methods of Warfare (concluded in Geneva 6/17/25)

TYC 6:319(C); WCC 2:77(C); PC 1952:15:33(E); SCMP 375:2(E)

52-31 **7/13/52** 6/28/57 Peking **Multilateral** Statement
"Recognition," subject to reservation, of Convention for the Amelioration of the Condition of the Wounded and Sick in Armed Forces in the Field (signed on behalf of China in Geneva 8/12/49 by representative of Republic of China)

PRC deposited instrument of ratification and reservation with Swiss Federal Council 12/28/56. Statement registered by Switzerland with UN Secretariat 2/9/57.

TYC 5:203(C); WCC 2:78(C); PC 1952:15:33(E); SCMP 375:2(E); UNTS 260:438(E,Fr, reservation only)

52-32 **7/13/52** 6/38/57 Peking **Multilateral** Statement
"Recognition," subject to reservation, of Convention for the Amelioration of the Condition of Wounded, Sick, and Shipwrecked Members of

Armed Forces at Sea (signed on behalf of China in Geneva 8/12/49 by representative of Republic of China)

See note above.

TYC 5:231(C); WCC 2:78(C); PC 1952:15:33(E); SCMP 375:2(E); UNTS 260:440(E,Fr, reservation only)

52-33 **7/13/52** 6/28/57 Peking **Multilateral** Statement
"Recognition," subject to reservation, of Convention relative to Treatment of Prisoners of War (signed on behalf of China in Geneva 8/12/49 by representative of Republic of China)

See note above.

TYC 5:255(C); WCC 2:78(C); PC 1952:15:33(E); SCMP 375:2(E); UNTS 260:442(E,Fr, reservation only)

52-34 **7/13/52** 6/28/57 Peking **Multilateral** Statement
"Recognition," subject to reservation, of Convention relative to the Protection of Civilian Persons in Time of War (signed on behalf of China in Geneva 8/12/49 by representative of Republic of China)

See note above.

TYC 5:333(C); WCC 2:78(C); PC 1952:15:33(E); SCMP 375:2(E); UNTS 260:444(E,Fr, reservation only)

52-35 **7/14/52** 10/25/52 Sofia **Bulgaria** Agreement
Cultural cooperation

TYC 2:185(C); JMJP 7/19/52; SCMP 378:4

52-36 **7/15/52** – Prague **Czechoslovakia** Protocol
Extension and revision of 1951 Agreement on Exchange of Goods and Payments [51-19]

TYC 2:122(C); JMJP 7/19/52; SCMP 377:5

52-37 **7/15/52** – Prague **Czechoslovakia** Protocol
General conditions for delivery of goods in 1952

TYC 2:114(C)

52-38 **7/21/52** – Budapest **Hungary** Protocol
Extension and revision of 1951 Agreement on Exchange of Goods and Payments [51-3]

TYC 2:10(C); JMJP 7/26/52; SCMP 382:7

52-39 **7/21/52** – Budapest **Hungary** Protocol
General conditions for delivery of goods in 1952

TYC 2:12(C)

52-40 **7/21/52** 7/21/52 Sofia **Bulgaria** Agreement
Exchange of goods and payments in 1952

TYC 2:83(C); JMJP 7/28/52; SCMP 384:6

52-41 **7/21/52** 7/21/52 Sofia **Bulgaria** Protocol
General conditions for delivery of goods in 1952

TYC 2:86(C)

52-42 **7/30/52** 7/30/52 Bucharest **Rumania** Agreement
Exchange of goods and payments in 1952

TYC 2:54(C); SCMP 388:39

52-43 **7/30/52** 7/30/52 Bucharest **Rumania** Protocol
General conditions for delivery of goods in 1952

TYC 2:57(C)

52-44 **8/9/52** – Berlin **France** Contract
Barter

Though not a formal governmental agreement, it was apparently approved in advance of signing by French as well as PRC government, in accordance with Agreement of 4/14/52 [52-13].

JMJP 8/20/52; SCMP 398:2

52-45 **8/9/52** 9/1/52 Moscow **USSR** Agreement
Training of PRC citizens in Soviet institutions of higher education

Exchange of Notes of same date provides for extension of this agreement to citizens of PRC who were studying in institutions of higher education in USSR before entry into force of this agreement. S/T p. 290

TYC 2:179(C); S/T p.289

52-46 **8/20/52(?)** - Peking **Hungary** Exchange of Notes
1952-53 plan for cultural cooperation

SCMP 399:1

52-47 **8/23/52** – Hong Kong **Portugal** Agreement
Settlement of military disputes on PRC–Macao border

SCMP 402:1

52-48 **9/15/52** – Moscow **USSR** Joint Communiqué
Talks culminating in two agreements listed below

WCC 2:88(C); JMST 1953, p. 197(C); PC 1952:19:7(E); SCMP 417:1(E);Izv 9/16/52(R); DIA 1952, p. 471(E); DAFR 1952, p. 293(E); RI 1952:38:998(It); S/T p. 290; Meissner, p. 171(G)

52-49 **9/15/52** – Moscow **USSR** Exchange of Notes
Extension of time limit for joint use of naval base at Port Arthur

Registered by USSR with UN Secretariat 1/3/56.

TYC 2:1(C); WCC 2:89(C); JMJP 9/16/52(C); JMST 1953, p. 197(C); PC 1952:19:8(E); SCMP 417:2(E); UNTS 226:46(C,R,E,Fr); BFSP 159:589(E); ND 2062:35(Fr);

BQ 2280:1(Fr); Izv 9/16/52(R); DIA 1952, p. 472(E); DAFR 1952, p. 295(E); RI 1952:38:998(It), 1959:7:271(It); S/T p.290; Meissner, p. 172(G); Beloff, p. 265(E)

52-50 **9/15/52** – Moscow **USSR** Joint Communiqué
Transfer of the Chinese Changchun Railway to PRC government

Provides for establishment of joint commission to complete transfer by end of 1952 under 1950 Agreement [50-5]. See Joint Communiqué and Final Protocol of 12/31/52 [52-64].

WCC 2:89(C); JMJP 9/16/52(C); JMST 1953, p. 197(C); PC 1952:19:7(E); SCMP 417:1(E); ND 2062:35(Fr); BQ 2280:1(Fr); Izv 9/16/52(R); DIA 1952, p. 417(E); DAFR 1952, p. 294(E); RI 1952:38:998(It), 1959:7:271(It); S/T, p. 290; Meissner, p. 172(G)

52-51 **9/15/52** 9/15/52 Moscow **USSR** **Mongolia** Agreement
Through rail traffic

Provides for construction of railway from Tsinin to Ulan Bator and establishment of direct rail communications between the three countries. Completion of project announced in Joint Communiqué of 1/4/56. See also Joint Communiqué of 10/12/54.

TYC 2:240(C); S/T p. 291

52-52 **9/21/52** 9/21/52 Moscow **USSR** **Finland** Agreement
Supply of goods and payments in 1952

Provides that Finland would send various pulp and paper products to PRC, for which it would receive automobiles, petroleum, and iron products from USSR, and PRC in turn would deliver certain unspecified products to USSR.

TYC 2:174(C); JMJP 7/27/52; SCMP 424:10; S/T p. 291

52-53 **9/21/52** 9/21/52 Moscow **USSR** Agreement
Trade

Specified goods to be delivered by PRC to USSR under tripartite agreement of same date [52-52].

S/T p. 291

52-54 **10/4/52** 12/29/52 Peking **Mongolia** Agreement
Economic and cultural cooperation in period 1952-62

Joint Communiqué also issued 10/4/52. WCC 2:92:(C); PC 1952:20:7(E)

TYC 2:7(C); JMJP 10/5/52; PC 1952:20:7(E); SCMP 429:1(E); BFSP 159:588(E); RI 1952:42:1106(It), 1959:7:277(It); Meissner, p. 172(G)

52-55 **10/4/52** 1/1/53 Peking **Ceylon** Agreement
Trade

TYC 2:173(C); JMJP 10/6/52; SCMP 429:8; CTS 1953:1(E)

52-56 **10/4/52** – Peking **Ceylon** Contract
Sale of rice to Ceylon

JMJP 10/6/52; SCMP 429:9

52-57 **10/13/52** – Peking **India** Contract
Sale of rice to India

SCMP 432:51

52-58 **10/23/52** – Peking **Chile** Agreement
Trade

Signed by representative of China National Import and Export Company and "Chilean delegate to Peace Conference of Asian and Pacific Regions and representative of Sino-Chilean Trade Corporation."

JMJP 10/24/52; SCMP 439:4

52-59 **11/6/52** – Peking **Vietnam (N)** Agreement
Exchange of mail

SCMP 449:13

52-60 **12/3/52** 1/1/53 Peking **Bulgaria** Agreement
Exchange of goods and payments in 1953

TYC 2:95(C); JMJP 12/7/52; SCMP 467:5

52-61 **12/3/52** 1/1/53 Peking **Bulgaria** Protocol
General conditions for delivery of goods in 1953

TYC 2:98(C)

52-62 **12/18/52** 1/1/53 Peking **Ceylon** Agreement
Exchange of Ceylonese rubber and PRC rice in period 1953-57

JMJP 12/20/52; SCMP 477:15; CTS 1953:1(E); H1:34

52-63 **12/18/52** – Peking **Ceylon** Contracts (2)
Deliveries of rubber and rice in 1953

JMJP 12/20/52; SCMP 477:15; H1:34

52-64 **12/31/52** – Harbin **USSR** Final Protocol
Soviet transfer of the Chinese Changchun Railway to PRC

Signed by Sino-Soviet Commission for the Transfer of the Chinese Changchun Railway. Joint Communiqué also issued.

WCC 2:116(C); JMJP 1/2/53; Pr 1/1/53; Meissner, p. 173(G); JMJP 1/3/53; SCMP 483:14(E); Izv 1/1/53; S/T p. 292

52-65 **12/31/52** – Port Arthur **USSR** (Miscellaneous)
Transfer of assets and operations of Soviet Foreign Insurance Administration in Northeast China (Manchuria) to Chinese People's Insurance Company

JMJP 3/1/53(C); JMST 1953, p. 198(C); SCMP 489:8; S/T p. 292

52-66 **12/31/52** 12/31/52 Peking **Japan** Protocol
Extension of 1952 Trade Accord to 6/30/53 [52-26]
JMJP 1/1/53; SCMP 483:21

1953

53-1 **1/9/53** 1/9/53 Peking **Rumania** Agreement
Scientific and technical cooperation
TYC 2:196(C); JMJP 1/10/53; SCMP 489:10

53-2 **1/16/53** 1/16/53 Peking **Mongolia** Agreement
Postal services
TYC 2:231(C); JMJP 1/17/53; SCMP 494:35

53-3 **1/16/53** 1/16/53 Peking **Mongolia** Agreement
Telecommunications
TYC 2:236(C); JMJP 1/17/53; SCMP 494:35

53-4 **1/19/53** 1/1/53 Peking **Rumania** Agreement
Exchange of goods and payments in 1953
TYC 2:66(C); SCMP 496:1

53-5 **1/19/53** 1/1/53 Peking **Rumania** Protocol
General conditions for delivery of goods in 1953
TYC 2:70(C)

53-6 **1/26/53** – Warsaw **Poland** –
1953 plan for cultural cooperation
SCMP 205:13

53-7 **2/9/53** – Berlin **Germany (E)** –
1953 plan for cultural cooperation
JMJP 2/12/53; SCMP 513:21; AGF p. 49; Dok 1:325

53-8 **2/24/53** – Peking **Mongolia** Protocol(?)
Exchange of goods and payments in 1953
Meissner, p. 195

53-9 **2/24/53** – Peking **Mongolia** Agreement
Noncommercial credit
JMJP 2/25/53; SCMP 519:11; Meissner, p. 192

53-10 **2/24/53** – Peking **Mongolia** Protocol
Bank procedure for implementation of Noncommercial Credit Agreement of same date [53-9]
Signed by representatives of People's Bank of China and Industrial and Commercial Bank of People's Republic of Mongolia.
JMJP 2/25/53; SCMP 519:11

53-11 **3/14/53** 3/14/53 Karachi **Pakistan** Agreement
Sale of cotton to PRC

Signed by Counsellor of PRC Embassy in Pakistan and Secretary of Pakistan Ministry of Commerce.

TYC 2:9(C); NCNA(E) 1272:147 (3/18/53); SCMP 533:8

53-12 **3/14/53** – Karachi **Pakistan** Contract
Sale of coal to Pakistan

See note above.

NCNA(E) 1272:147 (3/18/53); SCMP 533:8

53-13 **3/21/53** – Moscow **USSR** Protocol
Turnover of goods in 1953

Joint Communiqué also issued 3/26/53. Meissner, p. 173(G)

TYC 2:44(C); JMJP 3/27/53; SCMP 540:1; Izv 3/26/53; S/T p. 294

53-14 **3/21/53** – Moscow **USSR** Agreement
Grant of Soviet loan to PRC

SIA 1953, p. 237; S/T p. 294 (note)

53-15 **3/21/53** – Moscow **USSR** Protocol
Delivery to PRC of industrial equipment and materials in 1953

JMJP 3/27/53; SCMP 540:1; Izv 3/26/53; S/T p. 294

53-16 **3/21/53** – Moscow **USSR** Agreement
Soviet technical assistance in expansion and construction of power stations

JMJP 3/27/53; SCMP 540:1; Izv 3/26/53; S/T p. 294

53-17 **3/30/53** 1/1/53 Peking **Hungary** Agreement
Exchange of goods and payments in 1953

TYC 2:15(C); JMJP 3/31/53; SCMP 543:5

53-18 **3/30/53** 1/1/53 Peking **Hungary** Protocol
General conditions for delivery of goods in 1953

TYC 2:18(C)

53-19 **4/11/53** – Panmunjom **UN** Agreement (military)
Korea (N)
Repatriation of sick and injured prisoners of war in Korea

Signed by senior member of Korean People's Army and Chinese People's Volunteers liaison group and by senior member of UN Command liaison group. Also issued: Understanding of Administrative Details for Repatriation Operation (SCMP 522:1 [E]); and KPA-CPV Communiqué reserving right to request that sick and injured POW's on KPA-CPV side not repatriated by virtue of paragraph 3 of Article 109 of Geneva Convention be handed over to a neutral state "so as to secure a just solution of the question of their repatriation after an armistice." SCMP 549:8(E)

JMJP 4/12/53(C); SCMP 549:6(E)

53-20 **4/30/53** 1/1/53 Peking **Germany (E)** Agreement
Exchange of goods and payments in 1953

TYC 2:159(C); SCMP 562:33; AGF p. 50; Dok 1:325

53-21 **4/30/53** 1/1/53 Peking **Germany (E)** Protocol
General conditions for delivery of goods in 1953

TYC 2:162(C)

53-22 **5/7/53** 1/1/53 Peking **Czechoslovakia** Agreement
Exchange of goods and payments in 1953

TYC 2:117(C); JMJP 5/8/53; SCMP 567:21

53-23 **5/7/53** 1/1/53 Peking **Czechoslovakia** Protocol
General conditions for delivery of goods in 1953

TYC 2:121(C)

53-24 **5/7/53** 5/7/53 Prague **Czechoslovakia** Agreement
Cooperation in radio broadcasting

TYC 2:192(C); JMJP 5/8/53; SCMP 567:22

53-25 **5/19/53** – Peking **Hungary** Exchange of Notes
1953 plan for cultural cooperation

JMJP 5/23/53; SCMP 577:31

53-26 **5/22/53** – Peking **Bulgaria** Exchange of Notes
Confirmation of 1953 plan for cultural cooperation

JMJP 5/29/53; SCMP 580:15

53-27 **5/25/53** 1/1/53 Peking **Poland** Agreement
Turnover of goods and payments in 1953

TYC 2:48(C); JMJP 5/27/53; SCMP 579:9; Horak, p. 89

53-28 **5/25/53** – Peking **Poland** Protocol
General conditions for delivery of goods in 1953

TYC 2:52(C)

53-29 **Summer 1953** – Moscow **USSR** Agreement
Economic and technical aid

Provides for Soviet aid on 141 industrial projects and for repayment by PRC. PRC acceptance of Soviet offer formally conveyed by Chairman Mao Tse-tung to Chairman Malenkov in letter of 9/15/53. Pr 9/18/53(R); Meissner, p. 173(G). Meissner (at p. 194) lists two separate documents: a technical aid agreement and a long-term credit agreement.

S/T p. 296; H1:22

53-30 **6/5/53** 6/5/53 Peking **Finland** Agreement
Trade in 1953-54

TYC 2:35(C); JMJP 6/6/53; SCMP 584:3; H12(3):25(G)

53-31 **6/5/53** 6/5/53 Peking **Finland** –
General conditions for delivery of goods by PRC

TYC 2:372(C)

53-32 **6/5/53** 6/5/53 Peking **Finland** Agreement
Payments

TYC 2:37(C); JMJP 6/6/53; SCMP 584:3; FTS(FFF) 1953:20:94(Sw,E); FTS(SAS) 1953:20:144(F,E); H12(3):29(G)

53-33 **6/5/53** 6/5/53 Peking **France** Agreement
Barter

Signed by representatives of China National Import and Export Company and French industrial and commercial delegation.

TYC 2:37(C); SCMP 586:9; H12(3):47(G)

53-34 **6/8/53** – Panmunjom **UN** **Korea(N)** Agreement (military)
Repatriation of prisoners of war in Korea

Signed by senior delegate of Korean People's Army and Chinese People's Volunteers and senior delegate of UN Command. Annexed to military armistice agreement of 7/27/53 [53-42].

TYC 2:403(C); JMJP 6/9/53(C); SCMP 585:1(E)

53-35 **6/9/53** – Bucharest **Rumania** –
1953 plan for cultural cooperation

SCMP 589:7

53-36 **6/24/53** – Peking **Czechoslovakia** Protocol
Scientific and technical cooperation

Signed at first session of Sino-Czechoslovak Joint Committee for Scientific and Technical Cooperation.

SCMP 597:7

53-37 **6/27/53** – Peking **Czechoslovakia** Exchange of Notes
Confirmation of 1953 plan for cultural cooperation

JMJP 7/7/53; SCMP 604:6

53-38 **7/3/53** – – **Germany (E)** Agreement
Exchange of weekly press clippings

AGF p. 50

53-39 **7/6/53** 7/6/53 Peking **UK** Accord
Trade

Signed by representative of China National Import and Export Company and sixteen members of British trade delegation.

TYC 2:380(C); JMJP 7/7/53; SCMP 604:1

53-40 **7/16/53** 8/1/53 Peking **Hungary** Agreement
Postal services

TYC 2:204(C); JMJP 7/17/53; SCMP 612:2

53-41 **7/16/53** 8/1/53 Peking **Hungary** Agreement
Telecommunications

TYC 2:211(C); JMJP 7/17/53; SCMP 612:2

53-42 **7/27/53** 7/27/53 Panmunjom **UN** **Korea (N)** Agreement (military)

Armistice in Korea (With Annex: Terms of Reference for Neutral Nations Repatriation Commission)

Signed formally by senior delegate of Korean People's Army and Chinese People's Volunteers and senior delegate of UN Command; copies submitted for signature by commanders of KPA-CPV and by commander of UN Command.

TYC 2:382(C); WCC 2:217(C); JMJP 7/28/53(C); JMST 1955, p. 301(C); SCMP 619:1(E, sum.); SCMP 442:31(E, draft); UST 4:234(E,K,C); TIAS 2782:3(E,K,C); UN Doc. A/24/31(E); RI 1959:7:288(It)

53-43 **7/27/53** 7/27/53 Panmunjom **UN** **Korea (N)** Agreement (military)

Temporary supplement to Korean Armistice Agreement of 7/27/53

WCC 2:240(C); JMJP 8/4/53; JMST 1955, p. 309(C); SCMP 619:7(E); UST 4:346(E,K,C); TIAS 2782:117(E,K,C)

53-44 **7/31/53** 1/1/54 Moscow **Multilateral** Agreement
Through railway freight traffic

Signed by USSR, Albania, Bulgaria, Czechoslovakia, Germany (E), Hungary, Korea (N), Mongolia, Poland, and Rumania.

TYC 2:297(C); S/T p. 298; Horak, p. 93

53-45 **7/31/53** 1/1/54 Moscow **Multilateral** Agreement
Through railway passenger traffic

See note above.

TYC 2:241(C)

53-46 **8/3/53** – Panmunjom **Multilateral** Agreement
Operation of Red Cross teams in Korea

Signed by delegate of Korean and PRC Red Cross Societies and delegates of national Red Cross Societies of countries participating in UN Command in Korea. Approved on same day by members of Joint Committee for Repatriation of POW's.

SCMP 624:6

53-47 **8/8/53** – Peking **Germany (E)** Protocol
Supplement to Agreement on Exchange of Goods and Payments in 1953 [53-20]
JMJP 8/9/53; SCMP 627:21; AGF p. 90; Dok 1:326

53-48 **8/18/53** 8/18/53 Peking **Czechoslovakia** Agreement
Cooperation for prevention of insect pests and plant diseases
TYC 2:201(C); JMJP 8/19/53; SCMP 634:8

53-49 **8/20/53** 8/20/53 Peking **Mongolia** Protocol (supplementary)
Turnover of goods and payments in 1953
TYC 2:140(C); JMJP 8/21/53; SCMP 636:9

53-50 **8/20/53** – Peking **Mongolia** Protocol
Clearance of trade in 1951 and 1952
SCMP 636:9

53-51 **8/25/53** 8/25/53 Peking **Vietnam (N)** Protocol
Opening of small-scale trading in border areas
TYC 2:138(C)

53-52 **9/21/53** – Peking **Ceylon** –
Extension of 1952 Trade Agreement to 12/31/55 [52-55]
JMJP 9/24/53; SCMP 656:9

53-53 **9/21/53** – Peking **Ceylon** Contracts (2)
Exchange of rice and rubber in 1954
JMJP 9/24/53; SCMP 656:9

53-54 **9/20/53** – London **UK** Exchange of Letters
9/29/53 Peking
Military incident in the Pearl River Delta
WCC 2:152(C); H12(3):90

53-55 **10/2/53** – Peking **Multilateral** Communiqué
Cooperation in radio broadcasting
Issued after twenty-fourth meeting of Board of Directors of In national Broadcasting Organization and ninth session of Techn Commission of IBO.
SCMP 662:29

53-56 **10/3/53** 10/3/53 Peking **Hungary** Agreement
Scientific and technical cooperation
TYC 2:195(C); JMJP 10/4/53; SCMP 662:28

53-57 **10/15/53** 10/15/53 Peking **Hungary** Agreement
Cooperation in radio broadcasting
:); JMJP 10/16/53; SCMP 669:9

53-58 **10/15/53** 10/15/53 Peking **Poland** Agreement
Cooperation in radio broadcasting

TYC 2:182(C); JMJP 10/16/53; SCMP 669:9

53-59 **10/15/53** 10/15/53 Peking **Rumania** Agreement
Cooperation in radio broadcasting

TYC 2:183(C); JMJP 10/16/53; SCMP 669:9

53-60 **10/15/53** 10/15/53 Peking **Bulgaria** Agreement
Cooperation in radio broadcasting

TYC 2:188(C); JMJP 10/16/53; SCMP 670:17

53-61 **10/15/53** – Bucharest **Rumania** Protocol
Scientific and technical cooperation

Signed at first session of Sino-Rumanian Joint Committee for Scientific and Technical Cooperation.

SCMP 671:11

53-62 **10/29/53** 10/29/53 Peking **Japan** Accord
Trade in 1953-54

Signed by representatives of China Committee for Promotion of International Trade and Japanese Diet Members' League for Promotion of Sino-Japanese Trade.

TYC 2:368(C); JMJP 10/30/53(C); PC 1953:22 Supp.(E); SCMP 679:2(E); A/D p. 305(E)

53-63 **10/30/53** 10/30/53 Berlin **Germany (E)** Agreement
Cooperation in technology and technical science

TYC 2:199(C); JMJP 11/2/53; SCMP 680:12; AGF p. 50; Dok 4:85(G)

53-64 **8/26/53** – – **USSR** Exchange of Notes
10/31/53
Modification of 1950 Agreement on Exchange of Mails and Parcels [50-2]

S/T p. 303

53-65 **11/23/53** – Peking **Korea (N)** Communiqué
Talks during Premier Kim Il Sung's visit: PRC assistance for restoration of North Korea's war damaged economy, communications and transport, promotion of technical cooperation, etc.

Meissner (at p.195) lists three separate documents: an economic and technical aid agreement; a scientific and technical cooperation agreement; and an economic and cultural cooperation agreement [53-66].

PRC agreed to annul North Korean debts to the value of 280 million yuan and, in addition, promised a gift of 800 million yuan over the period 1954-57 in the form of commodities.

WCC 2:167(C); JMST 1955, p. 320(C); SCMP 694:3(E); ND 1912:6(Fr); DIA 1953, p. 455(E); Meissner, p. 177(G)

53-66 **11/23/53** 12/9/53 Peking **Korea (N)** Agreement
Economic and cultural cooperation in 1954-64

Apparently took effect from date of later of two ratifications, namely by PRC Government Council on 12/9/53, though instruments of ratification were not exchanged until 1/14/54.

TYC 2:6(C); WCC 2:168(C); JMJP 11/24/53(C); SCMP 694:2(E); BFSP 160:637(E); ND 1912:5(Fr); DIA 1953, p. 454(E); RI 1953:49:1188(It), 1959:7:295(It) A/D p. 311(E); Meissner, p. 178(G)

53-67 **11/28/53** 11/28/53 Peking **Germany (E)** –
1954 plan for cultural cooperation

Communiqué also issued (text at sources cited)

SCMP 697:18; Meissner, p. 181

53-68 **11/30/53** 1/4/54 Peking **Indonesia** Agreement
Trade in 1953-54

TYC 2:33(C); JMJP 1/18/54(C); SCMP 729:3(E); A/D p. 312(E)

53-69 **12/10/53** – – **Germany (E)** –
Banking arrangement to implement noncommercial payments

AGF p. 50

1954

54-1 **1/1/54** – Moscow **Multilateral** Agreement
Through railway traffic

Signed by USSR, Poland, Germany (E), Czechoslovakia, Hungary, Rumania, Bulgaria, Albania, Mongolia, and Korea (N).

SCMP 727:11; SIA 1954, p. 238

54-2 **1/23/54** – Moscow **USSR** Protocol
Exchange of goods in 1954

Communiqué also issued 1/23/54.

JMJP 1/25/54; SCMP 734:21; Izv 1/26/54; S/T p. 306; Meissner, p. 182

54-3 **1/23/54** – Moscow **USSR** Protocol
Delivery to PRC of Soviet industrial equipment and materials in 1954

SCMP 734:21; Izv 1/26/54; SIA 1954, p. 238; S/T p. 306

54-4 **1/25/54** – Peking **Korea (N)** Agreement
Through railway traffic

Referred to as border railway agreement by JMJP.

JMJP 1/29/54; SCMP 738:6

54-5 **2/19/54** 1/1/54 Warsaw **Poland** Agreement
Turnover of goods and payments in 1954
TYC 3:47(C); JMJP 2/22/54; SCMP 752:6; Horak, p. 89

54-6 **2/19/54** 1/1/54 Warsaw **Poland** Protocol
Extension and revision of Protocol on General Conditions for Delivery of Goods in 1953 [53-28]
TYC 3:51(C)

54-7 **2/23/54** – Peking **Poland** –
1954 plan for cultural cooperation
JMJP 2/26/54; SCMP 755:2

54-8 **3/25/54** 1/1/54 Sofia **Bulgaria** Agreement
Exchange of goods and payments in 1954
TYC 3:75(C); JMJP 3/30/54; SCMP 778:19

54-9 **3/25/54** 1/1/54 Sofia **Bulgaria** Protocol
General conditions for delivery of goods in 1954
TYC 3:78(C); JMJP 3/30/54; SCMP 778:20

54-10 **3/25/54** – Sofia **Bulgaria** Protocol
Clearance of trade
JMJP 3/30/54; SCMP 778:20

54-11 **3/30/54** 5/1/54 Peking **Korea (N)** Agreement
Parcel post
TYC 3:188(C); JMJP 3/31/54; SCMP 778:19

54-12 **3/30/54** 1/1/54 Berlin **Germany (E)** Agreement
Exchange of goods and payments in 1954
TYC 3:142(C); JMJP 4/2/54; SCMP 780:4; AGF p. 51; Dok 2:368

54-13 **3/30/54** 1/1/54 Berlin **Germany (E)** Protocol
General conditions for delivery of goods in 1954
TYC 3:145(C)

54-14 **4/7/54** 4/7/54 Ulan Bator **Mongolia** Protocol
Mutual supply of goods and payments in 1954
TYC 3:121(C); JMJP 4/10/54; SCMP 786:8

54-15 **4/7/54** 1/1/54 Ulan Bator **Mongolia** Protocol
General conditions for delivery of goods
TYC 3:122(C)

54-16 **4/19/54** 1/1/54 Bucharest **Rumania** Agreement
Exchange of goods and payments in 1954
TYC 3:57(C); JMJP 4/24/54; SCMP 794:24

54-17 **4/19/54** 1/1/54 Bucharest **Rumania** Protocol
General conditions for delivery of goods in 1954

TYC 3:61(C)

54-18 **4/22/54** 4/22/54 Rangoon **Burma** Agreement
Trade in period 1954-57

TYC 3:133(C); JMJP 4/23/54; SCMP 793:13

54-19 **4/22/54** – Rangoon **Burma** Exchange of Notes
Principle of trade balance

TYC 3:135(C)

54-20 **4/27/54** 1/1/54 Prague **Czechoslovakia** Agreement
Exchange of goods and payments in 1954

TYC 3:93(C); JMJP 4/30/54; SCMP 797:18

54-21 **4/27/54** 1/1/54 Prague **Czechoslovakia** Protocol
Extension and revision of Protocol on General Conditions for Delivery of Goods in 1953 [53-23]

TYC 3:97(C)

54-22 **4/29/54** 6/3/54 Peking **India** Agreement
Trade and intercourse between Tibet and India

Under Article 6, became effective upon ratification. Instruments of ratification were exchanged on 8/17/54. First PRC treaty to invoke "five principles of peaceful coexistence." Registered by India with UN Secretariat 4/28/58. Communiqué also issued 4/29/54. On 12/15/61 Indian government rejected PRC proposal to open negotiations for new agreement to replace the original, which accordingly expired on 6/3/62, in accordance with Article 6. A/D p. 301(E)

TYC 3:1(C); WCC 3:12(C); JMJP 4/30/54(C); JMST 1955, p. 341(C); SCMP 798:3(E); UNTS 299:70(E,Fr); India, Lok Sabha Secretariat, *Foreign Policy of India 1947-64* (1966), p. 198(E); BFSP 161:518(E); ND 1912:1(Fr), 2562:6(Fr); RI 1959:7:278(It); PI(M) 44:201(Sp), 67:277(Sp); A/D p. 283(E); V-P(2):449(G); Wint, p. 751(E)

54-23 **4/29/54** 4/29/54 Peking **India** Exchange of notes
Withdrawal of Indian armed guards from Tibet, transfer by India of postal, telegraph, and telephone equipment, etc.

Registered by India with UN Secretariat 4/28/58. On 4/30/54, India waived right to compensation for postal, telegraph, and telephone equipment.

TYC 3:4(C); WCC 3:15(C); SCMP 798:5(E); UNTS 299:76(E,Fr); India, Lok Sabha Secretariat, *Foreign Policy of India 1947-64* (1966), p. 203(E); PI(M) 44:204(Sp); BFSP 161:521(E); ND 1912:4(Fr), 2562:7(Fr); AsR 2629(E, sum.); RI 1959:7:279(It)

54-24 **4/30/54** – Budapest **Hungary** Protocol
Extension and revision of Agreement on Exchange of Goods and Payments in 1953 [53-17]
TYC 3:20(C); JMJP 4/30/54; SCMP 799:35

54-25 **4/30/54** 1/1/54 Budapest **Hungary** Protocol
Extension and revision of Protocol on General Conditions for Delivery of Goods in 1953 [53-18]
TYC 3:23(C)

54-26 **5/4/54** – Sofia **Bulgaria** –
1954 plan for cultural cooperation
JMJP 5/8/54; SCMP 802:7

54-27 **5/17/54** – Peking **Rumania** Contract
Exchange of films
Signed by representatives of Film Distribution Bureau of Rumanian People's Republic and China Film Distribution and Exhibition Company.
JMJP 5/19/54; SCMP 810:22

54-28 **5/17/54** – Peking **Rumania** Contract
Exchange of newsreel materials
See note above.
JMJP 5/19/54; SCMP 810:22

54-29 **5/19/54** – Peking **Mongolia** Exchange of Notes
1954 plan for cultural cooperation
SCMP 814:31

54-30 **5/20/54** – Peking **Korea (N)** Agreement
Currency exchange rate
Signed by representative of People's Bank of China, Vice-Minister of Finance of Korea (N), and representative of Central Bank of Korea (N).
JMJP 5/21/54; SCMP 813:16

54-31 **5/20/54** – Peking **Korea (N)** Protocol
Currency exchange along border
See note above.
JMJP 5/21/54; SCMP 813:16

54-32 **5/20/54** – Peking **Korea (N)** Protocol
Noncommercial remittances between People's Bank of China and Central Bank of Korea (N)
See note above.
SCMP 813:16

54-33 **5/28/54** – Peking **Rumania** –
1954 plan for cultural cooperation

JMJP 5/29/54; SCMP 819:24

54-34 **5/29/54** – Peking **USSR** Contract
Distribution of Soviet films in PRC

Signed by representatives of All-Union Association for Import and Export of Films of USSR and China Film Distribution and Exhibition Company.

JMJP 5/30/54; SCMP 819:28; H1:21

54-35 **6/10/54** 6/10/54 Berlin **Germany (E)** Agreement
Cooperation in radio broadcasting

TYC 3:162(C); SCMP 827:53; AGF p. 51

54-36 **6/17/54** 6/17/54 Peking **Finland** –
General conditions for delivery of goods by PRC

Signed by representatives of several PRC export companies and of Finnish Ministry of Industry and Commerce.

TYC 3:197(C)

54-37 **6/21/54** 6/21/54 Helsinki **Finland** Agreement
Trade in 1954-55

TYC 3:43(C); JMJP 6/22/54; SCMP 833:52

54-38 **6/23/54** – Peking **Germany (E)** Protocol
Scientific and technical cooperation

Signed at first session of Sino-German Standing Committee for Cooperation in Technology and Technical Sciences. Communiqué also issued 6/23/54.

JMJP 6/24/54; SCMP 835:27; AGF p. 51; Dok 2:368;
Meissner, p. 182 (G)

54-39 **6/28/54** – New Delhi **India** Joint Statement
Talks during Premier Chou En-lai's visit: adherence to five principles of peaceful coexistence (Panch Shila)

TYC 3:7(C); WCC 3:113(C); JMJP 6/29/54(C); JMST 1955, p. 339(C); PC 1954:14 Supp.(E); SCMP 838:5(E); India, Lok Sabha Secretariat, *Foreign Policy of India 1947-64* (1966), p. 294(E); BFSP 162:369(E); ADTJ 074:6(Fr); DIA 1954, p. 313(E); RI 1954:28:859(It), 1959:7:279(It); A/D p. 7(E); Wint, p. 753(E)

54-40 **6/29/54** – Rangoon **Burma** Joint Statement
Talks during Premier Chou En-lai's visit: adherence to five principles of peaceful coexistence (Panch Shila)

TYC 3:13(C); WCC 3:155(C); JMJP 6/30/54(C); JMST 1955, p. 340(C); PC 1954:14 Supp.(E); SCMP 839:2(E); DIA 1954, p. 314(E); RI 1943:28:860(It); A/D p. 9(E)

54-41 **6/30/54** 6/30/54 Peking **Korea (N)** Protocol
General conditions for delivery of goods

TYC 3:105(C)

54-42 **7/5/54** – Peking **Vietnam (N)** Communiqué
Geneva Conference on Indo-China

WCC 3:117(C); JMST 1955, p. 340(C); SCMP 843:1(E)

54-43 **7/7/54** – Peking **Vietnam (N)** Protocol
Exchange of goods in 1954

JMJP 7/9/54; SCMP 844:2

54-44 **7/7/54** 7/7/54 Peking **Vietnam (N)** Protocol
Small-scale trading in border areas

TYC 3:102(C); JMJP 7/9/54; SCMP 844:2

54-45 **7/7/54** – Peking **Vietnam (N)** Protocol
Currency exchange along border

Signed by representatives of People's Bank of China and Vietnam State Bank.

SCMP 844:2

54-46 **7/17/54** – Prague **Czechoslovakia** –
1954 plan for cultural cooperation

JMJP 7/19/54; SCMP 851:9

54-47 **7/20/54** 7/20/54 Warsaw **Poland** Agreement
Scientific and technical cooperation

Communiqué also issued.

TYC 3:171(C); JMJP 7/23/54; SCMP 854:29; Horak, p. 94; Meissner, p. 182

54-48 **7/21/54** – Geneva **Multilateral** Final Declaration
Restoration of peace in Indo-China

Signed at Geneva Conference on Indo-China by USSR, UK, France, Cambodia, Vietnam (N), and Laos. The signatories of this Declaration associated themselves with the armistice agreements for Laos, Cambodia, and Vietnam, also signed on 7/21/54. The Conference was also attended by the US and Vietnam (S). The US issued a separate declaration.

TYC 3:14(C); WCC 3:79(C); JMST 1955, p. 328(C); PC 1954:15 Supp.(E); SCMP 853:2(E); DIA 1954, p. 138(E); A/D p. 467(E); Maki, p. 203(E)

54-49 **7/21/54** – Peking **India** Agreement
Tobacco trade

Signed by representatives of Indian tobacco trade delegation and China

National Import and Export Company.
SCMP 856:46

54-50 **7/25/54** – Berlin **Germany (E)** Communiqué
Talks during Premier Chou En-lai's visit: rearmament of Germany (W) and Japan, Geneva Conference on Indo-China, etc.
WCC 3:122(C); JMST 1955, p. 340(C); PC 1954:17 Supp. (E); SCMP 856:40(E); Dok 2:394(G)

54-51 **8/21/54** 8/21/54 Moscow **USSR** Agreement
Cooperation in radio broadcasting
TYC 3:157(C); JMJP 8/23/54; SCMP 874:33; S/T p. 315

54-52 **8/31/54** – Peking **Hungary** Exchange of Notes
1954 plan for cultural cooperation
SCMP 880:17

54-53 **8/31/54** – – **Germany (E)** Protocol (supplementary)
Exchange of goods in 1954
AGF p. 51; Dok 2:400

54-54 **9/1/54** 9/1/54 Djakarta **Indonesia** Protocol
Trade
TYC 3:37(C); JMJP 1/20/55(C); SCMP 972:7(E)

54-55 **9/1/54** 9/1/54 Djakarta **Indonesia** Agreement
Payments
TYC 3:38(C); JMJP 1/20/55(C); SCMP 972:9(E)

54-56 **9/2/54** – Prague **Czechoslovakia** Protocol
Scientific and technical cooperation
Signed at second session of Sino-Czechoslovak Joint Committee for Scientific and Technical Cooperation.
JMJP 9/4/54; SCMP 885:36

54-57 **9/4/54** – Peking **Korea (N)** Protocol
Exchange of goods in 1954
JMJP 9/7/54; SCMP 883:55

54-58 **10/8/54** – Peking **Ceylon** Contracts (2)
Rice and rubber trade in 1955
JMJP 10/9/54; SCMP 905:15

54-59 **10/10/54(?)** – – **Albania** –
Economic aid by PRC (in form of gift of ten million rubles and credit of fifty million rubles over period 1955-60)
FEER 1/19/61, p. 85

54-60 **10/12/54** – Peking **USSR** Communiqué
Talks culminating in signature of eight documents listed below

WCC 3:174(C); JMJP 10/12/54(C); JMST 1955, p. 296(C); PC 1954:21 Supp.(E); SCMP 906:1(E); ADTJ 0121:2(Fr); ND 2062:36(Fr); Izv 10/12/54(R); DIA 1954, p. 321(E); RI 1954:43:1252(It); S/T p. 317; Meissner, p. 179(G)

54-61 **10/12/54** – Peking **USSR** Joint Declaration
Sino-Soviet cooperation, Geneva Conference on Indo-China, Taiwan, Korean unification, SEATO, etc.

Registered by USSR with UN Secretariat 1/3/56.

TYC 3:9(C); WCC 3:175(C); JMST 1955, p. 296(C); PC 1954:21 Supp.(E); SCMP 906:2(E); UNTS 226:58(R,C,E,Fr); BFSP 161:626(E); ADTJ 0121:2(Fr); ND 2062:36(Fr); Izv 10/12/54(R); DIA 1954, p. 322(E); RI 1954:43:1252(It), 1959:7:272(It); S/T p. 317; V-P(2):469(G); Meissner, p. 179(G)

54-62 **10/12/54** – Peking **USSR** Joint Declaration
Criticism of Japanese Peace Treaty of 1951, common policy of peaceful coexistence with Japan, etc.

See note above.

TYC 3:11(C); WCC 3:177(C); JMST 1955, p. 297(C); PC 1954:21 Supp.(E); SCMP 906:4(E); UNTS 226:70(R,C,E,Fr); BFSP 161:629(E); ADTJ 0121:2(Fr); ND 2062:37(Fr); Izv 10/12/54(R); DIA 1954, p. 323(E); RI 1954:43:1253(It), 1959:7:272(It); S/T p. 317; A/D p. 87(E); V-P(2):470(G); Meissner, p. 180(G)

54-63 **10/12/54** – Peking **USSR** Joint Communiqué
Withdrawal of Soviet troops from Port Arthur and return of naval base to PRC

See note above. Withdrawal of Soviet troops completed 5/24/55.

TYC 2:2(C); WCC 3:179(C); JMST 1955, p. 298(C); PC 1954:21 Supp.(E); SCMP 906:5(E); UNTS 226:52(R,C,E,Fr); BFSP 161:628(E); ADTJ 0121:3(Fr); ND 2062:37(Fr); Izv 10/12/54(R); DIA 1954, p. 327(E); RI 1954:43:1253(It), 1959:7:273(It); S/T p. 317; V-P(2):470(G); Meissner, p. 180(G)

54-64 **10/12/54** – Peking **USSR** Joint Communiqué
Transfer to PRC of Soviet shares in Sino-Soviet Petroleum Company, Non-Ferrous Metals Company, Shipbuilding Company, and Civil Aviation Company

WCC 3:179(C); JMST 1955, p. 298(C); PC 1954:21 Supp.(E); SCMP 906:5(E); ADTJ 0121:3(Fr); ND 2062:37(Fr); Izv 10/12/54(R); DIA 1954, p. 325(E); RI 1954:43:1253(It), 1959:7:273(It); S/T p. 317; Meissner, p. 183(G)

54-65 **10/12/54** 10/12/54 Peking **USSR** Agreement
Scientific and technical cooperation

Joint Communiqué also issued 10/12/54. PC 1954:21 Supp.(E); SCMP 906:6(E); ADTJ 0121:3(Fr); ND 2062:38(Fr); DIA 1954, p. 326(E); Izv 10/12/54(R); RI 1959:7:273(It); Meissner, p. 183(G)

TYC 3:170(C); WCC 3:180(C); S/T p. 318

54-66 **10/12/54** – Peking **USSR** Joint Communiqué
Construction of the Lanchow-Urumchi-Alma Ata Railway, and organization of through traffic

WCC 3:181(C); JMST 1955, p. 299(C); PC 1954:21 Supp.(E); SCMP 906:7(E); ADTJ 0121:4(Fr); ND 2062:38(Fr); Izv 10/12/54(R); DIA 1954, p. 325(E); RI 1959:7:273(It); Meissner, p. 183(G)

54-67 **10/12/54** – Peking **USSR** **Mongolia** Joint Communiqué
Construction of railway from Chining (Tsinin) to Ulan Bator, and organization of through traffic

WCC 3:182(C); JMST 1955, p. 299(C); PC 1954:21 Supp.(E); SCMP 906:8(E); ADTJ 0121:4(Fr); ND 2062:38(Fr); DIA 1954, p 326(E); Pr 10/12/54(R); RI 1959:7:273(It); Meissner, p. 184(G)

54-68 **10/12/54** – Peking **USSR** Agreement
Long-term credit for supply to PRC of industrial equipment and materials

SCMP 906:1; Izv 10/12/54; S/T p. 318

54-69 **10/12/54** – Peking **USSR** Protocol
Economic and technical assistance

SCMP 906:1; Izv 10/12/54; S/T p. 318

54-70 **10/14/54** 10/14/54 Peking **Albania** Agreement
Scientific and technical cooperation

TYC 3:172(C); JMJP 10/16/54; SCMP 909:21

54-71 **10/14/54** 2/21/55 Peking **Albania** Agreement
Cultural cooperation

TYC 3:160(C); JMJP 10/16/54; SCMP 909:21

54-72 **10/14/54** 10/14/54 New Delhi **India** Agreement
Trade in period 1954-56

TYC 3:28(C); JMJP 10/15/54(C); SCMP 908:2(E); BFSP 161:524(E); ND 1977:25 (Fr); AsR 474, 2629; A/D p. 289(E)

54-73 **10/14/54** – New Delhi **India** Exchange of Notes
Transit of goods of PRC origin through India to Tibet region of PRC

TYC 3:31(C); SCMP 908:7(E); BFSP 161:530(E); ND 1977:27(Fr); A/D p. 292(E)

54-74 **10/14/54** – New Delhi **India** Exchange of Notes
Agreement to discuss questions concerning inspection of commodities, navigation, insurance, and transit of merchants

TYC 3:33(C); SCMP 908:9(E); ND 1977:28(Fr); A/D p. 294(E)

54-75 **10/15/54** – Peking **Rumania** Protocol
Scientific and technical cooperation

Signed at second session of Sino-Rumanian Joint Committee for Scientific and Technical Cooperation.

JMJP 10/17/54; SCMP 909:21

54-76 **10/19/54** – New Delhi **India** Accord
Exchange of tobacco and raw silk

Signed by representatives of PRC trade delegation and Indian Ministry of Commerce and Industry.

JMJP 10/22/54; SCMP 913:5

54-77 **11/3/54** 11/3/54 Peking **Burma** Protocol (with payments and accounting procedure annexed)
Exchange of Burmese rice and PRC export commodities in 1954-55

TYC 3:137(C); JMJP 11/4/54; SCMP 922:10

54-78 **11/3/54** – Peking **Burma** Contract
Purchase of rice from Burma

Signed by representative of China National Cereals, Oils, and Fats Company and Commerce Secretary of Burma.

JMJP 11/4/54; SCMP 922:10

54-79 **12/3/54** 12/3/54 Tirana **Albania** Agreement
Exchange of goods and payments in 1955

TYC 3:53(C); JMJP 12/8/54; SCMP 943:9

54-80 **12/3/54** 12/3/54 Tirana **Albania** Agreement
Long-term credit to Albania

TYC 3:55(C); JMJP 12/8/54; SCMP 943:9; Meissner, p. 196(G)

54-81 **12/3/54** – Tirana **Albania** Protocol
1955 plan for scientific and technical cooperation

Signed at first meeting of Sino-Albanian Joint Committee for Cooperation in Technology and Technical Science.

JMJP 12/12/54; SCMP 946:26

54-82 **12/12/54** – Peking **Burma** Communiqué
Talks during Premier U Nu's visit: establishment of consulates, air service, restoration of highway traffic, postal agreement, increase in trade in 1955-57, border questions, etc.

WCC 3:216(C); JMJP 12/13/54(C); JMST 1956, p. 387(C); PC 1955:1 Supp.(E); SCMP 946:20(E); ND 1977:29(Fr); DIA 1954, p. 333(E)

54-83 **12/13/54** 12/13/54 Peking **Finland** Protocol
Supplement to Trade Agreement of 6/21/54 [54-37]
TYC 3:46(C); JMJP 12/14/54; SCMP 947:17

54-84 **12/15/54** – New Delhi **India** Contract
Export of silk to India
JMJP 12/19/54; SCMP 951:17

54-85 **12/16/54** 1/1/55 Peking **Mongolia** Protocol
Mutual supply of goods in 1955
TYC 3:131(C); JMJP 12/17/54; SCMP 950:4

54-86 **12/24/54** 1/1/55 Peking **Vietnam (N)** Agreement
Postal services
TYC 3:177(C)

54-87 **12/24/54** – Peking **Vietnam (N)** Protocol (supplementary)
Postal services
TYC 3:182(C)

54-88 **12/24/54** 12/24/54 Peking **Vietnam (N)** Agreement
Telecommunications
TYC 3:183(C)

54-89 **12/24/54** – Peking **Vietnam (N)** Protocol
Aid to Vietnam (N) for restoration of posts and telecommunications
SCMP 956:1

54-90 **12/24/54** 12/24/54 Peking **Vietnam (N)** Protocol
PRC aid to Vietnam (N) for restoration of railway connection between Hanoi and PRC border
TYC 3:194(C); SCMP 956:2

54-91 **12/24/54** – Peking **Vietnam (N)** Protocol
PRC aid to Vietnam (N) for civil aviation and weather observation
NCNA(E) 1826:226 (12/29/54); H1:29

54-92 **12/24/54** – Peking **Vietnam (N)** Protocol
PRC aid to Vietnam (N) for highway construction
SCMP 956:1; H1:29

54-93 **12/24/54** – Peking **Vietnam (N)** Protocol
PRC aid to Vietnam (N) for water conservation
SCMP 956:1; H1:29

54-94 **12/27/54** – Berlin **Germany (E)** –
1955 plan for cultural cooperation
JMJP 12/30/54; SCMP 957:9 AGF p. 51; Dok 2:407

54-95 **12/27/54** 9/1/54 Berlin **Germany (E)** Protocol
Exchange of students (graduate and undergraduate)
TYC 3:166(C); SCMP 957:10; AGF p. 51

54-96 **12/28/54** 12/28/54 Peking **Hungary** Agreement
Cooperation to prevent insect pests and plant diseases
TYC 3:174(C); JMJP 12/30/54; SCMP 956:26

54-97 **12/28/54** – Moscow **USSR** Protocol
Scientific and technical cooperation
Referred to in JMJP as "Protocol providing for mutual obligations in scientific and technical aid conducted in various departments of national economy of the contracting parties." Signed at first meeting of Sino-Soviet Joint Committee for Scientific and Technical Cooperation.
JMJP 1/2/55; SCMP 959:30; URSS 151:19; Izv 1/18/55

54-98 **12/29/54** – Peking **Indonesia** Joint Communiqué
Preliminary negotiations on dual nationality
WCC 3:223(C); JMJP 12/30/54; SCMP 957:9

54-99 **12/30/54** 12/30/54 Peking **USSR** Agreement
Regular air services
TYC 3:192(C); JMJP 12/31/54; SCMP 958:1; S/T p. 321; Tass 12/30/54

54-100 **12/30/54** – Peking **USSR** Protocol
Termination of Sino-Soviet Civil Aviation Joint Stock Company and transfer of Soviet shares to PRC
Soviet shares formally transferred 12/31/54.
SCMP 958:2; S/T p. 321

54-101 **12/30/54(?)** – Urumchi **USSR** Protocol
Termination of Sino-Soviet Joint Stock Company for Non-Ferrous and Rare Metals and transfer of Soviet shares to PRC
Soviet shares formally transferred 1/1/55.
SCMP 958:3; S/T p. 321

54-102 **12/31/54** – Urumchi **USSR** Protocol
Termination of Sino-Soviet Petroleum Joint Stock Company and transfer of Soviet shares to PRC
SCMP 959:32; S/T p. 321

54-103 **12/31/54** – Port Arthur **USSR** Protocol
Termination of Sino-Soviet Joint Stock Company for Shipbuilding and Repair and transfer of Soviet shares to PRC
SCMP 959:33; S/T p. 321

54-104 **12/31/54** – Peking **Korea (N)** Protocol
Granting of aid and credit by PRC to Korea (N) in 1955
JMJP 1/2/55; SCMP 959:45

54-105 **12/31/54** – Peking **Korea (N)** Protocol
Exchange of goods in 1955
SCMP 959:45

54-106 **12/31/54** 12/31/54 Peking **Korea (N)** Protocol
General conditions for delivery of goods
TYC 3:111(C)

1955

55-1 **1/10/55** – Peking **United Nations** Joint Communiqué
Talks during UN Secretary-General Hammarskjold's visit: "questions pertinent to the relaxation of world tension"
WCC 3:244(C); JMJP 1/11/55 (C); JMST 1956, p. 400(C); SCMP 965:1(E); AsR 13(E); RI 1955:3:102(It)

55-2 **1/10/55** – Peking **Hungary** Protocol
Scientific and technical cooperation
Signed at first meeting of Sino-Hungarian Committee for Scientific and Technical Cooperation.
JMJP 1/11/55; SCMP 965:4; AsR 26

55-3 **1/20/55** 1/1/55 Peking **Rumania** Agreement
Exchange of goods and payments in 1955
TYC 4:81(C); JMJP 1/23/55; SCMP 975:9; ECMM 23:44; AsR 39

55-4 **1/20/55** 1/1/55 Peking **Rumania** Protocol
General conditions for delivery of goods in 1955
TYC 4:86(C)

55-5 **1/20/55** – Budapest **Hungary** Protocol
1955 plan for cultural cooperation
JMJP 1/23/55; SCMP 975:10

55-6 **1/27/55** 1/1/55 Peking **Bulgaria** Agreement
Exchange of goods and payments in 1955
TYC 4:100(C); JMJP 1/28/55; SCMP 976:12; ECMM 23:44; AsR 39

55-7 **1/27/55** 1/1/55 Peking **Bulgaria** Protocol
General conditions for delivery of goods in 1955
TYC 4:103(C)

55-8 **2/11/55** – Moscow **USSR** Protocol
Exchange of goods in 1955
JMJP 2/13/55; SCMP 987:16; ECMM 23:44; Izv 2/12/55; S/T p. 323

55-9 **2/11/55** – Warsaw **Poland** –
1955 plan for cultural cooperation
JMJP 2/15/55; SCMP 988:21

55-10 **2/12/55** 1/1/55 Moscow **USSR** Protocol
General conditions for delivery of goods
TYC 4:46(C)

55-11 **2/17/55** – Peking **Bulgaria** –
1955 plan for cultural cooperation
JMJP 2/18/55; SCMP 991:17

55-12 **3/1/55** – Peking **Czechoslovakia** Exchanges of Notes
1955 plan for cultural cooperation
JMJP 3/8/55; SCMP 1002:16

55-13 **3/2/55** – Tirana **Albania** –
1955 plan for cultural cooperation
JMJP 3/6/55; SCMP 1001:8

55-14 **3/10/55** – Bucharest **Rumania** –
1955 plan for cultural cooperation
JMJP 3/14/55; SCMP 1007:17

55-15 **3/14/55** – Ulan Bator **Mongolia** Exchange of Notes
·1955 plan for cultural cooperation
JMJP 3/16/55; SCMP 1008:20

55-16 **3/21/55** 1/1/55 Peking **Poland** Agreement
Turnover of goods and payments in 1955
TYC 4:62(C); JMJP 3/22/55; SCMP 1012:13; ECMM 23:44; AsR 138

55-17 **3/21/55** 1/1/55 Peking **Poland** Protocol
General conditions for delivery of goods in 1955
TYC 4:66(C)

55-18 **3/23/55** 3/23/55 Sofia **Bulgaria** Agreement
Scientific and technical cooperation
TYC 4:212(C); JMJP 3/25/55; SCMP 1015:5; AsR 138

55-19 **3/28/55** – Peking **Burma** Contracts (3)
Trade

Signed by representatives of China National Metals and Electrical Supplies Import Company, China National Sundries Export Company, and China National Silk Company, and of Burmese Government Purchasing Mission. Joint Communiqué also issued. SCMP 1020:12(E)

JMJP 4/1/55; SCMP 1020:11; ECMM 23:44; AsR 138

55-20 **4/1/55** 4/1/55 Lhasa **India** Protocol
Transfer to PRC of Indian postal, telegraph, and public telephone services and equipment in Tibet

Joint Communiqué also issued 4/1/55. WCC 3:337(C); NCNA(E) 1905:17 (4/4/55)(E); SCMP 1021:1(E); AsR 138; A/D p. 422(E).

TYC 4:228(C); SCMP 1021:2

55-21 **4/6/55** 1/1/55 Peking **Czechoslovakia** Agreement
Exchange of goods and payments in 1955

TYC 4:128(C); JMJP 4/7/55; SCMP 1024:10; ECMM 23:45

55-22 **4/6/55** 1/1/55 Peking **Czechoslovakia** Protocol
General conditions for delivery of goods

TYC 4:132(C)

55-23 **4/15/55** – Peking **Japan** Joint Communiqué
Talks on fishery regulation in Yellow and East China Seas

Issued by representatives of China Fishery Association and Japan-China Fishery Association of Japan.

JMJP 4/16/55(C); SCMP 1029:36(E); H12(1):167(G)

55-24 **4/15/55** 6/14/55 Peking **Japan** Agreement
Fishery regulation in Yellow and East China Seas

See note above.

TYC 4:265(C); JMJP 4/16/55(C); SCMP 1029:38(E, sum.); H12(1):150(G)

55-25 **4/15/55** – Peking **Japan** Exchange of Letters
Demarcation of PRC military and conservation zones closed to Japanese fishing vessels

See note above.

TYC 4:280(C); JMJP 4/17/55(C); SCMP 1029:39(E, sum.); H12(1):160(G)

55-26 **4/15/55** – Peking **Japan** Exchange of Memoranda
Avoidance of fishery disputes in Yellow and East China Seas

See note above. Sets out parties' differing views on need for regulating competition in specified fishing areas.

TYC 4:276(C); JMJP 4/17/55(C); SCMP 1029:40(E); H12(1):163(G)

55-27 **4/21/55** – Peking **Korea (N)** Contract
Sale and distribution of films

Signed by representatives of China Film Distribution and Exhibition Company and Korean Film Distribution Agency.

SCMP 1034:43

55-28 **4/22/55** 1/20/60 Bandung **Indonesia** Treaty
Dual nationality

Communiqué also issued. WCC 3:275(C); JMST 1956, p. 385(C); SCMP 1033:27(E)

TYC 8:12(C); WCC 3:276(C); JMJP 4/26/55(C); JMST 1956, p. 385(C); PC 1955:10 Supp.(E); CB 326:1(G); BFSP 162:415(E); DIA 1955, p. 465(E); RI 1959:7:280(It); A/D p. 231(E); WGO 2:85; IA 1955:6:151(E)

55-29 **4/24/55** – Bandung **Multilateral** Final Communiqué of Bandung Conference

Economic and cultural cooperation, human rights and self-determination, problems of dependent peoples, world peace, etc.

Signed by Afghanistan, Burma, Cambodia, Ceylon, Egypt, Ethiopia, Gold Coast, India, Indonesia, Iran, Iraq, Japan, Jordan, Laos, Lebanon, Liberia, Libya, Nepal, Pakistan, Phillipines, Saudi Arabia, Sudan, Syria, Thailand, Turkey, Vietnam (N), Vietnam (S), and Yemen. Bandung Conference invoked ten principles for development of friendly relations between states.

TYC 4:13(C); WCC 3:254(C); JMJP 4/25/55(C); JMST 1956, p. 377(C); PC 1955:10 Supp.(E); SCMP 1033:11(E); DIA 1955, p. 429(E); A/D p. 22(E); Wint, p. 798(E)

55-30 **4/24/55** 1/1/55 Peking **Germany (E)** Agreement

Exchange of goods and payments in 1955

TYC 4:166(C); JMJP 4/25/55; SCMP 1033:46; ECMM 23:45; Dok 2:413(G)

55-31 **4/24/55** 1/1/55 Peking **Germany(E)** Protocol

General conditions for delivery of goods in 1955

TYC 4:169(C)

55-32 **4/26/55** 1/1/55 Peking **Hungary** Agreement

Exchange of goods and payments in 1955

TYC 4:23(C); JMJP 4/28/55; SCMP 1035:15; ECMM 23:45

55-33 **4/26/55** 1/1/55 Peking **Hungary** Protocol

General conditions for delivery of goods in 1955

TYC 4:27(C)

55-34 **4/27/55** – Moscow **USSR** Agreement

Soviet technical assistance to PRC in peaceful use of atomic energy

JMJP 5/1/55; NCNA(E) 1929:10 (5/3/55); SCMP 1038:16; Pr 4/30/55; S/T p. 326

55-35 **4/28/55** – Djakarta **Indonesia** Joint Statement

Talks during Premier Chou En-lai's visit: Bandung Resolution, Dual Nationality Treaty, Sino-Indonesian relations, etc.

WCC 3:283(C); JMJP 4/29/55(C); JMST 1956, p. 386(C); PC 1955:10 Supp.(E); SCMP 1037:2(E); DIA 1955, p. 469(E); A/D p. 30(E)

55-36 **5/4/55** 5/4/55 Tokyo **Japan** Agreement (with Appendix)
Trade in 1955

In letter delivered on same day, Chairman of Japanese Association for Promotion of International Trade and member of Standing Committee of Japanese Diet Members' League for Promotion of Sino-Japanese Trade affirmed that Prime Minister Hatoyama had given assurances of Japanese government's support and assistance to Trade Agreement. TYC 4:262(C); SCMP 1041:2(E)

TYC 4:258(C); JMJP 5/5/55(C); SCMP 1041:47(E); ECMM 23:45; AsR 205; Contemp. Japan 23:10-12:804(E)

55-37 **5/24/55** – Port Arthur **USSR** Final Protocol
Withdrawal of Soviet armed forces from the jointly used Chinese naval base and the transfer of Soviet installations at Port Arthur

Signed by Sino-Soviet Joint Military Commission established by Agreement of 2/14/50. Joint Communiqué also issued 5/25/55. WCC 3:302(C); JMJP 5/26/55(C); JMST 1957, p. 370(C); SCMP 1056:1(E); ADTJ 0212:2(Fr); DIA 1955, p. 470(E); S/T p. 329

JMJP 5/25/55; SCMP 1055:1; Izv 5/26/55; S/T p. 329

55-38 **5/25/55** 8/1/55 Peking **Vietnam (N)** Agreement
Through railway traffic

TYC 4:247(C); SCMP 1058:38; AsR 242

55-39 **5/31/55** – Peking **Egypt** Minutes
Talks on cultural cooperation

Signed by PRC Acting Minister of Culture and Egyptian Minister for WAKFS (Religious Foundations). Submitted to governments for examination and final decision.

JMJP 6/1/55; SCMP 1059:7; AsR 242

55-40 **6/3/55** 1/20/60 Peking **Indonesia** Exchange of Notes
Implementation of 1955 Treaty on Dual Nationality

TYC 8:17(C); WCC 3:310(C); JMJP 6/16/55(C); SCMP 1070:20(E); BFSP 162:421(E); ADTJ 0222:2(Fr); DIA 1955, p. 471(E); A/D p. 236(E)

55-41 **6/8/55** – Peking **Poland** Minutes
Talks between Academies of Sciences to develop scientific cooperation

JMJP 6/9/55; SCMP 1065:7

55-42 **6/11/55(?)** – Peking(?) **Poland** Protocol
Scientific and technical cooperation

Signed at second meeting of Sino-Polish Standing Committee for Scientific and Technical Cooperation.

JMJP 6/12/55

55-43 **6/13/55(?)** – Peking **USSR** Protocol
Scientific and technical cooperation

Signed at second meeting of Sino-Soviet Joint Committee for Scientific and Technical Cooperation. Communiqué also issued 7/6/55.

JMJP 7/5/55; SCMP 1082:24; ADTJ 0229:1; Izv 7/6/55; AsR 310

55-44 **6/22/55** – Pyongyang **Korea (N)** –
1955 plan for cultural cooperation

JMJP 7/13/55

55-45 **6/24/55** 6/24/55 Peking **Sweden** Exchange of Notes
Establishment of consular relations

Registered by Sweden with UN Secretariat 2/3/56.

UNTS 228:154(E,C,Fr)

55-46 **7/7/55** – Peking **Vietnam (N)** Joint Communiqué
Talks during President Ho Chi-minh's visit: Geneva Agreements on Indo-China, economic and technical aid by PRC (including gift of 800 million yuan in goods and services), etc.

Parties reiterate pledge to implement Geneva Agreements on Indo-China despite alleged violations, invoke five principles of peaceful coexistence.

TYC 4:3(C); WCC 3:319(C); JMJP 7/8/55(C); JMST 1957, p. 370(C); PC 1955:15 Supp.(E); SCMP 1085:9(E); ADTJ 0231:2(Fr); DIA 1955, p. 475(E); AsR 298; RI 1955:29:772(It); Maki, p. 208(E)

55-47 **7/7/55** – Peking **Vietnam (N)** Protocol
Cultural cooperation

TYC 4:204(C)

55-48 **7/7/55** 7/7/55 Peking **Vietnam (N)** Protocol
Exchange of goods by local state-owned trading companies in border areas

TYC 4:157(C)

55-49 **7/7/55** 7/7/55 Peking **Vietnam (N)** Protocol
Small-scale trading in border areas

TYC 4:154(C)

55-50 **7/11/55** 7/11/55 Sofia **Bulgaria** Agreement
Cooperation for prevention of insect pests and plant diseases

TYC 4:220(C); SCMP 1088:28; AsR 321

55-51 **7/12/55** – Pyongyang **Korea (N)** Exchange of Notes
1955 plan for cultural cooperation

SCMP 1087:36

55-52 **7/16/55** – Hanoi **Vietnam (N)** Contract
Distribution of PRC films in Vietnam (N)

JMJP 7/18/55; SCMP 1090:27

55-53 **7/30/55** 8/1/55 Bucharest **Rumania** Agreement
Postal services and telecommunications

TYC 4:229(C); JMJP 8/1/55; SCMP 1101:31

55-54 **8/8/55** 5/1/55 Peking **Finland** Agreement
Trade in 1955-56

TYC 4:43(C); JMJP 8/19/55; SCMP 1105:11; ECMM 23:45

55-55 **8/10/55** – Cairo **Egypt** Contract
Purchase of Egyptian cotton by PRC

Signed by representatives of China National Import and Export Company and Egyptian Cotton Commission.

JMJP 8/11/55; SCMP 1107:9

55-56 **8/16/55** 12/16/55 Peking **USSR** Agreement (with two annexes)
Cooperation in examination, prevention, and control of insect pests and plant diseases

TYC 4:214(C); JMJP 8/17/55; SCMP 1111:26; S/T p. 334

55-57 **8/20/55** – Berlin **Germany (E)** Protocol
Scientific and technical cooperation

Signed at second session of Sino-German Standing Committee for Cooperation in Technology and Technical Sciences.

JMJP 8/25/55; SCMP 1115:21; Dok 3:393(G)

55-58 **8/22/55** 9/23/55 Peking **Egypt** Agreement
Trade in 1955-58

Agreement provides that it shall come into effect "after the approval of the two governments." Egypt ratified 9/14/55, PRC 9/23/55

TYC 4:123(C); JMJP 8/23/55; SCMP 1151:64(E); ECMM 23:45; BFSP 162:407(E); AsR 450

55-59 **8/22/55** 9/23/55 Peking **Egypt** Protocol
Trade in 1955-56

See note above.

TYC 4:127(C); SCMP 1151:67(E); BFSP 162:411(E); AsR 450

55-60 **8/23/55** – Peking **Egypt** Contract
Purchase of Egyptian cotton by PRC

Signed by representatives of China National Import and Export Company, Egyptian Cotton Commission, and Misr Cotton Exporting Society of Egypt.

JMJP 8/24/55; SCMP 1116:7

55-61 **8/23/55** – Peking **Egypt** Contract
Importation by Egypt of rolled steel from PRC

Signed by representatives of Egyptian government trade delegation and China National Metals and Electrical Supplies Import Company.

JMJP 8/24/55; SCMP 1116:7

55-62 **8/26/55** – Peking **Egypt** Joint Communiqué
Trade talks

JMJP 8/26/55(C); SCMP 1118:20(E)

55-63 **9/10/55** – Geneva **USA** Agreed Announcement
Repatriation of PRC citizens in US and US citizens in PRC

Made by PRC Ambassador Wang Ping-nan and US Ambassador U. Alexis Johnson after ambassador-level negotiations at Geneva.

TYC 4:1(C); WCC 3:345(C); JMJP 9/11/55(C); JMST 1956, p. 393(C); PC 1955:18 Supp.(E); SCMP 1127:1(E); DSB 33:456(E); DIA 1955, p. 463(E); DAFR 1956, p. 316(E); AsR 416(E); RI 1955:38:998(It), 1959:7:306(It); H12(3):149(G)

55-64 **9/14/55** – Sofia **Bulgaria** Agreement
Postal services and telecommunications

Effective on ratification; date of ratification unknown.

TYC 4:238(C); JMJP 9/16/55; SCMP 1131:24; AsR 417

55-65 **9/16/55** – – **Germany (E)** –
Additional deliveries of goods in 1955

AGF p. 52; Dok 3:393(G)

55-66 **9/28/55** 9/28/55 Peking **Albania** Agreement
Cooperation in radio broadcasting

TYC 4:202(C); JMJP 9/30/55; SCMP 1140:40

55-67 **9/28/55** – Peking **Albania** –
1956 plan for cultural cooperation

JMJP 9/30/55; SCMP 1140:40

55-68 **10/12/55(?)** 6/1/55 Peking **Ceylon** Agreement
Increase in rubber prices for period June-December 1955

Joint Communiqué on trade talks also issued 10/16/55. SCMP 1151:62(E)

SCMP 1151:62; ECMM 23:45; AsR 449

55-69 **10/14/55** – Peking **Ceylon** Contracts (2)
Exchange of PRC rice and Ceylonese rubber in 1956

SCMP 1151:62; ECMM 23:45

55-70 **10/15/55** – Peking **Japan** Protocol
Supplement to Trade Agreement of 5/4/55 [55-36]

TYC 4:263(C)

55-71 **10/16/55(?)** – Peking **Ceylon** Agreement
Decrease in PRC rice prices

AsR 462

55-72 **10/17/55** – Peking **Japan** Joint Communiqué
Talks during visit of Japanese Diet Mission: promotion of diplomatic, economic, and cultural relations, etc.

Signed by Peng Chen, Secretary-General of Standing Committee of National People's Congress of PRC, and Eikichi Kanbayashiyama, Leader of Japanese Diet Mission. Urges normalization of diplomatic relations, abolition of trade restrictions, establishment of permanent trade organizations in Tokyo and Peking, further promotion of cultural exchanges, exchange of corpses of each other's nationals, and unrestricted travel to and from their home country of nationals residing in each other's country. PRC announces intention to make final disposition of Japanese war criminals.

WCC 3:377(C); JMJP 10/18/55(C); SCMP 1151:56(E)

55-73 **10/17/55** – Ulan Bator **Mongolia** Protocol
USSR

Opening of through rail traffic between PRC and the Soviet Union through Mongolia

JMJP 10/29/55; SCMP 1160:50; AsR 497

55-74 **10/17/55** – Ulan Bator **Mongolia** Agreement
Border railways

SCMP 1160:50; AsR 497

55-75 **10/17/55** – Ulan Bator **Mongolia** Protocol
Through railway traffic

SCMP 1160:50; AsR 497

55-76 **10/27/55** – Bucharest **Rumania** Protocol
Scientific and technical cooperation

Signed at third session of Sino-Rumanian Joint Committee for Scientific and Technical Cooperation.

JMJP 10/29/55; SCMP 1159:37

55-77 **11/8/55** 11/8/55 Rangoon **Burma** Agreement
Air transport

Registered by Burma with UN Secretariat 7/18/58. Joint Communiqué also issued 11/8/55. SCMP 1168:32(E)

TYC 4:251(C); JMJP 11/10/55; SCMP 1168:32; UNTS 306:36(E,F); AsR 497

55-78 **11/8/55** – Rangoon **Burma** Protocol
Air transport

See note above.

UNTS 306:50(E,F)

55-79 **11/8/55** – Rangoon **Burma** Exchange of Notes
Nationality of pilots

See note above.

UNTS 306:56(E,F)

55-80 **11/11/55(?)** – Rangoon **Burma** Protocol
Air services

JMJP 11/15/55; SCMP 1170:34

55-81 **11/11/55** 1/1/56 Prague **Czechoslovakia** Agreement
Exchange of goods and payments in 1956

TYC 4:150(C); JMJP 11/12/55; SCMP 1169:44

55-82 **11/11/55(?)** – Peking **Bulgaria** Protocol
Scientific and technical cooperation

Signed at first session of Sino-Bulgarian Joint Committee for Scientific and Technical Cooperation.

SCMP 1171:21

55-83 **11/16/55** – Peking **Japan** Joint Communiqué
Talks during visit of delegation of National League for Protection of Japanese Constitution: promotion of peaceful coexistence, restoration of diplomatic relations, etc.

Signed by representatives of Chinese People's Institute of Foreign Affairs and National League for Protection of Japanese Constitution.

WCC 3:379(C); JMJP 11/17/55(C); SCMP 1172:20(E); DIA 1955, p. 485(E)

55-84 **11/20/55** 1/1/56 Berlin **Germany (E)** Agreement
Exchange of goods and payments in 1956

TYC 4:182(C); JMJP 11/22/55; SCMP 1175:20; AsR 522; Dok 3:396(G)

55-85 **11/20/55** 1/1/56 Berlin **Germany (E)** Protocol
General conditions for delivery of goods in 1956

TYC 4:186(C)

55-86 **11/25/55** – Peking **Vietnam (N)** Agreement
Currency exchange rate

JMJP 11/26/55; SCMP 1178:37; H1:28

55-87 **11/25/55** – Peking **Vietnam (N)** Protocol
Currency exchange along border

JMJP 11/26/55; SCMP 1178:37

55-88 **11/25/55** – Peking **Vietnam (N)** Protocol
Noncommercial remittances between People's Bank of China and Vietnam National Bank

JMJP 11/26/55; SCMP 1178:37; H1:28

55-89 **11/25/55** – Peking **Vietnam (N)** Protocol
Settlement of trade balances

JMJP 11/26/55; SCMP 1178:37

55-90 **11/27/55** – Peking **Japan** Agreement
Establishment of liaison facilities to promote cultural exchanges

Signed by representatives of Chinese People's Association for Cultural Relations with Foreign Countries and National League for Protection of Japanese Constitution.

WCC 3:380(C); JMJP 11/28/55(C); SCMP 1178:30

55-91 **11/29/55** – Peking **USSR** Arrangement
Acquisition of each other's film copyrights

SCMP 1180:44; H1:21

55-92 **11/30/55** 2/17/56 Damascus **Syria** Agreement
Trade

Joint Communiqué on trade also issued 11/30/55. SCMP 1182:27(E)

TYC 4:118(C); JMJP 12/2/55; PC 1956:1:45; SCMP 1182:28; ECMM 23:45; STS 57:1(Fr); AsR 543; H12(2):64(G)

55-93 **11/30/55** 2/17/56 Damascus **Syria** Agreement
Payments

TYC 4:120(C); JMJP 12/2/55; PC 1956:1:45;SCMP 1182:28;ECMM 23:45; STS 57:3(Fr); AsR 543; H12(2):67(G)

55-94 **12/3/55** – Peking **Czechoslovakia** Protocol
Scientific and technical cooperation

Signed at third meeting of Sino-Czechoslovak Joint Committee for Scientific and Technical Cooperation. Joint Communiqué also issued. SCMP 1188:58(E)

JMJP 12/10/55; SCMP 1188:58

55-95 **12/17/55** – Peking **Uruguay** Joint Statement
Promotion of trade relations

Signed by Assistant Minister of Foreign Trade of PRC and Uruguayan Consul in Hong Kong.

SCMP 1193:49

55-96 **12/21/55** – Peking **Korea (N)** Agreement
Currency exchange rate
JMJP 12/22/55; SCMP 1196:16

55-97 **12/21/55** – Peking **Korea (N)** Protocol
Noncommercial remittances between People's Bank of China and Central Bank of Korea
JMJP 12/22/55; SCMP 1196:16

55-98 **12/21/55** 1/1/56 Ulan Bator **Mongolia** Agreement
Cooperation in radio broadcasting
TYC 4:207(C); JMJP 12/24/55; SCMP 1197:14

55-99 **12/21/55** 1/1/56 Warsaw **Poland** Agreement
Turnover of goods and payments in 1956
TYC 4:77(C); JMJP 12/24/55; SCMP 1197:17; Horak, p. 101

55-100 **12/21/55** 1/1/56 Warsaw **Poland** Protocol
Extension of Protocol of 3/21/55 on general conditions for delivery of goods [55-17]
TYC 4:81(C)

55-101 **12/25/55** – Peking **Germany (E)** Joint Statement
Talks during Premier Grotewohl's visit: unification of Germany, PRC representation in UN, international tensions, peaceful coexistence, etc.
TYC 4:9(C); WCC 3:355(C); JMJP 12/26/55(C); JMST 1957, p. 372(C); PC 1956:2 Supp.(E); SCMP 1198:38(E); RI 1956:1:16(It); Dok 3:418(G), 4:89(G)

55-102 **12/25/55** 2/10/56 Berlin **Germany (E)** Treaty
Friendship and cooperation
TYC 4:7(C); YHTY 87(C,G); WCC 3:359(C); JMJP 12/26/55(C); JMST 1957, p. 373(C); PC 1956:2 Supp.(E); SCMP 1198:33(E); BFSP 162:413(E); ADTJ 0302:1(Fr); AGF p. 52; RI 1959:7:276(It); Dok 3:424(G), 4:95(G); V-P(2):510(G, sum.); IA 1956:1:159(E)

55-103 **12/25/55** 2/1/56 Peking **Germany (E)** Agreement
Cultural cooperation
TYC 4:209(C); JMJP 12/26/55; SCMP 1198:30; AGF p. 52; Dok 4:98(G)

55-104 **12/25/55** 2/1/56 Peking **Germany (E)** Agreement
Examination, prevention, and control of insect pests and plant diseases
TYC 4:223(C); JMJP 12/26/55; SCMP 1198:30; AGF p. 53; Dok 4:100(G)

55-105 **12/27/55** – Moscow **USSR** Protocol
Exchange of goods in 1956

TYC 4:60(C); JMJP 12/29/55; SCMP 1200:34; Izv 12/28/55; S/T p. 345; H1:22; IA 1956:1:259

55-106 **12/27/55** – Moscow **USSR** Exchange of Notes
Revision of Protocol of 2/12/55 on general conditions for delivery of goods [55-10]

SCMP 1200:34

55-107 **12/29/55** 12/29/55 Rangoon **Burma** Protocol (with payments and accounting procedure)
Exchange of Burmese rice and PRC export commodities for 1955-56

Press Communiqué also issued 12/29/55. SCMP 1201:54(E); Burma Wkly. Bull. 4:40:320 (1/5/56)(E); AsR 625(E)

TYC 4:162(C); JMJP 12/31/55

55-108 **12/30/55** – – **Vietnam (N)** Contract
Purchase of five airliners and aircraft equipment from PRC

Signed by representatives of Vietnam Export and Import Company and China Technical Import Company.

SCMP 1205:41

55-109 **12/30/55** – – **Vietnam (N)** Contract
Aid by PRC technicians in Vietnam (N)

See note above.

SCMP 1205:41

55-110 **12/31/55** 8/4/56 Beirut **Lebanon** Agreement
Trade

Communiqué also issued 1/3/56. SCMP 1202:42(E); JMJP 1/4/56(C)

TYC 4:159(C); JMJP 3/4/56(C); ND 2242:14(Fr); H12(2):51(G); A/M/K 4:29(Fr,A)

55-111 **12/31/55** – Beirut **Lebanon** Exchange of Letters
Establishment of PRC Trade Mission in Beirut

A/M/K 4:23(Fr,A); H12(2):55(G)

55-112 **12/31/55** – Beirut **Lebanon** Exchange of Letters
Trade involving third countries

A/M/K 4:19(Fr,A); H12(2):57(G)

1956

56-1 **1/3/56** – Peking **Czechoslovakia** –
1956 plan for cultural cooperation

JMJP 1/4/56; SCMP 1202:42

56-2 **1/3/56** 1/1/56 Bucharest **Rumania** Agreement
Exchange of goods and payments in 1956

TYC 5:69(C); SCMP 1203:25

56-3 **1/3/56** 1/1/56 Bucharest **Rumania** Protocol
General conditions for delivery of goods in 1956

TYC 5:73(C)

56-4 **1/4/56** – Peking **USSR** **Mongolia** Joint Communiqué
Completion of Ulan Bator-Chining (Tsinin) Railway and opening of through traffic between three countries

Through rail service began 1/1/56.

JMST 1957, p. 373(C); SCMP 1203:15; Izv 1/4/56(R)

56-5 **1/4/56** – Moscow **USSR** Agreement
Technical cooperation in civil aviation

JMJP 1/6/56; SCMP 1204:34; Izv 1/5/56; S/T p. 346

56-6 **1/4/56** – Moscow **USSR** Communiqué
Scientific and technical cooperation

Issued after third meeting of Sino-Soviet Joint Committee for Scientific and Technical Cooperation. USSR undertook to build nuclear reactor in PRC. Protocol signed in late December 1955.

SCMP 1203:24; Izv 1/5/56(R)

56-7 **12/29/55 / 1/10/56** – Rangoon **Burma** Exchange of Notes
Extension of Article 7 of 1954 Trade Agreement [54-18]

TYC 3:136(C); H12(1):34

56-8 **1/12/56** – Peking **Korea (N)** Protocol
Exchange of goods in 1956

JMJP 1/13/56; SCMP 1209:33

56-9 **1/12/56** – Peking **Korea (N)** Protocol
Material aid to Korea (N)

JMJP 1/13/56; SCMP 1209:33

56-10 **1/14/56** 1/14/56 Peking **Korea (N)** Protocol
Transport of timber on rivers Yalu and Tumen

TYC 5:24(C)

56-11 **1/19/56** – Rangoon **Burma** Contract
Purchase of Burmese rice by PRC

Signed by Commercial Counsellor of PRC Embassy in Burma (for China National Cereals, Oils, and Fats Export Company) and Chairman of State Agricultural Marketing Board of Union of Burma.

JMJP 1/23/56; SCMP 1215:46

56-12 **1/19/56** – Sofia **Bulgaria** –
1956 plan for cultural cooperation
SCMP 1215:49

56-13 **1/21/56** 1/1/56 Sofia **Bulgaria** Agreement
Exchange of goods and payments in 1956
TYC 5:88(C); JMJP 1/22/56; SCMP 1215:49

56-14 **1/21/56** 1/1/56 Sofia **Bulgaria** Protocol
General conditions for delivery of goods in 1956
TYC 5:91(C)

56-15 **1/27/56** 1/1/56 Budapest **Hungary** Agreement
Exchange of goods and payments in 1956
TYC 5:34; JMJP 2/1/56; SCMP 1220:39

56-16 **1/27/56** 1/1/56 Budapest **Hungary** Protocol
General conditions for delivery of goods in 1956
TYC 5:38(C)

56-17 **1/27/56** – Peking **Hungary** –
1956 plan for cultural cooperation
JMJP 2/1/56; SCMP 1220:39

56-18 **1/28/56** – Peking **Poland** –
1956 plan for cultural cooperation
JMJP 2/3/56; SCMP 1220:38

56-19 **2/2/56** – Peking **Germany (E)** –
1956 plan for cultural cooperation
JMJP 2/3/56; SCMP 1224:31; Dok 3:456

56-20 **2/7/56** 1/1/56 Ulan Bator **Mongolia** Protocol
Mutual supply of goods in 1956
TYC 5:133(C); JMJP 2/9/56; SCMP 1227:23; AsR 678

56-21 **2/7/56** 1/1/56 Ulan Bator **Mongolia** Protocol
General conditions for delivery of goods
TYC 5:135(C)

56-22 **2/13/56** – Bucharest **Rumania** –
1956 plan for cultural cooperation
JMJP 2/19/56; SCMP 1231:39

56-23 **2/14/56** 10/1/56 Belgrade **Yugoslavia** Agreement
Postal services
TYC 5:174(C); JMJP 2/19/56; SCMP 1233:39; YTS 1957:69:64(S-C,E)

56-24 **2/14/56** 10/1/56 Belgrade **Yugoslavia** Agreement
Telecommunications

TYC 5:182(C); JMJP 2/19/56; SCMP 1233:39; YTS 1957:69:64(S-C,E)

56-25 **2/17/56** 2/17/56 Belgrade **Yugoslavia** Agreement
Trade

TYC 5:113(C); JMJP 2/19/56; SCMP 1233:40; YTS 1957:63:27(S-C,E); AsR 705

56-26 **2/17/56** – Belgrade **Yugoslavia** Exchange of Letters
Agreement that in event of dispute over interpretation between Serbo-Croatian and Chinese texts of Trade Agreement of 2/17/56, English translation should be taken as basis for settlement [56-25]

YTS 1957:63:29(S-C,E)

56-27 **2/17/56** – Belgrade **Yugoslavia** Agreement
Payments

TYC 5:115(C); JMJP 2/19/56; SCMP 1233:40; YTS 1957:63:30(S-C,E); AsR 705

56-28 **2/17/56** – Belgrade **Yugoslavia** Exchange of Letters
Agreement that in event of dispute over interpretation between Serbo-Croatian and Chinese texts of Payments Agreement of 2/17/56, English translation should be taken as basis for settlement [56-27]

YTS 1957:63:32(S-C,E)

56-29 **2/17/56** – Belgrade **Yugoslavia** Agreement
Scientific and technical cooperation

TYC 5:165(C); JMJP 2/19/56; SCMP 1233:40; YTS 1957:65:47(S-C,E); AsR 705

56-30 **2/17/56** – Belgrade **Yugoslavia** Exchange of Letters
Agreement that in event of dispute over interpretation between Serbo-Croatian and Chinese texts of Scientific and Technical Cooperation Agreement of 2/17/56, English translation should be taken as basis for settlement [56-29]

YTS 1957:65:48(S-C,E)

56-31 **2/18/56** – Peking **Cambodia** Joint Communiqué
Talks during Premier Norodom Sihanouk's visit: Sino-Cambodian relations, five principles of peaceful coexistence, international situation, etc.

TYC 5:15(C); WCC 4:48(C); JMJP 2/19/56(C); JMST 1957, p. 388(C); PC 1956:5 Supp.(E); SCMP 1233:31(E); AsR 681

56-32 **2/19/56** – Peking **France** Joint Statement
Trade talks

Signed by representatives of French Economic Mission to PRC and China Committee for Promotion of International Trade.

JMJP 2/21/56; SCMP 1234:29(E); AsR 733(E)

56-33 **2/19/56** – Peking **France** Protocol
Commercial payments procedures

See note above.

TYC 5:405(C); SCMP 1234:29; AsR 733; H12(3):49(G)

56-34 **2/19/56** – Peking **France** Protocol
Payments

See note above.

TYC 5:406(C); JMJP 2/21/56; SCMP 1234:29; AsR 733; H12(3):50(G)

56-35 **2/24/56** – Peking **Poland** Exchange of Notes
Changes in postal and telegram services

TYC 5:148(C)

56-36 **2/25/56** 2/25/56 Peking **Poland** Protocol
Technical cooperation in postal services and telecommunications

TYC 5:173(C); SCMP 1237:33

56-37 **2/25/56** 4/1/56 Ulan Bator **Mongolia** Agreement
Parcel post

TYC 5:187(C); SCMP 1237:34

56-38 **2/29/56** – Budapest **Hungary** Protocol
Scientific and technical cooperation

Signed at second session of Sino-Hungarian Committee for Scientific and Technical Cooperation.

JMJP 3/4/56; SCMP1243:29

56-39 **3/11/56** – Peking **Albania** Protocol
Scientific and technical cooperation

Signed at second meeting of Sino-Albanian Joint Committee for Cooperation in Technology and Technical Science.

JMST 1957, p. 364

56-40 **3/13/56** 1/1/56 Peking **Albania** Protocol
Exchange of goods and payments in 1956

TYC 5:66(C); SCMP 1249:26

56-41 **3/19/56** 3/19/56 Karachi **Pakistan** Contract
Supply of coal by PRC to Pakistan

PakTS 1956:12:1(E); AsR 825

56-42 **3/26/56** 3/26/56 Moscow **Multilateral** Agreement
Establishment of Joint Institute for Nuclear Research

Signed by USSR, Albania, Bulgaria, Czechoslovakia, Germany (E), Hungary, Korea (N), Mongolia, Poland, and Rumania. Vietnam (N) acceded 9/20/56. Registered by USSR with UN Secretariat 2/1/57. Statute of Institute adopted 9/26/56. PRC withdrew from Institute in July 1966. Communiqué also issued.

TYC 10:408(C); JMJP 7/13/56(C); SCMP 1263:3; UNTS 259:126(R,E,Fr); Izv 7/12/56(R); AsR 767; S/T p. 351; V-P(2):521(G, sum.)

56-43 **3/27/56** – Sofia **Bulgaria** Exchange of Notes
Revision of Protocol on General Conditions for Delivery of Goods in 1955 [55-7]

TYC 5:104(C)

56-44 **3/31/56** 4/1/56 Peking **Finland** Exchange of Notes
Reciprocal grant of most-favored-nation treatment in customs duties and navigation

TYC 5:61(C); JMJP 4/1/56; SCMP 1261:53; FTS(FFF) 1956:5:66(Sw.,E); FTS(SAS) 1956:5:68(F,E); BFSP 162:890(E); H12(3):32(G)

56-45 **4/5/56** 4/5/56 Peking **Vietnam (N)** Agreement
Civil air transport

TYC 5:194(C); JMJP 4/6/56; SCMP 1264:37; AsR 770

56-46 **4/7/56** – Peking **USSR** Joint Communiqué
Talks culminating in signature of two documents listed below

WCC 4:56(C); JMJP 4/8/56(C); JMST 1957, p. 367(C); SCMP 1265:30(E); Izv 4/8/56(R); RI 1959:7:273(It); S/T p. 352

56-47 **4/7/56** – Peking **USSR** Agreement
Soviet aid on construction projects in PRC

JMJP 4/8/56; SCMP 1265:30; SIA 1955-56, p. 244; Izv 4/10/56; AsR 781; IA 1956:7:135

56-48 **4/7/56** – Peking **USSR** Agreement
Cooperation in construction of Lanchow-Aktogai railway and through-traffic service from 1960

JMJP 4/8/56; SCMP 1265:30; SIA 1955-56, p. 244; Izv 4/10/56; IA 1956:7:135

56-49 **4/12/56** – Khartoum **Sudan** Communiqué
Trade talks

JMJP 4/15/56; SCMP 1270:34(E); H12(2):183(G)

56-50 **4/12/56** – Khartoum **Sudan** Exchange of Letters
Development of trade relations

TYC 5:59(C); JMJP 4/29/56(C); SCMP 1281:32(E); H12(2):181(G)

56-51 **4/15/56** 9/25/56 Cairo **Egypt** Agreement
Cultural cooperation

TYC 5:159(C); JMJP 4/17/56; SCMP 1380:20(E); AsR 1086(E); H12(2):6(G)

56-52 **4/16/56** – Peking **Egypt** Communiqué
Trade talks

JMJP 4/17/56(C); SCMP 1271:32(E)

56-53 **4/23/56** – Warsaw **Poland** Protocol
Scientific and technical cooperation

Signed at third session of Sino-Polish Standing Committee for Scientific and Technical Cooperation.

JMJP 4/27/56; SCMP 1278:34

56-54 **4/24/56** 6/10/56 Peking **Cambodia** Agreement
Trade

TYC 5:105(C); JMJP 4/25/56; SCMP 1303:22(E) AsR 890(E); H12(1):179(G)

56-55 **4/24/56** 6/10/56 Peking **Cambodia** Agreement
Payments

TYC 5:107(C); JMJP 4/25/56; SCMP 1303:23 (E, sum.); AsR 890(E); H12(1):182(G)

56-56 **4/27/56** – Belgrade **Yugoslavia** Contract
Distribution of films

SCMP 1281:35

56-57 **4/27/56** – Belgrade **Yugoslavia** Contract
Exchange of newsreel materials

SCMP 1281:35

56-58 **4/28/56** – Bucharest **Rumania** Exchange of Notes
Revision of Protocol on General Conditions for Delivery of Goods in 1955 [55-4]

TYC 5:86(C)

56-59 **4/29/56** – Peking **Cambodia** Joint Communiqué
Trade talks

SCMP 1281:28(E); A/D p. 314(E)

56-60 **4/29/56** – Budapest **Hungary** Exchange of Notes
Revision of Protocol on General Conditions for Delivery of Goods in 1955 [55-33]

TYC 5:54(C)

56-61 **5/8/56** – Peking **Japan** Joint Communiqué
Fishery talks

Issued by representatives of China Fishery Association and Japan-China Fishery Association of Japan.

SCMP 1287:27

56-62 **5/8/56** – Peking **Japan** Protocol
Extension of 1955 Agreement on Fishery Regulation in Yellow and East China Seas to 6/13/57 [55-24]

Signed by representatives of China Fishery Association of PRC and Japan-China Fishery Association of Japan.

TYC 5:410(C); JMJP 5/9/56(C); SCMP1287:27

56-63 **5/8/56** – Peking **Japan** Exchange of Notes
Extension of fishery agreement by 1955 Exchange of Letters to 6/13/57 [55-25]

See note above.

TYC 5:411(C); SCMP 1287:27

56-64 **5/8/56** – Peking **Japan** Exchange of Notes
Extension of fishery agreement by 1955 Exchange of Memoranda to 6/13/57 [55-26]

See note above.

TYC 5:413(C); SCMP 1287:27

56-65 **5/10/56** 5/10/56 Karachi **Pakistan** Contract
Supply of coal by PRC to Pakistan

Supplements contract of 3/19/56 [56-41].

PakTS 1956:13:1(E); AsR 825

56-66 **5/20/56** – Cairo **Egypt** –
1956-57 plan for cultural cooperation

JMJP 5/22/56; SCMP 1295:30

56-67 **5/22/56** – – **Germany (E)** Protocol
Additional deliveries of goods in 1956

AGF p. 53; Dok 3:456

56-68 **5/30/56** – Pyongyang **Korea (N)** –
1956 plan for cultural cooperation

SCMP 1301:22

56-69 **6/1/56** – Peking **UK** Exchange of Notes
Trademark registration

TYC 5:68(C); H12(3):100(G)

56-70 **6/12/56** 6/12/56 Peking **Multilateral** Agreement
Cooperation in fishery, oceanographic, and limnological research in western Pacific region

Established Fishery Research Commission for Western Pacific. Signed by USSR, Korea (N), and Vietnam (N). Mongolia acceded 12/15/58. Amendment proposed at 1959 Conference in Hanoi. Approved by PRC 4/30/60, in effect 8/8/62. TYC 11:131(C)

TYC 5:169(C); JMJP 6/13/56(C); SCMP 1310:20 (E, sum.); Izv 6/13/56

56-71 **6/12/56** 5/25/57 Damascus **Syria** Agreement
Cultural cooperation

TYC 5:158(C); SCMP 1311:31; STS 84:1(Fr); H12(2):63(G)

56-72 **6/12/56** – Damascus **Syria** –
1956-57 plan for cultural cooperation

JMJP 6/15/56; SCMP 1311:31

56-73 **6/14/56** – Peking **USSR** Exchange of Notes
Delivery of commodities

TYC 5:64(C)

56-74 **6/18/56** 6/18/56 Hanoi **Vietnam (N)** Protocol
General conditions for delivery of goods

Articles 15 to 20 did not become effective until 7/1/56.

TYC 5:122(C)

56-75 **6/21/56** – Peking **Cambodia** Joint Communiqué
Economic aid talks

WCC 4:72(C); JMST 1957, p. 388(C); PC 1956:14 Supp.(E); SCMP 1318:45(E); AsR 941(E); A/D p. 314(E); H12(1):187(G)

56-76 **6/21/56** 6/21/56 Peking **Cambodia** Agreement
Economic aid by PRC (gift of 800 million rials in 1956-57 for construction of factories, etc.)

TYC 5:109(C); SCMP 1318:46; BFSP 162:885(Fr); AsR 941(E); H12(1):183(G)

56-77 **6/21/56** 6/21/56 Peking **Cambodia** Protocol
Implemention of Economic Aid Agreement of 6/21/56 [56-76]

TYC 5:111(C); SCMP 1318:46; BFSP 162:887(Fr); H12(1):185(G)

56-78 **6/21/56** – Poznan **Poland** Agreement
Trade

SCMP 1318:54

56-79 **6/23/56** – Peking **USSR** Protocol
Scientific and technical cooperation

Signed at fourth session of Sino-Soviet Joint Committee for Scientific and Technical Cooperation. Communiqué also issued. Pr 6/23/56(R)

SCMP 1326:29

56-80 **6/28/56** – Sofia **Multilateral** Regulations
Establishment of Organization for Cooperation of Railways

Signed by USSR, Mongolia, Poland, Rumania, Czechoslovakia, Bulgaria, Germany (E), Hungary, Korea (N), Albania, and Vietnam (N). Ratified by PRC 5/18/57. Revised regulations adopted by conference at Peking 6/7/57. Operations began in September 1957. Regulations further revised and adopted by conference at Ulan Bator in June 1962.

TYC 6:314(C); S/T p. 359

56-81 **6/28/56** – Tientsin **Japan** Joint Communiqué
Repatriation of Japanese war criminals, return of corpses, visiting rights between nationals residing in each other's country and their relatives, etc.

Signed by representatives of Chinese Red Cross Society and of Japanese Red Cross Society, Japan-China Friendship Association, and Japanese Peace Liaison Committee.

WCC 4:470(C); SCMP 1323:28 (E, sum.)

56-82 **7/3//56** 1/1/57 Moscow **USSR** Agreement
Korea (N)
Rescue of persons, ships, and aircraft at sea in Pacific region

Denounced by PRC 6/24/67. Lost effect 1/1/68. Izv 7/19/67

TYC 5:199(C); JMJP 7/4/56; SCMP 1324:23; Izv 7/4/56

56-83 **7/4/56** – Peking **Czechoslovakia** Protocol
Exchange of essential goods for period 1958-62

JMJP 7/7/56; SCMP 1325:33

56-84 **7/5/56** 12/7/56 Moscow **USSR** Agreement
Cultural cooperation

Registered by USSR with UN Secretariat 3/25/57.

TYC 5:152(C); JMJP 7/7/56; SCMP 1326:30; UNTS 263:131(R,C,E,Fr); Izv 7/6/56; AsR 930

56-85 **7/13/56** – Moscow **USSR** –
1956 plan for cultural cooperation

JMJP 7/15/56; SCMP 1331:33

56-86 **7/14/56** 9/1/56 Peking **Poland** Agreement
Exchange of students

TYC 5:154(C)

56-87 **7/25/56** – Peking **USSR** Protocol (supplementary)
Mutual supply of goods in 1956

JMJP 7/26/56; SCMP 1339:23; Izv 7/27/56

56-88 **7/26/56** – Hanoi **Vietnam (N)** Agreement
Exchange of goods and payments in 1956

JMJP 7/27/56; SCMP 1340:30

56-89 **7/26/56** – Hanoi **Vietnam (N)** Protocol
Economic aid by PRC to Vietnam (N) in 1956

JMJP 7/27/56; SCMP 1340:30

56-90 **7/26/56** – Hanoi **Vietnam (N)** Protocol
Technical assistance by PRC to Vietnam (N)

JMJP 7/27/56; SCMP 1340:30

56-91 **7/31/56** 5/1/56 Helsinki **Finland** Agreement
Trade in 1956-57

TYC 5:63(C); JMJP 8/5/56; SCMP 1343:29

56-92 **8/13/56** 6/13/56 Pyongyang **Korea (N)** Agreement
Cooperation in radio broadcasting

TYC 5:162(C); SCMP 1352:34

56-93 **8/18/56** – Peking **USSR** Agreement
Joint investigation and development of natural resources of Heilungkiang River Valley

Established Sino-Soviet Joint Academic Committee for Research on the Productivity of the Heilungkiang River Basin, which had its fourth and last session in April 1962.

SCMP 1355:49; Pr 8/19/56; AsR 990

56-94 **8/25/56** – Peking **Laos** Joint Statement
Talks during Prince Souvanna Phouma's visit: PRC support for Laotian policy of peace and neutralism, joint support of five principles of peaceful coexistence (Panch Shila), development of economic and cultural relations, etc.

TYC 5:13(C); WCC 4:102(C); JMJP 8/26/56(C); JMST 1957, p. 389(C); PC 1956:18 Supp.(E); SCMP 1360:30(E); AsR 989; RI 1956:36:1085(It); H12(1):191(G)

56-95 **8/28/56** – Peking **India** Agreement
Sale of rice by PRC to India

SCMP 1362:32

56-96 **8/29/56** 8/29/56 Ulan Bator **Mongolia** Agreement
Economic and technical aid by PRC (including gift of 160 million rubles for period 1956-59)

TYC 5:144(C); JMJP 8/30/56; SCMP 1363:26

56-97 **9/2/56** 9/2/56 Yenchi **Korea (N)** Protocol
Joint conservation on Tumen River

TYC 5:29(C)

56-98 **9/5/56** – Prague **Czechoslovakia** Protocol
Scientific and technical cooperation

Signed at fourth session of Sino-Czechoslovak Joint Committee for Scientific and Technical Cooperation.

SCMP 1367:39

56-99 **9/13/56** – Vienna **Austria** Protocol
Promotion of trade

Signed by representatives of China Committee for Promotion of International Trade and Austrian Association on East-West Trade.

TYC 5:409(C); SCMP 1373:34; H12(3):69(G)

56-100 **9/14/56** – Peking **Ceylon** Joint Communiqué
Development of diplomatic, economic, and cultural relations

TYC 5:22(C); WCC 4:106(C); JMJP 9/17/56(C); JMST 1957, p. 390(C); SCMP 1373:30(E)

56-101 **9/16/56** – Sofia **Bulgaria** Protocol
Scientific and technical cooperation

Signed at second session of Sino-Bulgarian Joint Committee for Scientific and Technical Cooperation.

SCMP 1375:35

56-102 **9/18/56** – Moscow **USSR** –
Conveyance of Manchurian archives by USSR to PRC

H1:21

56-103 **9/20/56** – Katmandu **Nepal** Joint Communiqué
Talks culminating in signature of three documents listed below

WCC 4:119(C); JMST 1957, p. 385(C); SCMP 1378:16(E)

56-104 **9/20/56** 1/17/58 Katmandu **Nepal** Agreement
Maintenance of friendly relations between PRC and Nepal, and trade and intercourse between Tibet region of PRC and Nepal

Abrogates all existing treaties and documents between China and Nepal, including those between Nepal and Tibet region of China.

TYC 5:4(C); WCC 4:120(C) JMJP 9/24/56(C); JMST 1957, p. 386(C); PC 1956:21 Supp.(E); SCMP 1378:17(E); Nepal Department of Publicity News Bull. 3:3:1 (9/20/56)(E); PI(M) 67:282(Sp); BFSP 162:892(E); ADTJ 0426:9; DIA 1956, p. 740(E); AsR 1071(E, sum.); A/D p. 328(E); H12(1):206(G); V-P(2):529(G, sum.); WGO 2:85; IA 1956:11:165(E)

56-105 **9/20/56** 9/20/56 Katmandu **Nepal** Exchange of Notes
Establishment of consulates-general, military withdrawal of Nepalese from Tibet, jurisdiction over and responsibility for each other's nationals by country of residence, trade expansion, nationality, and other questions

TYC 5:7(C); WCC 4:123(C); PC 1956:21 Supp.(E); WCMP 1378:21(E); BFSP 162:896(E); ADTJ 0426:9; DIA 1956, p. 743(E); A/D p. 331(E); H12(1):210(G); IA 1956:11:167(E)

56-106 **9/20/56** – Katmandu **Nepal** Exchange of Notes
Exchange of diplomatic envoys

TYC 5:10(C); WCC 4:127(C); SCMP 1378:20(E); BFSP 162:896(E); H12(1):213(G); IA 1956:11:168(E)

56-107 **9/23/56** – Dubna **Multilateral** Statute
Joint Institute of Nuclear Research

Statute (and Table of Personnel) signed by USSR, Poland, Czechoslovakia, Rumania, Bulgaria, Albania, Germany (E), Hungary, Korea (N), Vietnam (N), and Mongolia. Institute established 3/26/56.

S/T p. 444; AGF p. 4

56-108 **10/3/56** – Peking **Malaya** **Singapore** Joint Communiqué
Trade talks

TYC 5:407(C); SCMP 1385:15(E); H12(1):203(G)

56-109 **10/5/56** – Berlin **Multilateral** Agreement
Cooperation of agricultural institutes of socialist countries

Signed by USSR, Germany (E), and other People's Republics.

H1:31; AGF p. 4

56-110 **10/7/56** – Peking **Nepal** Joint Statement
Talks during Premier Tanka Prasad Acharya's visit: economic and cultural relations, five principles of peaceful coexistence (Panch Shila), etc.

TYC 5:12(C); WCC 4:134(C); JMJP 10/8/56(C); JMST 1957, p. 387(C); SCMP 1387:30(E); AsR 1061(E)

56-111 **10/7/56** 10/7/56 Peking **Nepal** Agreement
Economic aid by PRC (including gift of sixty million Indian rupees over three years, one-third in cash, two-thirds in goods and services)

TYC 5:32(C); JMJP 11/4/56(C); JMST 1957, p. 387(C); PC 1956:21 Supp.(E); SCMP 1407:36(E); BFSP 1955-56, p. 899(E); ADFO 0456:3(Fr); DIA 1956, p. 746(E); AsR 1133(E); A/D p. 334(E); H12(1):220(G)

56-112 **10/7/56** – Peking **Nepal** Exchange of Notes
Cash payments under Economic Aid Agreement of 10/7/56 [56-111]

JMJP 11/4/56(C); AsR 1133(E)

56-113 **10/7/56** – Peking **Nepal** Exchange of Notes
Foreign exchange facilities to Nepalese traders in Tibet

TYC 5:33(C); JMJP 11/4/56(C); JMST 1957, p. 387(C); SCMP 1407:37(E); BFSP 1955-56, p. 901(E); AsR 1133(E)

56-114 **10/14/56** – Peking **Indonesia** Joint Press Communiqué
Talks during President Sukarno's visit: expansion of trade relations, international tensions, etc.

WCC 4:138(C); JMJP 10/15/56(C); JMST 1957, p. 377(C); SCMP 1392:18(E)

56-115 **10/15/56** – Peking **Japan** Joint Statement
Trade talks

Signed by representatives of China Committee for Promotion of International Trade, and of the Japanese Association for Promotion of International Trade and the Japanese Diet Members' League for Promotion of Sino-Japanese Trade.

TYC 5:404(C); JMJP 10/16/56(C); SCMP 1392:36(E); H12(1):139(G)

56-116 **10/22/56** – Peking/Cairo **Egypt** Joint Communiqué
Trade talks

JMJP 10/23/56(C); SCMP 1397:32(E); H12(2):15(G)

56-117 **10/22/56** 9/23/56 Cairo **Egypt** Protocol
Trade in 1956-57

TYC 5:120(C); JMJP 10/25/56(C); SCMP 1397:22

56-118 **10/22/56** 9/23/56 Cairo **Egypt** Agreement
Payments

TYC 5:118(C); JMJP 10/25/56(C); SCMP 1397:32; H12(2):16(G)

56-119 **10/22/56** – Cairo **Egypt** Exchange of Letters
Annulment of Article 4 of 1955 Trade Agreement [55-58]

H12(2):14(G)

56-120 **10/22/56** – Tirana **Albania** Protocol
Scientific and technical cooperation

Signed at third meeting of Sino-Albanian Joint Committee for Cooperation in Technology and Technical Science.

SCMP 1401:31

56-121 **10/23/56** – Peking **Pakistan** Joint Statement
Talks during Premier Suhrawardy's visit: development of Sino-Pakistani relations, peaceful coexistence, etc.

TYC 5:1(C); WCC 4:145(C); JMJP 10/24/56(C); JMST 1957, p. 385(C); PC 1956:22 Supp.(E); SCMP 1398:24(E); AsR 1097; RI 1956:44:1342 (It)

56-122 **10/24/56** – Peking **Germany (E)** Agreement
Cooperation between Academies of Sciences

SCMP 1399:26; AGF p. 53

56-123 **10/29/56** – Warsaw **Poland** Protocol
Cooperation between Academies of Sciences

SCMP 1403:33

56-124 **10/31/56** 12/21/56 Peking **Multilateral** Minutes
Conference on postal services, telecommunications, hydrography, and meteorology

Signed by Mongolia, Korea (N), USSR, and Vietnam (N).

TYC 5:166(C); SCMP 1404:37

56-125 **First week of November** – Peking **Egypt** –
Gift by PRC (twenty million Swiss francs) following Suez crisis

SCMP 1415:31; FEER 1/19/61, p. 85

56-126 **11/3/56** 2/9/57 Peking **Indonesia** Agreement
Trade

Joint Communiqué on trade talks also issued. SCMP 1406:51(E)

TYC 5:55(C); JMJP 11/5/56; SCMP 1406:51; H12(1):127(G)

56-127 **11/3/56** – Peking **Indonesia** Exchange of Notes
Extension of 1954 Payments Agreement to 10/31/57 [54-55]

SCMP 1406:52; H12(1):129(G)

56-128 **11/3/56** – Peking **Indonesia** Exchange of Notes
Supply of export commodities to PRC over next three years in settlement of Indonesia's debit balance

SCMP 1406:52; H12(1):130(G)

56-129 **11/3/56** – Peking **Indonesia** Exchange of Notes
Economic and technical cooperation

TYC 5:57(C); SCMP1406:52; H12(1):131(G)

56-130 **11/7/56** – Peking **Czechoslovakia** Agreement
Cooperation between Academies of Sciences

SCMP1409:24

56-131 **11/9/56** – Peking **Burma** Joint Press Communiqué
Talks during Premier U Nu's visit: settlement of boundary question, etc.

Parties agreed to withdraw their armed forces from designated border areas.

WCC 4:161(C); JMJP 11/10/56(C); JMST 1957, p. 384(C); SCMP 1411:52(E); Burma Wkly. Bull. 5:32:253 (11/15/56)(E); AsR 1121; A/D p. 187(E)

56-132 **11/22/56** – Hanoi **Vietnam (N)** Joint Communiqué
Talks during Premier Chou En-lai's visit: Suez crisis, Hungarian uprising, struggle in Vietnam, Sino-Vietnamese relations, etc.

TYC 5:18(C); WCC 4:166(C); JMJP 11/23/56(C); JMST 1957, p. 373(C); SCMP 1418:15(E); ADTJ 0441:5(Fr); AsR 1192(E); RI 1956:48:1519(It); A/D p. 37(E, abbrev.)

56-133 **11/27/56** – Phnom Penh **Cambodia** Joint Communiqué
Talks during Premier Chou En-lai's visit: international tensions, five principles of peaceful coexistence (Panch Shila), Sino-Cambodian relations, etc.

TYC 5:16(C); WCC 4:173(C); JMJP 11/28/56(C); JMST 1957, p. 389(C); SCMP 1421:22(E); AsR 1197(E)

56-134 **11/29/56** – Peking **Japan** Joint Communiqué
Fishery talks

Issued by delegation of China Fishery Association and Japan-China Fishery Association of Japan.

JMJP 12/1/56; SCMP 1423:44

56-135 **12/8/56** – Prague **Czechoslovakia** –
1957 plan for cultural cooperation

SCMP 1429:39

56-136 **12/12/56** – Peking **Rumania** Protocol
Scientific and technical cooperation

Signed at fourth session of Sino-Rumanian Joint Committee for Scientific and Technical Cooperation.

JMJP 12/15/56; SCMP 1435:36

56-137 **11/26/56** – – **Albania** Exchange of Notes
12/19/56
Free grant of PRC aid

AsR 3912

56-138 **12/20/56** – Rangoon **Burma** Joint Statement
Talks during Premier Chou En-lai's visit: settlement of boundary question, etc.

TYC 5:21(C); WCC 4:200(C); JMJP 12/21/56(C); JMST 1957, p. 384(C); SCMP 1438:33(E); ADTJ 0456:4(Fr); Burma Wkly. Bull. 5:38:302 (12/27/56)(E); RI 1957:1:29(It); H12(1):18(G, abbrev.)

56-139 **12/20/56** – Hanoi **Vietnam(N)** Agreement
Maritime transport

TYC 5:196(C); SCMP 1438:37

56-140 **12/20/56** – Warsaw **Poland** –
1957 plan for cultural cooperation

SCMP 1438:38

56-141 **12/22/56** 1/1/57 Peking **Mongolia** Protocol
Mutual supply of goods in 1957
TYC 5:148(C); SCMP 1439:36

56-142 **12/24/56** – Karachi **Pakistan** Joint Statement
Talks during Premier Chou En-lai's visit: international tensions, Sino-Pakistani relations, etc.
TYC 5:2(C); WCC 4:206(C); JMJP 12/25/56(C); JMST 1957, p. 385(C); SCMP 1440:20(E); ADTJ 0457:1(Fr); AsR 1235(E); A/D p. 31(E)

56-143 **12/24/56** – Moscow **USSR** Protocol
Scientific and technical cooperation
Signed at fifth meeting of Sino-Soviet Joint Committee for Scientific and Technical Cooperation. Communiqué also issued 12/26/56. Izv 12/26/56(R)
JMJP 12/26/56; SCMP 1440:38

56-144 **12/29/56** – Colombo **Ceylon** Joint Communiqué
Trade talks
SCMP 1442:44(E); AsR 1213; H12(1):56(G, sum.)

56-145 **12/29/56** – Colombo **Ceylon** Exchange of Notes
Extension of 1952 Trade Agreement [52-55]
TYC 5:150(C); JMJP 12/31/56; SCMP 1442:44

56-146 **12/29/56** – Colombo **Ceylon** Contracts (2)
Exchange of PRC rice and Ceylonese sheet rubber in 1957
JMJP 12/31/56; AsR 1213

1957

57-1 **1/4/57** – Peking **Yugoslavia** Protocol
Exchange of goods in 1957
TYC 6:164(C); JMJP 1/5/57; SCMP 1446:30; YTS 1958:5:41(S-C,E)

57-2 **1/4/57** – Peking **Yugoslavia** Exchange of Notes
Cooperation in air transport and marine insurance
TYC 6:165(C); YTS 1958:5:43(S-C,E)

57-3 **1/4/57** – Peking **Yugoslavia** Statute
Sino-Yugoslav Committee for Scientific and Technical Cooperation
Adopted at first session of Sino-Yugoslav Committee for Scientific and Technical Cooperation.
SCMP 1446:30; YTS 1958:3:65(S-C,E)

57-4 **1/8/57** – Moscow **Germany (E)** Press Communiqué
Talks during Moscow meeting of Premiers Chou En-lai and Grotewohl: international tensions, Suez crisis, Hungarian uprising, etc.

WCC 4:217(C); JMJP 1/10/57(C); JMST 1958, p. 406(C); SCMP 1449:39(E); ADTJ 0457:2(Fr); AsR 1246; RI 1957:3:90(It); Dok 5:329(G)

57-5 **1/11/57** – Moscow **USSR Hungary** Joint Communiqué
Talks by party and government leaders: socialist solidarity, etc.

WCC 4:218(C); JMJP 1/12/57(C); SCMP 1451:42(E); Pr 1/12/57(R); AsR 1246

57-6 **1/16/57** – Warsaw **Poland** Joint Statement
Talks during Premier Chou En-lai's visit: Suez crisis, Hungarian uprising, etc.

TYC 6:17(C); WCC 4:223(C); JMJP 1/17/57(C); JMST 1958, p. 409(C); SCMP 1454:30(E); ADTJ 0458:4(Fr); AsR 1246(E); Horak, p. 109

57-7 **1/17/57** – Budapest **Hungary** Joint Statement
Talks during Premier Chou En-lai's visit: international tensions, Hungarian uprising, Suez crisis, etc.

TYC 6:2(C); WCC 4:234(C); JMJP 1/18/57(C); JMST 1958, p. 404(C); SCMP 1455:27(E); AsR 1246; RI 1957:4:130(It)

57-8 **1/18/57** – Moscow **USSR** Joint Statement
Talks during Premier Chou En-lai's visit: international tensions, Suez crisis, Hungarian uprising, socialist solidarity, etc.

Reaffirms parties' adherence to principles of peaceful coexistence, defends Warsaw Treaty as defensive military alliance, and urges disarmament agreement between great powers.

TYC 6:10(C); WCC 4:245(C); JMJP 1/20/57(C); JMST 1958, p. 401(C); SCMP 1456:34(E); BFSP 163:386(E); ADTJ 0461:2(Fr); Pr 1/19/57(R); DIA 1957, p. 467(E); AsR 1269(E, abbrev.); RI 1959:7:274(It)

57-9 **1/18/57** – Peking **USSR** –
1957 plan for cultural cooperation

SCMP 1456:50

57-10 **1/22/57** – Kabul **Afghanistan** Joint Communiqué
Talks during Premier Chou En-lai's visit: Sino-Afghanistan relations, Bandung Conference principles, etc.

TYC 6:26(C); WCC 4:253(C); JMJP 1/24/57(C); JMST 1958, p. 415(C); SCMP 1459:33(E); ADTJ 0467:4(Fr); AsR 1269; RI 1957:6:191(It)

57-11 **1/24/57** – Pyongyang **Korea (N)** Protocol
Exchange of goods in 1957

SCMP 1460:28

57-12 **1/24/57** – Pyongyang **Korea (N)** Protocol
PRC economic aid to Korea (N)
SCMP 1460:28

57-13 **1/28/57** 1/1/57 Peking **Bulgaria** Agreement
Exchange of goods and payments in 1957
TYC 6:143(C); JMJP 1/29/57; SCMP 1462:32

57-14 **1/28/57** 1/1/57 Peking **Bulgaria** Protocol
General conditions for delivery of goods in 1957
TYC 6:147(C)

57-15 **1/29/57** – Katmandu **Nepal** Joint Communiqué
Talks during Premier Chou En-lai's visit: Sino-Nepalese relations, peaceful coexistence, etc.
TYC 6:1(C); WCC 4:258(C); JMJP 1/30/57(C); JMST 1958, p. 416(C); SCMP 1464:31(E); ADFO 0481:10; AsR 1301(E); RI 1957:6:191(It)

57-16 **2/5/57** – Colombo **Ceylon** Joint Statement
Talks during Premier Chou En-lai's visit: Kashmir dispute, peaceful coexistence, etc.
Diplomatic relations established two days later.
TYC 6:42(C); WCC 4:262(C); JMJP 2/7/57(C); JMST 1958, p. 416(C); SCMP 1466:30(E); AsR 1294(E); RI 1957:7:219(It)

57-17 **2/15/57** 4/1/57 Peking **USSR** Protocol
Further cooperation in postal services and telecommunications
TYC 1:122(C); JMJP 2/16/57; SCMP 1474:35; Pr 2/16/57

57-18 **2/15/57** – Peking **USSR** Protocol
Soviet technical assistance in postal services and telecommunications
SCMP 1474:35; Pr 2/16/57

57-19 **2/20/57** – Peking **Bulgaria** –
1957 plan for cultural cooperation
JMJP 2/21/57; SCMP 1477:35

57-20 **2/21/57** – Peking **Rumania** –
1957 plan for cultural cooperation
JMJP 2/22/57; SCMP 1478:34

57-21 **March** – Peking **Germany (E)** Protocol
Scientific and technical cooperation
Signed at third session of Sino-German Standing Committee for Cooperation in Technology and Technical Sciences.
JMJP 3/18/57; NCNA(E) 2582:183 (3/18/57)

57-22 **3/6/57** 1/1/57 Prague **Czechoslovakia** Agreement
Exchange of goods and payments in 1957
TYC 6:169(C); JMJP 3/8/57; SCMP 1486:19

57-23 **4/14/57** – Peking **Switzerland** Exchange of Notes
3/8/57
Trademark registration
TYC 6:178(C); H12(3):81(G)

57-24 **3/8/57** – Ulan Bator **Mongolia** –
1957 plan for cultural cooperation
JMJP 3/10/57; SCMP 1488:29

57-25 **3/8/57** 1/1/57 Peking **Albania** Protocol
Exchange of goods and payments in 1957
TYC 6:110(C); JMJP 3/9/57; SCMP 1488:30

57-26 **3/8/57** – Peking **Albania** Protocol
Use of PRC's economic aid to Albania
JMJP 3/9/57; SCMP 1488:30

57-27 **3/8/57** 3/8/57 Peking **Albania** Protocol
General conditions for delivery of goods in 1957
TYC 6:112(C)

57-28 **3/27/57** – Peking **Czechoslovakia** Joint Communiqué
Talks during Premier Siroky's visit: world tensions, peaceful coexistence, etc.
TYC 6:33(C); WCC 4:308(C); JMJP 3/28/57(C); JMST 1958, p. 410(C); SCMP 1501:17(E); AsR 1385

57-29 **3/27/57** 8/1/57 Peking **Czechoslovakia** Treaty
Friendship and cooperation
TYC 6:40(C); YHTY 93(C,Czech); WCC 4:314(C); JMJP 3/28/57(C); JMST 1958, p. 410(C); PC 1957:8:40; SCMP 1501:15(E); ADTJ 0489:1(Fr); AsR 1385; RI 1957:14:447(It), 1959:7:277(It)

57-30 **3/27/57** 8/9/57 Peking **Czechoslovakia** Agreement
Cultural cooperation
TYC 6:212(C); SCMP 1501:17

57-31 **3/27/57** 8/9/57 Peking **Czechoslovakia** Agreement
Cooperation in public health work
TYC 6:230(C); SCMP 1501:17

57-32 **3/27/57** – Peking **USSR** Protocol
Transfer of Peking Red Cross hospital to PRC
JMJP 3/28/57

57-33 **3/30/57** – Hanoi **Vietnam (N)** –
1957 plan for cultural cooperation
JMJP 3/31/57; SCMP 1503:35

57-34 **4/1/57** 1/1/57 Warsaw **Poland** Agreement
Turnover of goods and payments in 1957
TYC 6:93(C); SCMP 1505:27

57-35 **4/1/57** 1/1/57 Warsaw **Poland** Protocol
General conditions for delivery of goods in 1957
TYC 6:97(C)

57-36 **4/5/57** 1/1/57 Peking **Germany (E)** Agreement
Exchange of goods and payments in 1957
TYC 6:184(C); SCMP 1508:23; Dok 5:331

57-37 **4/5/57** 1/1/57 Peking **Germany (E)** Protocol
General conditions for delivery of goods in 1957
TYC 6:187(C)

57-38 **4/6/57** – Peking **Sweden** Exchange of Notes
4/8/57
Trademark registration
Registered by Sweden with UN Secretariat 5/8/62.
TYC 6:180(C); UNTS 428:268(C,E,Fr)

57-39 **4/10/57** – Moscow **USSR** Protocol
General conditions for delivery of goods in 1957
TYC 6:77(C)

57-40 **4/10/57** 4/10/57 Pyongyang **Korea (N)** Agreement
Examination, prevention, and control of insect pests and plant diseases
TYC 6:225(C); SCMP 1511:23

57-41 **4/11/57** – Peking **Poland** Joint Statement
Talks during Chairman Cyrankiewicz' visit: implementation of Geneva Agreements on Indo-China, etc.
TYC 6:21(C); WCC 4:319(C); JMJP 4/12/57(C); JMST 1958, p. 408(C); NCNA(E) 2607:102 (4/12/57)(E); SCMP 1512:24(E); ADTJ 0497:2(Fr); DIA 1957, p. 497(E); AsR 1433(E); RI 1957:16:508(It)

57-42 **4/11/57** – Moscow **USSR** Protocol
Exchange of goods in 1957
NCNA(E) 2608:117 (4/13/57); SCMP 1512:40; Pr, Izv 4/12/57; CDSP 9:15:18; S/T p. 381

57-43 **4/11/57** – Moscow **USSR** Exchange of Notes
Application of 1950 Trade Agreement [50-17]
TYC 6:92(C); AsR 1421

57-44 **4/12/57** – Moscow **USSR** –
1957 plan for cooperation in radio broadcasting
SCMP 1512:40

57-45 **4/12/57** – Hanoi **Vietnam (N)** Agreement
Transit of PRC cargoes through Vietnam (N) from Southwest Yunnan to other parts of PRC
Vietnam (N) grants exemption from customs duties.
SCMP 1512:58

57-46 **4/19/57** 1/1/57 Peking **Rumania** Agreement
Exchange of goods and payments in 1957
TYC 6:121(C); JMJP 4/20/57; SCMP 1516:37

57-47 **4/19/57** 1/1/57 Peking **Rumania** Protocol
General conditions for delivery of goods in 1957
TYC 6:124(C)

57-48 **4/25/57** – Hanoi **Vietnam (N)** Joint Communiqué
Fishery regulation in Gulf of Tonkin
TYC 6:276(C); SCMP 1519:24

57-49 **5/13/57** – Budapest **Hungary** Agreement
Grant of long-term credit by PRC and loan of 100 million rubles
SCMP 1532:22; FEER 1/19/61, p. 85

57-50 **5/15/57** – Hanoi **Vietnam (N)** Contract
Mutual supply of books, newspapers, periodicals, records, scores, and prints
Signed by representatives of International Bookstore of China and the Books and Periodicals Import and Export Agency of Vietnam.
SCMP 1533:21

57-51 **5/25/57** – New Delhi **India** Exchange of Letters
Extension of 1954 Trade Agreement to 12/31/58 [54-72]
TYC 6:68(C); JMJP 5/26/57; SCMP 1541:34; H12(1):95(G); A/D p. 295(E)

57-52 **5/25/57** – New Delhi **India** Exchange of Letters
Promotion of trade relations between state foreign trade companies
TYC 6:71(C); SCMP 1541:34; A/D p. 298(E)

57-53 **5/26/57** – Peking **USSR** Communiqué
Talks during President Voroshilov's visit: socialist solidarity, etc.

JMJP 5/27/57(C); JMST 1958, p. 396(C); SCMP 1540:21(E);
Izv 5/28/57(R); AsR 1494(E)

57-54 **5/31/57** 5/1/57 Peking **Albania** Agreement
Postal services and telecommunications

TYC 6:237(C); JMJP 6/1/57; SCMP 1544:39

57-55 **5/10/57** – Tokyo/Peking **Japan** Exchange of Notes
5/30/57
Extension of 1955 Fishery Agreement [55-24]

Signed by representatives of China Fishery Association and Japan-China Fishery Association of Japan.

TYC 6:330(C); JMJP 6/7/57; SCMP 1548:35; AsR 1522

57-56 **5/10/57** – Tokyo/Peking **Japan** Exchange of Notes
5/30/57
Extension of fishery agreement by 1955 Exchange of Letters [55-25]

See note above.

TYC 6:331(C); SCMP 1548:35; AsR 1522

57-57 **5/10/57** – Tokyo/Peking **Japan** Exchange of Notes
5/30/57
Exchange of fishery agreement by 1955 Exchange of Memoranda [55-26]

See note above.
TYC 6:333(C); SCMP 1548:35; AsR 1522

57-58 **6/7/57** – Lhasa **India** Exchange of Notes
Return of real estate in Yatung

H12(1):89

57-59 **6/7/57** 7/1/57 Pyongyang **Korea (N)** Agreement
Extension of 1949 Postal Agreement [49-1]

TYC 6:243(C); SCMP 1549:30

57-60 **6/7/57** 7/1/57 Pyongyang **Korea (N)** Agreement
Extension of 1949 Telecommunications Agreement [49-3]

TYC 6:249(C); SCMP 1549:30

57-61 **6/7/57** – Peking **Multilateral** Regulations (revised)
Cooperation in railway service

Originally adopted at conference held in Sofia June 23-28, 1956.

TYC 6:314(C); AGF p. 5

57-62 **6/7/57** 12/20/57 Peking **Yugoslavia** Agreement
Cultural cooperation

TYC 6:210(C); JMJP 6/8/57; SCMP 1549:30

57-63 **6/7/57** – Peking **Yugoslavia** –
1957 plan for cultural cooperation

JMJP 6/8/57; SCMP 1549:30

57-64 **5/15/57** – – **Cambodia** Exchange of Notes
6/7/57
Extension of 1956 Trade and Payments Agreements to 6/16/58 [56-54,55]
TYC 6:163(C); H12(1):189

57-65 **6/8/57** 1/1/57 Budapest **Hungary** Agreement
Exchange of goods and payments in 1957
TYC 6:48(C); SCMP 1549:32

57-66 **6/8/57** 1/1/57 Budapest **Hungary** Protocol
General conditions for delivery of goods in 1957
TYC 6:52(C)

57-67 **6/15/57** – Peking **Germany (E)** –
1957 plan for cultural cooperation
JMJP 6/16/57; SCMP 1554:36

57-68 **6/22/57** – Phnom Penh **Cambodia** Contract
Implementation of 1956 Trade Agreement in 1957-58 [56-54]
Signed by representatives of People's Bank of China and State Bank of Cambodia.
SCMP 1559:26

57-69 **7/3/57** 12/5/57 Damascus **Syria** Agreement
Revision of 1955 Trade and Payments Agreements [55-92,93]
Communiqué also issued 7/12/57. JMJP 7/12/57
TYC 6:161(C); SCMP 1565:41; STS 57:6(Fr); H12(2):69(G)

57-70 **7/17/57** – Peking **USSR** Protocol
Scientific and technical cooperation
Signed at sixth meeting of Sino-Soviet Joint Committee for Scientific and Technical Cooperation. Communiqué also issued 7/18/57. Pr 7/18/57(R)
JMJP 7/18/57; SCMP 1574:49

57-71 **7/18/57** – Budapest **Hungary** –
1957 plan for cultural cooperation
SCMP 1576:52

57-72 **7/28/57** 10/18/57 Kabul **Afghanistan** Agreement
Exchange of goods and payments in period 1957-59
Under Article 14, effective after ratification by both parties. Afghanistan ratified on 10/1/57. PRC State Council on 10/18/57. Afghanistan notified by PRC on 10/23/57; PRC notified by Afghanistan on 1/29/58.
TYC 6:139(C); JMJP 7/30/57; SCMP 1581:28; H12(1):7(G)

57-73 **7/31/57** 1/1/57 Hanoi **Vietnam (N)** Agreement
Mutual supply of goods and payments in 1957
TYC 6:173(C); JMJP 8/1/57; SCMP 1584:44

57-74 **7/31/57** – Hanoi **Vietnam (N)** Protocol
Material aid by PRC to Vietnam (N)
JMJP 8/1/57; SCMP 1584:44

57-75 **7/31/57** 7/31/57 Hanoi **Vietnam (N)** Protocol
Exchange of goods by local state-owned trading companies in border areas
TYC 6:175(C)

57-76 **7/31/57** – Hanoi **Vietnam (N)** Exchange of Notes
Extension of 1955 Protocol on Small-Scale Trade in Border Areas [55-49]
TYC 6:177(C)

57-77 **8/3/57** – Peking **Hungary** Protocol
Scientific and technical cooperation
Signed at third meeting of Sino-Hungarian Committee for Scientific and Technical Cooperation.
JMJP 8/4/57; SCMP 1586:35

57-78 **8/7/57** – Peking **Finland** Exchange of Notes
Extension of 1956 Trade Agreement to 10/31/57 [56-91]
TYC 6:73(C); H12(3):34(G)

57-79 **8/7/57** – Peking **Finland** Exchange of Notes
Interpretation of Article 8 of 1953 Payments Agreement [53-32]
TYC 6:74(C); H12(3):35

57-80 **8/15/57** – Belgrade **Yugoslavia** Exchange of Notes
8/26/57
Interpretation of Article 9 of 1956 Trade Agreement applied to Trade Protocol of 1/4/57 [56-25; 57-1]
YTS 1958:5:43(S-C,E)

57-81 **9/10/57** – Bucharest **Rumania** Communique
Scientific and technical cooperation
Signed at fifth session of Sino-Rumanian Joint Committee for Scientific and Technical Cooperation.
JMJP 9/14/57; SCMP 1610:40

57-82 **9/12/57** – Peking **Czechoslovakia** Protocol
Scientific and technical cooperation
Signed at fifth session of Sino-Czechoslovak Joint Committee for Scientific and Technical Cooperation.
JMJP 9/17/57; SCMP 1613:41

57-83 **9/19/57** 1/1/58 Peking **Ceylon** Agreement (with schedules)
Trade and payments in period 1958-62

Registered by Ceylon with UN Secretariat 7/13/59.

TYC 6:203(C); JMJP 10/4/57(C); SCMP 1616:35;UNTS 337:139(C,E,Fr); CTS 1957:8:2(E); AsR 1683; A/D p. 317(E)

57-84 **9/19/57** – Peking **Ceylon** Exchange of Letters
Import control regulations

See note above.

UNTS 337:143(C,E,Fr); CTS 1957:8:6(E); A/D p. 321(E)

57-85 **9/19/57** – Peking **Ceylon** Exchange of Letters
Trade involving third countries

See note above.

UNTS 337:144(C,E,Fr); CTS 1957:8:7(E); A/D p. 321(E)

57-86 **9/19/57** 1/1/58 Peking **Ceylon** Protocol
Exchange of goods in 1958

See note above.

TYC 6:207(C); JMJP 10/4/57(C); SCMP 1616:35; UNTS 337:145(C,E,Fr); CTS 1957:8:4(E); AsR 1683; A/D p. 323(E)

57-87 **9/19/57** 1/1/58 Peking **Ceylon** Agreement
Economic aid by PRC

See note above.

TYC 6:208(C); JMJP 10/4/57(C); SCMP 1616:35; UNTS 337:171(C,E,Fr); CTS 1957:9(E); SIA 1957, p. 334; AsR 1683; A/D p. 316(E)

57-88 **9/20/57** – Peking **Ceylon** Communiqué
Economic talks

JMJP 9/21/57(C); PC 1957:20:44; SCMP 1617:27(E); AsR 1682(E); H12(1):65

57-89 **9/26/57** – Berlin **Germany (E)** Protocol
Delivery and supply of complete sets of equipment in 1958

SCMP 1622:40; AGF p. 53; Dok 5:332

57-90 **9/27/57** 10/12/57 Peking **Germany (W)** Agreement
Trade

Signed by representatives of China Committee for Promotion of International Trade and Eastern Committee of West German Economy. Implementation arranged in official letters from governmental departments of PRC and Germany (W) 8/20/56 and 9/26/57. TYC 6:325(C)

TYC 6:323(C); SCMP 1622:40; H12(3):4(G)

57-91 **9/27/57** – Peking **Germany (W)** Exchange of Notes
Application of Trade Agreement of 9/27/57 to West Berlin area [57-90]

See note above.

TYC 6:326(C); H12(3):7(G)

57-92 **9/27/57** – Peking **Germany (W)** Exchange of Notes
Arbitration procedure under Trade Agreement of 9/27/57 [57-90]

See note above.

TYC 6:328(C); H12(3):8(G)

57-93 **10/3/57** – Ulan Bator **Mongolia** Protocol
Through rail service

Signed at meeting of a joint committee for cooperation in administration of railway linking PRC and Mongolia.

SCMP 1626:49

57-94 **10/3/57** – Ulan Bator **Mongolia** **USSR** Protocol
Operation of through railway traffic

Signed at conference of railway representatives.

SCMP 1626:50

57-95 **10/4/57** – Peking **Hungary** Joint Statement
Talks during Premier Kadar's visit: international tensions, UN intervention in Hungary's domestic affairs, etc.

TYC 6:6(C); WCC 4:383(C); JMJP 10/5/57(C); JMST 1958, p. 405(C); SCMP 1627:29(E); ADTJ 0569:4(Fr); AsR 1682(E); RI 1957:41:1224(It)

57-96 **10/8/57** – Pyongyang **Korea (N)** Protocol
Tumen River project

SCMP 1632:38

57-97 **10/11/57** – Peking **Bulgaria** Joint Statement
Talks during Premier Yugov's visit: international situation, peaceful coexistence, etc.

TYC 6:29(C); WCC 4:387(C); JMJP 10/12/57(C); JMST 1958, p. 412(C); SCMP 1632:19(E); ADTJ 0572:2(Fr); AsR 1717(E)

57-98 **10/11/57** – Peking **Bulgaria** Agreement
Exchange of goods and payments in period 1958-60

SCMP 1632:19

57-99 **10/13/57(?)** – Peking **Morocco** Agreement
Exchange of goods in 1958

SCMP 1633:37

57-100 **10/23/57** – Peking **Multilateral** Statement
"Acceptance" of 1930 International Load Line Convention for Shipping (and revision of Appendix Two proposed by Australia)

TYC 6:294(C); SCMP 1640:2

57-101 **10/26/57** – Peking **Afghanistan** Joint Communiqué
Talks during visit of Premier Daud Khan: principles of Bandung Conference, Sino-Afghanistan relations, etc.

TYC 6:27(C); WCC 4:394(C); JMJP 10/28/57(C); JMST 1958, p. 416(C); SCMP 1641:39(E); AsR 1737(E)

57-102 **10/29/57** 10/29/57 Peking **Poland** Protocol
Cooperation in public health work

TYC 6:229(C); JMJP 10/30/57; SCMP 1643:38

57-103 **11/1/57** – Peking **Yugoslavia** –
General conditions for implementation of scientific and technical cooperation

YTS 1958:8:65(S-C,E)

57-104 **11/1/57** 11/1/57 Rangoon/Peking **Burma** Agreement
Postal services

TYC 6:255(C); SCMP 1646:49; H12(1):43(G)

57-105 **11/1/57** 11/1/57 Rangoon/Peking **Burma** Agreement
Parcel post

TYC 6:260(C); SCMP 1646:49; H12(1):47

57-106 **11/1/57** – Peking **Japan** Joint Statement
Trade talks between China Committee for Promotion of International Trade and Japanese Trade Mission

Japanese mission consisted of representatives of Japanese Diet Members' League for Promotion of Sino-Japanese Trade, Japanese Association for Promotion of International Trade, and Japan-China Export and Import Association. After discussing PRC draft for fourth Sino-Japanese trade agreement, both parties agreed to prepare memorandum concerning establishment of permanent private trade mission in each other's country which would be integral part of trade agreement. Talks adjourned to allow Japanese delegates to return to Tokyo for consultations. See note on entry of 3/5/58 [58-24].

TYC 6:321(C); JMJP 11/4/57(C); SCMP 1646:45(E)

57-107 **11/4/57** – Peking **Poland** Protocol
Scientific and technical cooperation

Signed at fourth session of Sino-Polish Standing Committee for Scientific and Technical Cooperation.

SCMP 1648:35

57-108 **11/8/57** – Stockholm **Sweden** Agreement
Trade

Took effect provisionally on 11/8/57, officially on 1/23/58 after exchange of notes.

TYC 6:181(C); SCMP 1679:1; H12(3):76(G)

57-109 **11/21/57** – Moscow **USSR** –
1958 plan for cultural cooperation
JMJP 11/23/57; SCMP 1659:39

57-110 **11/27/57** – Peking **Poland** –
1958 plan for educational cooperation
SCMP 1663:60

57-111 **12/1/57** 12/1/57 Peking **Denmark** Agreement (with annexes)
Trade and payments
Registered by Denmark with UN Secretariat 8/22/58.
TYC 6:44(C); SCMP 1664:59; UNTS 309:243(C,Danish,E,Fr)

57-112 **12/1/57** – Peking **Denmark** Exchange of Notes
Reciprocal most-favored-nation treatment in customs duties and navigation
See note above.
TYC 6:45(C); SCMP 1664:59; UNTS 309:248(C,Danish,E,Fr)

57-113 **12/2/57** – Peking **Poland** –
1958 plan for cultural cooperation
JMJP 12/3/57; SCMP 1665:53

57-114 **12/11/57** 12/11/57 Moscow **USSR** Protocol
Cooperation between Academies of Sciences in period 1958-62
TYC 6:215(C); JMJP 12/13/57; SCMP 1673:46; AsR 1810

57-115 **12/11/57** – Moscow **USSR** Protocol
1958 plan for cooperation between Academies of Sciences
JMJP 12/13/57; SCMP 1673:46

57-116 **12/11/57** – Peking **Vietnam (N)** –
1958 plan for cultural cooperation
JMJP 12/12/57; SCMP 1672:35

57-117 **12/16/57** 6/30/58 Moscow **Multilateral** Agreement
Establishment of Organization for Cooperation in Postal Services and Telecommunications among Socialist Countries
Signed by Albania, Bulgaria, Hungary, Vietnam (N), USSR, Mongolia, Poland, Rumania, Czechoslovakia, Germany (E), and Korea (N). Ratified by PRC 4/1/58.
TYC 6:271(C); AGF p. 6

57-118 **12/16/57** 3/22/58 Berlin **Germany (E)** Agreement
Cooperation in public health work
TYC 6:234(C); SCMP 1675:44; Dok 5:333(G)

57-119 **12/18/57** 11/1/57 Peking **Finland** Agreement
Trade in 1957-58

TYC 6:76(C); SCMP 1677:31; H12(3):36

57-120 **12/21/57** 4/19/58 Moscow **USSR** Agreement
Regime of commercial navigation on border waterways and tributary streams and lakes

Registered by USSR with UN Secretariat 7/14/58.

TYC 6:278(C); JMJP 12/23/57; SCMP 1679:40; UNTS 305:215(R,C,E,Fr); Izv 12/22/57; S/T p. 395

57-121 **12/21/57** – Peking **Egypt** Communiqué
Trade talks

JMJP 12/22/57(C); SCMP 1679:49(E); H12(2):20(G)

57-122 **12/21/57** 9/23/57 Peking **Egypt** Protocol
Trade in 1958

TYC 6:166(C); JMJP 12/22/57; SCMP 1679:49; AsR 1846; H12(2):19

57-123 **12/21/57** – Peking **Egypt** Exchange of Letters
Revision of Article 3 of 1956 Payments Agreement [56-118]

TYC 6:168(C); H12(2):19(G)

57-124 **12/23/57** – Peking **Multilateral** Statement
"Acceptance" of 1948 International Regulations for Preventing Collisions at Sea

Subject to reservation that regulations do not apply to nonpowered vessels.

TYC 6:313(C); SCMP 1681:1

57-125 **12/27/57** – Belgrade **Yugoslavia** Protocol
Scientific and technical cooperation

Signed at second session of Sino-Yugoslav Committee for Scientific and Technical Cooperation.

JMJP 1/4/58; SCMP 1683:38; YTS 1958:8:71(S-C,E)

57-126 **12/30/57** – Peking **Poland** –
1958 plan for cooperation between Academies of Sciences

JMJP 12/31/57; SCMP 1685:47

57-127 **12/30/57** – Moscow **USSR** Protocol
Settlement of noncommercial payments

SCMP 1685:46; Izv 1/1/58

57-128 **12/30/57** – Peking **Korea (N)** –
1958-59 plan for cultural cooperation

JMJP 12/31/57; SCMP 1684:45

57-129 **12/31/57** 12/31/57 Pyongyang **Korea (N)** Agreement
Scientific and technical cooperation

TYC 6:218(C); JMJP 1/4/58; SCMP 1684:46

57-130 **12/31/57** 12/31/57 Pyongyang **Korea (N)** Agreement
Cooperation in hydrological work

TYC 6:219(C); SCMP 1684:46

1958

58-1 **1/9/58** – Peking **Sudan** Joint Communiqué
Trade talks

Issued 1/9/58, signed 12/30/57.

TYC 6:72(C); JMJP 1/9/58(C); SCMP 1690:38(E); H12(2):183(G)

58-2 **1/12/58** – Peking **Yemen** Joint Communiqué
Talks during visit of Deputy Premier Mohammed al-Badr: international tensions, peaceful coexistence, foreign aid, disarmament, PRC representation in UN, etc.

TYC 7:1(C); WCC 5:3(C); JMJP 1/13/58(C); JMST 1959, p. 351(C); PR 3/25/58, p. 19; SCMP 1691:37(E); AsR 1846

58-3 **1/12/58** 5/15/58 Peking **Yemen** Treaty
Friendship

Replaced by 1964 Treaty of Friendship [64-78].

TYC 7:3(C); WCC 5:5(C); JMJP 1/13/58(C); PR 3/25/58, p. 19; SCMP 1691:39(E); BFSP 163:871(E); AsR 1846; H12(2):38(G)

58-4 **1/12/58** 5/15/58 Peking **Yemen** Treaty
Commerce

TYC 7:28(C); JMJP 1/13/58(C); PR 3/25/58, p. 19; SCMP 1692:24(E); BFSP 163:877; AsR 1846; H12(2):4(G)

58-5 **1/12/58** 5/15/58 Peking **Yemen** Agreement
Scientific and cultural cooperation

TYC 7:31(C); JMJP 1/13/58(C); PR 3/25/58, p. 19; SCMP 1692:21(E); BFSP 163:874(E); AsR 1846; H12(2):45(G)

58-6 **1/17/58** 1/17/58 Ulan Bator **Mongolia** Agreement
Air communications

TYC 7:179(C); SCMP 1696:35

58-7 **1/18/58** – Moscow **USSR** Agreement
Joint research in science and technology and assistance to PRC

Referred to as protocol in JMJP.

WCC 5:285; JMJP 1/19/58; PR 4/1/58, p. 12; SCMP 1696:34; Izv 1/19/58

58-8 **1/18/58** – Moscow **USSR** Protocol
Cooperation between Academies of Agricultural Sciences
WCC 5:285; SCMP 1696:35; Pr 1/19/58

58-9 **1/18/58** – Moscow **USSR** Protocol
Cooperation in scientific and technical research between Ministries of Higher Education
WCC 5:285; SCMP 1696:35; Izv 1/19/58

58-10 **1/21/58** 1/1/58 Peking **Korea (N)** Protocol
Exchange of goods in 1958
TYC 7:120(C); JMJP 1/22/58; SCMP 1698:35

58-11 **1/21/58** 1/1/58 Peking **Korea (N)** Protocol
General conditions for delivery of goods
TYC 7:122(C)

58-12 **1/24/58** – Ulan Bator **Mongolia** Agreement
Technical cooperation in civil aviation
SCMP 1701:36

58-13 **1/24/58** – Ulan Bator **Mongolia** Protocol
Air transport and mutual services
SCMP 1701:36

58-14 **1/28/58** 1/1/58 Peking **Mongolia** Protocol
Exchange of goods in 1958
TYC 7:136(C); SCMP 1703:38

58-15 **1/31/58** 2/1/58 Peking/Rangoon **Burma** Agreement
Telecommunications
TYC 7:174(C); H12(1):47

58-16 **2/15/58** 2/15/58 Peking **Finland** Exchange of Letters
Revision of 1953 Payments Agreement [53-32]
TYC 7:49(C); H12(3):36(G)

58-17 **2/16/58** – Peking **Czechoslovakia** –
1958 plan for cultural cooperation
SCMP 1717:45

58-18 **2/19/58** – Pyongyang **Korea (N)** Joint Statement
Withdrawal of Chinese People's Volunteers from Korea (N)
Confirming Statement of 2/20/58 issued by General Headquarters of CPV. SCMP 1718:41(E)
TYC 7:18(C); WCC 5:37(C); PR 3/4/58, p. 21(E); SCMP 1717:13(E); ZD 1958:2:477(P,E); DIA 1958, p. 477; A/D p. 44(E)

58-19 **2/21/58** 7/11/58 Peking **Mongolia** Agreement
Cultural cooperation
TYC 7:164(C); JMJP 2/22/58; PR 3/4/58, p. 17; SCMP 1719:46

58-20 **2/21/58** – Peking **Mongolia** –
1958 plan for cultural cooperation
JMJP 2/22/58; SCMP 1719:46

58-21 **2/21/58** 2/21/58 Rangoon **Burma** Agreement
Trade
TYC 7:161(C); JMJP 2/23/58; SCMP 1719:48; AsR 1922; H12(1):34

58-22 **2/22/58** – Warsaw **Poland** Agreement
Noncommercial payments
SCMP 1719:49

58-23 **2/28/58** – Belgrade **Yugoslavia** Protocol
Exchange of goods in 1958
TYC 7:93(C); PR 3/11/58, p. 20; SCMP 1724:44; YTS 1958:10:19(S-C,E)

58-24 **3/5/58** 3/5/58 Peking **Japan** Agreement (with Memorandum)
Trade
Signed by representatives of China Committee for Promotion of International Trade and Japanese trade delegation. Provides for establishment of permanent "people's commercial agency" in each other's country. On 4/5/58 Japanese Premier Kishi issued statement that Japanese government would "respect the spirit" of the document and provide "support and assistance" within the framework of Japanese domestic law. But it was later explained that the Japanese government could not recognize the PRC commercial agency's right to hoist the PRC flag in Japan and support could not be given to certain other parts of the Agreement (SCMP 1752:27). In return, the PRC government stopped issuing export and import permits for trade with Japan. SCMP 1772:45(E); ADFO 0657:1(Fr); H12(1):148
TYC 7:197(C); WCC 5:261(C); JMJP 2/6/58(C); PR 3/11/58, p. 20; SCMP 1727:55(E); Contemp. Japan 25:3:520(E); H12(1):143(G)

58-25 **3/12/58** 1/1/58 Tirana **Albania** Protocol
Exchange of goods and payments in 1958
TYC 7:54(C); SCMP 1733:46

58-26 **3/12/58** – Tirana **Albania** Exchange of Notes
Extension of Protocol on General Conditions for Delivery of Goods in 1957 [57-27]
TYC 7:56(C); PR 3/25/58, p. 19

58-27 **3/13/58** 1/1/58 Sofia **Bulgaria** Protocol
Exchange of goods and payments in 1958
TYC 7:84(C); PR 3/25/58, p. 19; SCMP 1735:34

58-28 **3/15/58** 3/15/58 Hanoi **Vietnam (N)** Agreement
Cooperation in radio broadcasting
TYC 7:166(C); SCMP 1735:41

58-29 **3/19/58** – Sofia **Bulgaria** –
1958 plan for cultural cooperation
SCMP 1739:18

58-30 **3/21/58** 1/1/58 Peking **Hungary** Agreement
Exchange of goods and payments in 1958
TYC 7:38(C); PR 4/1/58, p. 20; SCMP 1740:25; AsR 1971

58-31 **3/22/58** – Berlin **Germany (E)** –
1958 plan for cultural cooperation
PR 4/8/58, p. 22; SCMP 1741:34

58-32 **3/24/58** – Peking **Multilateral** Agreement
Joint research on high-tension electrical equipment under tropical conditions
Signed by USSR, Hungary, Poland, Czechoslovakia, and Germany (E).
SCMP 1741:35; Izv 3/25/58

58-33 **2/19/58** – Phnom Penh/Peking **Cambodia** Exchange of Notes
3/26/58
Extension of 1956 Economic Aid Agreement [56-76]
TYC 7:90(C); H12(1):189(G)

58-34 **3/27/58** – Berlin **Germany (E)** Agreement
Noncommercial payments
SCMP 1744:42; AGF p. 53; Dok 6:300(G)

58-35 **3/29/58** – Belgrade **Yugoslavia** –
1958 plan for cultural cooperation
PR 4/15/58, p. 18; SCMP 1744:56; YTS 1959:4:68(S-C,E)

58-36 **3/30/58** 1/1/58 Bucharest **Rumania** Agreement
Exchange of goods and payments in 1958
TYC 7:65(C); PR 4/8/58, p. 21; SCMP 1745:26; AsR 2018

58-37 **3/30/58** 1/1/58 Bucharest **Rumania** Protocol
General conditions for delivery of goods in 1958
TYC 7:69(C)

58-38 **3/31/58** 1/1/58 Peking **Vietnam (N)** Agreement
Mutual supply of goods and payments in 1958
TYC 7:138(C); PR 4/8/58, p. 21; SCMP 1745:28

58-39 **3/31/58** – Peking **Vietnam (N)** Exchange of Notes
Revision of 1956 Protocol on General Conditions for Delivery of Goods [56-74]
TYC 7:140(C)

58-40 **3/31/58** – Peking **Vietnam (N)** Agreement
PRC aid in industrial construction or reconstruction projects
JMJP 4/1/58; PR 4/8/58, p. 21; SCMP 1745:28; AsR 2018

58-41 **3/31/58** – Peking **Vietnam (N)** Protocol
PRC aid to Vietnam (N) in 1958
JMJP 4/1/58; PR 4/8/58, p. 21; SCMP 1745:28; AsR 2018

58-42 **4/3/58** – Budapest **Hungary** –
1958 plan for cultural cooperation
PR 4/15/58, p. 18; SCMP 1748:57

58-43 **4/5/58** 1/1/58 – **Poland** Protocol
Extension of Protocol on General Conditions for Delivery of Goods in 1957 [57-35]
TYC 7:50(C); PR 4/15/58, p. 17

58-44 **4/6/58** – Changchun **Korea (N)** Accord
Flood control plan for Tumen River
JMJP 4/8/58; SCMP 1748:63

58-45 **4/7/58** – Peking **Poland** Communiqué
Trade talks during visit of Polish government delegation
WCC 5:80(C); JMST 1959, p. 336(C); SCMP 1749:50(E)

58-46 **4/7/58** – Peking **Poland** Agreement
Trade in period 1959-62
JMJP 4/8/58; PR 4/15/58, p. 17; SCMP 1749:49; AsR 2018; Horak, p. 123

58-47 **4/7/58** 1/1/58 Peking **Poland** Agreement
Turnover of goods and payments in 1958
TYC 7:51(C); SCMP 1749:49

58-48 **4/7/58** – Peking **Rumania** Joint Statement
Talks during visit of Chairman Stoica: international tensions, disarmament, German question, socialist solidarity, etc.
TYC 7:10(C); WCC 5:82(C); JMJP 4/9/58(C); JMST 1959, p. 337(C); PR 4/15/58, p. 58(E, sum.); SCMP 1750:43(E); ZD 1958:6:1096(P,E); ADTJ 0642:1(Fr)

58-49 **3/25/58** – Peking **Denmark** Exchange of Notes
4/12/58
Trademark registration
TYC 7:37(C); H12(3):17(G)

58-50 **4/12/58** – Bucharest **Rumania** –
1958 plan for cultural cooperation
SCMP 1752:40

58-51 **4/16/58** 1/1/58 Peking **Czechoslovakia** Agreement
Exchange of goods and payments in 1958
TYC 7:98(C); JMJP 4/18/58; PR 4/22/58, p. 21; SCMP 1755:54

58-52 **4/16/58** 1/1/58 Peking **Czechoslovakia** –
General conditions for delivery of goods
TYC 7:101(C)

58-53 **4/17/58** – Djakarta **Indonesia** Exchange of Notes
Loan by PRC to Indonesia
Exchanged between Vice-Premier of Indonesia and PRC ambassador in Djakarta.
PR 4/22/58, p. 20

58-54 **4/21/58** – Peking **Hungary** Agreement
Trade in period 1959-62
JMJP 4/22/58; PR 4/22/58, p. 20; SCMP 1757:46

58-55 **4/23/58** – Peking **USSR** Joint Communiqué
Trade talks
WCC 5:95(C); JMST 1959, p. 315(C); SCMP 1764:47(E)

58-56 **4/23/58** 7/25/58 Peking **USSR** Treaty
Commerce and navigation
Registered by USSR with UN Secretariat 10/2/58. Also appended: Annex on legal status of PRC and Soviet trade delegations in each other's country. TYC 7:47(C); SCMP 1760:34(E); UNTS 313:142 (R,C,E,Fr)
TYC 7:42(C); WCC 5:95(C); JMJP 4/24/58(C); SCMP 1760:29(E); UNTS 313:136(R,C,E,Fr); BFSP 163:866(E); AsR 2041(E); WGO 1:24

58-57 **4/23/58** – Peking **USSR** Protocol
Exchange of goods in 1958
JMJP 4/24/58(C); PR 4/22/58, p. 20; SCMP 1764:47; Pr, Izv 4/24/58; AsR 2041

58-58 **4/23/58** 1/1/58 Berlin **Germany (E)** Agreement
Exchange of goods and payments in 1958
TYC 7:142(C); PR 5/6/58, p. 19; SCMP 1760:44; Dok 6:302

58-59 **4/29/58** – Peking **Albania** –
1958-59 plan for cultural cooperation
SCMP 1763:46

58-60 **5/7/58** – Prague **Czechoslovakia** Protocol
Exchange of daily necessities

SCMP 1769:45

58-61 **May** – New Delhi **India** Agreement
Trade in 1958-59

Signed by representatives of PRC and Indian state trading companies.

PR 5/27/58, p. 21; SCMP 1776:35

58-62 **5/17/58** – Peking **Hungary** Agreement
Cooperation between Academies of Sciences

TYC 7:168; JMJP 5/18/58; SCMP 1777:37

58-63 **5/22/58** 1/1/58 Berlin **Germany (E)** Protocol
General conditions for delivery of goods in 1958

TYC 7:144(C)

58-64 **6/3/58** – Karachi **Pakistan** Contract
Barter of PRC coal for Pakistan cotton

PR 6/10/58, p. 20; SCMP 1787:52; AsR 2096

58-65 **6/4/58** 6/4/58 Peking **Norway** Agreement
Trade and payments

Grants reciprocal most-favored-nation treatment in customs duties and navigation.

TYC 7:94(C); JMJP 6/5/58; PR 6/10/58, p. 20; SCMP 1787:52; AsR 2115; H12(3):64(G)

58-66 **6/4/58** – Peking **Albania** Protocol
Scientific and technical cooperation

Signed at fourth meeting of Sino-Albanian Joint Committee for Cooperation in Technology and Technical Science.

SCMP 1795:51

58-67 **6/5/58** – Peking **Multilateral** Statement
"Adherence" to 1929 Warsaw Convention for the Unification of Certain Rules relating to International Carriage by Air

Adopted by Standing Committee of National People's Congress of PRC. Instrument of accession deposited with Polish government on 7/19/58.

TYC 7:196(C); SCMP 1788:49

58-68 **6/12/58** – Budapest **Hungary** Protocol
Trade

PR 6/24/58, p. 19; SCMP 1794:50

58-69 **6/16/58** – Peking **Norway** Exchange of Letters
Application of Article 5 of Trade and Payments Agreement of 6/4/58 [58-65]

Signed by representatives of banks of PRC and Norway.

SCMP 1796:40

58-70 **6/9/58** 6/16/58 Phnom Penh **Cambodia** Exchange of Notes
6/28/58 Peking
Extension of 1956 Trade and Payments Agreements to 6/16/59 [56-54, 55]

TYC 7:92(C)

58-71 **7/4/58** – Moscow **USSR** Protocol
Scientific and technical cooperation

Signed at seventh session of Sino-Soviet Joint Committee for Scientific and Technical Cooperation.

PR 7/15/58, p. 19; SCMP 1807:51; Izv, Pr 7/6/58

58-72 **7/21/58** – Peking **Rumania** Agreement
Trade in period 1958-62

JMJP 7/22/58; PR 7/29/58, p. 21

58-73 **7/31/58** – Berlin **Germany (E)** Protocol
Scientific and technical cooperation

Signed at fourth session of Sino-German Standing Committee for Cooperation in Technology and Technical Sciences.

PR 8/12/58, p. 20; SCMP 1828:45

58-74 **8/3/58** – Peking **USSR** Joint Communiqué
Talks during Chairman Khrushchev's visit: international situation, peaceful coexistence, disarmament, etc.

TYC 7:5(C); WCC 5:144(C); JMJP 8/4/58(C); JMST 1959, p. 314(C); PR 8/12/58, p. 6(E); SCMP 1827:25(E); ZD 1958:7-9:1317(P,E); ADTJ 0686:2(Fr); Pr 8/4/58(R); DIA 1958, p. 516(E); DAFR 1958, p. 266(E); AsR 2191(E); RI 1959:7:275(It)

58-75 **8/8/58** – Moscow **USSR** Agreement
Soviet technical aid in construction or expansion of forty-seven industrial projects in PRC

Superseded by more extensive agreement of 2/7/59 [59-24].

JMJP 8/12/58; PR 8/19/58, p. 21; SCMP 1833:42; Pr, Izv 8/12/58; AsR 2197

58-76 **8/8/58** – Karachi **Pakistan** Agreement
Barter of PRC rice for Pakistan cotton and jute

PR 8/19/58, p. 21; SCMP 1832:48

58-77 **8/8/58** – Budapest **Hungary** Agreement
Mutual purchase of film distribution rights

SCMP 1832:48

58-78 **8/15/58(?)** – Prague **Czechoslovakia** Protocol
Scientific and technical cooperation

Signed at sixth meeting of Sino-Czechoslovak Joint Committee for Scientific and Technical Cooperation.

PR 9/23/58, p. 21; SCMP 1837:57

58-79 **8/22/58** – Budapest **Hungary** Protocol
Scientific and technical cooperation

Signed at fourth meeting of Sino-Hungarian Committee for Scientific and Technical Cooperation.

PR 9/23/58, p. 21; SCMP 1841:52

58-80 **8/24/58** – Peking **Cambodia** Joint Statement
Talks during Premier Norodom Sihanouk's visit: trade, PRC economic aid, neutralist policy of Cambodia, Chinese nationals in Cambodia, etc.

TYC 7:15(C); WCC 5:152(C); JMJP 8/25/58(C); JMST 1959, p. 349(C); PR 8/2/58, p. 14(E); SCMP 1841:35(E); ZD 1958:7-9:1335(P,E); DIA 1958, p. 519(E); AsR 2249(E); A/D p. 32(E); H12(1):174(G, abbrev.)

58-81 **8/25/58** 8/25/58 Peking **UAR** Agreement
Postal services

TYC 7:170(C); SCMP 1842:61

58-82 **9/15/58** – Warsaw **Poland** Protocol
Scientific and technical cooperation

Signed at fifth session of Sino-Polish Standing Committee for Scientific and Technical Cooperation.

PR 9/23/58, p. 21; SCMP 1856:37

58-83 **9/17/58** 9/17/58 Colombo **Ceylon** Exchange of Notes
PRC loan for flood relief and rehabilitation

PR 9/30/58, p. 25; CTS 1958:11(E); AsR 2371; H12(1):66(G)

58-84 **9/25/58** 9/25/58 Tunis **Tunisia** Agreement
Exchange of goods in 1959

Signed by Chinese Vice-Minister of Foreign Trade and Tunisian Under-Secretary of State for Planning.

TYC 7:96(C); JMJP 9/27/58; PR 10/7/58, p. 20; SCMP 1866:48; AsR 2371; H12(2):194(G)

58-85 **9/27/58** – Peking **Korea (N)** Agreement
Exchange of main commodities in period 1959-62

JMJP 9/28/58; PR 10/7/58, p. 19; SCMP 1865:48; AsR 2371

58-86 **9/27/58** – Peking **Korea (N)** Agreement
PRC grant of loan as aid in construction of power station on Yalu River

JMJP 9/28/58; PR 10/7/58, p. 19; SCMP 1865:48; AsR 2371

58-87 **9/27/58** – Peking **Korea (N)** Agreement
PRC grant of loan for two industrial plants, machinery, and equipment
JMJP 9/28/58; PR 10/7/58, p. 19; SCMP 1865:48; AsR 2371

58-88 **9/27/58** – Peking **Korea (N)** Protocol
PRC supply of whole sets of equipment and machinery for joint construction of power station on Yalu River
PR 10/7/58, p. 19; SCMP 1865:48

58-89 **12/24/57** 10/4/58 Peking **Pakistan** Exchange of Letters
4/9/58
10/4/58
Grant of reciprocal most-favored-nation treatment
TYC 7:35(C); H12(1):233(G)

58-90 **10/5/58** – Budapest **Hungary** Agreement
Tourism
SCMP 1873:72

58-91 **10/9/58** – – **Germany (E)** Agreement
Purchase of film distribution rights
AGF p. 54

58-92 **10/10/58** – Bucharest **Rumania** Agreement
Cooperation in radio and television broadcasting
SCMP 1875:61

58-93 **10/13/58** – Djakarta **Indonesia** Contract
Sale of rice by PRC
Signed by representatives of PRC Commercial Counsellor's Office and Indonesian Food Foundation.
PR 10/21/58, p. 21

58-94 **10/17/58** – Pyongyang **Korea (N)** Joint Communiqué
Withdrawal of Chinese People's Volunteers from Korea (N) and turnover of barracks, etc., to Korea (N)
Signed by Commanders of CPV and Korean (N) Minister of Defense.
JMJP 10/18/58(C); JMST 1959, p. 327(C); PR 10/21/58, p. 20

58-95 **10/18/58** – Peking **Korea (N)** Protocol
Scientific and technical cooperation
Signed at first meeting of Sino-Korean Committee for Scientific and Technical Cooperation
SCMP 1880:49

58-96 **10/27/58** – Rabat **Morocco** Agreement
Trade
JMJP 11/2/58; PR 11/4/58, p. 23; H12(2):158

58-97 **November** – – **Indonesia** –
Extension of 1956 Trade Agreement [56-126]
AsR 2407

58-98 **11/13/58** – Peking **Bulgaria** Protocol
Scientific and technical cooperation
Signed at third session of Sino-Bulgarian Joint Committee for Scientific and Technical Cooperation.
PR 11/25/58, p. 18; SCMP 1897:39

58-99 **11/19/58** 1/1/59 Peking **Korea (N)** Protocol
Exchange of goods in 1959
TYC 7:133(C); JMJP 11/20/58; PR 11/25/58, p. 19; SCMP 1900:47; AsR 2402

58-100 **11/27/58** – Peking **Bulgaria** –
1959 plan for cultural cooperation
JMJP 11/28/58; SCMP 1905:34

58-101 **12/8/58** – Peking **Korea (N)** Joint Statement
Talks during Premier Kim Il Sung's visit: Korean unification, etc.
TYC 7:24(C); WCC 5:214(C); JMJP 12/9/58(C); JMST 1959, p. 338(C); PR 12/16/58, p. 16(E); SCMP 1912:33(E); ZD 1958:10-12:374(P,E); AsR 2431(E); A/D p. 49(E)

58-102 **12/8/58** – Kunming **Vietnam (N)** Protocol
Border railways
Signed at session of Sino-Vietnamese Joint Committee on Border Railways.
SCMP 1913:50

58-103 **12/9/58** – Ulan Bator **Multilateral** Protocol
Rail transportation in 1959
Signed at Railway Transport Planning Conference attended by delegates from Korea (N), Mongolia, Vietnam (N), and USSR.
SCMP 1913:54

58-104 **12/15/58** 2/8/59 Cairo **UAR** Agreement
Trade in period 1959-61
TYC 7:57(C); JMJP 12/17/58; SCMP 1917:51; STS 109:1(Fr); AsR 2463; H12(2):74

58-105 **12/15/58** 2/8/59 Cairo **UAR** Agreement
Payments
TYC 7:60(C); JMJP 12/17/58; SCMP 1917:51; STS 109:3(Fr); AsR 2463; H12(2):76

58-106 **12/15/58** 2/8/59 Cairo **UAR** Protocol
Trade in 1959

TYC 7:64(C); JMJP 12/17/58; PR 12/23/58, p. 31; SCMP 1917:51; AsR 2463; H12(2):80

58-107 **12/16/58(?)** – Pyongyang **Korea (N)** Protocol
Barter in border areas

Signed by representatives of Kirin and Liaoning Provinces in PRC and Korean Union of Producers' Cooperatives.

SCMP 1919:32

58-108 **12/18/58** 1/1/59 Peking **Bulgaria** Protocol
Exchange of goods and payments in 1959

TYC 7:87(C); JMJP 12/19/58; PR 12/23/58, p. 31; SCMP 1920:31

58-109 **12/18/58** – Peking **Bulgaria** Protocol
Extension and revision of 1957 Agreement on Exchange of Goods and Payments for 1958-60 [57-98]

SCMP 1920:31

58-110 **12/20/58** – Peking **Algeria** (in exile) Joint Communiqué
Talks during visit of Mahmoud Cherif, member of "Provisional Government of Republic of Algeria": Algerian independence, nuclear tests, etc.

PRC recognized "Provisional Government of Republic of Algeria" on 9/22/58.

TYC 7:9(C); WCC 5:218(C); JMJP 12/21/58(C); JMST 1959, p. 353(C); PR 12/23/58, p. 24(E); SCMP 1921:38(E); DIA 1958, p. 533(E); H12(2):85(G)

58-111 **12/27/58** 1/1/59 Pyongyang **Korea (N)** Agreement
Currency exchange rate and noncommercial payments

SCMP 1925:49

58-112 **12/27/58** 1/1/59 Pyongyang **Korea (N)** Protocol
Currency exchange in border areas

SCMP 1925:49

58-113 **12/27/58** 1/1/59 Pyongyang **Korea (N)** Protocol
Noncommercial remittances between People's Bank of China and Central Bank of Korea (N)

SCMP 1925:49

58-114 **12/29/58** – Peking **Korea (N)** Protocol
Clearance of accounts for PRC aid in period 1954-57

JMJP 11/1/59; SCMP 1926:43

58-115 **12/29/58** – Peking **Mongolia** Agreement
Economic and technical aid
JMJP 12/30/58; SCMP 1926:45; AsR 2469

58-116 **12/29/58** – Peking **Mongolia** Protocol
Economic and technical aid
JMJP 12/30/58; PR 1/6/59, p. 30; SCMP 1926:45; AsR 2469

1959

59-1 **January** – – **Czechoslovakia** –
1959 plan for cultural cooperation
PR 1/27/59, p. 21

59-2 **1/3/59** 2/2/59 Baghdad **Iraq** Agreement
Trade and payments
Effective on notification of ratification. Ratifications exchanged in Baghdad 2/7/59 TYC 8:55(C) Communiqué also issued.
TYC 8:53(C); WCC 6:1(C); JMJP 1/5/59; PR 1/13/59, p. 21; SCMP 1930:34; AsR 2463; H12(2):28(G)

59-3 **1/3/59** – Baghdad **Iraq** Exchange of Letters
Trade involving third countries
JMJP 1/5/59; H12(2):30(G)

59-4 **1/5/59** – Ulan Bator **Mongolia** –
1959 plan for cultural cooperation
JMJP 1/6/59

59-5 **1/9/59** – Peking **Hungary** –
1959 plan for cultural cooperation
JMJP 1/10/59; PR 1/27/59, p. 21; SCMP 1934:32

59-6 **1/16/59** – Peking **Albania** Agreement
Trade in period 1961-65
WCC 6:5(C); JMJP 1/17/59; PR 1/20/59, p. 22; SCMP 1938:32; AsR 2472

59-7 **1/16/59** – Peking **Albania** Agreement
PRC loan in period 1961-65 (repayable with commodities in period 1981-90)
WCC 6:5(C); JMJP 1/17/59; PR 1/20/59, p. 22; SCMP 1938:32; AsR 2472

59-8 **1/16/59** 1/1/59 Peking **Albania** Protocol
Exchange of goods and payments in 1959
TYC 8:72(C); PR 1/20/59, p. 22; SCMP 1938:32

59-9 **1/16/59** – Peking **Albania** Protocol
Use of PRC loan and gift to Albania in 1959
PR 1/20/59, p. 22; SCMP 1938:32

59-10 **1/16/59** – Peking **Albania** Protocol
Clearance of account on PRC loan and commodity gift in 1958
PR 1/20/59, p. 22; SCMP 1938:32

59-11 **1/16/59** 7/30/59 Hanoi **Vietnam (N)** Agreement
Cultural cooperation in period 1959-64
TYC 8:152(C); JMJP 1/17/59; PR 1/27/59, p. 21; SCMP 1938:38

59-12 **1/16/59** – Hanoi **Vietnam (N)** –
1959 plan for cultural cooperation
JMJP 1/17/59; SCMP 1938:38

59-13 **1/17/59** – Peking **USSR** Protocol
Scientific and technical cooperation
Signed at eighth session of Sino-Soviet Joint Committee for Scientific and Technical Cooperation. Joint Communiqué also issued 1/17/59. SCMP 1939:48(E); AsR 2516(E)
JMJP 1/20/59; PR 1/27/59, p. 21; SCMP 1939:48; AsR 2516; G/S p. 134

59-14 **1/17/59** – Peking **USSR** Protocol
Exchange of technical information and experts
SCMP 1939:48

59-15 **1/21/59** – Dubna **Multilateral** Protocol
Further scientific cooperation among members of Joint Institute for Nuclear Research
Signed by USSR, Mongolia, Vietnam (N), Korea (N), Albania, Poland, Germany (E), Rumania, Czechoslovakia, Hungary, and Bulgaria.
G/S p. 134

59-16 **1/23/59** – Tai'zz **Yemen** Protocol
PRC aid in construction of road in Yemen
PR 2/3/59, p. 23

59-17 **1/23/59** – Tai'zz **Yemen** Protocol
PRC aid in construction of textile factory in Yemen
PR 2/3/59, p. 23

59-18 **1/27/59** – Peking **Germany (E)** Joint Statement
Talks during Premier Grotewohl's visit: Soviet proposals for unified Germany, demilitarization of West Berlin, etc.
TYC 8:6(C); WCC 6:12(C); JMJP 1/28/59(C); JMST 1959, p. 339(C); PR 2/3/59, p. 16(E); SCMP 1945:27(E); ZD 1959:1-2:145(P,E); AsR 2531(E); AGF p. 54

59-19 **1/27/59** 6/4/59 Peking **Germany (E)** Treaty
Consular

TYC 8:26(C); WCC 6:16(C); JMJP 1/28/59; PR 2/3/59, p. 22; SCMP 2088:5(E); AsR 2531; AGF p. 54; WGO 3:213

59-20 **1/30/59** – Warsaw **Poland** –
1959 plan for cultural cooperation

PR 2/10/59, p. 19; SCMP 1949:40

59-21 **1/30/59** 1/1/59 Ulan Bator **Mongolia** Protocol
Mutual supply of goods in 1959

TYC 8:102(C); JMJP 2/9/59; PR 2/17/59, p. 18

59-22 **2/5/59** 1/1/59 Peking **Germany (E)** Agreement
Exchange of goods and payments in 1959

TYC 8:106(C); JMJP 2/6/59; PR 2/17/59, p. 18; SCMP 1952:44

59-23 **2/5/59** 1/1/59 Peking **Germany (E)** Protocol
General conditions for delivery of goods in 1959

TYC 8:108(C)

59-24 **2/7/59** – Moscow **USSR** Agreement
Further expansion of Soviet economic and technical aid during period 1959-67

Signed by Premier Chou En-lai and Chairman Khrushchev.

WCC 6:12(C); JMJP 2/8/59; JMST 1959, p. 317; PR 2/17/59, p. 12; SCMP 1953:43; AsR 2547; G/S p. 136

59-25 **2/13/59** – Peking **Rumania** Agreement
Currency exchange rate and noncommercial payments

JMJP 2/14/59; PR 2/24/59, p. 26; SCMP 1958:34

59-26 **2/14/59** 1/1/59 Warsaw **Poland** Protocol
General conditions for delivery of goods in 1959

TYC 8:56(C)

59-27 **2/18/59** – Peking **Vietnam (N)** Agreement
Trade in period 1960-62

JMJP 2/19/59; PR 2/24/59, p. 26; SCMP 1959:37; AsR 2573

59-28 **2/18/59** 1/1/59 Peking **Vietnam (N)** Agreement
Mutual supply of goods and payments in 1959

TYC 8:104(C); JMJP 2/19/59; PR 2/24/59, p. 26; SCMP 1959:37; AsR 2573

59-29 **2/18/59** – Peking **Vietnam (N)** Agreement
Economic and technical aid (including long-term loan of 300 million yuan)

JMJP 2/19/59; PR 2/24/59, p. 26; SCMP 1959:37; AsR 2573

59-30 **2/18/59** – Peking **Vietnam (N)** Exchange of Notes
PRC aid of 100 million yuan without compensation to Vietnam (N)
JMJP 2/19/59; PR 2/24/59, p. 26; SCMP 1959:37; AsR 2573

59-31 **2/18/59** – Peking **Vietnam (N)** Protocol
Economic and technical aid
JMJP 2/19/59; PR 2/24/59, p. 26; SCMP 1959:37; AsR 2573

59-32 **2/18/59** – Peking **Vietnam (N)** Protocol
PRC technical aid
JMJP 2/19/59; PR 2/24/59, p. 26; SCMP 1959:37; AsR 2573

59-33 **2/18/59** – Peking **Vietnam (N)** Protocol
PRC aid in 1959
JMJP 2/19/59; PR 2/24/59, p. 26; SCMP 1959:37; AsR 2573

59-34 **2/18/59** 2/18/59 Peking **Korea (N)** Agreement
Air transport
TYC 8:173(C); JMJP 2/19/59; PR 2/24/59, p. 27; SCMP 1959:46

59-35 **2/18/59** – Peking **Korea (N)** Protocol
Reciprocal air services
JMJP 2/19/59; SCMP 1959:46

59-36 **2/18/59** – Peking **Korea (N)** Protocol
Technical cooperation in civil aviation
SCMP 1959:46

59-37 **2/20/59** – Warsaw **Poland** –
1959 plan for cooperation between Academies of Sciences
JMJP 2/22/59; PR 3/17/59, p. 20; SCMP 1964:48

59-38 **2/21/59** 5/18/59 Pyongyang **Korea (N)** Agreement
Cultural cooperation
TYC 8:150(C); JMJP 2/22/59; PR 3/3/59, p. 20; SCMP 1964:47; AsR 2577

59-39 **2/23/59** – Damascus **Syria (UAR)** Agreement
Exchange of newsreels
Applies to Syrian region of UAR, on whose behalf signed by representative of "Central Arab Studio of Second Bureau of First Army."
SCMP 1962:32

59-40 **2/26/59** – Moscow **USSR** Protocol
Exchange of goods in 1959
JMJP 2/27/59; PR 3/3/59, p. 20; SCMP 1965:30; AsR 2573; G/S p. 138

59-41 **3/3/59** – Prague **Czechoslovakia** Agreement
Scientific cooperation in 1959-61
TYC 8:167(C); JMJP 3/6/49; SCMP 1968:32

59-42 **3/3/59** – Prague **Czechoslovakia** –
1959 plan for cooperation between Academies of Sciences
JMJP 3/6/59; PR 3/31/59, p. 22; SCMP 1968:32

59-43 **3/6/59** – Warsaw **Poland** Agreement
Turnover of goods and payments in 1959
JMJP 3/8/59; PR 3/17/59, p. 20; SCMP 1972:36; AsR 2588

59-44 **3/9/59** – Leipzig **Germany (E)** Contract
Supply by Germany (E) of equipment for power stations in 1959-62
PR 3/31/59, p. 22; SCMP 1975:46

59-45 **3/9/59** – Leipzig **Germany (E)** Protocol
Supply by Germany (E) of two cement plants
SCMP 1975:46

59-46 **3/10/59** – Peking **Rumania** –
1959 plan for cultural cooperation
JMJP 3/11/59; PR 3/31/59, p. 22; SCMP 1973:42

59-47 **3/11/59** – Harbin **USSR** –
Joint use of Amur River
SCMP 1975:47

59-48 **3/12/59** 1/1/59 Prague **Czechoslovakia** Agreement
Exchange of goods and payments in 1959
TYC 8:99(C); PR 3/31/59, p. 22; SCMP 1975:47

59-49 **3/17/59** 1/1/59 Budapest **Hungary** Agreement
Exchange of goods and payments in 1959
TYC 8:33(C); JMJP 3/19/59; PR 3/31/59, p. 22; SCMP 1977:33

59-50 **3/17/59** 1/1/59 Budapest **Hungary** Protocol
General conditions for delivery of goods in 1959
TYC 8:36(C)

59-51 **3/17/59** – Berlin **Germany (E)** Agreement
Cooperation between Academies of Sciences
TYC 8:170(C); JMJP 3/19/59; PR 3/31/59, p. 22; SCMP 1978:38

59-52 **3/17/59** – Berlin **Germany (E)** –
1959 plan for cooperation between Academies of Sciences
JMJP 3/19/59; SCMP 1978:38

59-53 **3/18/59** – Peking **Yugoslavia** Protocol
Exchange of goods in 1959
TYC 8:98(C); JMJP 3/19/59; SCMP 1978:33; YTS 1960:1:54(S-C,E); WGO 3:9

59-54 **3/18/59** – Peking **USSR** –
1959 plan for cultural cooperation
JMJP 3/19/59; PR 3/31/59, p. 22; SCMP 1978:42; G/S p. 140

59-55 **3/22/59** 1/1/59 Peking **Rumania** Protocol
Exchange of goods and payments in 1959
TYC 8:74(C); JMJP 3/23/59; PR 3/31/59, p. 22; SCMP 1980:53

59-56 **3/22/59** 1/1/59 Peking **Rumania** Protocol
General conditions for delivery of goods in 1959
TYC 8:78(C)

59-57 **3/26/59** 3/26/59 Peking **Ceylon** Agreement
Air transport
TYC 8:175(C); JMJP 3/27/59; SCMP 1984:43; CTS 1959:2:2(E); AsR 2648; H12(1):71

59-58 **3/26/59** – Peking **Ceylon** Protocol
Air transport
JMJP 3/27/59; SCMP 1984:43; CTS 1959:2:6(E); H12(1):71

59-59 **3/26/59** – Peking **Ceylon** Exchange of Notes
Nationality of pilots
H12(1):71

59-60 **4/3/59** – Budapest **Hungary** –
1959 plan for cooperation between Academies of Sciences
SCMP 1988:41

59-61 **4/4/59** – Baghdad **Iraq** Agreement
Cultural cooperation
Ratified by PRC 6/19/59; in effect after mutual notification of ratifications, date unknown.
TYC 8:133(C); JMJP 4/5/59; PR 4/14/59, p. 21; SCMP 1988:43; H12(2):25(G)

59-62 **4/6/59** 4/6/59 Budapest **Hungary** Agreement
Cooperation in radio broadcasting
TYC 8:130(C)

59-63 **4/8/59** – Baghdad **Iraq** –
1959 plan for cultural cooperation
PR 4/14/59, p. 21; SCMP 1992:37

59-64 **4/13/59** – Bucharest **Rumania** Agreement
Cooperation between Academies of Sciences
TYC 8:162(C)

59-65 **4/13/59(?)** – Prague **Czechslovakia** Agreement
Trade in period 1960-62
SCMP 1994:41

59-66 **4/15/59** 4/15/59 Warsaw **Poland** Agreement
Cooperation in radio and television broadcasting
TYC 8:136(C); JMJP 4/17/59; SCMP 1996:53

59-67 **4/15/59** – Warsaw **Poland** Protocol (supplementary)
Cooperation in radio and television broadcasting
TYC 8:139(C)

59-68 **4/20/59** – Tirana **Albania** Agreement
Noncommercial payments
SCMP 2000:59

59-69 **4/23/59** – Sofia **Bulgaria** Agreement
Cooperation between Academies of Sciences
TYC 8:164(C)

59-70 **4/25/59** 4/25/59 Berlin **Germany (E)** Agreement
Cooperation in radio and television broadcasting
TYC 8:155(C); SCMP 2003:48; AGF p. 54

59-71 **4/25/59** – Berlin **Germany (E)** Protocol
Television cooperation
TYC 8:160(C); AGF p. 55

59-72 **4/28/59** – Warsaw **Multilateral** Communiqué
Forthcoming Summit Conference on Germany and West Berlin
Signed by Warsaw Treaty countries, viz., USSR, Albania, Bulgaria, Hungary, Germany (E), Poland, Rumania, and Czechoslovakia.
WCC 6:52(C); JMJP 4/30/59(C); JMST 1959, p. 311(C); SCMP 2005:45(E); BFSP 164:253(E); DIA 1959, p. 583(E)

59-73 **4/30/59** 4/30/59 Prague **Czechoslovakia** Agreement
Cooperation in radio and television broadcasting
TYC 8:147(C); SCMP 2006:36

59-74 **5/6/59** – Peking **Hungary** Communiqué
Talks during visit of Hungarian party and government delegates, led by Premier Muennich: Sino-Hungarian relations
WCC 6:64(C); SCMP 2010:36(E)

59-75 **5/6/59** 11/2/59 Peking **Hungary** Treaty
Friendship and cooperation

TYC 8:1(C); YHTY 98(C,Hungarian); WCC 6:62(C); JMJP 5/7/59(C); JMST 1959, p. 340(C); PR 5/12/59, p. 22(E); SCMP 2010:39(E); ZD 1959:4-6:724(P,E); WGO 2:14

59-76 **5/15/59** 11/1/58 Helsinki **Finland** Agreement
Trade in 1958-59

TYC 8:69(C); PR 5/26/59, p. 23; SCMP 2018:41; H12(3):37

59-77 **5/20/59** – Peking **Czechoslovakia** Protocol
Scientific and technical cooperation

Signed at seventh meeting of Sino-Czechoslovak Joint Committee for Scientific and Technical Cooperation.

JMJP 5/21/59; PR 5/26/59, p. 22; SCMP 2020:40

59-78 **5/21/59** – Pyongyang **Korea (N)** Protocol
Scientific and technical cooperation

Signed at second meeting of Sino-Korean Committee for Scientific and Technical Cooperation.

JMJP 5/27/59; PR 6/9/59, p. 22; SCMP 2021:37

59-79 **5/25/59** – New Delhi **India** Exchange of Letters
Extension of 1954 Trade Agreement until 12/31/59 [54-72]

JMJP 5/27/59; SCMP 2024:31; AsR 2707; A/D p. 299(E); H12(1):98(G)

59-80 **5/30/59** – Phnom Penh **Cambodia** Exchange of Notes
6/1/59
Extension of 1956 Trade and Payments Agreements [56-54,55]

TYC 8:93(C)

59-81 **6/1/59** – Peking **USSR** –
1959 plan for cooperation between Academies of Sciences

PR 6/9/59, p. 22; SCMP 2028:42

59-82 **6/13/59** – Peking/Colombo **Ceylon** Joint Communiqué
Talks on trade in 1959

JMJP 6/14/59; SCMP 2037:30(E)

59-83 **6/13/59** 1/1/59 Colombo **Ceylon** Protocol
Exchange of goods in 1959

TYC 8:125(C); JMJP 6/14/59; PR 6/23/59, p. 22; SCMP 2037:31; CTS 1959:11(E); AsR 2743; H12(1):67(G)

59-84 **6/13/59** – Colombo **Ceylon** Contracts (2)
Exchange of PRC rice and Ceylon rubber

JMJP 6/14/59; SCMP 2037:31; AsR 2743

59-85 **6/20/59** – Hanoi **Vietnam (N)** Agreement
Currency exchange rate and noncommercial payments
JMJP 6/22/59; SCMP 2042:29

59-86 **6/23/59** 12/19/59 Peking **USSR** Treaty
Consular
TYC 8:20(C); WCC 6:72(C); JMJP 6/25/59; PR 6/30/67, p. 22; SCMP 2046:23; UNTS 356:83(R,C,E,Fr); WGO 2:14, 3:213

59-87 **6/27/59** – Hanoi **Vietnam (N)** Protocol
Joint survey of Gulf of Tonkin
PR 7/7/59, p. 21; SCMP 2047:35

59-88 **7/4/59** – Peking **USSR** Protocol
Scientific and technical cooperation
Signed at ninth sesssion of Sino-Soviet Joint Committee for Scientific and Technical Cooperation.
JMJP 7/8/59; PR 7/14/59, p. 22; SCMP 2053:28; G/S p. 148

59-89 **7/11/59** 7/11/59 Tirana **Albania** Agreement
Cooperation in radio broadcasting
TYC 8:140(C); JMJP 7/13/59; SCMP 2056:30

59-90 **8/6/59** 8/6/59 Sofia **Bulgaria** Agreement
Cooperation in radio and television broadcasting
TYC 8:143(C); PR 8/18/59, p. 20; SCMP 2074:35

59-91 **8/25/59** – Peking **Korea (N)** Agreement
Fishery regulation in Yellow Sea
JMJP 8/26/59; PR 9/1/59, p. 24; SCMP 2088:35; AsR 2997

59-92 **8/28/59** – Peking **Bulgaria** Protocol
Scientific and technical cooperation
Signed at fourth session of Sino-Bulgarian Joint Committee for Scientific and Technical Cooperation.
SCMP 2092:41; AsR 2926

59-93 **9/9/59** – Peking **Afghanistan** Joint Communiqué
Talks during visit of Foreign Minister Sardar Mohammed Naim: principles of Bandung Conference and UN Charter, support for further US-Soviet exchanges of visits
TYC 8:5(C); WCC 6:189(C); PR 9/22/59, p. 21(E, sum.); SCMP 2099:58(E); AsR 2926(E); H12(1):3(G)

59-94 **9/30/59** – Peking **Morocco** Agreement
Trade in 1959-60
SCMP 2112:45

59-95 **10/7/59** – Peking **Guinea** Agreement
Cultural cooperation

In force on mutual notification of approval, date unknown. Establishment of diplomatic relations announced in Joint Communiqué issued on 10/4/59.

TYC 8:127(C); PR 10/13/59, p. 26; SCMP 2116:35; AsR 2959

59-96 **10/7/59** – Peking **Guinea** –
Plan for cultural cooperation in fourth quarter of 1959

SCMP 2116:35

59-97 **10/11/59** – Peking **Indonesia** Joint Communiqué
Talks during Foreign Minister Subandrio's visit: peaceful coexistence and Bandung principles, Taiwan, West Irian, PRC representation in UN, approval of Khrushchev-Eisenhower meeting, disarmament, Chinese nationals in Indonesia

TYC 8:3(C); WCC 6:430(C); JMJP 10/12/59(C); JMST 1959, p. 350(C); PR 10/20/59, p. 12(E); SCMP 2117:33(E); AsR 2996(E); A/D p. 60(E); H12(1):108(G)

59-98 **10/12/59** – Peking **USSR** Protocol
Scientific and technical cooperation

Signed at tenth session of Sino-Soviet Joint Committee for Scientific and Technical Cooperation. Communiqué also issued 10/12/59. SCMP 2118:45(E)

JMJP 10/3/59; PR 10/20/59, p. 23; SCMP 2118:44; AsR 2971

59-99 **10/12/59** – Peking **Rumania** Protocol
Scientific and technical cooperation

Signed at sixth session of Sino-Rumanian Joint Committee for Scientific and Technical Cooperation. Communiqué also issued 10/12/59. SCMP 2119:39(E)

PR 10/20/59, p. 23; SCMP 2119:39; AsR 2971

59-100 **Mid-October** – Peking **Japan** Agreement
Emergency shelter for fishing boats

Signed by representatives of Chinese People's Association for Cultural Relations with Foreign Countries and Japan-China Friendship Association of Japan, apparently between 10/15/59 and 10/24/59 during Japanese delegates' visit to attend National Day celebrations in PRC. Specific provisions were adopted on basis of this Agreement, which was later replaced by Fishery Agreement of 11/9/63 [63-129].

SCMP 3100:47; CB 724:3

59-101 **11/1/59** – Peking **Poland** Protocol
Scientific and technical cooperation

Signed at sixth sesssion of Sino-Polish Standing Committee for Scientific and Technical Cooperation. Communiqué also issued 11/1/59.

JMJP 11/2/59; PR 11/17/59, p. 26; SCMP 2132:39

59-102 **11/10/59** – Peking **Hungary** –
1960 plan for cooperation between Academies of Sciences
JMJP 11/11/59; PR 12/8/59, p. 21; SCMP 2137:30

59-103 **11/17/59** – Peking **Hungary** Protocol
Scientific and technical cooperation
Signed at fifth session of Sino-Hungarian Committee for Scientific and Technical Cooperation. Communiqué also issued 11/17/59.
JMJP 11/19/59; PR 12/8/59, p. 21: SCMP 2142:45

59-104 **11/21/59** – Phnom Penh **Cambodia** Exchange of Notes
Reciprocal tariff concessions
Represents culmination of notes exchanged on 9/17/59, 10/14/59, 10/20/59, and 11/14/59.
TYC 8:95(C)

59-105 **12/5/59** – Sofia **Bulgaria** –
1960 plan for cultural cooperation
JMJP 12/8/59; SCMP 2154:38

59-106 **12/5/59** – Peking **Multilateral** Protocol(s)
Technical aspects of railway construction
Signed by USSR, Bulgaria, Hungary, Vietnam (N), Germany (E), Korea (N), Poland, and Czechoslovakia.
SCMP 2153:44

59-107 **12/10/59** – Prague **Czechoslovakia** Agreement
Cooperation in agricultural research between Academies of Sciences
PR 12/29/59, p. 23; SCMP 2158:42

59-108 **12/11/59** 12/11/59 Budapest **Hungary** Agreement
Civil aviation
PR 12/29/59, p. 23; SCMP 2158:44

59-109 **12/11/59** – Moscow(?) **Multilateral** Agreement
Arrangements of state banks for currency exchange and cash movements
Signed by USSR, Albania, Bulgaria, Czechoslovakia, Korea (N), Germany (E), Hungary, Mongolia, Poland, Rumania, and Vietnam (N).
AGF p. 8

59-110 **12/12/59** – Moscow **USSR** Agreement
Currency exchange and cash movements
G/S p. 161

59-111 **12/16/59** 11/1/59 Peking **Finland** Agreement
Trade in 1959-60
TYC 8:71(C); SCMP 2161:34; H12(3):37

59-112 **12/22/59** – Ulan Bator **Mongolia** Agreement
Noncommercial payments
JMJP 12/24/59; SCMP 2166:36

59-113 **12/31/59** – Moscow **USSR** –
1960 plan for cultural cooperation
JMJP 1/1/60; PR 1/12/60, p. 22; SCMP 2171:40; G/S p. 164

59-114 **12/31/59** – Peking **Cuba** Contract
PRC purchase of Cuban sugar
Signed by China National Foodstuffs Export Company and Cuban trade authorities.
JMJP 1/12/60; PR 1/19/60, p. 22; SCMP 2177:32

59-115 **12/31/59** – Peking **Vietnam (N)** Protocol
PRC technical aid in 1959
JMJP 1/25/60; SCMP 2187:37

1960

60-1 **1/3/60** – Colombo **Ceylon** Agreement (?)
Exchange of Ceylon rubber and PRC rice
AsR 3116

60-2 **1/18/60** 6/18/60 Peking **Germany (E)** Treaty
Commerce and navigation
TYC 9:134(C); WCC 7:8(C); JMJP 1/19/60; PR 1/26/60, p. 30; SCMP 2182:38; AsR 3153; AGF p. 56; Dok 8:333(G); WGO 3:213

60-3 **1/18/60** – Peking **Germany (E)** Agreement
Exchange of goods in 1960-62
JMJP 1/19/60; PR 1/26/60, p. 30; SCMP 2182:38; AsR 3153; AGF p. 56

60-4 **1/19/60** – Peking **Germany (E)** Communiqué
Talks during visit of government delegation to PRC: West German and Japanese militarist policies, etc.
WCC 7:12(C); PR 1/26/60, p. 26; SCMP 2184:41(E); AsR 3153(E); Dok 8:331(G)

60-5 **1/20/60** – Peking **Indonesia** Joint Press Communiqué
Signing of protocol on exchange of ratifications of 1955 Dual Nationality Treaty [55-28]
PR 2/2/60, p. 16(E); SCMP 2187:35(E); A/D p. 260(E)

60-6 **1/28/60** – Peking **Burma** Joint Communiqué
Talks during Premier Ne Win's visit: Sino-Burmese relations

WCC 7:27(C); JMJP 1/29/60(C); PR 2/2/60, p. 12(E); SCMP 2188:47(E); ZD 1960:2:301(P,E); AsR 3151(E); H12(1):20

60-7 **1/28/60** 5/14/60 Peking **Burma** Treaty
Friendship and mutual nonaggression

TYC 9:44(C); YHTY 3(C,E); WCC 7:23(C); JMJP 2/1/60(C); JMST 1960, p. 318(C); PR 2/2/60, p. 12(E); SCMP 2188:47; CB 612:1(E); BFSP 164:649(E); ZD 1960:2:304(P,E); Burma Wkly. Bull. 8:41:387 (1/29/60)(E); AsR 3151(E); A/D p. 55(E); H12(1):19(G); FEER 2/11/60, p. 292(E); IA 1960:3:99(E)

60-8 **1/28/60** 5/14/60 Peking **Burma** Agreement
Boundary

TYC 9:65(C); WCC 7:25(C); JMJP 2/1/60(C); JMST 1960, p. 319(C); PR 2/2/60, p. 14(E); SCMP 2188:47; CB 612:2(E); BFSP 164:651(E); ZD 1960:2:307(P,E); Burma Wkly. Bull. 8:41:386 (1/29/60)(E); SIA 1959-60, p. 262; AsR 3151(E); A/D p. 188(E); H12(1):20(G); WGO 3:213; FEER 2/11/60, p. 292(E); IA 1960:3:100(E)

60-9 **1/29/60** 1/29/60 Moscow **USSR** Agreement
Forest protection and prevention of forest fires

TYC 9:148(C); PR 2/9/60, p. 21; SCMP 2190:49; Chichvarin (ed.), *Mezhdunarodnye soglasheniya po okhrane prirody (sbornik dokumentov)* (Moscow, 1966), p. 244(R)

60-10 **2/2/60** 1/1/60 Peking **Czechslovakia** Protocol
Exchange of goods and payments in 1960

TYC 9:118(C); PR 2/9/60, p. 21; SCMP 2191:53

60-11 **2/5/60** – Peking **Korea (N)** –
1960 plan for cultural cooperation

PR 2/23/60, p. 22; SCMP 2194:50

60-12 **2/8/60** 1/1/60 Peking **Ceylon** Protocol
Exchange of goods in 1960

PR 2/16/60, p. 21; SCMP 2195:47; CTS 1960:3(E); H12(1):70

60-13 **2/11/60** – – **Poland** Protocol
Exchange of goods in 1960-61

Reported by Trybuna Ludu 2/12/60. Cf. Agreement of 2/22/60 [60-21].

Horak, p. 123

60-14 **2/11/60** – Peking **Poland** –
1960-61 plan for cultural cooperation

PR 2/16/60, p. 21; SCMP 2198:48

60-15 **2/16/60** – Bucharest **Rumania** –
1960 plan for cultural cooperation

JMJP 2/18/60; PR 2/23/60, p. 22; SCMP 2201:30

60-16 **2/16/60** – Peking **Vietnam (N)** –
1960 plan for cultural cooperation
JMJP 2/17/60; PR 2/23/60, p. 22; SCMP 2201:31

60-17 **2/16/60** – Budapest **Hungary** –
1960 plan for cultural cooperation
JMJP 2/18/60; PR 2/23/60, p. 22; SCMP 2202:32

60-18 **2/18/60** – Peking **Czechoslovakia** –
1960 plan for cooperation between Academies of Sciences
JMJP 2/19/60; SCMP 2203:37

60-19 **2/19/60** – Peking **Czechoslovakia** –
1960 plan for cultural cooperation
JMJP 2/20/60; SCMP 2204:54

60-20 **2/20/60** – Moscow **USSR** –
1960 plan for cooperation between Academies of Sciences
JMJP 2/22/60; SCMP 2205:46

60-21 **2/22/60** – Peking **Poland** Agreement
Turnover of goods and payments in 1960
JMJP 2/24/60; PR 3/1/60, p. 24; SCMP 2206:41

60-22 **2/22/60** 1/1/60 Peking **Poland** Protocol
Extension of Protocol on General Conditions for Delivery of Goods in 1959 [59-26]
TYC 9:90(C)

60-23 **2/23/60** 1/1/60 Peking **Mongolia** Protocol
Mutual supply of goods in 1960
TYC 9:126(C); JMJP 2/24/60; PR 3/1/60, p. 24; SCMP 2206:40

60-24 **2/23/60** – Peking **Mongolia** Exchange of Notes
Revision of 1956 Protocol on General Conditions for Delivery of Goods [56-21]
TYC 9:128(C)

60-25 **2/23/60** – Peking **Mongolia** –
1960 plan for cultural cooperation
JMJP 2/24/60; SCMP 2206:40

60-26 **2/24/60** – Peking **UAR** Joint Communiqué
Trade talks
JMJP 2/25/60(C); SCMP 2206:41(E); H12(2):81(G)

60-27 **2/24/60** – Peking **UAR** Protocol
Trade in 1960
JMJP 2/25/60; PR 3/1/60, p. 24; SCMP 2206:41; AsR 3235

60-28 **2/24/60** – Moscow **USSR** –
1960 plan for scientific and technical cooperation
JMJP 2/26/60; PR 3/1/60, p. 24; SCMP 2207:41; G60:126

60-29 **2/28/60** 1/1/60 Peking **Hungary** Agreement
Exchange of goods and payments in 1960
TYC 9:86(C); JMJP 2/29/60; SCMP 2209:30

60-30 **2/28/60** – Peking **Hungary** Protocol
General conditions for delivery of goods in 1960
TYC 9:89(C)

60-31 **2/29/60** 1/1/60 Pyongyang **Korea (N)** Protocol
Mutual supply of goods in 1960
TYC 9:121(C); JMJP 3/1/60; PR 3/22/60, p. 26; SCMP 2210:46

60-32 **2/29/60** – Peking **Rumania** –
1960 plan for cooperation between Academies of Sciences
JMJP 3/1/60; PR 3/22/60, p. 26; SCMP 2210:46

60-33 **2/29/60** – Peking **Finland** –
Establishment of direct telegraphic services between Shanghai and Helsinki
JMJP 3/3/60

60-34 **3/4/60** – Tirana **Albania** –
1960 plan for cultural cooperation
PR 3/22/60, p. 26; SCMP 2213:40

60-35 **3/7/60** 1/1/60 Hanoi **Vietnam (N)** Agreement
Mutual supply of goods and payments
TYC 9:123(C); JMJP 3/8/60; PR 3/22/60, p. 26; SCMP 2215:42

60-36 **3/7/60** – Hanoi **Vietnam (N)** Protocol
Mutual supply of goods and payments in 1960
TYC 9:125(C); JMJP 3/8/60; SCMP 2215:42

60-37 **3/7/60** – Hanoi **Vietnam (N)** Protocol
PRC aid to Vietnam (N) in 1960
JMJP 3/8/60; SCMP 2215:42

60-38 **3/7/60** – Hanoi **Vietnam (N)** –
Trade in border areas
JMJP 3/8/60; SCMP 2215:42

60-39 **3/15/60** 1/1/60 Peking **Rumania** Protocol
Exchange of goods and payments in 1960
TYC 9:91(C); JMJP 3/16/60; PR 3/22/60, p. 26; SCMP 2221:44

60-40 **3/15/60** 1/1/60 Peking **Rumania** Protocol
General conditions for delivery of goods in 1960
TYC 9:95(C)

60-41 **3/15/60** 1/1/60 Tirana **Albania** Protocol
Exchange of goods and payments in 1960
TYC 9:110(C); JMJP 3/17/60; SCMP 2221:37

60-42 **3/15/60** – Tirana **Albania** Protocol
Albanian use of PRC loan and other aid funds in 1960
JMJP 3/17/60; SCMP 2221:37

60-43 **3/15/60** – Tirana **Albania** Exchange of Notes
Extension of Protocol on General Conditions for Delivery of Goods in 1957 [57-27]
TYC 9:112(C)

60-44 **3/15/60** – Peking **Bulgaria** –
1960 plan for cooperation between Academies of Sciences
JMJP 3/16/60; SCMP 2221:38

60-45 **3/15/60** 1/1/60 Sofia **Bulgaria** Protocol
Exchange of goods in 1960
TYC 9:113(C); JMJP 3/17/60; PR 3/22/60, p. 26; SCMP 2222:38

60-46 **3/21/60** – Peking **Nepal** Joint Communiqué
Talks during Premier Koirala's visit: five principles of peaceful coexistence, Sino-Nepalese relations
Parties agreed to establish embassies in Peking and Katmandu.
TYC 9:4(C); WCC 7:47(C); JMJP 3/22/60; PR 3/29/60, p. 7(E); SCMP 2227:38(E); ZD 1960:3:485(P,E); AsR 3264(E); H12(1):216

60-47 **3/21/60** 4/28/60 Peking **Nepal** Agreement
Boundary
TYC 9:63(C); WCC 7:49(C); JMJP 3/25/60(C); JMST 1960, p. 319(C); PR 3/29/60, p. 8(E); SCMP 2227:40(E); BFSP 164:664(E); ZD 1960:3:490(P,E); AsR 3265(E); A/D p. 207(E); H12(1):214(G); WGO 3:213; Wint, p. 762(E); UA 12:4:392

60-48 **3/21/60** 3/21/60 Peking **Nepal** Agreement
Economic aid
TYC 9:84(C); WCC 7:51(C); JMJP 3/25/60(C); JMST 1960, p. 320(C); PR 3/22/60, p. 10(E); SCMP 2227:42(E); AsR 3265(E); A/D p. 335(E); H12(1):222(G); UA 12:4:393

60-49 **3/23/60** 1/1/60 Berlin **Germany (E)** Protocol
Exchange of goods and payments in 1960

Communiqué also issued. Dok 8:339(G)
TYC 9:139(C); JMJP 3/25/60; SCMP 2226:42; AGF p. 95

60-50 **3/23/60** – Berlin **Germany (E)** Protocol
General conditions for delivery of goods in 1960
TYC 9:141(C)

60-51 **3/25/60** – Berlin **Germany (E)** –
1960 plan for cultural cooperation
SCMP 2228:39

60-52 **3/25/60** – Belgrade **Yugoslavia** Protocol
Exchange of goods in 1960
TYC 9:117(C); SCMP 2229:55; YTS 1961:2:15(S-C); WGO 3:209

60-53 **3/28/60** – Peking **Vietnam (N)** Protocol
PRC aid to Vietnam (N) in establishment of farms and agricultural school
JMJP 3/29/60; PR 4/19/60, p. 29

60-54 **3/29/60** – Peking **USSR** Protocol
Exchange of goods in 1960
JMJP 3/30/60; PR 4/5/60, p. 32; SCMP 2230:47; G60:131

60-55 **4/13/60** – Peking **Germany (E)** Protocol
Scientific and technical cooperation
Signed at fifth session of Sino-German Standing Committee for Cooperation in Technology and Technical Sciences. Communiqué also issued.
JMJP 4/16/60; PR 4/26/60, p. 46; SCMP 2242:43; AGF p. 55; Dok 8:340

60-56 **4/19/60** – Rangoon **Burma** Joint Communiqué
Talks during Premier Chou En-lai's visit: peaceful coexistence, Sino-Burmese relations, etc.
TYC 9:46(C); WCC 7:75(C); JMJP 4/20/60(C); JMST 1960, p. 335(C); PR 4/26/60, p. 42(E); SCMP 2244:34(E); Burma Wkly. Bull. 18:52:472 (4/20/60)(E); AsR 3299(E)

60-57 **4/25/60** – New Delhi **India** Joint Communiqué
Talks during Premier Chou En-lai's visit: Sino-Indian boundary issues
Agreed that PRC and Indian officials meet for further discussion of boundary question.
TYC 9:11(C); WCC 7:80(C); JMJP 4/26/60(C); JMST 1960, p. 335(C); PR 5/3/60, p. 17(E); SCMP 2247:38(E); BFSP 164:584(E); DIA 1960, p. 489(E); AsR 3301(E); H12(1):89(G)

60-58 **4/28/60** 11/13/61 Katmandu **Nepal** Treaty
Peace and friendship

TYC 10:13(C); YHTY 7(C,Nepalese,E); WCC 7:96(C); JMJP 4/30/60(C); JMST 1960, p. 320(C); PR 5/3/60, p. 6(E); SCMP 2251:38(E); BFSP 164:667(E); DIA 1960, p. 500(E); SIA 1959-60, p. 222; ND 2722:22; AsR 3330; A/D p. 56(E); H12(1):21(G)

60-59 **4/29/60** – Katmandu **Nepal** Joint Communiqué
Talks during Premier Chou En-lai's visit: Sino-Nepalese relations, peaceful coexistence, etc.

TYC 9:6(C); WCC 7:103(C); JMJP 4/30/60(C); JMST 1960, p. 335(C); PR 5/3/60, p. 6(E); SCMP 2251:37(E); AsR 3330; H12(1):218(G)

60-60 **5/6/60** 5/6/60 Peking **Mongolia** Agreement
Cooperation in radio broadcasting

TYC 9:143(C); JMJP 5/7/60; SCMP 2256:44

60-61 **5/7/60** 6/8/61 Prague **Czechoslovakia** Treaty
Consular

Registered by Czechoslovakia with UN Secretariat 8/7/61.

TYC 9:52(C); JMJP 5/8/60; PR 5/17/60, p. 41; SCMP 2256:36; UNTS 402:210(Czech,C,E,Fr); WGO 3:208, 4:274

60-62 **5/8/60** – Phnom Penh **Cambodia** Joint Statement
Talks during Premier Chou En-lai's visit: Cambodian neutralist policy, peaceful coexistence, etc.

TYC 9:23(C); WCC 7:107(C); JMJP 5/9/60(C); JMST 1960, p. 336(C); PR 5/17/60, p. 30(E); SCMP 2257:17(E); AsR 3335

60-63 **5/14/60** – Hanoi **Vietnam (N)** Joint Communiqué
Talks during Premier Chou En-lai's visit: international tensions, disarmament, support for Soviet policies, socialist solidarity, peaceful coexistence, Indo-China, etc.

TYC 9:31(C); WCC 7:121(C); JMJP 5/15/60(C); JMST 1960, p. 336(C); PR 5/17/60, p. 23(E); SCMP 2261:37(E); AsR 3369(E)

60-64 **5/15/60** – Peking **Iraq** –
1960 plan for cultural cooperation

JMJP 5/16/60; PR 5/31/60, p. 29; SCMP 2262:42

60-65 **5/19/60** – Peking **Algeria** (in exile) Joint Communiqué
Talks during visit of Krim Belkacem, Vice-Premier and Foreign Minister of Provisional Government of Republic of Algeria: national liberation movements, Algerian independence, etc.

TYC 9:18(C); WCC 7:158(C); JMJP 5/20/60(C); PR 5/24/60, p. 16(E); SCMP 2265:36(E); AsR 3460(E); H12(2):87(G, abbrev.)

60-66 **5/23/60** 8/2/60 Peking **Korea (N)** Agreement
Border river navigation

TYC 9:153(C); JMJP 5/24/60; PR 7/12/60, p. 27; SCMP 2267:42; WGO 4:274

60-67 **5/23/60** – Peking **Mongolia** Protocol
Clearing of accounts under 1956 Agreement on Economic and Technical Aid

JMJP 5/25/60; SCMP 2268:41

60-68 **5/25/60** – Peking **Iraq** Joint Communiqué
Trade talks

JMJP 5/27/60(C); SCMP 2271:34(E); AsR 3460; H12(2):32(G)

60-69 **5/25/60** – Peking **Iraq** Agreement
Trade in 1960-61

JMJP 5/26/60; PR 5/31/60, p. 29; SCMP 2270:33; AsR 3460; H12(2):31

60-70 **5/25/60** – Peking **Iraq** Agreement
Payments in 1960-61

JMJP 5/26/60; PR 5/31/60, p. 29; SCMP 2270:33; AsR 3460; H12(2):31

60-71 **5/31/60** – Ulan Bator **Mongolia** Joint Statement
Talks during Premier Chou En-lai's visit: proletarian internationalsim, international tensions, Sino-Mongolian relations, etc.

TYC 9:39(C); WCC 7:130(C); JMJP 6/1/60(C); JMST 1960, p. 338(C); PR 6/7/60, p. 11(E); SCMP 2273:41(E); AsR 3414(E)

60-72 **5/31/60** 10/12/60 Ulan Bator **Mongolia** Treaty
Friendship and mutual assistance

TYC 9:37(C); YHTY 14(C,Mongolian); WCC 7:135(C); JMJP 6/1/60(C); JMST 1960, p. 321(C); PR 6/7/60, p. 10(E); SCMP 2273:40(E); BFSP 164:663(E); ND 2722:25(Fr); AsR 3414(E)

60-73 **5/31/60** – Ulan Bator **Mongolia** Agreement
PRC economic and technical aid to Mongolia including loan of 200 million rubles)

JMJP 6/1/60; SCMP 2273:39

60-74 **5/31/60** 5/31/60 Ulan Bator **Mongolia** Agreement
Scientific and technical cooperation

TYC 9:146(C); SCMP 2273:43

60-75 **6/3/60** – Conakry **Guinea** –
1960 plan for cultural cooperation

JMJP 6/7/60; SCMP 2276:41

60-76 **6/10/60** – Peking **USSR** Agreement
Cooperation between Academies of Medical Sciences
JMJP 6/11/60; SCMP 2278:38

60-77 **7/4/60** – Pyongyang **Korea (N)** Agreement
Cooperation between Academies of Sciences
JMJP 7/5/60; PR 7/12/60, p. 27; SCMP 2293:35

60-78 **7/4/60** – Pyongyang **Korea (N)** –
1960 plan for cooperation between Academies of Sciences
SCMP 2293:35

60-79 **7/6/60** – Rangoon **Burma** Communiqué
Boundary demarcation
Issued after first session of Sino-Burmese Joint Boundary Committee.
JMJP 7/7/60(C); PR 7/12/60, p. 26; SCMP 2295:38(E); Burma Wkly. Bull. 9:12:90 (7/21/60)(E)

60-80 **6/23/60** – Phnom Penh **Cambodia** Exchange of Notes
7/6/60
Extension of 1956 Trade, Payments, and Economic Aid Agreements [56-54,55,76]
TYC 9:116(C)

60-81 **7/23/60** 7/23/60 Havana **Cuba** Agreement
Trade and payments
After ratification by PRC (9/30/60) and Cuba (9/17/60), made retroactive to date of signature.
TYC 10:238(C); JMJP 7/26/60; PR 7/26/60, p. 6; SCMP 2307:30(E. sum.); AsR 3483; H12(3):121(G)

60-82 **7/23/60** 7/23/60 Havana **Cuba** Agreement
Scientific and technical cooperation
See note above.
TYC 10:402(C); JMJP 7/26/60; PR 7/26/60, p. 6; SCMP 2307:30; AsR 3483; H12(3):130(G)

60-83 **7/23/60** 11/23/60 Havana **Cuba** Agreement
Cultural cooperation
TYC 10:388(C); JMJP 7/26/60; PR 7/26/60, p. 6; SCMP 2307:30; AsR 3483; H12(3):116(G)

60-84 **7/25/60** – Mutankiang **USSR** Protocol
Border railway
Signed at meeting of Sino-Soviet Border Through Railway Traffic Committee.
SCMP 2310:37; G60:143

60-85 **8/2/60** – Peking **Burma** Communiqué
Boundary demarcation

Issued after second session of Sino-Burmese Joint Boundary Committee.

JMJP 8/3/60(C); PR 8/2/60, p. 11(E); SCMP 2313:40(E)

60-86 **8/26/60** – Peking **Multilateral** Protocol
Passenger rail service in 1960-61

Signed at conference of eastern section of railway transport committee of Railway Cooperation Organization of Socialist Countries, attended by delegates from USSR, Mongolia, and (presumably) Korea (N) and Vietnam (N).

SCMP 2330:23

60-87 **8/26/60** – Kabul **Afghanistan** Joint Communiqué
Talks during visit of Vice-Premier and Foreign Minister Ch'en Yi: Sino-Afghanistan relations, principles of Bandung Conference and UN Charter, etc.

TYC 9:16(C); WCC 7:219(C); JMJP 8/28/60(C); JMST 1961, p. 177(C); PR 8/30/60, p. 6(E); SCMP 2330:24(E); H12(1):5

60-88 **8/26/60** 12/12/60 Kabul **Afghanistan** Treaty
Friendship and mutual nonaggression

TYC 9:12(C); YHTY 18(C,Afghan,E); WCC 7:214(C); JMJP 2/13/60(C); JMST 1961, p. 136(C); PR 12/20/60, p. 18(E); SCMP 2399:22(E); BFSP 164:594(E); ZD 1960:10:1785(P,E); DIA 1960, p. 502(E); AsR 3723(E), 3839(E); H12(1):4(G)

60-89 **8/26/60** 12/12/60 Kabul **Afghanistan** Exchange of Notes
Abrogation of 1944 Treaty of Friendship

TYC 9:14(C); YHTY 25(C,Afghan,E); SCMP 2399:24(E); ZD 1960:10:1788(P,E); H12(1):6(G)

60-90 **8/26/60** – Kabul **Afghanistan** Agreement
Extension of Agreement on Exchange of Goods and Payments for 1957-59 [57-72]

Text of 1957 Agreement re-signed.

SCMP 2330:24; AsR 3539; H12(1):11

60-91 **9/5/60** – Rangoon **Burma** Communiqué
Boundary demarcation

Issued after third session of Sino-Burmese Joint Boundary Committee.

PR 9/14/60, p. 41; SCMP 2335:26(E); Burma Wkly. Bull. 9:20:159 (9/15/60)(E)

60-92 **9/13/60** – Peking **Guinea** Joint Communiqué
Talks during President Sekou Touré's visit: five principles of peaceful coexistence, anticolonialism, etc.

TYC 9:1(C); WCC 7:238(C); JMJP 9/14/60(C); JMST 1961, p. 179(C); PR 9/14/60, p. 9(E); SCMP 2341:24(E); ADTJ 1004:1(Fr); AsR 3567(E)

60-93 **9/13/60** 7/1/61 Peking **Guinea** Treaty
Friendship

TYC 10:1(C); YHTY 57(C,Fr); WCC 7:240(C); JMJP 9/14/60(C); JMST 1961, p. 136(C); PR 9/14/60, p. 10(E); SCMP 2341:29 (E); BFSP 164:661(E); ZD 1960:8-9:1463(P,E); AsR 3568(E); H12(2):125(G); WGO 4:274

60-94 **9/13/60** 9/13/60 Peking **Guinea** Agreement
Economic and technical aid

TYC 9:80(C); WCC 7:242(C); JMJP 9/14/60; PR 9/14/60, p. 11(E); SCMP 2341:27(E); BFSP 164:662; AsR 3568(E); WGO 4:274

60-95 **9/13/60** 9/13/60 Peking **Guinea** Agreement
Trade and payments

TYC 9:82(C); JMJP 9/14/60; PR 9/14/60, p. 12(E); SCMP 2341:26(E); BFSP 164:662; AsR 3568(E); H12(2):127(G)

60-96 **9/20/60** – Ulan Bator **Mongolia** Agreement
Dispatch of more PRC workers to help Mongolian construction

SCMP 2345:19

60-97 **9/24/60** – Peking **Burma** Joint Press Communiqué
Signing of forthcoming Boundary Treaty (on 10/1/60), exchange of visits by Premier Chou En-lai and U Nu, and gifts by each government to inhabitants of border areas in other's country

TYC 9:47(C); WCC 7:252(C); JMJP 9/24/60(C); PR 9/27/60, p. 11(E); SCMP 2348:20(E); Burma Wkly. Bull. 9:23:177(E); H12(1):23

60-98 **10/1/60** 1/4/61 Peking **Burma** Treaty
Boundary

TYC 9:68(C); WCC 7:272(C); JMJP 10/2/60(C); JMST 1961, p. 137(C); PR 10/4/60, p. 29(E); SCMP 2354:36(E, sum.); CB 636:1(E); BFSP 164:654; ZD 1961:11:1768(P,E); Burma Wkly. Bull. 9:24:187 (10/13/60)(E); AsR 3616(E); A/D p. 191(E); H12(1):23(G); Wint, p. 776(E)

60-99 **10/1/60** – Peking **Burma** Exchange of Notes
Boundary questions, cultivation of transfrontier lands, nationality, etc.

TYC 9:78(C); WCC 7:280(C); JMJP 10/2/60(C); JMST 1961, p. 139(C); SCMP 2354:39; CB 636:9(E); Burma Wkly. Bull. 9:24:189 (10/13/60)(E); A/D p. 202(E); H12(1):27(G)

60-100 **10/4/60** – Peking **Burma** Joint Communiqué
Talks during Premier U Nu's visit: Sino-Burmese relations, five principles of peaceful coexistence, etc.

TYC 9:48(C); WCC 7:286(C); JMJP 10/5/60(C); JMST 1961, p. 172(C); PR 10/4/60, p. 25(E); SCMP 2355:24(E); Burma Wkly. Bull. 9:24:185 (10/13/60)(E); AsR 3618(E); H12(1):28

60-101 **10/5/60** – Peking **Algeria** (in exile) Joint Communiqué
Talks during visit of Premier Ferhat Abbas of Provisional Government of Republic of Algeria: peaceful coexistence, national liberation movements, etc.

TYC 9:20(C); WCC 7:289(C); JMJP 10/6/60(C); JMST 1961, p. 178(C); PR 10/11/60, p. 16(E); SCMP 2356:28(E); AsR 3627(E); H12(2):89(G, abbrev.)

60-102 **10/6/60** – Peking **Burma** Communiqué
Boundary demarcation

Issued after fourth session of Sino-Burmese Joint Boundary Committee.

JMJP 10/7/60(C); SCMP 2357:18(E)

60-103 **10/9/60** – Peking **Poland** Agreement
Cooperation between Academies of Sciences

JMJP 10/10/60; SCMP 2358:41

60-104 **10/9/60** – Peking **Poland** –
1961 plan for cooperation between Academies of Sciences

PR 10/18/60, p. 24; SCMP 2358:41

60-105 **10/13/60** – Peking **Korea (N)** Agreement
Granting of loans by PRC to Korea (N)

JMJP 10/14/60; PR 10/18/60, p. 8; SCMP 2361:37; AsR 3643

60-106 **10/13/60** – Peking **Korea (N)** Agreement
Supply of whole sets of equipment and technical aid by PRC to Korea (N)

JMJP 10/14/60; SCMP 2361:37; AsR 3643

60-107 **10/18/60** – Peking **Korea (N)** Protocol
Scientific and technical cooperation

Signed at third meeting of Sino-Korean Committee for Scientific and Technical Cooperation.

PR 10/25/60, p. 20; SCMP 2364:33; AsR 3724

60-108 **10/18/60** – Tirana **Albania** Protocol
Scientific and technical cooperation

Signed at fifth meeting of Sino-Albanian Joint Committee for Cooperation in Technology and Technical Science.

JMJP 10/21/60; PR 10/25/60, p. 20; SCMP 2365:25

60-109 **10/20/60** – Budapest **Hungary** Protocol
Scientific and technical cooperation

Signed at sixth meeting of Sino-Hungarian Committee for Scientific and Technical Cooperation.

PR 11/1/60, p. 26; SCMP 2366:26

60-110 **10/24/60** – Rangoon **Burma** Communiqué
Trade talks

JMJP 10/25/60(C); PR 11/1/60, p. 26; SCMP 2367:18(E); Burma Wkly. Bull. 9:27:262 (11/3/60)(E); AsR 3643, 3723; H12(1):34(G)

60-111 **10/24/60** – Rangoon **Burma** Accord (with Exchange of Letters)
PRC purchase of rice from Burma

JMJP 10/25/60; PR 11/1/60, p. 26; SCMP 2367:18; AsR 3643, 3723; H12(1):35

60-112 **10/24/60** – Peking **Albania** –
1961-62 plan for cultural cooperation

JMJP 10/26/60; PR 11/1/60, p. 26; SCMP 2368:20

60-113 **10/26/60** – Katmandu **Nepal** Communiqué
Boundary demarcation

Issued after first session of Sino-Nepalese Joint Boundary Committee.

JMJP 10/29/60(C); PR 11/1/60, p. 16(E); SCMP 2372:26(E); AsR 3670

60-114 **11/5/60** – Sofia **Bulgaria** Protocol
Scientific and technical cooperation

Signed at fifth session of Sino-Bulgarian Joint Committee for Scientific and Technical Cooperation.

JMJP 11/9/60; PR 11/15/60, p. 26; SCMP 2378:32

60-115 **11/10/60** 11/1/60 Rabat **Morocco** Agreement
Trade in 1960-61

JMJP 11/12/60; PR 11/22/60, p. 25; SCMP 2380:28; AsR 3744

60-116 **11/15/60** – Shumchun **Hong Kong** Agreement(?)
Supply of water from Kwangtung Province to Hong Kong for indefinite period

Signed by representatives of Hong Kong Administration and People's Commune of Paoan County, Kwangtung Province.

AsR 3692

60-117 **11/28/60** – Peking **Multilateral** Press Communiqué
Cooperation in fishery research in western Pacific

Issued after fifth session of Fisheries Research Commission for Western Pacific, attended by delegates from USSR, Mongolia, Korea (N), and Vietnam (N).

SCMP 2389:35

60-118 **11/28/60** 11/28/60 Peking **Vietnam (N)** Agreement
Scientific and technical cooperation

TYC 9:145(C); JMJP 11/29/60; PR 12/13/60, p. 53; SCMP 2389:39

60-119 **11/28/60** – Peking **Vietnam (N)** –
Common measures for implementation of Scientific and Technical Cooperation Agreement of 11/28/60 [60-118]

Signed by representatives of Science and Technology Committee of PRC and National Scientific Research Board of Vietnam (N).

PR 12/13/60, p. 53; SCMP 2389:39

60-120 **11/28/60** – Peking **Vietnam (N)** Protocol
1960 plan for scientific and technical cooperation

See note above.

PR 12/13/60, p. 53; SCMP 2389:39

60-121 **11/30/60** – Peking **Cuba** Joint Communiqué
Trade talks

TYC 9:7(C); JMJP 12/1/60(C); SCMP 2391:30(E); AsR 3703(E)

60-122 **11/30/60** – Peking **Cuba** Agreement
Economic aid by PRC (including interest-free loan of 240 million rubles in period 1961-65)

WCC 7:347(C); JMJP 12/1/60; SCMP 2391:29; SIA 1959-60, p. 499; AsR 3703

60-123 **11/30/60** – Peking **Cuba** Protocol
Trade in 1960

SCMP 2391:29

60-124 **11/30/60** – Peking **Cuba** Protocol
Implementation of Scientific and Technical Cooperation Agreement of 7/23/60 [60-82]

JMJP 12/1/60; SCMP 2391:29

60-125 **11/30/60** – Rabat **Tunisia** Agreement
Trade in 1960-61

JMJP 12/2/60; SCMP 2392:31

60-126 **11/30/60** – Warsaw **Poland** Protocol
Scientific and technical cooperation

Signed at seventh session of Sino-Polish Standing Committee for Scientific and Technical Cooperation.

SCMP 2393:35

60-127 **12/15/60** 12/24/60 Djakarta **Indonesia** "Arrangement"
Implementation of 1955 Dual Nationality Treaty [55-28]

In accordance with Article 13, came into force on date of publication, though ratifications were exchanged three days earlier (12/21/60).

TYC 9:58(C); WCC 7:355(C); JMJP 12/24/60(C); JMST 1961, p. 141(C); PR 12/27/60, p. 9(E); SCMP 2408:32(E); ADTJ 1058:1(Fr); DIA 1960, p. 495(E); SIA 1959-60, p. 275; AsR 3735(E); A/D p. 270(E); H12(1):113(G); RGDIP 65:688(Fr)

60-128 **12/19/60** – Peking **Cambodia** Joint Statement
Talks during visit of Prince Norodom Sihanouk, Head of State of Cambodia: five principles of peaceful coexistence, principles of Bandung Conference, Cambodian neutralism, anticolonialism, etc.

TYC 9:27(C); JMJP 12/22/60(C); JMST 1961, p. 171(C); PR 12/27/60, p. 6(E); SCMP 2406:28(E); AsR 3731(E); H12(1):175(G, abbrev.)

60-129 **12/19/60** 5/2/61 Peking **Cambodia** Treaty
Friendship and mutual nonaggression

TYC 9:25(C); YHTY 33(C,Cambodian,Fr); WCC 7:370(C); JMJP 5/3/61(C); JMST 1961, p. 135(C); PR 5/5/61, p. 10(E); SCMP 2491:35(E); BFSP 164:651; ZD 1961:5-6:646(P,E); AsR 4067(E); A/D p. 36(E); H12(1):177(G)

60-130 **12/19/60** – Peking **Cambodia** Protocol
Economic and technical aid by PRC

PR 12/20/60, p. 14; SCMP 2404:21; H12(1):190

60-131 **12/19/60** – Peking **Cambodia** Protocol
Application of 1956 Economic Aid Agreement [56-76]

PR 12/20/60, p. 14; SCMP 2404:21; H12(1):190

60-132 **12/19/60** – Peking **Cambodia** Agreement
Cooperation in navigation

PR 12/20/60, p. 14; SCMP 2404:21; H12(1):190

60-133 **12/19/60** – Peking **Cambodia** Exchange of Letters
Dispatch by PRC of railway and agriculture experts and technicians

PR 12/20/60, p. 14; SCMP 2404:21; H12(1):190

60-134 **12/24/60** – Peking **Burma** Communiqué
Boundary demarcation

Issued after fifth session of Sino-Burmese Joint Boundary Committee.

SCMP 2409:26(E); Burma Wkly. Bull. 9:35:336 (12/29/60)(E)

1961

61-1 **1/9/61** – Peking/Rangoon **Burma** Joint Communiqué
Talks during Premier Chou En-lai's visit: economic and technical aid, Laos, peaceful coexistence, etc.

TYC 10:36(C); WCC 8:5(C); JMJP 1/10/61(C); JMST 1961, p. 173(C); PR 1/13/61, p. 6(E); SCMP 2416:39(E); Burma Wkly. Bull. 9:38:357(E); ADTJ 1067:2(Fr); AsR 3771(E)

61-2 **1/9/61** 10/1/61 Rangoon **Burma** Agreement
Economic and technical cooperation

TYC 10:369(C); WCC 8:9(C); JMJP 1/10/61(C); PR 1/13/61, p. 8(E); SCMP 2416:32(E); Burma Wkly. Bull. 9:38:359(E); ADTJ 1067:4(Fr); AsR 3772(E); A/D p. 343(E); H12(1):35(G)

61-3 **1/9/61** 1/9/61 Rangoon **Burma** Agreement
Payments

TYC 10:311(C); JMJP 1/10/61(C); PR 1/13/61, p. 9(E); SCMP 2416:34(E); Burma Wkly. Bull. 9:38:360(E); ADTJ 1067:5(Fr); AsR 3772(E); A/D p. 343(E); H12(1):37(G)

61-4 **1/21/61** – Havana **Cuba** Contract
Purchase of Cuban sugar

JMJP 1/24/61; SCMP 2427:31

61-5 **1/21/61** – Havana **Cuba** Contract
Export to PRC of Cuban copper ore

SCMP 2427:31

61-6 **1/27/61** 1/27/61 Peking **Burma** Agreement
Trade in 1961-66

TYC 10:372(C); WCC 8:125(C); JMJP 2/1/61(C); SCMP 2432:19(E); Burma Wkly. Bull. 9:41:383(E); A/D p. 345(E); H12(1):39(G)

61-7 **1/31/61** – Peking **Albania** Exchange of Notes
Extension of Protocol on General Conditions for Delivery of Goods in 1957 [57-27]

TYC 10:289(C)

61-8 **1/31/61** – Peking **Vietnam (N)** Press Communiqué
Economic and trade talks culminating in signing of six documents listed below

WCC 8:131(C); JMJP 2/1/61(C); JMST 1961, p. 164(C); SCMP 2433:28(E); AsR 3911(E); A/D p. 326(E)

61-9 **1/31/61** – Peking **Vietnam (N)** Agreement
PRC loans over period 1961-67

JMJP 2/1/61; SCMP 2433:28; AsR 3911

61-10 **1/31/61** – Peking **Vietnam (N)** Protocol
PRC technical aid and supply of complete sets of equipment

JMJP 2/1/61; SCMP 2433:28; AsR 3911

61-11 **1/31/61** – Peking **Vietnam (N)** Protocol
Mutual supply of goods in 1961

JMJP 2/1/61; SCMP 2433:29; AsR 3911

61-12 **1/31/61** 1/31/61 Peking **Vietnam (N)** Protocol
Transit of cargo
TYC 10:357(C); JMJP 2/1/61; SCMP 2433:29; AsR 3911

61-13 **1/31/61** – Peking **Vietnam (N)** Exchange of Notes
Extension of 1955 Protocol on Small-Scale Trading in Border Areas [55-49]
TYC 10:358(C); SCMP 2433:29; AsR 3911

61-14 **1/31/61** – Peking **Vietnam (N)** Exchange of Notes
Extension of 1955 Protocol on Exchange of Goods between Local State Trading Companies in Border Areas [55-48]
TYC 10:360(C); SCMP 2433:29

61-15 **2/2/61** – Peking **Albania** Press Communiqué
Economic and trade talks
SCMP 2434:24(E); ADTJ 1077:1(Fr); AsR 3912(E)

61-16 **2/2/61** 7/22/61 Peking **Albania** Treaty
Commerce and navigation
TYC 10:290(C); WCC 8:132(C); JMJP 2/3/61; PR 2/10/61, p. 5; SCMP 2434:23; Gazeta Zyrtare e Republikës Popullore të Shqipërisë, 1961:307(Albanian); AsR 3911; WGO 4:274

61-17 **2/2/61** 1/1/61 Peking **Albania** Protocol
Exchange of goods and payments in 1961
TYC 10:297(C); JMJP 2/3/61; PR 2/10/61, p. 5; SCMP 2434:23; AsR 3912

61-18 **2/2/61** 2/2/61 Peking **Albania** Agreement
Loan by PRC to Albania
TYC 10:295(C); JMJP 2/3/61; PR 2/10/61, p. 5; SCMP 2434:23; AsR 3912

61-19 **2/2/61** – Peking **Albania** Protocol (No. 1)
Albania's use of PRC loan in accordance with Loan Agreement of same date [61-18]
JMJP 2/3/61; PR 2/10/61; SCMP 2434:23; AsR 3912

61-20 **2/2/61** – Peking **Albania** Protocol
Albania's use of PRC loan in 1961
JMJP 2/3/61; PR 2/10/61, p. 5; SCMP 2434:23; AsR 3912

61-21 **2/2/61** – Peking **Albania** Protocol
Settlement of commodities supplied by PRC in 1960 in accordance with 1954 Credit Agreement and with Notes exchanged in November and December 1956 [54-80; 56-137]
PR 2/10/61, p. 5; SCMP 2434:23; AsR 3912

61-22 **2/4/61** – Peking **USSR** –
1961 plan for cultural cooperation

JMJP 2/5/61; PR 2/10/61, p. 20; SCMP 2435:36; AsR 3911; G61:120

61-23 **2/5/61** 1/1/61 Cairo **UAR** Protocol
Trade in 1961

TYC 10:299(C); JMJP 2/7/61; PR 3/10/61, p. 23; SCMP 2436:25; AsR 3845; FIYB 1962:4:1

61-24 **2/15/61** – Peking **Cuba** Agreement
Exchange of television films

JMJP 2/22/61

61-25 **2/15/61** – Peking **Nepal** Communiqué
Boundary demarcation

Signed at second session of Sino-Nepalese Joint Boundary Committee.

JMJP 2/18/61(C); SCMP 2443:39(E); AsR 3851

61-26 **2/24/61** – Prague **Czechoslovakia** Protocol
Scientific and technical cooperation

Signed at eighth session of Sino-Czechoslovak Joint Committee for Scientific and Technical Cooperation.

JMJP 2/26/61; SCMP 2447:22

61-27 **2/28/61** 2/28/61 Bamako **Mali** Agreement
Trade and payments

TYC 10:327(C); JMJP 3/4/61; PR 3/10/61, p. 23; SCMP 2456:27(E); AsR 3889(E, sum.); H12(2):150(G); WGO 4:274

61-28 **2/28/61** – Bamako **Mali** Exchange of Letters
Grant of long-term credit by PRC to Mali

H12(2):155

61-29 **3/2/61** – Peking **USSR** Press Communiqué
Economic and trade talks

JMJP 3/3/61(C); SCMP 2451:25(E)

61-30 **3/4/61** – Peking **Mali** Joint Communiqué
Trade talks

JMJP 3/4/61(C); JMST 1961, p. 179(C); SCMP 2452:30(E); ADTJ 1072:2(Fr); AsR 3863; H12(2):155(G)

61-31 **3/7/61** – Vientiane/Peking **Laos** Exchange of Notes
3/8/61
Exchange of cultural and economic delegations

H12(1):198

61-32 **3/8/61** – Havana **Cuba** Exchange of Letters
Remittance of money by Chinese in Cuba to their relatives in PRC
TYC 10:243(C); H12(3):127(G)

61-33 **3/8/61** – Peking **Hungary** –
1961 plan for cultural cooperation
JMJP 3/9/61; PR 3/24/61, p. 21; SCMP 2455:24

61-34 **3/8/61** 1/1/61 Peking **Bulgaria** Protocol
Exchange of goods and payments in 1961
TYC 10:322(C); JMJP 3/9/61; PR 3/24/61, p. 21; SCMP 2456:20

61-35 **3/17/61** – Peking **Rumania** –
1961 plan for cultural cooperation
JMJP 3/19/61; PR 3/24/61, p. 21; SCMP 2462:29

61-36 **3/18/61** – Peking **Korea (N)** Protocol
Mutual supply of goods in 1961
JMJP 3/19/61; PR 3/24/61, p. 21

61-37 **3/18/61** – Peking **Korea (N)** Protocol
PRC supply of complete sets of equipment and technical aid to Korea (N)
JMJP 3/29/61; JMST 1961, p. 131

61-38 **3/20/61** 3/20/61 – **USSR** Agreement
Currency exchange and cash movements
Signed by representatives of People's Bank of China and Soviet State Bank.
TYC 10:269(C)

61-39 **3/27/61** – Budapest **Hungary** –
1961-62 plan for cooperation between Academies of Sciences
JMJP 4/2/61; SCMP 2469:21

61-40 **3/28/61** – Peking **Korea (N)** Protocol
PRC aid in several light industrial construction projects
PR 4/7/61, p. 18; SCMP 2470:36

61-41 **3/31/61** – Pyongyang **Korea (N)** –
1961 plan for cultural cooperation
JMJP 4/1/61; PR 4/7/61, p. 18; SCMP 2471:33

61-42 **4/1/61** – Djakarta **Indonesia** Joint Communiqué
Talks during Foreign Minister Ch'en Yi's visit: anti-imperialism, West Irian, Taiwan, PRC representation in UN, five principles of peaceful coexistence, ten principles of Bandung Conference, etc.
TYC 10:9(C); WCC 8:154(C); JMJP 4/4/61(C); JMST 1961, p. 175(C); SCMP 2472:35(E); AsR 3939(E); A/D p. 67(E)

61-43 **4/1/61** 6/14/61 Djakarta **Indonesia** Treaty
Friendship
TYC 10:7(C); YHTY 40(C, Indonesian); WCC 8:152(C); JMJP 6/15/61(C); PR 4/7/61, p. 7(E); SCMP 2520:28(E); ZD 1961:5-6:650(P,E); AsR 4068(E); A/D p. 62(E); H12(1):117(G); Wint, p. 791(E)

61-44 **4/1/61** 6/14/61 Djakarta **Indonesia** Agreement
Cultural cooperation
TYC 10:390(C); JMJP 6/16/61(C); PR 6/16/58, p. 11(E); SCMP 2520:29(E); AsR 4081(E); A/D p. 64(E); H12(1):119(G)

61-45 **4/4/61** 5/1/61 Peking **Norway** Exchange of Notes
Exemption of visa fees
NoTS 1961, p. 274(E,N)

61-46 **4/4/61** – Colombo **Ceylon** Joint Communiqué
Trade talks
JMJP 4/5/61(C); JMST 1961, p. 177(C); SCMP 2473:20(E); H12(1):70(G)

61-47 **4/4/61** 1/1/61 Colombo **Ceylon** Protocol
Exchange of goods in 1961
TYC 10:384(C); JMJP 4/5/61; PR 4/14/61, p. 22; SCMP 2473:21; CTS 1962:21(S,E); AsR 3935; H12(1):70(G)

61-48 **4/4/61** – Prague **Czechoslovakia** –
1961 plan for cultural cooperation
JMJP 4/6/61; PR 4/23/61, p. 23; SCMP 2474:25

61-49 **4/7/61** – Ulan Bator **Mongolia** –
1961 plan for cultural cooperation
JMJP 4/8/61; PR 4/28/61, p. 23; SCMP 2475:34

61-50 **4/7/61** – Moscow **USSR** Protocol
Exchange of goods in 1961
JMJP 4/9/61; PR 4/14/61, p. 6; SCMP 2476:38; AsR 3935; G61:127

61-51 **4/7/61** – Moscow **USSR** Agreement
Postponement of repayment by PRC of debts owed to USSR on trade deals contracted in 1960
SIA 1961, p. 195; AsR 3949; G61:127

61-52 **4/7/61** – Moscow **USSR** Protocol
Delivery of raw sugar from USSR to PRC
SIA 1961, p. 195; G61:127

61-53 **4/8/61** – Moscow **USSR** Joint Communiqué
Trade talks

Refers to various undesignated trade agreements that supplement protocol of 4/7/61. See also SCMP 2475:35.

WCC 8:161(C); JMJP 4/9/61(C); JMST 1961, p. 153(C); PR 4/14/61, p. 6(E, sum.); SCMP 2476:37(E); URSS 226:15(Fr); DIA 1961, p. 254(E)

61-54 **4/10/61** – Prague **Czechoslovakia** –
1961 plan for cooperation between Academies of Sciences

JMJP 4/12/61; SCMP 2477:29

61-55 **4/11/61** 11/1/60 Helsinki **Finland** Agreement
Trade in 1960-61

TYC 10:319(C); JMST 1961, p. 134; SCMP 2479:34

61-56 **4/11/61** – Helsinki **Finland** Exchange of Notes
Amendment of 1953 Payments Agreement [53-32]

TYC 10:321(C); H12(3):38(G)

61-57 **4/16/61** – Peking **Burma** Joint Communiqué
Talks during Premier U Nu's visit: technical aid, support for convening Geneva Conference on Laos, Kuomintang troops in Burma, etc.

TYC 10:41(C); WCC 8:167(C); JMJP 4/18/61(C); JMST 1961, p. 174(C); SCMP 2481:26(E); Burma Wkly. Bull. 9:52:461(E); AsR 3948(E); H12(1):29(G)

61-58 **4/18/61** – Peking **Indonesia** Exchange of Notes
Economic and technical cooperation

Refers to draft of agreement signed 10/11/61 [61-134].

SCMP 2482:41; AsR 3949

61-59 **4/18/61** – Hanoi **Vietnam (N)** –
1961 plan for cultural cooperation

JMJP 4/21/61; PR 4/28/61, p. 23; SCMP 2482:44

61-60 **4/20/61** – Peking **Cuba** –
1961 plan for cultural cooperation

JMJP 4/21/61; PR 4/28/61, p. 23; SCMP 2484:50

61-61 **4/20/61** – Sofia **Bulgaria** –
1961-62 plan for cooperation between Academies of Sciences

JMJP 4/25/61; PR 4/28/61, p. 23; SCMP 2485:23

61-62 **4/23/61** – Peking **Albania** Protocol
Supply of complete sets of equipment and technical assistance by PRC to Albania

JMJP 4/26/61; PR 4/28/61, p. 23; SCMP 2485:19

61-63 **4/23/61** – Peking **Albania** Protocol
Living conditions of specialists, technicians, and trainees

JMJP 4/24/61; PR 4/28/61, p. 23; SCMP 2485:19

61-64 **4/23/61** – Peking **Albania** Protocol
Use of PRC loan by Albanian Government under Loan Agreement of 2/2/61 [61-18]

JMJP 4/26/61; PR 4/28/61, p. 23; SCMP 2485:19

61-65 **4/23/61** – Peking **Albania** Exchange of Notes
Supply of grains and other principal foodstuffs by PRC to Albania

JMJP 4/26/61; SCMP 2486:18

61-66 **4/25/61** – Peking **Albania** Press Communiqué
Economic talks

WCC 8:172(C); JMJP 4/26/61(C); JMST 1961, p. 166(C); SCMP 2486:17(E)

61-67 **4/25/61** – Hangchow **Laos** Joint Statement
Talks during visit of Premier Souvanna Phouma and Prince Souphanouvong, Chairman of Neo Lao Haksat: support for convening Geneva Conference on Laotian situation, anti-imperialism, etc.

TYC 10:22(C); WCC 8:26(C); JMJP 4/26/61(C); JMST 1961, p. 170(C); PR 4/28/61, p. 6(E); SCMP 2486:24(E); AsR 4015(E)

61-68 **4/26/61** – Ulan Bator **Mongolia** Communiqué
Trade talks

JMJP 4/27/61(C); JMST 1961, p. 155(C); SCMP 2487:32(E)

61-69 **4/26/61** 3/2/62 Ulan Bator **Mongolia** Treaty
Commerce

TYC 10:361(C); WCC 9:305(C); JMJP 4/27/61; PR 5/5/61, p. 23; SCMP 2488:38; AsR 4035

61-70 **4/26/61** 1/1/61 Ulan Bator **Mongolia** Protocol
Exchange of goods in 1961

TYC 10:367(C); JMJP 4/27/61; PR 5/5/61, p. 23; SCMP 2488:38; AsR 4036

61-71 **4/28/61** – Bucharest **Rumania** –
1961 plan for cooperation between Academies of Sciences

JMST 1961, p. 132; SCMP 2490:39

61-72 **5/4/61** – Canton **Ceylon** Minutes
Talks on administration of air services

Signed by representatives of General Bureau of Civil Aviation of PRC and Ceylonese Airline Company.

JMJP 5/6/61

61-73 **5/9/61** – Peking **Burma** Communiqué
Boundary demarcation

Issued after sixth session of Sino-Burmese Joint Boundary Committee.

JMJP 5/10/61(C); SCMP 2496:29

61-74 **5/10/61** – Peking **Germany (E)** –
1961 plan for cultural cooperation

JMJP 5/11/61; PR 5/26/61, p. 21; SCMP 2497:26; AGF p. 55; Dok 9:468

61-75 **3/10/61** 4/1/61 Warsaw **Poland** Agreement
5/15/61 Peking
Currency exchange and cash movements

TYC 10:272(C)

61-76 **5/15/61** 1/1/61 Peking **Germany (E)** Protocol
Exchange of goods and payments in 1961

TYC 10:377(C); JMST 1961, p. 131; PR 5/26/61, p. 21; SCMP 2500:37; AGF p. 56; Dok 9:469

61-77 **5/15/61** – Peking **Germany (E)** Protocol
General conditions for delivery of goods

TYC 10:379(C)

61-78 **5/25/61** – Peking **Bulgaria** –
1961 plan for cultural cooperation

JMJP 5/26/61; PR 6/2/61, p. 25; SCMP 2508:32

61-79 **5/25/61** 5/25/61 Peking **USSR** Agreement
Cooperation in radio and television broadcasting

TYC 10:396(C); JMJP 5/26/61; PR 6/2/61, p. 25; SCMP 2508:43; G61:131

61-80 **5/26/61** – Moscow **USSR** Agreement
Cooperation between Academies of Sciences

G61:131

61-81 **6/4/61** – Peking **Burma** Joint Press Communiqué
Transfer of border territories

Communiqué confirms completion of transfer by local leaders on 6/4/61.

TYC 10:51(C); WCC 8:179(C); JMJP 6/6/61(C); JMST 1961, p. 141(C); PR 6/9/61, p. 10(E); SCMP 2513:38(E); Burma Wkly. Bull. 10:7:49(E); A/D p. 204(E)

61-82 **6/15/61** – Peking **Vietnam (N)** Joint Communiqué
Talks during visit of Premier Pham Van Dong: anti-imperialism, US intervention in Vietnam (S), Geneva Conference on Laos, PRC representation in UN, etc.

TYC 10:31(C); WCC 8:188(C); JMJP 6/17/61(C); JMST 6/17/61(C); SCMP 2522:41(E); AsR 4055(E)

61-83 **6/15/61** – Peking **Indonesia** Joint Press Communiqué
Talks during visit of President Sukarno: peaceful coexistence, West Irian, PRC representation in UN, Geneva Conference on Laos, etc.

TYC 10:11(C); WCC 8:193(C); JMJP 6/16/61(C); JMST 1961, p. 175(C); SCMP 2521:31(E); AsR 4068(E); A/D p. 69(E)

61-84 **6/15/61** 6/15/61 – **Germany (E)** Agreement
Currency exchange and cash movements

TYC 10:381(C)

61-85 **6/18/61** – Peking **Nigeria** Communiqué
Economic talks

TYC 10:248(C); WCC 8:195(C); JMJP 6/22/61(C); JMST 1961, p. 181(C); SCMP 2523:35; H12(2):62(G)

61-86 **6/19/61** – Moscow **USSR** Agreement
Economic cooperation

PR 7/7/61, p. 20; SCMP 2524:45; AsR 4080; G61:136

61-87 **6/19/61** 6/19/61 Moscow **USSR** Agreement
Scientific and technical cooperation

TYC 10:404(C); JMJP 6/21/61; PR 7/7/61, p. 20; SCMP 2524:45; AsR 4080; G61:136

61-88 **6/21/61** – Moscow **USSR** Protocol
Cooperation between Academies of Sciences

TYC 10:405(C); JMJP 6/22/61; PR 7/7/61, p. 21; SCMP 2525:39; G61:136

61-89 **6/21/61** – Moscow **USSR** –
Plan for cooperation between Academies of Sciences

JMJP 6/22/61; SCMP 2525:39; G61:136

61-90 **6/22/61** – Moscow **USSR** Communiqué
Talks on economic, scientific, and technical cooperation

WCC 8:197(C); JMJP 6/23/61(C); JMST 1961, p. 154(C); SCMP 2526:40(E)

61-91 **6/26/61** – Ulan Bator **Mongolia** Protocol
Handing over of PRC aid projects to Mongolia

SCMP 2530:38

61-92 **7/4/61** – Conakry **Guinea** Contract
Exchange and distribution of films

Signed by representatives of China Film Distribution and Exhibition Company and Guinean National Office of Cinematography (Ministry of Information and Tourism).

JMJP 7/8/61; SCMP 2536:35

61-93 **7/7/61** 1/1/61 Bucharest **Rumania** Protocol
Exchange of goods and payments in 1961
TYC 10:300(C); JMJP 7/9/61; PR 7/14/61, p. 23; SCMP 2537:42

61-94 **7/7/61** 1/1/61 Bucharest **Rumania** Protocol
General conditions for delivery of goods in 1961
TYC 10:304(C)

61-95 **7/10/61** 1/1/61 Warsaw **Poland** Protocol
General conditions for delivery of goods
TYC 10:276(C)

61-96 **7/11/61** 9/10/61 Peking **Korea (N)** Treaty
Friendship, cooperation, and mutual assistance
TYC 10:25(C); YHTY 45(C,K); WCC 8:213(C); JMJP 7/12/61(C); JMST 1961, p. 134(C); PR 7/14/61, p. 5(E); SCMP 2540:39(E); CCD 53:12(E); ZD 1961:7:842(P,E); ADTJ 1124:1(Fr); DIA 1961, p. 258(E); AsR 4140(E); A/D p. 53(E); WGO 4:274

61-97 **7/12/61** – Bamako **Mali** Contract
Distribution of PRC films in Mali
Signed by representatives of China Film Distribution and Exhibition Company and Mali Ministry of Interior, Information, and Tourism.
JMST 1962, p. 108; SCMP 2540:47

61-98 **7/13/61** – Warsaw **Poland** Agreement
Turnover of goods and payments in 1961
JMJP 7/15/61; PR 7/28/61, p. 23; SCMP 2541:44

61-99 **7/14/61** – Peking **Tunisia** Accord
Organization of week-long festival of PRC films in Tunisia
Signed by representatives of PRC Ministry of Culture and Tunisian friendship delegation.
JMJP 7/17/61

61-100 **6/27/61** 7/15/61 Peking **Hungary** Agreement
7/15/61 Budapest
Currency exchange and cash movements
TYC 10:259(C)

61-101 **7/15/61** – Peking **Korea (N)** Joint Communiqué
Talks during Premier Kim Il Sung's visit: revisionism, world communist movement, anti-imperialism, Taiwan, etc.

TYC 10:27(C); WCC 8:217(C); JMJP 7/16/61(C); JMST 1961, p. 164(C); PR 7/21/61, p. 7(E); SCMP 2541:38(E); AsR 4140(E)

61-102 **7/15/61** 1/1/61 Budapest **Hungary** Protocol
Exchange of goods and payments in 1961
TYC 10:263(C); JMJP 7/16/61; PR 7/28/61, p. 23; SCMP 2541:35

61-103 **7/15/61** – Peking **Yugoslavia** Protocol
Exchange of goods in 1961
TYC 10:325(C); JMJP 7/16/61; SCMP 2541:50; YTS 1962:1:94(S-C,E); WGO 4:103

61-104 **7/20/61** – Hanoi **Vietnam (N)** Protocol
1961 plan for scientific and technical cooperation
JMJP 7/21/61; PR 7/28/61, p. 23; SCMP 2545:39

61-105 **8/3/61** – Phnom Penh **Cambodia** Exchange of Notes
Extension of 1956 Trade and Payments Agreements [56-54,55]
TYC 10:326(C); JMST 1962, p. 107

61-106 **8/7/61** – Colombo **Ceylon** Exchange of Letters
PRC aid in construction of cotton mill in Ceylon
SCMP 2558:27; H12(1):71

61-107 **8/18/61** – Peking **Ghana** Joint Communiqué
Talks during President Nkrumah's visit: anti-imperialism, national liberation movements, Algeria, Congo, peaceful coexistence, Taiwan, PRC representation in UN, etc.
TYC 10:18(C); WCC 8:231(C); JMJP 8/19/61(C); JMST 1961, p. 180(C); PR 8/25/61, p. 5(E); SCMP 2566:32(E); AsR 4272(E); H12(2):107(G)

61-108 **8/18/61** 3/28/62 Peking **Ghana** Treaty
Friendship
TYC 10:17(C); YHTY 61(C,E); WCC 8:230(C); JMJP 8/22/61(C); JMST 1961, p. 136(C); PR 8/25/61, p. 7(E); SCMP 2567:27(E); ZD 1961:8:1079(P,E); DIA 1961, p. 646(E); AsR 4272; H12(2):106(G); WGO 4:274

61-109 **8/18/61** 8/18/61 Peking **Ghana** Agreement
Economic and technical cooperation
TYC 10:250(C); WCC 8:235(C); JMJP 8/22/61; SCMP 2567:32(E); AsR 4272; H12(2):118(G); WGO 4:274

61-110 **8/18/61** 8/18/61 Peking **Ghana** Agreement
Trade and payments
TYC 10:252(C); JMJP 8/22/61; SCMP 2567:28(E); AsR 4272; H12(2):113(G)

61-111 **8/18/61** 3/2/62 Peking **Ghana** Agreement
Cultural cooperation

TYC 10:392(C); JMJP 8/22/61; SCMP 2567:34(E); AsR 4272; H12(2):110(G); WGO 4:274

61-112 **8/21/61** – Peking **Brazil** Agreement
Trade and payments

Signed by representatives of People's Bank of China and Brazilian Bank.

JMJP 8/22/61; PR 8/25/61, p. 22; SCMP 2567:22; AsR 4273

61-113 **8/24/61** – Katmandu **Nepal** Communiqué
Boundary demarcation

Signed at third session of Sino-Nepalese Joint Boundary Committee.

JMJP 8/30/61(C); SCMP 2572:34(E); AsR 4177

61-114 **8/26/61** – Peking **USSR** Communiqué
Trade talks

WCC 8:237(C); JMJP 8/27/61(C); JMST 1961, p. 154(C); SCMP 2570:31(E); AsR 4189(E); G61:141

61-115 **8/31/61** – Huhehot **Mongolia** Protocol
Railway conference **USSR**

JMJP 9/2/61

61-116 **8/31/61** – Huhehot **Mongolia** Protocol
Joint railways

Signed at meeting of Sino-Mongolian Joint Boundary Railway Committee.

JMJP 9/2/61

61-117 **9/5/61** – Peking **Ethiopia** Communiqué
Talks on promotion of political, economic, and cultural cooperation

TYC 10:399(C); WCC 8:245(C); JMJP 9/8/61(C); JMST 1962, p. 162(C); PR 9/5/61, p. 22; SCMP 2578:35(E); H12(2):93(G)

61-118 **9/5/61** – Katmandu **Nepal** Protocol
Economic aid

JMJP 9/7/61; SCMP 2576:33; AsR 4196; A/D p. 337(E)

61-119 **9/5/61** – Katmandu **Nepal** Exchange of Letters
Working conditions for PRC experts and technicians in Nepal

Referred to in Article 5 of Protocol of 9/5/61 [61-118].

A/D p. 339

61-120 **9/11/61** – – **Cuba** Agreement
Exchange of feature films

JMST 1962, p. 109; PR 9/22/61, p. 23

61-121 **9/11/61** – – **Cuba** Agreement
Exchange of newsreels and documentary films
JMST 1962, p. 109; PR 9/22/61, p. 23

61-122 **9/18/61** – Conakry **Guinea** Protocol
Economic and technical aid
JMJP 9/20/61; SCMP 2585:26; AsR 4225

61-123 **9/20/61** – Peking **Poland** Protocol
Scientific and technical cooperation
Signed at eighth session of Sino-Polish Standing Committee for Scientific and Technical Cooperation.
SCMP 2586:42

61-124 **9/21/61** – Kabul **Afghanistan** Protocol
Exchange of goods and payments in 1961
JMJP 9/24/61; SCMP 2588:29

61-125 **9/22/61** 9/22/61 Peking **Mali** Agreement
Economic and technical cooperation
TYC 10:333(C); JMJP 9/23/61; SCMP 2588:37; AsR 4240

61-126 **9/7/61** – Copenhagen **Denmark** Exchange of Notes
9/23/61
Reciprocal tax exemptions to students, etc.
Official text is in English. Registered by Denmark with UN Secretariat 11/29/62.
TYC 10:237(C); JMST 1962, p. 109; UNTS 446:4(E,F)

61-127 **10/2/61** – Peking **Cuba** Joint Communiqué
Talks during visit of President Dorticos: anti-imperialism, PRC representation in UN, Guantanamo Base, Taiwan, etc.
TYC 10:2(C); WCC 8:267(C); JMJP 10/3/62(C); JMST 1962, p. 163(C); PR 10/6/61, p. 9(E); SCMP 2594:25(E); ZD 1961:10:1562(P,E); AsR 4273(E)

61-128 **10/5/61** 10/5/61 Peking **Nepal** Treaty
Boundary
TYC 10:45(C); WCC 8:271(C); JMJP 10/13/61(C); JMST 1962, p. 109(C); PR 10/20/61, p. 5(E); SCMP 2601:26(E); BFSP 164:667; ZD 1961:10:1572(P,E); ADTJ 1185:1(Fr); AsR 4296(E); PI(M) 67:289(Sp); A/D p. 209(E); H12(1):219(G); RGDIP 66:462(Fr)

61-129 **10/6/61** – Peking **USSR** Protocol
Scientific and technical cooperation in first half of 1962
Signed at eleventh session of Sino-Soviet Joint Committee for Scientific and Technical Cooperation. Communiqué also issued. SCMP 2597:49(E)
JMJP 10/7/61; SCMP 2597:48; AsR 4247; G61:143

61-130 **10/6/61** – Peking **USSR** –
Plan for cooperation between Academies of Sciences during fourth quarter of 1961 and first half of 1962
JMJP 10/7/61; PR 10/13/61, p. 22; SCMP 2597:48

61-131 **10/7/61** – – **Laos** Agreement (?)
Establishment of Consulates-General in Phong Saly and Kunming
JMJP 10/8/61; PR 10/13/61, p. 23; SCMP 2597:44

61-132 **10/7/61** 1/1/62 Peking **Ceylon** Protocol
Exchange of goods in 1962
TYC 10:386(C); JMJP 10/9/61; PR 10/13/61, p. 23; SCMP 2598:29; CTS 1962:12(S,E)

61-133 **10/8/61** – Peking **Ceylon** Joint Communiqué
Trade talks
SCMP 2598:29(E, sum.)

61-134 **10/11/61** 1/8/62 Peking **Indonesia** Agreement
Economic and technical cooperation
TYC 10:245(C); WCC 9:297(C); JMJP 10/12/61; SCMP 2600:34

61-135 **10/13/61** 2/22/62 Peking **Burma** Protocol
Boundary demarcation
TYC 10:52(C); JMJP 10/14/61; JMST 1962, p. 111(C, sum.); PR 10/20/61, p. 8; SCMP 2602:23 (E, sum.); AsR 4299(E, sum.); A/D p. 204(E, sum.)

61-136 **10/14/61** – Peking **Burma** Joint Communiqué
Talks during Premier U Nu's visit: PRC representation in UN, five principles of peaceful coexistence, etc.
TYC 10:43(C); WCC 8:278(C); JMJP 10/15/61(C); SCMP 2602:31(E); ZD 1961:11:1795(P,E); AsR 4299(E)

61-137 **10/15/61** – Peking **Nepal** Joint Communiqué
Talks during King Mahendra's visit: five principles of peaceful coexistence, ten principles of Bandung Conference, Sino-Nepalese economic cooperation, etc.
TYC 10:15(C); WCC 8:279(C); JMJP 10/16/61(C); JMST 1962, p. 156(C); SCMP 2603:43(E); AsR 4296(E)

61-138 **10/15/61** 10/15/61 Peking **Nepal** Agreement
Economic and technical aid by PRC in construction of highway from Tibetan border to Katmandu in Nepal
TYC 10:423(C); WCC 8:281(C); JMJP 10/29/61(C); JMST 1962, p. 156(C); PR 11/3/61, p. 18; SCMP 2611:32(E); AsR 4298(E, sum.); H12(1):224(G); A/D p. 339(E)

61-139 **10/18/61** – Baghdad **Iraq** Joint Communiqué
Trade talks

Confirms extension of Payments Agreement of 5/25/60 for one year in accordance with Article 7(1).

JMJP 10/19/61(C); JMST 1962, p. 157(C); SCMP 2604:31(E); H12(2):33(G)

61-140 **10/18/61** 12/18/61 Baghdad **Iraq** Agreement
Extension of 1960 Trade Agreement [60-69]

TYC 10:268(C); JMJP 10/19/61; PR 10/27/61, p. 17; SCMP 2605:35; H12(2):32

61-141 **10/20/61** 1/1/61 Prague **Czechoslovakia** Protocol
Exchange of goods and payments in 1961-62

TYC 10:335(C); JMST 1962, p. 107

61-142 **10/20/61** 10/20/61 Prague **Czechoslovakia** Protocol
General conditions for delivery of goods

TYC 10:338(C)

61-143 **10/21/61** 1/1/62 Havana **Cuba** Agreement
Telecommunications

TYC 10:418(C); JMST 1962, p. 109; SCMP 2607:29

61-144 **10/21/61** 1/1/62 Havana **Cuba** Agreement
Postal services

TYC 10:414(C); JMST 1962, p. 109; PR 10/27/61, p. 17; SCMP 2607:29

61-145 **10/27/61** – Rabat **Morocco** Agreement
Payments

JMJP 10/29/61; PR 11/3/61, p. 18; SCMP 2611:32; H12(2):158; Maroc: Revue du Ministre des Affaires Etrangères (NS) 1963:7:32

61-146 **10/30/61** – Pyongyang **Korea (N)** Protocol
Scientific and technical cooperation

Signed at fourth session of Sino-Korean Scientific and Technical Cooperation Committee.

JMJP 11/2/61; PR 11/10/61, p. 19; SCMP 2614:30

61-147 **11/1/61** 8/18/61 Peking **Ghana** Protocol
Implementation in 1961-62 of Trade and Payments Agreement of 8/18/61 [61-110]

TYC 10:258(C); JMJP 11/2/61; PR 11/10/61, p. 19; SCMP 2615:28

61-148 **11/1/61** – Peking **Ghana** Exchange of Letters
1962 plan for cultural cooperation

JMST 1962, p. 108; PR 11/10/61, p. 19; SCMP 2615:29

61-149 **11/1/61** – Peking **Ghana** Exchange of Letters
Trade
PR 11/10/61, p. 19; SCMP 2615:28

61-150 **11/1/61** – Peking **Ghana** Exchange of Letters
Economic and technical cooperation
PR 11/10/61, p. 19; SCMP 2615:28

61-151 **11/1/61** – Peking **Ghana** "Undertaking"
Technical banking arrangement on accounting procedures between People's Bank of China and Bank of Ghana for implementation of Economic and Technical Cooperation Agreement of 8/18/61 [61-109]
JMJP 11/2/61; SCMP 2615:29

61-152 **11/1/61** – Peking **Ghana** "Undertaking"
Technical banking arrangement between People's Bank of China and Bank of Ghana for implementation of Trade and Payments Agreement of 8/18/61 [61-110]
JMJP 11/2/61; SCMP 2615:29

61-153 **11/2/61** – Peking **Ghana** Joint Communiqué
Trade talks
JMJP 11/3/61(C); JMST 1962, p. 159(C)

61-154 **11/24/61** 11/24/61 Peking **Korea (N)** Protocol
Extension of 1956 Protocol for transportation of timber on Yalu and Tumen Rivers [56-10]
TYC 10:233(C); JMJP 11/25/61; SCMP 2629:34

61-155 **11/25/61** – Baghdad **Iraq** –
1961-62 plan for cultural cooperation
JMJP 11/28/61; PR 12/8/61, p. 18; SCMP 2630:32

61-156 **December(?)** – – **Ceylon** Agreement(?)
Exchange of Ceylonese sheet rubber for rice from PRC
AsR 4356

61-157 **12/13/61** – Peking **Burma** Protocol
Economic and technical cooperation
JMJP 12/14/61; PR 12/22/61, p. 22; SCMP 2643:31; AsR 4367

61-158 **12/13/61** – Peking **Burma** Protocol
Purchase of Burmese rice in 1962
JMJP 12/14/61; PR 12/22/61, p. 22; SCMP 2643:31; AsR 4367

61-159 **12/21/61** – Peking **Burma** Exchange of Letters
Supplement to Agreement of 1/9/61 on Economic and Technical Cooperation [61-2]
JMJP 12/22/61; SCMP 2648:26

61-160 **12/21/61** – Peking **Burma** Exchange of Letters
Technical cooperation
JMJP 12/22/61; SCMP 2648:26

61-161 **12/26/61** – Peking **Albania** Agreement
Establishment of Sino-Albanian Shipping Joint Stock Company
Company began business 4/2/62.
JMJP 12/27/61; PR 1/5/62, p. 26; SCMP 2650:30; AsR 4367

1962

62-1 **1/8/62** 1/1/62 Pyongyang **Korea (N)** Protocol
Mutual supply of goods in 1962
TYC 11:90(C); JMJP 1/10/62; PR 1/19/62, p. 22; SCMP 2658:28

62-2 **1/13/62** – Peking **Albania** Agreement
Granting of loan by PRC
JMJP 1/14/62; PR 1/19/62, p. 10; SCMP 2661:20

62-3 **1/13/62** – Peking **Albania** Exchange of Notes
Supply of complete sets of equipment and technical aid by PRC
Supplements Protocol of 4/23/61 [61-62].
JMJP 1/14/62; PR 1/19/62, p. 10; SCMP 2661:20

62-4 **1/13/62** – Peking **Albania** Protocol
Exchange of goods and payments in 1962
JMJP 1/14/62; PR 1/19/62, p. 10; SCMP 2661:20

62-5 **1/13/62** – Peking **Albania** Protocol
Use of PRC credits by Albania in 1962
Supplements Loan Agreements of 1/16/59 and 2/2/61.
JMJP 1/14/62; PR 1/19/62, p. 10; SCMP 2661:20

62-6 **1/13/62** – Peking **Albania** Protocol
Scientific and technical cooperation
Signed at sixth meeting of Sino-Albanian Joint Committee for Cooperation in Technology and Technical Science.
JMJP 1/14/62; PR 1/19/62, p. 10; SCMP 2661:20

62-7 **1/13/62** – Peking **Mongolia** –
1962 plan for cultural cooperation
JMJP 1/14/62; PR 1/26/62; SCMP 2661:32

62-8 **1/13/62** – Khang Khay **Laos** Agreement
Construction by PRC of highway between Yunnan Province and Phong Saly

Signed by representatives of Souvanna Phouma's regime in name of "Kingdom of Laos."

JMJP 1/14/62; PR 1/19/62, p. 22; SCMP 2662:31; AsR 4470; WGO 5:114

62-9 **1/13/62** – Khang Khay **Laos** Agreement
Air transport

See note above.

JMJP 1/14/62; PR 1/19/62, p. 22; SCMP 2662:32; AsR 4470; WGO 5:114

62-10 **1/15/62** – Peking **Albania** Press Communiqué
Economic talks

JMJP 1/16/62(C); JMST 1962, p. 134(C); SCMP 2663:21(E)

62-11 **1/20/62** – Hanoi **Vietnam (N)** Protocol
Mutual supply of goods and payments in 1962

JMJP 1/21/62; PR 1/26/62, p. 21; SCMP 2668:32

62-12 **1/20/62** – Hanoi **Vietnam (N)** Exchange of Notes
Extension of 1955 Protocol on Small-Scale Trading in Border Areas [55-49]

TYC 11:97(C)

62-13 **1/20/62** – Hanoi **Vietnam (N)** Exchange of Notes
Extension of 1955 Protocol on Exchange of Goods between Local State Trading Companies in Border Areas [55-48]

TYC 11:99(C)

62-14 **1/23/62** – Moscow **USSR** –
1962 plan for cultural cooperation

JMJP 1/25/62; SCMP 2669:32; AsR 4429; G62:131

62-15 **1/27/62** 1/27/62 Havana **Cuba** Agreement
Cooperation in radio and television broadcasting

TYC 11:120(C); JMJP 1/30/62; SCMP 2672:26; H12(3):119(G)

62-16 **1/27/62** – Havana **Cuba** Protocol
Radio and television cooperation in 1962

JMJP 1/30/62; SCMP 2672:26

62-17 **2/2/62** – Budapest **Hungary** –
1962 plan for cultural cooperation

JMJP 2/4/62; PR 2/16/62, p. 21; SCMP 2676:32

62-18 **2/7/62** – Colombo **Ceylon** Exchange of Notes
Reciprocal recognition of ship's papers

TYC 11:140(C)

62-19 **2/17/62** – Bucharest **Rumania** –
1962 plan for cultural cooperation
JMJP 2/18/62; SCMP 2684:32

62-20 **2/25/62** 1/1/62 Peking **Mongolia** Protocol
Mutual supply of goods in 1962
TYC 11:108(C); JMJP 2/26/62; PR 3/2/62, p. 18; SCMP 2689:28; AsR 4489

62-21 **2/28/62** – Warsaw **Poland** –
1962 plan for cultural cooperation
JMJP 3/1/62; PR 3/9/62, p. 19; SCMP 2691:31

62-22 **1/18/62** 3/7/62 Prague **Czechoslovakia** Agreement
3/7/62 Peking
Currency exchange and cash movements
TYC 11:82(C)

62-23 **3/11/62** – Baghdad **Iraq** Contract
Purchase of dates
Signed by representatives of Commercial Counsellor of PRC Embassy and Iraqi Dates Organization.
PR 3/23/62, p. 20; SCMP 2699:31

62-24 **3/17/62** 1/1/62 Peking **UAR** Agreement
Trade
Provides that Agreement would be made effective retroactively after notification of ratifications. UAR notified 6/6/62 of PRC ratification of 6/1/62; PRC notified 10/30/62 of UAR ratification of 9/25/62.
TYC 11:61(C); JMJP 3/18/62; PR 3/23/62, p. 20; SCMP 2703:30; FIYB 1964:4:1

62-25 **3/17/62** 1/1/62 Peking **UAR** Agreement
Payments
See note above.
TYC 11:64:(C); JMJP 3/18/62; PR 3/23/62, p. 20; SCMP 2703:30; FIYB 1964:4:1

62-26 **3/17/62** 1/1/62 Peking **UAR** Protocol
Trade in 1962
TYC 11:68(C); JMJP 3/18/62; PR 3/23/62, p. 20; SCMP 2703:30; FIYB 1964:4:1

62-27 **3/18/62** – Tai'zz **Yemen** Protocol
Supply of highway maintenance experts by PRC to Yemen
JMJP 3/21/62; PR 3/23/62, p. 20; SCMP 2705:28

62-28 **3/27/62** 1/1/62 Peking **Poland** Protocol
Extension of 1961 Protocol on General Conditions for Delivery of Goods [61-95]
TYC 11:60(C)

62-29 **3/28/62** – Peking **Poland** Agreement
Turnover of goods and payments in 1962
JMJP 3/29/62; PR 4/6/62, p. 20; SCMP 2711:29; AsR 4586

62-30 **3/29/62** 11/1/61 Peking **Finland** Agreement
Trade in 1961-62
TYC 11:74(C); JMJP 3/30/62; PR 4/6/62, p. 21; SCMP 2712:29; AsR 4586

62-31 **3/30/62** 1/1/62 Sofia **Bulgaria** Protocol
Exchange of goods and payments in 1962
TYC 11:76(C); JMJP 4/1/62; PR 4/6/62, p. 20; SCMP 2713:23

62-32 **3/30/62** – Sofia **Bulgaria** Protocol
Amendment of Protocol on General Conditions for Delivery of Goods in 1957 [57-14]
TYC 11:79(C)

62-33 **3/30/62** 1/1/62 Peking **Hungary** Agreement
Exchange of goods and payments in 1962
TYC 11:37(C); JMJP 3/31/62; SCMP 2713:24; AsR 4586

62-34 **3/30/62** 1/1/62 Peking **Hungary** Protocol
General conditions for delivery of goods in 1962
TYC 11:40(C)

62-35 **4/3/62** – Peking **Czechoslovakia** –
1962 plan for cultural cooperation
JMJP 4/4/62; PR 4/6/62, p. 20; SCMP 2715:27

62-36 **4/11/62** – Tirana **Albania** Agreement
Cooperation between New China News Agency and Albanian Telegraph Agency
Signed by Counsellor of PRC Embassy in Albania and Director of Albanian Telegraph Agency.
JMJP 4/14/62; SCMP 2722:28

62-37 **4/17/62** – Peking **USSR** Joint Resolutions
Joint survey of Heilungkiang River Valley
Final reports approved at fourth session of Sino-Soviet Joint Academic Committee for Research on Productivity of Heilungkiang River Basin. Completes joint survey work undertaken in accordance with Agreement of 8/18/56 [56-93].
SCMP 2724:36

62-38 **4/18/62** – Sofia **Bulgaria** –
1962 plan for cultural cooperation
JMJP 4/20/62; PR 4/27/62, p. 23; SCMP 2726:28

62-39 **4/20/62** – Peking **USSR** Protocol
Exchange of goods in 1962

JMJP 4/21/62; PR 4/27/62, p. 22; SCMP 2726:38; AsR 4586; G62:138

62-40 **4/25/62** – Havana **Cuba** Protocol
Trade in 1962

Joint Communiqué also issued 4/25/62. SCMP 2730:28(E, sum.)

JMJP 4/27/62; SCMP 2730:28

62-41 **4/27/62(?)** – Peking **Multilateral** Protocol
Railway transport

Signed at International Railway Transport Conference on Through Freight Traffic attended by delegates from USSR, Vietnam (N), Korea (N), and Mongolia.

PR 5/4/62, p. 23; SCMP 2730:34

62-42 **4/30/62** – Peking **Korea (N)** –
1962 plan for cultural cooperation

JMJP 5/1/62; PR 5/11/62, p. 21; SCMP 2732:39

62-43 **5/3/62** – Peking **Pakistan** Press Communiqué
Agreement to conduct negotiations on boundary question

TYC 11:14(C); WCC 9:322(C); JMJP 5/4/62(C); JMST 1962, p. 155(C); PR 5/11/62, p. 10(E); SCMP 2734:33(E); A/D p. 217(E)

62-44 **5/5/62** – Peking **Vietnam (N)** –
1962 plan for cultural cooperation

JMJP 5/7/62; PR 5/11/62, p. 21; SCMP 2735:43

62-45 **5/7/62** – Peking **USSR** Accord
Shipping survey and registration

Signed by Directors of Registries of Shipping.

JMJP 5/17/62; JMST 1962, p. 106; SCMP 2743:30

62-46 **5/7/62** – Tirana **Albania** Protocol
Shipping

Signed at first meeting of Administrative Council of Sino-Albanian Shipping Joint Stock Company.

JMJP 5/11/62; SCMP 2738:20

62-47 **5/13/62** – Peking **USSR** Protocol
Implementation of 1961 Agreement on Economic Cooperation [61-86]

JMJP 5/14/62; SCMP 2741:34; G62:140

62-48 **5/22/62** – Warsaw **Poland** –
1962 plan for cooperation between Academies of Sciences

JMJP 5/24/62; SCMP 2748:28

62-49 **5/23/62** 5/23/62 Peking **Sudan** Agreement
Trade
TYC 11:56(C); JMJP 5/24/62; PR 6/1/62, p. 22; SCMP 2748:31; AsR 4657

62-50 **2/9/62** – Phnom Penh **Cambodia** Exchange of Notes
5/23/62
Reciprocal recognition of ship's papers
TYC 11:139(C)

62-51 **5/28/62** 1/1/63 Colombo **Ceylon** Exchange of Notes
Extension of 1957 Economic Aid Agreement [57-87]
TYC 11:114(C); JMJP 5/29/62; PR 6/8/62, p. 23; CTS 1962:16(S,E); AsR 4693

62-52 **5/29/62** 1/1/62 Peking **Rumania** Protocol
Exchange of goods and payments in 1962
TYC 11:69(C); JMJP 5/30/62; PR 6/8/62, p. 22; SCMP 2752:30; AsR 4682

62-53 **5/29/62** – Peking **Rumania** Protocol
Extension of Protocol on General Conditions for Delivery of Goods in 1961 [61-94]
TYC 11:73(C)

62-54 **5/31/62** – Peking **Mongolia** Joint Arrangement
Implementation of 1960 Agreement on Scientific and Technical Cooperation [60-74]
Signed at first meeting of Sino-Mongolian Executive Organ for Scientific and Technical Cooperation.
JMST 1962, p, 106; PR 6/22/62, p. 20; SCMP 2755:28; AsR 4719

62-55 **6/4/62** – Peking **Mongolia** Protocol
1962 plan for scientific and technical cooperation
See note above.
JMST 1962, p. 106; SCMP 2755:28; AsR 4719

62-56 **6/15/62** – Peking **Korea (N)** –
1962 plan for cooperation between Academies of Sciences
JMJP 6/16/62; SCMP 2763:23

62-57 **6/22/62** – Ulan Bator **Multilateral** (Miscellaneous)
Adoption and revision of various regulations on railway cooperation and administration
Signed at seventh session of Railway Cooperation Organization of Socialist Countries attended by delegates from Bulgaria, Hungary, Vietnam (N), Germany (E), Korea (N), Poland, Rumania, USSR, Czechoslovakia, Mongolia, and PRC.
TYC 11:141, 145, 148(C); SCMP 2768:28; G62:144

62-58 **6/23/62** – Moscow **USSR** Protocol
1962-63 plan for scientific and technical cooperation

Signed at twelfth session of Sino-Soviet Committee on Scientific and Technical Cooperation.

JMJP 6/25/62; PR 6/29/62, p. 21; SCMP 2769:38; AsR 4719; G62:145

62-59 **6/25/62** – Warsaw **Poland** Protocol
Scientific and technical cooperation

Signed at ninth session of Sino-Polish Standing Committee for Scientific and Technical Cooperation.

JMJP 6/27/62; PR 7/13/62, p. 20; SCMP 2770:26

62-60 **6/28/62** – Belgrade **Yugoslavia** Protocol
Exchange of goods in 1962

TYC 11:80(C); JMST 1962, p. 107; SCMP 2772:31; YTS 1963:424(S-C,E); WGO 6:141

62-61 **7/1/62** – Peking **Czechoslovakia** Protocol
Scientific and technical cooperation

Signed at ninth session of the Sino-Czechoslovak Joint Committee for Scientific and Technical Cooperation.

JMJP 7/3/62; PR 7/13/62, p. 20; SCMP 2774:27

62-62 **7/2/62** – Phnom Penh **Cambodia** Exchange of Notes
7/5/62
Extension of 1956 Trade and Payments Agreements [56-54,55]

TYC 11:81(C); JMST 1963, p. 202

62-63 **7/9/62** – Conakry **Guinea** Protocol
Trade in 1962

JMJP 7/11/62; SCMP 2778:24

62-64 **7/17/62** 1/1/62 Peking **Czechoslovakia** Protocol
Exchange of goods and payments in 1962

TYC 11:86(C); JMJP 7/18/62; SCMP 2783:23

62-65 **7/17/62(?)** – Bucharest **Rumania** Protocol
Scientific and technical cooperation

Signed at seventh session of Sino-Rumanian Joint Committee for Scientific and Technical Cooperation. Communiqué also issued 7/17/62.

JMJP 7/20/62; PR 8/3/62, p. 17; SCMP 2785:25

62-66 **7/18/62** – Kabul **Afghanistan** Protocol
Exchange of goods and payments in 1962

JMJP 7/21/62; SCMP 2786:23

62-67 **7/19/62** – Peking **Czechoslovakia** Exchange of Notes
7/20/62
Extension of 1952 Agreement on Scientific and Technical Cooperation [52-19]
TYC 11:126(C); JMST 1963, p. 201

62-68 **7/20/62** – Havana **Cuba** –
1962 plan for cultural cooperation
JMJP 7/22/62; SCMP 2786:24

62-69 **7/20/62** – Berlin **Germany (E)** Protocol
Scientific and technical cooperation
Signed at sixth session of Sino-German Standing Committee for Cooperation in Technology and Technical Sciences. Communiqué also issued 7/21/62.
JMJP 7/24/62; PR 8/3/62, p. 17; SCMP 2788:26; Dok 10:587

62-70 **7/21/62** – Moscow **USSR** –
1962 plan for cooperation between Academies of Sciences
JMJP 7/23/62; PR 8/3/62, p. 17; SCMP 2787:38

62-71 **7/23/62** 7/23/62 Geneva **Multilateral** Declaration
Neutrality of Laos
Signed by Burma, Cambodia, Canada, France, India, Poland, Thailand, UK, USA, USSR, Vietnam (N), Vietnam (S), and PRC. Registered by UK with UN Secretariat 3/14/63.
TYC 11:3(C); WCC 9:278(C); JMJP 7/23/62(C); PR 7/27/62, p. 5; SCMP 2788:26; UNTS 456:302(E,C,Fr,L,R,); DSB 1962:1207:259(E); DAFR 1962, p. 284(E); A/D p. 485(E)

62-72 **7/23/62** 7/23/62 Geneva **Multilateral** Protocol
Withdrawal of foreign forces from Laos
Signed by Laos and all states enumerated in note above. Registered by UK with UN Secretariat 3/14/63.
TYC 11:7(C); WCC 9:281(C); JMJP 7/23/62(C); SCMP 2788:26; UNTS 456:324(E,C,Fr,L,R); DSB 1962:1207:261(E); DAFR 1962, p. 288(E)

62-73 **7/30/62** – Bamako **Mali** Contract
Distribution of PRC films in Mali
Signed by representatives of China Film Distribution and Exhibition Company and Mali National Office of Cinematography.
JMJP 8/11/62; SCMP 2800:25

62-74 **7/30/62** – Bamako **Mali** Contract
Exchange of newsreel materials
See note above.
JMJP 8/11/62; SCMP 2800:25

62-75 **7/31/62** – Peking **Vietnam (N)** Protocol
Scientific and technical cooperation

Signed at second session of Sino-Vietnamese Executive Organ for Scientific and Technical Cooperation.

JMJP 8/2/62; SCMP 2794:38

62-76 **8/1/62** 9/17/62 Colombo **Ceylon** Exchange of Letters
Extension of 1958 Exchange of Notes on PRC Loan for Flood Relief and Rehabilitation [58-83]

JMST 1963, p. 202; CTS 1962:18:3(S,E); AsR 4791

62-77 **8/4/62** 1/1/62 Berlin **Germany (E)** Protocol
Exchange of goods and payments in 1962

TYC 11:110(C); JMJP 8/6/62; SCMP 2797:22; AGF p. 56; Dok 10:372

62-78 **8/4/62** – Berlin **Germany (E)** Protocol
General conditions for delivery of goods in 1962

TYC 11:113(C)

62-79 **8/14/62** 8/14/62 Katmandu **Nepal** Exchange of Notes
Choice of nationality, transfrontier cultivation, and transfrontier pasturing by border inhabitants

TYC 11:15(C); JMJP 8/17/62(C); JMST 1963, p. 309(C); PR 8/31/62, p. 21; SCMP 2804:28(E, sum.); AsR 4797

62-80 **8/14/62** – Berlin **Germany (E)** –
1962 plan for cultural cooperation

JMST 1963, p. 201; SCMP 2804:23; AGF p. 56; Dok 10:595

62-81 **8/22/62** – Peking **Vietnam (N)** Protocol
Protection of fishery resources in Red River

JMJP 8/23/62; PR 8/31/62, p. 21; SCMP 2808:20

62-82 **8/23/62** – Havana **Cuba** Protocol
Implementation of 1960 Agreement on Scientific and Technical Cooperation [60-82]

JMJP 8/26/62; SCMP 2810:22

62-83 **8/28/62** – Moscow **USSR** Protocol
Verification of mutual deliveries of goods in first half of 1962

JMJP 8/30/62; SCMP 2813:31; G62:150

62-84 **9/8/62** – Peking **Poland** Minutes
Talks on performance of Trade Agreement of 3/28/62 [62-29]

JMJP 9/9/62; SCMP 2818:33

62-85 **Sept.** – Conakry **Guinea** Contract
Distribution and exhibition of PRC films in Guinea

Signed by representatives of China Film Distribution and Exhibition Company and Guinean Ministry of Information and Tourism.

JMJP 9/20/62; SCMP 2824:27

62-86 **Sept.** – Conakry **Guinea** Contract
Exchange of newsreel materials

See note above.

JMJP 9/20/62; SCMP 2824:27

62-87 **9/13/62** – Peking **Bulgaria** Protocol
Scientific and technical cooperation

Signed at sixth session of the Sino-Bulgarian Joint Committee for Scientific and Technical Cooperation.

JMST 1963, p. 200; SCMP 2821:31

62-88 **9/15/62** – Colombo **Ceylon** Press Communiqué
Trade talks

JMJP 9/18/62; SCMP 2823:21

62-89 **9/22/62(?)** – Peking **Korea (N)** Protocol
Scientific and technical cooperation

Signed at fifth session of Sino-Korean Committee on Scientific and Technical Cooperation.

JMJP 9/23/62; PR 9/28/62, p. 21; SCMP 2827:30

62-90 **9/30/62** – Peking **Czechoslovakia** Agreement
Cooperation between Academies of Sciences in 1962-66

TYC 11:127(C); JMJP 10/1/62; PR 10/5/62, p. 22; SCMP 2833:23

62-91 **9/30/62** – Peking **Czechoslovakia** –
1962-63 plan for cooperation between Academies of Sciences

JMJP 10/1/62; SCMP 2833:23

62-92 **10/3/62** – Peking **Ceylon** Joint Communiqué
Conference concerning trade and economic and technical cooperation

JMJP 10/4/62; SCMP 2835:23(E); AsR 4862

62-93 **10/3/62** 1/1/63 Peking **Ceylon** Agreement
Trade and payments in 1962-67

TYC 11:115(C); JMJP 10/4/62; PR 10/12/62, p. 22; SCMP 2835:23; CTS 1965:7(S,E); AsR 4862; WGO 5:114

62-94 **10/3/62** 10/3/62 Peking **Ceylon** Agreement
Economic and technical cooperation

JMJP 10/4/62; PR 10/12/62, p. 22; SCMP 2835:23; CTS 1965:9(S,E); AsR 4862; WGO 5:114

62-95 **10/3/62** 1/1/63 Peking **Ceylon** Protocol
Exchange of goods in 1963

TYC 11:118(C); JMJP 10/4/62; PR 10/12/62, p. 22; SCMP 2823:22; CTS 1965:8(S,E); AsR 4862

62-96 **10/3/62** – Peking **Ceylon** Contracts (2)
Exchange of rice and rubber in 1963

SCMP 2835:23

62-97 **10/18/62** – Accra **Ghana** Protocol
Economic and technical cooperation

JMJP 10/20/62; PR 10/26/62, p. 23; SCMP 2845:22

62-98 **11/1/62** 1/1/62 Peking **Indonesia** Agreement
Radio and television broadcasting cooperation

TYC 11:121(C); JMJP 11/2/62; SCMP 2854:30; WGO 5:114

62-99 **11/5/62** – Peking **Korea (N)** Communiqué
Trade talks

WCC 9:378(C); JMJP 11/6/62(C); JMST 1963, p. 259(C); SCMP 2857:31(E)

62-100 **11/5/62** 12/15/62 Peking **Korea (N)** Treaty
Commerce and navigation

TYC 11:92(C); WCC 9:380(C); JMJP 11/6/62; PR 11/9/62, p. 24; SCMP 2856:41; WGO 5:114

62-101 **11/5/62** – Peking **Korea (N)** Agreement
Mutual supply of major goods in period 1963-67

JMJP 11/6/62; PR 11/9/62, p. 24; SCMP 2856:41

62-102 **11/5/62** – Peking **Korea (N)** Protocol
Mutual supply of goods in 1963

Parties also signed two other documents, presumably commercial in nature.

JMJP 11/6/62; PR 11/9/62, p. 24; SCMP 2856:41

62-103 **11/9/62** 11/9/62 Peking **Japan** Memorandum
Expansion of trade in period 1963-67

Signed by Liao Cheng-chih and Tatsunosuke Takasaki following trade talks in September 1962 between Premier Chou En-lai and Kenzo Matsumara, adviser of Japanese Liberal Democratic Party and member of Lower House of the Diet.

TYC 11:157(C); JMJP 11/10/62(C); JMST 1963, p. 283(C); SCMP 2860:39(E)

62-104 **11/9/62** – Bamako **Mali** Protocol
Economic and technical cooperation

JMJP 11/11/62; SCMP 2860:44; AfD 869

62-105 **12/1/62** – Peking **USSR** Protocol
Air transport and reciprocal services
JMJP 12/2/62; SCMP 2873:39

62-106 **12/4/62** – Peking **Laos** Joint Press Communiqué
Talks during visit of Prince Phoumi Nosavan, Vice-Premier and Minister of Finance of Provisional Government of National Union of Laos: economic and technical aid, five principles of peaceful coexistence, support for 1962 Geneva Agreements on Laos, etc.

PRC agree to furnish long-term loan, technical aid, and equipment for construction of industrial projects.

TYC 11:1(C); WCC 9:295(C); JMJP 12/5/62(C); JMST 1963, p. 286(C); PR 12/7/62, p. 20(E); SCMP 2876:26(E)

62-107 **12/5/62** – Peking **Vietnam (N)** Communiqué
Trade talks
WCC 9:394(C); JMJP 12/6/62(C); JMST 1963, p. 253(C); SCMP 2876:30(E)

62-108 **12/5/62** 2/15/63 Peking **Vietnam (N)** Treaty
Commerce and navigation
TYC 11:100(C); WCC 9:396(C); JMJP 12/6/62; PR 12/14/62, p. 26; SCMP 2876:29; Vietnam Info. Bull. 1963:8:3

62–109 **12/5/62** – Peking **Vietnam (N)** Protocol
Mutual supply of goods and payments in 1963
JMJP 12/6/62; PR 12/14/62, p. 26; SCMP 2876:29

62-110 **12/5/62** – Peking **Vietnam (N)** Exchange of Notes
Extension of 1955 Protocol on Small-Scale Trading in Border Areas [55-49]
TYC 11:105(C); JMJP 12/6/62

62-111 **12/5/62** – Peking **Vietnam (N)** Exchange of Notes
Extension of 1955 Protocol on Exchange of Goods between Local State Trading Companies in Border Areas [55-48]
TYC 11:107(C); JMJP 12/6/62

62-112 **12/11/62** – Tirana **Albania** –
1963-64 plan for cultural cooperation
JMJP 12/13/62; PR 12/21/62, p. 22; SCMP 2881:21; AsR 4982

62-113 **12/12/62** – Tirana **Albania** Protocol
Scientific and technical cooperation

Signed at seventh meeting of Sino-Albanian Joint Committee for Cooperation in Technology and Technical Science.

JMJP 12/15/62; PR 12/21/62, p. 22; SCMP 2882:25

62-114 **12/13/62** 6/14/63 Dar es Salaam **Tanganyika** Agreement
Cultural cooperation

TYC 11:123(C); JMJP 12/15/62; PR 7/19/63, p. 28; SCMP 2882:29

62-115 **12/14/62** – Peking **Hungary** Protocol
Scientific and technical cooperation

Signed at seventh meeting of Sino-Hungarian Committee for Scientific and Technical Cooperation.

JMJP 12/16/62; SCMP 2883:32

62-116 **12/24/62** – Hanoi **Vietnam (N)** –
1963-64 plan for cultural cooperation

JMJP 12/26/62; SCMP 2889:41; Vietnam Info. Bull. 1963:2:2

62-117 **12/26/62** 3/25/63 Peking **Mongolia** Treaty
Boundary

TYC 11:19(C); WCC 9:405(C); JMJP 3/26/63(C); JMST 1963, p. 204(C); PR 3/29/63, p. 27(E); SCMP 2889:32; CB 707:1(E); AsR 5013(E, sum.); WGO 5:114

62-118 **12/27/62** – Peking **Japan** Protocol
Trade

Signed by representatives of China Council for Promotion of International Trade, and of Japan-China Trade Promotion Association, Japan International Trade Promotion Association, and Kansai Council of Japan International Trade Promotion Association. Memorandum also issued. SCMP 2890:30(E)

TYC 11:158(C); JMJP 12/28/62(C); JMST 1963, p. 284(C); PR 1/11/63, p. 20; SCMP 2890:29(E)

62-119 **12/28/62** – Peking **Pakistan** Joint Communiqué
"Agreement in principle" on location and alignment of PRC-Pakistan boundary

TYC 11:14(C); WCC 9:421(C); JMJP 12/28/62(C); JMST 1963, p. 308(C); PR 12/28/62, p. 8(E); SCMP 2890:43(E); AsR 5021

62-120 **12/31/62** – Rangoon **Burma** Joint Communiqué
Trade talks

JMST 1963, p. 202; SCMP 2893:18(E)

62-121 **12/31/62** – Rangoon **Burma** Protocol
Trade in 1963

JMJP 1/1/63; PR 1/18/63, p. 20; SCMP 2893:18

1963

63-1 **1/5/63** – Karachi **Pakistan** Agreement
Trade

Joint Communiqué on trade talks also issued 1/5/63. SCMP 2895:30(E); AsR 5034

JMJP 1/6/63; PR 1/11/63, p. 20; SCMP 2895:29; AsR 5034; WGO 5:114

63-2 **1/5/63** 5/30/63 Peking **UAR** Agreement
Telecommunications

TYC 12:230(C); JMJP 1/6/63; SCMP 2895:31; H12(2):82

63-3 **1/8/63** – Peking **Ceylon** Joint Communiqué
Talks during Mrs. Bandaranaike's visit: Sino-Indian border dispute

Premier Chou En-lai gives "positive response" to Colombo Conference proposals presented by Premier Bandaranaike as chairman of Conference.

TYC 12:61(C); WCC 10:135(C); JMJP 1/8/63(C); JMST 1963, p. 312(C); SCMP 2896:20(E); ZD 1963:6:741(P,E); AsR 5049(E)

63-4 **1/8/63** – Peking **Indonesia** Joint Communiqué
Talks during Foreign Minister Subandrio's visit: Sino-Indian border dispute, Sino-Indonesian relations, etc.

TYC 12:3(C); WCC 10:137(C); JMJP 1/8/63(C); JMST 1963, p. 290(C); SCMP 2896:27(E)

63-5 **1/10/63** 5/26/63 Baghdad **Iraq** Accord
Renewal of 1960 Trade Agreement [60-69]

Joint Communiqué also issued 1/10/63. JMJP 1/12/63; SCMP 2899:31(E)

TYC 12:143(C); PR 1/18/63, p. 20; SCMP 2899:30; AsR 5086; H12(2):34

63-6 **1/10/63** 5/15/64 Mogadishu **Somalia** Agreement
Cultural cooperation

Joint Communiqué on visit of PRC cultural and friendship delegation also issued 1/14/63. JMJP 1/15/63; SCMP 2900:30

TYC 12:211(C); JMJP 1/13/63; SCMP 2899:33; H12(2):176

63-7 **1/13/63** – Katmandu **Nepal** Protocol
Construction of Katmandu-Lhasa highway

JMJP 1/15/63; PR 1/18/63, p. 20; SCMP 2900:29; AsR 5045

63-8 **1/17/63** – Peking **Albania** Protocol
Exchange of goods and payments in 1963

JMJP 1/19/63; SCMP 2903:24

63-9 **1/17/63** – Peking **Albania** Protocol
Albania's use of PRC loans in 1963

Joint Communiqué also issued 1/18/63. SCMP 2904:20(E)

JMJP 1/19/63; PR 1/25/63, p. 19; SCMP 2903:24

63-10 **1/20/63** 1/20/63 Peking **Nepal** Protocol
Boundary demarcation

TYC 12:67(C); JMJP 1/21/63; JMST 1963, p. 210; PR 1/25/63, p. 9; SCMP 2906:28(E, sum.); AsR 5050(E, sum.)

63-11 **1/22/63** – Peking **Japan** Memorandum
Fishery regulation in Yellow and East China Seas

Signed by representatives of China Fishery Association, Chinese People's Association for Cultural Relations with Foreign Countries, and Japan-China Fishery Association of Japan.

JMJP 1/23/63; PR 2/8/63, p. 21; SCMP 2909:27(E)

63-12 **1/23/63** – Peking **Ghana** Joint Press Communiqué
Talks during visit of Ghanaian government goodwill delegation; Sino-Indian dispute, principles of peaceful coexistence, PRC representation in UN, etc.

TYC 12:9(C); WCC 10:153(C); JMJP 1/24/63(C); JMST 1963, p. 317(C); SCMP 2908:23(E); H12(2):201

63-13 **2/8/63** – Prague **Multilateral** Agreement
Noncommercial payments

Signed at conference of Finance Ministers of Socialist countries by delegates from USSR, Albania, Bulgaria, Czechoslovakia, Vietnam (N), Germany (E), Hungary, Korea (N), Mongolia, Poland, and Rumania.

NT 1963:7:36

63-14 **2/18/63** 2/18/63 Tirana **Albania** Agreement
Inspection and prevention of insect pests and plant diseases

TYC·12:224(C); JMJP 2/22/63; PR 3/15/63, p. 79; SCMP 2926:14; WGO 5:114

63-15 **2/21/63** 7/8/63 Peking **Syria** Agreement
Trade

TYC 12:164(C); JMJP 2/22/63; PR 3/1/63, p. 5; SCMP 2927:33; STS 157:1 (Fr); AsR 5152

63-16 **2/21/63** 7/8/63 Peking **Syria** Agreement
Payments

TYC 12:169(C); JMJP 2/22/63; PR 3/1/63, p. 5; SCMP 2927:33; STS 158:1 (Fr); AsR 5152

63-17 **2/21/63** 7/8/63 Peking **Syria** Agreement
Economic and technical cooperation

TYC 12:171(C); WCC 10:164(C); JMJP 2/22/63; PR 3/1/63, p. 5; SCMP 2927:33; STS 159:1 (Fr); AsR 5152

63-18 **2/22/63** – Peking **Cuba** Protocol
Trade and payments in 1963

JMJP 2/23/63; PR 3/1/63, p. 4; SCMP 2927:25; AsR 5159; H12(3):128

63-19 **2/22/63** 2/22/63 Peking **Cuba** Protocol
General conditions for delivery of goods

TYC 12:125(C); JMJP 2/23/63; PR 3/1/63, p. 4; SCMP 2927:25; AsR 5159; H12(3):128

63-20 **2/22/63** – Peking **Cuba** Agreement
Loan by PRC to Cuba

JMJP 2/23/63; PR 3/1/63, p. 4; SCMP 2927:25; AsR 5159

63-21 **2/23/63** – Kunming **Vietnam (N)** Protocol
Border railways

Signed at sixth session of Sino-Vietnamese Joint Committee on Border Railways.

JMJP 2/25/63; PR 3/15/63, p. 79; SCMP 2928:28

63-22 **2/23/63** – Peking **USSR** –
1963 plan for cultural cooperation

Signed by representative of the Chinese People's Association for Cultural Relations with Foreign Countries and Soviet Ambassador to PRC.

JMJP 2/24/63; PR 3/15/63, p. 79; NT 1963:8:32

63-23 **2/24/63** – Peking **Syria** Exchange of Notes
Adjustment of PRC loan (under Economic and Technical Cooperation Agreement of 2/21/63) in event of change of gold standard value of Swiss franc [63-17]

TYC 12:174(C);

63-24 **2/26/63** – Peking **Cuba** Joint Communiqué
Economic talks

JMJP 2/26/63(C); SCMP 2929:22(E)

63-25 **2/27/63** – Peking **Cambodia** Joint Communiqué
Talks during visit of Prince Norodom Sihanouk: Sino-Indian border dispute, Cambodian and Laotian neutrality, Taiwan, etc.

TYC 12:26(C); WCC 10:167(C); JMJP 2/27/63(C); JMST 1963, p. 290(C); PR 3/15/63, p. 70(E); SCMP 2930:17(E); ZD 1963:1-2:131(P,E); AsR 5158

63-26 **2/28/63** – Havana **Cuba** Agreement
Purchase of films from each other

JMJP 3/2/63; PR 3/15/63, p. 79; H12(3):120

63-27 **3/2/63** – Peking **Afghanistan** Press Communiqué
Agreement to hold negotiations on border treaty

TYC 12:121(C); WCC 10:174(C); JMJP 3/2/63(C); JMST 1963, p. 315(C); SCMP 2932:20(E)

63-28 **3/2/63** 3/2/63 Peking **Pakistan** Agreement
Boundary between "China's Sinkiang and the contiguous areas the defense of which is under the actual control of Pakistan"

TYC 12:64(C); WCC 10:170(C); JMJP 3/3/63(C); JMST 1963, p. 209(C); PR 3/15/63, p. 67(E); SCMP 2932:29(E); CCD 90:64(E, Article 2 only); ZD 1963:3:192(P,E); AsR 5183(E); PI(M) 67:287(Sp); A/D p. 218(E); WGO 5:114; Wint, p. 765(E); RGDIP 67:723(Fr); ILM 2:3:541(E); AJIL 57:713(E)

63-29 **3/3/63** – Khartoum **Sudan** Contract
Exchange of newsreel material

Signed by representatives of China Film Distribution and Exhibition Company and Film Production Unit of Sudanese Ministry of Information and Labor.

JMJP 3/7/63; PR 3/22/63, p. 18; SCMP 2934:36

63-30 **3/4/63** – Peking **Pakistan** Joint Communiqué
Talks during Foreign Minister Bhutto's visit: Boundary Agreement of 3/2/63, Sino-Indian border dispute, Kashmir, etc.

TYC 12:1(C); WCC 10:177(C); JMJP 3/5/63(C); JMST 1963, p. 308(C); PR 3/15/63, p. 66(E); SCMP 2933:32(E); ZD 1963:3:201(P,E); AsR 5185

63-31 **3/5/63** 1/1/63 Peking **Bulgaria** Agreement
Exchange of goods and payments in 1963

TYC 12:161(C); JMJP 3/6/63; PR 3/15/63, p. 79; SCMP 2934:23; WGO 5:114

63-32 **3/10/63** – Peking **Laos** Joint Communiqué
Talks during King Vatthana's visit: Laotian neutrality, technical aid, PRC representation in UN, etc.

TYC 12:10(C); WCC 10:181(C); JMJP 3/11/63(C); JMST 1963, p. 287(C); PR 3/15/63, p. 74(E); SCMP 2938:21(E); ZD 1963:3:205(P,E)

63-33 **3/11/63** – Vientiane **Laos** Agreement
Exchange of information

Signed by representatives of New China News Agency and Laotian Ministry of Information, Publicity, and Tourism.

JMJP 3/14/63; PR 3/29/63, p. 27; SCMP 2940:24

63-34 **3/18/63** 1/1/63 Ulan Bator **Mongolia** Protocol
Mutual supply of goods in 1963
TYC 12:196(C); JMJP 3/20/63; PR 3/29/63, p. 27; SCMP 2943:23

63-35 **3/20/63** – Peking **Bulgaria** –
1963 plan for cultural cooperation
JMJP 3/21/63; PR 3/29/63, p. 27; SCMP 2945:23

63-36 **3/26/63** 3/26/63 Accra **Ghana** Agreement
Maritime transport
TYC 12:234(C)

63-37 **3/27/63** – Pyongyang **Korea (N)** –
1963 plan for cultural cooperation
JMJP 3/28/63; PR 4/5/63, p. 27; SCMP 2950:24

63-38 **3/30/63** – Ulan Bator **Mongolia** –
1963 plan for cultural cooperation
JMJP 3/31/63; PR 4/5/63, p. 27; SCMP 2952:27

63-39 **3/30/63** – Peking **Morocco** Agreement
Trade
JMJP 3/31/63; PR 4/5/63, p. 27; SCMP 2952:28; Maroc: Revue du Ministre des Affaires Etrangères (NS) 7:32 (1963); H12(2): 158; WGO 5:114

63-40 **4/8/63** 1/1/63 Bucharest **Rumania** Agreement
Exchange of goods and payments in 1963
TYC 12:145(C); JMJP 4/10/63; PR 4/19/63, p. 27; SCMP 2959:21; AsR 5331; WGO 5:114

63-41 **4/8/63** – Bucharest **Rumania** Protocol
Extension of Protocol on General Conditions for Delivery of Goods in 1961 [61-94]
TYC 12:149(C)

63-42 **4/10/63** 1/1/63 Budapest **Hungary** Agreement
Exchange of goods and payments in 1963
TYC 12:139(C); JMJP 4/11/63; PR 4/19/63, p. 27; SCMP 2960:23; WGO 5:114

63-43 **4/10/63** – Budapest **Hungary** Protocol
Extension of Protocol on General Conditions for Delivery of Goods in 1962 [62-34]
TYC 12:143(C)

63-44 **4/19/63** 1/1/63 Prague **Czechoslovakia** Agreement
Exchange of goods and payments in 1963
TYC 12:183(C); JMJP 4/20/63; PR 4/26/63, p. 12; SCMP 2965:26; WGO 5:114

63-45 **4/20/63** – Djakarta **Indonesia** Joint Statement
Talks during Chairman Liu Shao-chi's visit: West Irian, Taiwan, anti-imperialism, GANEFO, etc.

TYC 12:5(C); WCC 10:197(C); JMJP 4/21/63(C); JMST 1963, p. 212(C); PR 4/26/63, p. 11(E); SCMP 2965:36(E); ZD 1963:4:419(P,E); ADTJ 1386:1(Fr); AsR 5250(E, abbrev.)

63-46 **4/20/63** – Peking **Poland** –
1963 plan for cultural cooperation

JMJP 4/21/63; PR 4/26/63, p. 12; SCMP 2965:50

63-47 **4/20/63** – Moscow **USSR** Protocol
Exchange of goods in 1963

JMJP 4/22/63; PR 4/26/63, p. 6; SCMP 2966:42; AsR 5245; NT 1963:17:32

63-48 **4/20/63** – Moscow **USSR** Protocol
Preterm payment by PRC of debt to USSR for trade transactions in 1960

JMJP 4/22/63; PR 4/26/63, p. 6; SCMP 2966:42

63-49 **4/21/63** – Moscow **USSR** Communiqué
Trade talks

SCMP 2967:38(E)

63-50 **4/25/63** – Rangoon **Burma** Joint Communiqué
Talks during Chairman Liu Shao-chi's visit: Burmese neutrality, Sino-Indian relations, etc.

TYC 12:57(C); WCC 10:203(C); JMJP 4/27/63(C); JMST 1963, p. 219(C); PR 5/3/63, p. 10(E); SCMP 2969:25(E); ZD 1963:4:428(P,E); AsR 5327(E)

63-51 **4/25/63** – Peking **UAR** Joint Communiqué
Talks during visit of Ali Sabri, Chairman of UAR Executive Council of Ministers: peaceful coexistence, anticolonialism, Palestine Arabs, Taiwan, Sino-Indian border dispute, PRC representation in UN, etc.

TYC 12:17(C); WCC 10:245(C); JMJP 4/26/63(C); JMST 1963, p. 315(C); PR 5/3/63, p. 15(E); SCMP 2969: 37(E); ADTJ 1395:1(Fr); AsR 5243; H12(2):201

63-52 **4/30/63** – Warsaw **Poland** Agreement
Transfer of goods and payments in 1963

JMJP 5/2/63; PR 5/17/63, p. 20; SCMP 2972:38; WGO 5:114

63-53 **5/2/63** – Peking **Albania** Protocol
Management of Sino-Albanian Shipping Joint Stock Company

Signed by representatives of PRC and Albanian Ministries of Communications.

JMJP 5/3/63; PR 5/17/63, p. 20; SCMP 2973:22

63-54 **5/2/63** – Peking **Guinea** Protocol
Trade in 1963

JMJP 5/3/63; SCMP 2973:26; H12(2):132

63-55 **5/2/63** – Peking **Guinea** Protocol (supplementary)
Economic and technical cooperation

JMJP 5/3/63; SCMP 2973:26; H12(2):132

63-56 **5/4/63** – Peking **Poland** Protocol
Scientific and technical cooperation

Signed at tenth session of Sino-Polish Standing Committee for Scientific and Technical Cooperation.

JMJP 5/6/63; PR 5/17/63, p. 20; SCMP 2975:45

63-57 **5/5/63** – Phnom Penh **Cambodia** Joint Statement
Talks during Chairman Liu Shao-ch'i's visit: Cambodian neutralist policy, Taiwan, PRC representation in UN, Laos, Sino-Indian border dispute, anti-imperialism, etc.

TYC 12:29(C); WCC 10:211(C); JMJP 5/7/63(C); JMST 1963, p. 222(C); PR 5/10/63, p. 9; SCMP 2975:36(E); CCD 96:75(E); ZD 1963:5:593(P,E); ADTJ 1395:2(Fr)

63-58 **5/15/63** 7/24/64 Peking **Mali** Agreement
Cultural cooperation

TYC 12:203(C); JMJP 5/16/63; SCMP 2982:26; H12(2):202; WGO 5:114

63-59 **5/15/63** – Peking **Mali** Contract
Exchange of documentary film material

Signed by representatives of China Film Distribution and Exhibition Company and Cinema Bureau of Mali Ministry of Information.

SCMP 2982:26

63-60 **5/15/63** – Peking **Mali** Contract
Distribution of PRC films in Mali

See note above.

SCMP 2982:26

63-61 **5/15/63** 5/15/63 Peking **Somalia** Agreement
Trade and payments

Joint Communiqué also issued 5/18/63. SCMP 2984:37(E)

TYC 12:178(C); JMJP 5/18/63; SCMP 2982:27; H12(2):176

63-62 **5/15/63** – Prague **Czechoslovakia** –
1963 plan for cultural cooperation

JMJP 5/17/63; PR 5/31/63, p. 23; SCMP 2983:27

63-63 **5/16/63** – Hanoi **Vietnam (N)** Joint Statement
Talks during Chairman Liu Shao-ch'i's visit: antirevisionism, reunification of Vietnam, etc.

TYC 12:47(C); WCC 10:228(C); JMJP 5/17/63(C); JMST 1963, p. 227(C); PR 5/24/63, p. 10(E); SCMP 2983:36(E); CCD 96:42(E); ZD 1963:5:603(P,E); ADTJ 1399:1(Fr); AsR 5314(E, abbrev.)

63-64 **5/17/63** – Peking **Mali** Protocol
PRC aid to National Film Board of Mali in production of weekly newsreels

JMJP 5/18/63; SCMP 3002:36; H12(2):202

63-65 **5/20/63** – Ulan Bator **Mongolia** Minutes
Boundary demarcation talks

Issued after first meeting of Sino-Mongolian Joint Boundary Demarcation Committee.

JMJP 5/21/63

63-66 **5/6/63** – Peking **Mongolia** Exchange of Notes
5/25/63
Change of executive organ under 1960 Agreement on Scientific and Technical Cooperation [60-74]

TYC 12:220(C)

63-67 **5/25/63** – Peking **Hungary** –
1963 plan for cultural cooperation

JMJP 5/26/63; PR 6/7/63, p. 31; SCMP 2899:28

63-68 **5/29/63** 1/1/63 Helsinki **Finland** Agreement
Trade in 1963

TYC 12:154(C); JMJP 5/31/63; PR 6/14/63, p. 25; SCMP 2992:27

63-69 **5/29/63** – Helsinki **Finland** Exchange of Notes
Further amendment of 1953 Payments Agreement [53-32, 61-56]

TYC 12:156(C)

63-70 **6/7/63** – Peking **Germany (E)** –
1963 plan for cultural cooperation

JMJP 6/8/63; PR 6/21/63, p. 39; SCMP 2998:24; AGF p. 56; Dok 11:376(G)

63-71 **6/8/63** 6/8/63 Peking **Rumania** Agreement
Scientific and technical cooperation

TYC 12:216(E); JMJP 6/11/63; PR 6/14/63, p. 5; SCMP 2999:27; AsR 5331

63-72 **6/8/63** – Peking **Rumania** Protocol
Scientific and technical cooperation

Signed at eighth session of Sino-Rumanian Joint Committee for Scientific and Technical Cooperation.

JMJP 6/11/63; SCMP 2999:27

63-73 **6/10/63** – Pyongyang **Korea (N)** –
1963 plan for cooperation between Academies of Sciences

JMJP 6/11/63; PR 6/21/63, p. 39; SCMP 2999:27

63-74 **6/13/63** – Peking **Pakistan** Press Communiqué
Boundary demarcation

Issued after first session of Sino-Pakistani Joint Boundary Demarcation Committee.

JMJP 6/14/63(C); SCMP 3001:29(E); AsR 5331

63-75 **6/15/63** – Phnom Penh **Cambodia** Exchange of Notes
Extension of 1956 Trade and Payments Agreements [56-54,55]

TYC 12:175(C)

63-76 **6/18/63** 4/9/64 Oslo **Norway** Agreement
Cultural cooperation

TYC 12:210(C); JMJP 6/20/63; PR 7/19/63, p. 28; SCMP 3005:23; NoTS 1964, p. 226(N); H12(3):63(G)

63-77 **6/19/63** – Peking **USSR** Protocol
1963-64 plan for scientific and technical cooperation

Signed at thirteenth session of Sino-Soviet Joint Committee for Scientific and Technical Cooperation. Communiqué also issued 6/19/63. SCMP 3005:23(E)

JMJP 6/20/63; PR 7/19/63, p. 28; SCMP 3005:23; AsR 5330

63-78 **6/19/63** – Peking **Bulgaria** –
1963 plan for cooperation between Academies of Sciences

JMJP 6/20/63; PR 7/19/63, p. 28; SCMP 3005:19

63-79 **6/21/63** – Pyongyang **Korea (N)** Protocol
Scientific and technical cooperation

Signed at sixth session of Sino-Korean Committee for Scientific and Technical Cooperation.

JMJP 6/23/63; PR 7/19/63, p. 28; SCMP 3008:32

63-80 **6/22/63** 1/1/63 Peking **Germany (E)** Agreement
Exchange of goods and payments in 1963

TYC 12:198(C); JMJP 6/24/63; PR 7/19/63, p. 28; SCMP 3008:20; AGF p. 56; Dok 11:608

63-81 **6/22/63** – Peking **Germany (E)** Protocol
General conditions for delivery of goods in 1963
TYC 12:200(C)

63-82 **6/23/63** – Peking **Korea (N)** Joint Statement
Talks during President Choi Yong Kun's visit: US imperialism, peaceful coexistence, etc.
TYC 12:36(C); WCC 10:256(C); JMJP 6/24/63(C); JMST 1963, p. 259(C); PR 6/28/63, p. 8(E); SCMP 3008:22(E); CCD 96:54(E); ZD 1963:6:713(P,E)

63-83 **6/25/63** – Peking **Cuba** Agreement
Cooperation between PRC Academy of Sciences and National Committee for Cuban Academy of Science
TYC 12:214(C); JMJP 6/26/63; PR 6/28/63, p. 4; SCMP 3009:24; H12(3):121

63-84 **6/25/63** – Peking **Cuba** –
1963-64 plan for cooperation between Academies of Sciences
JMJP 6/26/63; SCMP 3009:24; H12(3):121

63-85 **7/5/63** – Peking **Rumania** –
1963 plan for cultural cooperation
JMJP 7/7/63; PR 7/12/63, p. 5; SCMP 3016:34; AsR 5352

63-86 **7/6/63** – Peking **Rumania** Agreement
Cooperation between Academies of Sciences
TYC 12:217(C); JMJP 7/8/63; PR 7/12/63, p. 5; SCMP 3016:35; AsR 5352

63-87 **7/6/63** – Peking **Rumania** –
1963-64 plan for cooperation between Academies of Sciences
JMJP 7/8/63; PR 7/12/63, p. 5; SCMP 3016:35

63-88 **7/14/63** 1/1/63 Cairo **UAR** Protocol
Trade in 1963-64
TYC 12:159(C); JMJP 7/16/63; PR 8/9/63, p. 24; SCMP 3021:38; AsR 5352; AfR 542; H12(2):201; FIYB 1965:4:38:

63-89 **7/15/63** – Prague **Czechoslovakia** Protocol
Scientific and technical cooperation
Signed at tenth session of Sino-Czechoslovak Joint Committee for Scientific and Technical Cooperation.
JMJP 7/19/63; PR 8/9/63, p. 24; SCMP 3023:25

63-90 **7/18/63** – Hanoi **Vietnam (N)** Protocol
Scientific and technical cooperation

Signed at third sesssion of Sino-Vietnamese Executive Organ for Scientific and Technical Cooperation.

JMJP 7/20/63; PR 8/9/63, p. 24; SCMP 3026:40; CCD 146:77

63-91 **7/24/63** – Peking **Cuba** –
1963 plan for cultural cooperation

JMJP 7/25/63; PR 8/9/63, p. 25; SCMP 3028:26; AsR 5378

63-92 **7/25/63** – Colombo **Ceylon** Agreement
Maritime transport

Provisionally effective 7/25/63; formally enters into force on notification of ratification, in accordance with Article 9, date unknown.

TYC 12:251(C); JMJP 7/27/63; PR 8/9/63, p. 25; SCMP 3030:22; AsR 5375

63-93 **8/1/63** – Rangoon **Burma** Agreement
Cooperation between New China News Agency and News Agency Burma

Signed by representatives of New China News Agency and Burmese Ministry of Information.

SCMP 3036:22

63-94 **8/3/63** – Kabul **Afghanistan** Joint Press Communiqué
Boundary negotiations

Minutes of talks also issued. JMJP 8/3/63

TYC 12:121(C); WCC 10:291(C); JMJP 8/4/63(C); SCMP 3035:28(E); AsR 5411(E)

63-95 **8/9/63** – Peking **Somalia** Agreement
Economic and technical cooperation

Joint Communiqué also issued 8/10/63.

JMJP 8/10/63; SCMP 3039:32; AsR 5401

63-96 **8/10/63** – Peking **Somalia** Joint Communiqué
Talks during Premier Shermarke's visit: anti-imperialism, PRC representation in UN, economic and technical assistance, etc.

TYC 12:33(C); WCC 10:295(C); JMJP 8/11/63(C); JMST 1964, p. 470(C); PR 8/16/63, p. 26(E); SCMP 3039:32(E); CCD 100:87(E); AsR 5401; AfR 569

63-97 **5/6/63** – Peking **Vietnam (N)** Exchange of Notes
8/10/63
Change of executive organs under 1960 Agreement on Scientific and Technical Cooperation [60-118]

TYC 12:222(C)

63-98 **8/17/63** – Prague **Czechoslovakia** Exchange of Notes
Extension of 1953 Agreement on Cooperation for Prevention of Insect Pests and Plant Diseases [53-48]

TYC 12:228(C)

63-99 **8/27/63** – Peking **Vietnam (N)** Agreement
Fishery cooperation in Gulf of Bakbo
JMJP 8/28/64; SCMP 3051:35

63-100 **8/28/63** – Rangoon **Burma** Exchange of Notes
Reciprocal recognition of ship's papers
TYC 12:249(C)

63-101 **8/29/63** – Karachi **Pakistan** Agreement
Air transport
Press Release also issued 8/29/63. SCMP 3053:29(E)
JMJP 8/31/63; PR 9/6/63, p. 4; SCMP 3053:29; AsR 5443

63-102 **8/30/63** – Karachi **Pakistan** Agreement
Air services
Signed by representatives of General Bureau of Civil Aviation of PRC and Pakistan International Airlines.
AsR 5444

63-103 **8/31/63** 8/31/63 Peking **Mali** Agreement
Cooperation in radio broadcasting
Signed by representatives of Broadcasting Administrative Bureau of China and National Broadcasting Station of Mali.
TYC 12:206(C); JMJP 9/1/63; SCMP 3053:28; AfR 592

63-104 **9/1/63** – – **Sudan** Accord
Establishment of direct telegraphic services between Shanghai and Khartoum
JMJP 9/2/63; JMST 1964, p. 338; CCD 146:86

63-105 **9/5/63** – Karachi **Pakistan** Press Communiqué
Boundary demarcation
Issued after second session of Sino-Pakistani Joint Boundary Demarcation Committee.
JMJP 9/6/63(C); SCMP 3056:33(E)

63-106 **9/11/63** 1/13/64 Algiers **Algeria** Agreement
Cultural cooperation
TYC 12:207(C); JMJP 9/13/63; SCMP 3060:24

63-107 **9/16/63** – – **Pakistan** Accord
Opening of direct telecommunications between Peking and Karachi
JMJP 9/17/63; JMST 1964, p. 337

63-108 **9/23/63** – Peking **Japan** Agreement
Trade in 1963-64 on basis of 1962 Liao-Takasaki Memorandum [62-103]

Communiqué on trade talks also issued 9/23/63. SCMP 3069:24(E); AsR 5515(E, sum.)

JMJP 9/24/63; PR 9/27/63, p. 4; SCMP 3069:24

63-109 **9/27/63** – Pyongyang **Korea (N)** Press Communiqué
Talks during Chairman Liu Shao-ch'i's visit: world communist movement, Sino-Korean relations, etc.

Reaffirms Joint Statement of 6/23/63 [63-82].

TYC 12:46(C); WCC 10:407(C); JMJP 9/28/63(C); JMST 1964, p. 343(C); SCMP 3072:38(E); CCD 96:54(E)

63-110 **9/27/63** – Bamako **Mali** –
1963 plan for cultural cooperation

JMJP 9/30/63; SCMP 3073:46

63-111 **9/30/63** – Karachi **Pakistan** Contract
Exchange of cement from PRC for jute from Pakistan

Joint Communiqué also issued 9/30/63. JMJP 10/9/63; AsR 5541

JMST 1964, p. 337; SCMP 3075:34; AsR 5541

63-112 **10/9/63** – Kabul **Afghanistan** Agreement
Exchange of goods and payments

JMJP 10/11/63; SCMP 3080:19

63-113 **10/9/63** – Kabul **Afghanistan** Protocol
Exchange of goods in 1963-64

JMJP 10/11/63; SCMP 3080:19

63-114 **10/10/63** 1/1/64 Peking **Ceylon** Protocol
Exchange of goods in 1964

Joint Communiqué also issued 10/10/63. SCMP 3080:20(E)

TYC 12:193(C); JMJP 10/11/63; SCMP 3080:20; CTS 1964:2(S,E); AsR 5514

63-115 **10/11/63** – Peking **UK** Accord
Exchange of television films

Signed by representatives of Peking Television Station and British Commonwealth International News Film Agency (and Reuters Ltd).

JMJP 10/12/63; SCMP 3081:23

63-116 **10/11/63** – Algiers **Algeria** Communiqué
PRC grant of long-term interest-free loan to Algeria

PR 10/18/63, p. 3; SCMP 3081:22(E)

63-117 **10/13/63(?)** – Harbin **USSR** Protocol
Border railways

Signed at 1963 session of Sino-Soviet Border Through Railway Traffic Committee.

JMJP 10/15/63; SCMP 3082:35; NYT 10/15/63, p. 8

63-118 **10/14/63** 1/1/64 Pyongyang **Korea (N)** Protocol
Mutual supply of goods in 1964

TYC 12:193(C); JMJP 10/15/63; SCMP 3082:32

63-119 **10/15/63** – Peking **Germany (E)** Protocol
Scientific and technical cooperation

Signed at seventh session of Sino-German Standing Committee for Cooperation in Technology and Technical Sciences.

JMJP 10/17/63; JMST 1964, p. 336; SCMP 3084:26; CCD 146:78; AGF p.56

63-120 **10/15/63** – Peking **Albania** Protocol
Scientific and technical cooperation

Signed at eighth session of Sino-Albanian Joint Committee for Cooperation in Technology and Technical Science.

JMJP 10/18/63; SCMP 3085:21; CCD 146:76

63-121 **10/16/63** – Peking **Indonesia** Exchange of Notes (and supplementary documents)
Economic and technical cooperation

JMJP 10/17/63; JMST 1964, p. 337; SCMP 3084:27; AsR 5514

63-122 **10/23/63** – Peking **Burma** Protocol
Purchase of Burmese rice by PRC in 1964

JMJP 10/24/63; SCMP 3088:22

63-123 **10/24/63** – Hanoi **Vietnam (N)** Protocol
Mutual supply of goods and payments in 1964

JMJP 10/26/63; SCMP 3090:44

63-124 **10/24/63** – Hanoi **Vietnam (N)** Exchange of Notes
Extension of 1955 Protocol on Small-Scale Trading in Border Areas [55-49]

TYC 12:190(C); JMST 1964, p. 335

63-125 **10/24/63** – Hanoi **Vietnam (N)** Exchange of Notes
Extension of 1955 Protocol on Exchange of Goods between Local State Trading Companies in Border Areas [55-48]

TYC 12:192(C); JMST 1964, p. 335

63-126 **10/28/63** 1/1/64 Peking **Finland** Agreement
Trade in 1964

TYC 12:157(C); JMJP 10/24/63; SCMP 3091:29; AsR 5592; H12(3):39(G)

63-127 **10/28/63** – Algiers **Algeria** Agreement
Economic and technical cooperation

JMJP 10/31/63; SCMP 3093:27

63-128 **11/5/63** – Peking **Yugoslavia** Protocol
Exchange of goods in 1963-64

TYC 12:176(C); JMJP 11/6/63; SCMP 3097:43; YTS 1964:885(S-C,E)

63-129 **11/9/63** – Peking **Japan** Agreement
Fishery regulation in Yellow and East China Seas

Signed by representatives of Chinese People's Association for Cultural Relations with Foreign Countries, China-Japan Friendship Association of PRC, China Fishery Association, Japan-China Friendship Association of Japan, and Japan-China Fishery Council of Japan. Parties also signed Appendices CB 724:7(E); and Joint Statement WCC 10:607(C); JMJP 11/10/63(C); JMST 1964, p. 45(C); SCMP 3100:47(E, sum.); CB 724:3(E); CCD 146:80. This agreement replaces 1959 Agreement on Emergency Sheltering of Fishing Vessels [59-100].

TYC 12:254(C); WCC 10:604(C); JMJP 11/10/63(C); JMST 1964, p. 448(C); PR 11/15/63, p. 4; SCMP 3100:46; CB 724:1(E); CCD 111:89(E)

63-130 **11/9/63** – Peking **Japan** Exchange of Letters
Exclusion of Japanese fishing boats from PRC military security areas and conservation zone

See note above.

TYC 12:267(C); JMJP 11/10/63(C); JMST 1964, p. 452(C); SCMP 3100:46; CB 724:4(E); CCD 111:92(E)

63-131 **11/9/63** – Peking **Japan** Exchange of Memoranda
Prevention of fishing disputes in Yellow Sea

TYC 12:270(C); JMJP 11/10/63(C); JMST 1964, p. 453(C); SCMP 3100:46; CB 724:6(E)

63-132 **11/14/63** – – **Cuba** Memorandum
Commodity list of import and export trade in 1964

JMST 1964, p. 336; CCD 146:78

63-133 **11/15/63** – Pyongyang **Korea (N)** Protocol
Border railways

Signed at 1963 session of Sino-Korean Border Railway Joint Committee.

JMST 1964, p. 336; SCMP 3104:27

63-134 **11/15/63** – Havana **Cuba** Protocol
Implementation of 1960 Scientific and Technical Cooperation Agreement [60-82]

Joint Press Communiqué also issued 11/15/63.

JMJP 11/17/63; SCMP 3104:25

63-135 **10/1/63** 11/20/63 Prague **Czechoslovakia** Agreement
11/20/63 Peking
Currency exchange and cash movements

TYC 12:186(C)

63-136 **11/22/63** 11/22/63 Peking **Afghanistan** Treaty
Boundary

TYC 12:122(C); WCC 10:429(C); JMJP 11/23/63(C); JMST 1964, p. 340(C); PR 11/29/63, p. 7(E); SCMP 3109:21(E); CCD 111:88(E, Articles 1 and 2 only); ZD 1963:11-12:1734(P,E); AsR 5579

63-137 **11/24/63** – Peking **Afghanistan** Press Communiqué
Boundary demarcation

Issued after first session of Sino-Afghan Joint Boundary Demarcation Committee.

JMJP 11/25/63; SCMP 3110:23(E, sum.)

63-138 **11/25/63** 11/25/63 Phnom Penh **Cambodia** Agreement
Air transport

TYC 12:236(C); JMJP 11/26/63; PR 11/29/63, p. 5; SCMP 3110:29; AsR 5580

63-139 **11/25/63** – Changchun **Korea (N)** Protocol
Cooperation in exploiting and utilizing the Yalu and Tumen Rivers in 1964

Signed at third session of Sino-Korean Joint Committee on Cooperation in Navigation on the Yalu and Tumen Rivers.

JMJP 11/26/63; JMST 1964, p. 336; SCMP 3110:36; CCD 146:78

63-140 **11/26/63** – Sofia **Bulgaria** Protocol
Scientific and technical cooperation

Signed at seventh session of Sino-Bulgarian Joint Committee for Scientific and Technical Cooperation.

JMJP 11/28/63; SCMP 3111:28

63-141 **11/26/63** 11/26/63 Phnom Penh **Cambodia** Protocol
Agency business and reciprocal services in civil aviation

Signed by representatives of PRC General Bureau of Civil Aviation and Royal Cambodian Airline Company.

TYC 12:242(C); JMJP 11/28/63; SCMP 3111:29

63-142 **11/28/63** – – **Indonesia** Accord
Joint filming and production of color documentary film of first Games of Newly Emerging Forces (GANEFO), to be held in Djakarta

Film released in March 1964. SCMP 3175:28, 3176:21

JMST 1964, p. 337; CCD 146:82

63-143 **11/29/63** – Peking **USSR** –
1963-64 plan for cooperation between Academies of Sciences
JMJP 11/30/63; SCMP 3112:31

63-144 **12/6/63** – Tirana **Albania** Protocol
Exchange of goods and payments in 1964
JMJP 12/10/63(C); PR 12/13/63, p. 4; SCMP 3118:22

63-145 **12/6/63** – Tirana **Albania** Protocol
Albania's use of PRC loan in 1964
JMJP 12/10/63; PR 12/13/63, p. 4; SCMP 3118:22

63-146 **12/6/63** – Tirana **Albania** Joint Communiqué
Trade talks
JMST 1964, p. 335; PR 12/13/63, p. 4; SCMP 3118:22; CCD 146:76

63-147 **12/11/63** – Peking **Afghanistan** Press Communiqué
Talks concerning establishment of air services
JMJP 12/12/63(C); SCMP 3120:25(E); AsR 5630

63-148 **12/11/63** – Budapest **Hungary** Protocol
Scientific and technical cooperation
Signed at eighth session of Sino-Hungarian Joint Committee for Scientific and Technical Cooperation. Communiqué also issued. JMJP 12/13/63(C)
JMJP 12/13/63; SCMP 3121:24

63-149 **12/21/63** – Cairo **UAR** Joint Communiqué
Talks during Premier Chou En-lai's visit: Bandung principles, anti-imperialism, disarmament, Sino-Indian border dispute, Palestine Arabs, Taiwan, PRC representation in UN, etc.
TYC 12:20(C); WCC 10:459(C); JMJP 12/23/63(C); JMST 1964, p. 369(C); PR 12/27/63, p. 9(E); SCMP 3128:34(E); CCD 116:44(E); ZD 1964:1:88(P,E); ADTJ 1486:1(Fr); AsR 5892(E)

63-150 **12/27/63** – Algiers **Algeria** Joint Communiqué
Talks during Premier Chou En-lai's visit: Korea, Palestine Arabs, foreign aid, disarmament, five principles of peaceful coexistence, ten Bandung principles, etc.
TYC 12:13(C); WCC 10:477(C); JMJP 12/29/63(C); JMST 1964, p. 378(C); PR 1/3/64, p. 31(E); SCMP 3131:25(E); ZD 1964:1:102(P,E); ADTJ 1486:3(Fr); AsR 5892(E, abbrev.)

63-151 **12/27/63** 1/1/64 Peking **Rumania** Agreement
Exchange of goods and payments in 1964
TYC 12:149(C); JMJP 12/28/63(C); PR 1/10/64, p. 5; SCMP 3130:40

63-152 **12/27/63** – Peking **Rumania** Protocol
Extension of Protocol on General Conditions for Delivery of Goods in 1961 [61-94]
TYC 12:153(C); JMST 1964, p. 336

63-153 **12/30/63** – Bamako **Mali** Protocol (supplementary)
Economic and technical cooperation
JMJP 1/1/64; SCMP 3133:44

63-154 **12/31/63** – Rabat **Morocco** Joint Communiqué
Talks during Premier Chou En-lai's visit: peaceful coexistence, disarmament, PRC representation in UN, abolition of foreign military bases, Palestine Arabs, etc.
TYC 12:59(C); WCC 10:482(C); JMJP 1/1/64(C); JMST 1964, p. 383(C); PR 1/3/64, p. 33(E); SCMP 3132:47(E); ZD 1964:1:111(P,E); ADTJ 1486:5(Fr); AsR 5892

1964

64-1 **Jan.** – – **Syria** Accord
Establishment of telecommunications between Peking and Damascus
JMJP 1/9/64

64-2 **Jan.** – Mexico City **Mexico** Contract
Exchange of films
Signed by representatives of China Film Distribution and Exhibition Company and Mexico Film Company.
SCMP 3141:25

64-3 **1/2/64** 1/2/64 Peking **Albania** Agreement
Cooperation in public health work
TYC 13:349(C); JMJP 1/4/64; SCMP 3134:24

64-4 **1/7/64** 1/1/64 Conakry **Guinea** Protocol
Trade in 1964
TYC 13:259(C); JMJP 1/9/64; SCMP 3137:31

64-5 **1/8/64** – Tirana **Albania** Joint Statement
Talks during Premier Chou En-lai's visit: anti-imperialism, revisionism, etc.
TYC 13:41(C); JMJP 1/11/64(C); JMST 1964, p. 356(C); PR 1/17/64, p. 13(E); SCMP 3139:17(E); CCD 116:50(E, abbrev.); ADTJ 1493:3(Fr); AsR 5641

64-6 **1/9/64** – Budapest **Hungary** Exchange of Notes
Extension of 1953 Agreement on Scientific and Technical Cooperation [53-56]
TYC 13:338(C)

64-7 **1/10/64** – Tunis **Tunisia** Joint Communiqué
Talks during Premier Chou En-lai's visit: Palestine Arabs, five principles of peaceful coexistence, disarmament, etc.

TYC 13:60(C); JMJP 1/12/64(C); JMST 1964, p. 385(C); PR 1/17/64, p. 24(E); SCMP 3139:43(E); CCD 116:60(E); ZD 1964:1:116(P,E); ADTJ 1493:6(Fr); AsR 5893

64-8 **1/14/64** – Havana **Cuba** Protocol
1964-65 plan for cultural cooperation

JMJP 1/17/64; SCMP 3142:16

64-9 **1/15/64** – Havana **Cuba** Protocol
Exchange of goods and payments in 1964

Press Communiqué also issued 1/16/64. JMJP 1/19/64(C); SCMP 3143:25(E, sum.); JPRS 28416 (Translations on Cuba, No. 235)(E); CCD 146:79

JMJP 1/17/64, p. 4; SCMP 3143:24

64-10 **1/16/64** – Accra **Ghana** Joint Communiqué
Talks during Premier Chou En-lai's visit: peaceful coexistence, disarmament, Sino-Indian dispute, Taiwan, etc.

TYC 13:22(C); JMJP 1/17/64(C); JMST 1964, p. 388(C); PR 1/24/64, p. 13(E); SCMP 3143:33(E); ZD 1964:1:119(P,E); ADTJ 1497:1(Fr); AsR 5893

64-11 **1/16/64** 10/30/63 Peking **Germany (E)** Protocol
Extension and amendment of 1953 Agreement on Cooperation in Technology and Technical Science [53-63]

TYC 13:346(C); AGF p. 56; Dok 12:726

64-12 **1/17/64** – Ulan Bator **Mongolia** Protocol
Scientific and technical cooperation

Signed at second meeting of Sino-Mongolian Executive Organ for Scientific and Technical Cooperation.

JMJP 1/19/64; SCMP 3144:39

64-13 **1/20/64** 1/1/64 Peking **Mongolia** Protocol
Mutual supply of goods in 1964

TYC 13:315(C); JMJP 1/22/64; SCMP 3145:27

64-14 **1/21/64** – Bamako **Mali** Joint Communiqué
Talks during Premier Chou En-lai's visit: foreign aid, national liberation movements, etc.

Enumerates eight principles of PRC's foreign aid policy.

TYC 13:11(C); JMJP 1/22/64(C); JMST 1964, p. 393(C); PR 1/31/64, p. 8(E); SCMP 3146:28(E); CCD 116:62(E, abbrev.); ZD 1964:1:129(P,E); ADTJ 1497:3(Fr); AsR 5893

64-15 **1/23/64** – Bucharest **Rumania** –
1964-65 plan for cultural cooperation

JMJP 1/25/64; SCMP 3148:47

64-16 **1/24/64** – Hanoi **Multilateral** Protocol
1964 plan for cooperation in railway transport

Signed at 1964 session of eastern section of railway transport committee of Railway Cooperation Organization of Socialist Countries, attended by delegates from Mongolia, Korea (N), Vietnam (N), and USSR. Meeting also adopted various supplementary documents on technical measures for fulfillment of transport plan.

SCMP 3149:34

64-17 **1/26/64** – Conakry **Guinea** Joint Communiqué
Talks during Premier Chou En-lai's visit: international situation, anticolonialism, Sino-Indian dispute, etc.

TYC 13:1(C); JMJP 1/29/64(C); JMST 1964, p. 396(C); PR 2/7/64, p. 26(E); SCMP 3152:26(E); ZD 1964:1:138(P,E); ADTJ 1502:1(Fr); AsR 5893

64-18 **1/28/64** – Djakarta **Indonesia** Contract
Implementation of 1961 Agreement on Economic and Technical Cooperation [61-134]

Signed by representatives of China Complete Set Equipment Export Company and Indonesian Team for Implementation of PRC Loans.

JMST 1964, p. 337; SCMP 3153:30; CCD 146:82

64-19 **1/30/64** – Khartoum **Sudan** Joint Communiqué
Talks during Premier Chou En-lai's visit: Palestine Arabs, PRC representation in UN, etc.

TYC 13:35(C); JMJP 1/31/64(C); JMST 1964, p. 402(C); PR 2/7/64, p. 30(E); SCMP 3153:40(E); ZD 1964:1:147(P,E); ADTJ 1502(Fr); AsR 5893

64-20 **1/31/64** 1/31/64 Peking **Hungary** Agreement
Cooperation in radio and television broadcasting

TYC 13:327(C); JMJP 2/1/64; SCMP 3153:30

64-21 **2/1/64** – Asmara **Ethiopia** Joint Communiqué
Talks during Premier Chou En-lai's visit: Second Afro-Asian Conference, disarmament, PRC representation in UN, normalization of Sino-Ethiopian relations, etc.

TYC 13:68(C); JMJP 2/2/64(C); JMST 1964, p. 404(C); PR 2/7/64, p. 31(E); SCMP 3154:34(E); CCD 116:66(E); ZD 1964:2:275(P,E); ADTJ 1502:4(Fr); AfR 723(E, sum.)

64-22 **2/4/64** – Mogadishu **Somalia** Joint Communiqué
Talks during Premier Chou En-lai's visit: African unity, etc.

TYC 13:66(C); JMJP 2/5/64(C); JMST 1964, p. 406(C); PR 2/14/64, p. 17(E); SCMP 3157:38(E); ZD 1964:2:280(P,E); ADTJ 1510:1(Fr)

64-23 2/5/64 – Peking **Poland** Agreement
Transfer of goods and payments in 1964
JMJP 2/7/64; SCMP 3157:30; CCD 146:79

64-24 2/5/64 – Accra **Ghana** Protocol
Exchange of goods in 1964
TYC 13:267(C); JMST 1964, p. 339(C)

64-25 2/6/64 – Peking **Vietnam (N)** Agreement
Cooperation between PRC Academy of Sciences and State Commission of Sciences and Technology of Vietnam (N)
JMJP 2/7/64; SCMP 3158:37

64-26 2/6/64 – Peking **Vietnam (N)** –
1964 plan for cooperation between PRC Academy of Sciences and State Commission of Sciences and Technology of Vietnam (N)
JMJP 2/7/64; SCMP 3158:37

64-27 2/17/64 – Karachi **Pakistan** Joint Communiqué
Boundary demarcation
Signed at third session of Sino-Pakistani Joint Boundary Demarcation Committee.
JMJP 2/19/64; SCMP 3164:35; AsR 5730

64-28 2/18/64 – Rangoon **Burma** Joint Communiqué
Talks during Premier Chou En-lai's visit: PRC representation in UN; Sino-Indian dispute, etc.
TYC 13:70(C); JMJP 2/19/64(C); JMST 1964, p. 414(C); PR 2/21/64, p. 7(E); SCMP 3164:28(E); CCD 116:67(E); ZD 1964:2:285(P,E); AsR 5759(E)

64-29 2/23/64 – Rawalpindi **Pakistan** Joint Communiqué
Talks during Premier Chou En-lai's visit: PRC representation in UN, Sino-Indian dispute, Kashmir, etc.
TYC 13:20(C); JMJP 2/25/64(C); JMST 1964, p. 416(C); PR 2/28/64, p. 8(E); SCMP 3167:35(E); CCD 116:71(E); ZD 1964:2:293(P,E); AsR 5729(E)

64-30 2/28/64 – Peking **Ceylon** Contract
Sale of cotton to Ceylon
JMJP 2/29/64; PR 3/6/64, p. 4; SCMP 3170:28

64-31 2/28/64 – Peking **Ceylon** Exchange of Notes
Economic cooperation and development of trade
JMST 1964, p. 338; SCMP 3170:28; CCD 146:84

64-32 **2/29/64** – Colombo **Ceylon** Joint Communiqué
Talks during Premier Chou En-lai's visit: PRC representation in UN, Taiwan, disarmament, Second Afro-Asian Conference, etc.

PRC agreed to provide additional economic aid to Ceylon.

TYC 13:75(C); JMJP 3/2/64(C); JMST 1964, p. 421(C); PR 3/6/64, p. 17(E); SCMP 3171:37(E); CCD 119:116; ZD 1964:2:297(P,E); AsR 5893

64-33 **2/29/64** – Moscow **USSR** –
1964 plan for cultural cooperation

JMJP 3/2/64; SCMP 3171:49; Izv 3/1/64; AsR 5748

64-34 **3/5/64** – Peking **Albania** Agreement
Agricultural cooperation

JMJP 3/7/64; SCMP 3175:34; PI(H) 1964:6:166

64-35 **3/8/64** – Peking **Pakistan** Protocol (and related documents)
Opening of direct air services

One of these documents has been described as an agreement on technical and business arrangements for direct air services between the airlines of PRC and Pakistan. CCD 146:83

JMJP 3/9/64; PR 3/20/64, p. 5; SCMP 3176:30; AsR 5731

64-36 **3/9/64** – Hanoi **Vietnam (N)** Protocol
Border railways

Signed at seventh session of Sino-Vietnamese Joint Committee on Border Railways.

JMJP 3/11/64; SCMP 3178:28; PI(H) 1964:6:166

64-37 **3/15/64** – Karachi **Pakistan** Press Communiqué
Boundary demarcation

Issued after third session of Sino-Pakistani Joint Boundary Demarcation Committee.

JMJP 3/17/64; SCMP 3182:35; CCD 146:83

64-38 **3/21/64** – Sofia **Bulgaria** –
1964 plan for cultural cooperation

JMJP 3/24/64; SCMP 3186:23

64-39 **3/24/64** – Budapest **Hungary** –
1964 plan for cultural cooperation

JMJP 3/25/64; SCMP 3188:26

64-40 **3/25/64** – Peking **Albania** Accord
Cooperation between PRC Academy of Sciences and State University of Tirana

JMJP 3/27/64; SCMP 3189:28

64-41 **3/25/64** – Peking **Albania** –
1964-65 plan for cooperation between PRC Academy of Sciences and State University of Tirana

JMJP 3/27/64; SCMP 3189:28

64-42 **3/28/64** 1/1/64 Peking **Hungary** Agreement
Exchange of goods and payments in 1964

TYC 13:274(C); JMJP 3/29/64; PR 4/3/64, p. 4; SCMP 3190:28

64-43 **3/30/64** – Peking **Poland** –
1963-64 plan for cooperation between Academies of Sciences

JMJP 4/1/64; SCMP 3191:27

64-44 **4/8/64** – Peking **Laos** Joint Communiqué
Talks during Premier Souvanna Phouma's visit: 1962 Geneva Agreement on Laos, support for conference to guarantee neutrality of Cambodia, etc.

TYC 13:31(C); JMJP 4/9/64(C); JMST 1964, p. 457(C); PR 4/10/64, p. 10(E); SCMP 3197:19(E); ADTJ 1525:1(Fr); AsR 5816

64-45 **4/11/64** – Cairo **UAR** –
1964-65 plan for cultural cooperation

JMJP 4/15/64; SCMP 3200:34; AsR 5844

64-46 **4/14/64** 1/1/64 Sofia **Bulgaria** Agreement
Exchange of goods and payments in 1964

TYC 13:301(C); JMJP 4/27/64

64-47 **4/14/64** – Peking **Algeria** –
1964 plan for cultural cooperation

JMJP 4/15/64; SCMP 3201:19

64-48 **4/14/64** 4/14/64 Peking **Algeria** Agreement
Cooperation in radio and television broadcasting

TYC 13:329(C); SCMP 3201:19

64-49 **4/15/64** – Djakarta **Multilateral** Final Communiqué
Preparatory meeting of Second Afro-Asian Conference

Meeting attended by delegates from Afghanistan, Algeria, Cambodia, Cameroon, Ceylon, Ethiopia, Ghana, Guinea, India, Indonesia, Iran, Iraq, Liberia, Morocco, Nepal, Pakistan, Philippines, Syria, and Tanzania.

JMJP 4/17/64(C); ZD 1964:4-5:765(P,E)

64-50 **4/18/64** – Peking **Korea (N)** –
1964-65 plan for cultural cooperation

JMJP 4/19/64; SCMP 3204:45

64-51 **4/19/64** – Peking **Japan** Minutes
Talks between staffs of Liao Cheng-chih and Tatsunosuke Takasaki: trade based on Liao-Takasaki Memorandum [62-103]
JMJP 4/20/64(C); SCMP 3205:28

64-52 **4/19/64** – Peking **Japan** Minutes
Talks between staffs of Liao Cheng-chih and Tatsunosuke Takasaki: exchange of correspondents
TYC 13:391; JMJP 4/20/64(C); JMST 1964, p. 454(C); SCMP 3205:27(E, sum.)

64-53 **4/19/64** – Peking **Japan** Minutes
Talks between staffs of Liao Cheng-chih and Tatsunosuke Takasaki: exchange of representatives and setting up of liaison offices
TYC 13:386(C); JMJP 4/20/64(C); JMST 1964, p. 454(C); SCMP 3205:27(E, sum.)

64-54 **4/24/64** – Peking **Czechoslovakia** Agreement
Exchange of goods and payments in 1964
JMJP 4/27/64; SCMP 3208:34; AsR 5844

64-55 **4/26/64** – Bamako **Mali** –
1964 plan for cultural cooperation
JMST 1964, p. 338; SCMP 3209:34

64-56 **4/27/64** – Katmandu **Nepal** Protocol (supplementary)
Amendment of 1960 Economic Aid Agreement [60-48]
Substitutes highway and other projects for those stipulated in 1961 Economic Aid Protocol [61-118].
JMJP 4/30/64; SCMP 3210:33; AsR 5819

64-57 **4/27/64** – Hanoi **Vietnam (N)** Contract
Books and periodicals trade in 1964-65
Signed by representatives of PRC publication trade delegation and Vietnam Publications Import and Export Company.
JMST 1964, p. 335; SCMP 3210:38

64-58 **4/29/64** – Peking **Korea (N)** –
1964 plan for cooperation between Academies of Sciences
JMJP 4/30/64; SCMP 3211:26

64-59 **4/29/64** – Peking **Vietnam (N)** Accord (supplementary)
1964 plan for cultural cooperation
JMJP 4/30/64; SCMP 3211:34

64-60 **5/6/64** – Canton **Netherlands** Exchange of Letters
Promotion of economic and trade relations

Signed by representatives of China Committee for Promotion of International Trade, and of Netherlands Central Council for Trade Promotion and Netherlands trade delegation.

JMJP 5/7/64; JMST 1964, p. 339; SCMP 3216:24

64-61 **5/9/64** – Peking **Indonesia** Joint Communiqué
Olympic Games

Signed by representatives of Physical Culture and Sports Committee of PRC and Physical Culture Ministry of Indonesia. Denounces action of International Olympic Committee against Indonesia, and upholds Games of Newly Emerging Forces (GANEFO).

JMST 1964, p. 337; SCMP 3218:21(E); CCD 146:83

64-62 **5/9/64** – Peking **Korea (N)** Agreement
Technical cooperation

JMJP 5/10/64; SCMP 3218:26

64-63 **4/20/64** – Khartoum **Sudan** Exchange of Notes
5/9/64
Amendment to 1962 Trade Agreement [62-49]

TYC 13:286(C)

64-64 **5/10/64** – Peking **Kenya** Agreement
Economic and technical cooperation

JMJP 5/11/64; SCMP 3219:31; PI(H) 1964:7:284; AfR 804

64-65 **5/12/64** – Peking **Mali** Protocol (supplementary)
Exchange of goods and payments

JMJP 5/13/64; SCMP 3220:28; CCD 146:87

64-66 **5/12/64** – Conakry **Guinea** –
1964 plan for cultural cooperation

JMJP 5/15/64; SCMP 3221:16

64-67 **5/13/64** – Peking **Indonesia** Joint Communiqué
Scientific and technical cooperation

Signed by representatives of Science and Technology Committee of PRC and Indonesian Ministry of National Scientific Research.

TYC 13:339(C); SCMP 3222:18; CCD 146:83

64-68 **5/13/64** – Peking **USSR** Protocol
Exchange of goods in 1964

JMJP 5/14/64; PR 5/22/64, p. 4; SCMP 3223:42; AsR 5906

64-69 **5/15/64** – Katmandu **Nepal** Exchange of Letters
Boundary demarcation procedures

AsR 5864

64-70 **5/13/64(?)** – Peking **USSR** Protocol
Trade payments

PRC uses favorable balance of trade in 1963 to pay 1960 trade arrears ahead of due date in 1965.

JMJP 5/17/64; SCMP 3223:42

64-71 **5/18/64** – Warsaw **Poland** –
1964 plan for cultural cooperation

JMJP 5/19/64; SCMP 3224:36

64-72 **5/19/64** – Peking **Sudan** Joint Communiqué
Talks during President Ibrahim Abboud's visit: Second Afro-Asian Conference, PRC representation in UN, etc.

TYC 13:38(C); JMJP 5/20/64(C); JMST 1964, p. 468(C); PR 5/22/64, p. 6(E); SCMP 3225:28(E); PI(H) 1964:7:285

64-73 **5/19/64** – Katmandu **Nepal** Agreement
Trade

Protocol also signed (in accordance with provision of Article VI of Agreement), and Communique issued.

JMJP 5/21/64; JMST 1964, p. 337; SCMP 3226:34; CCD 146:84; AsR 5874

64-74 **5/23/64** – Tirana **Albania** Protocol
Shipping

Signed at third meeting of Administrative Council of Sino-Albanian Shipping Joint Stock Company.

JMST 1964, p. 335; SCMP 3228:22

64-75 **5/25/64** – Peking **Iraq** –
1964-65 plan for cultural cooperation

JMJP 5/26/64; SCMP 3228:31

64-76 **5/27/64** – Peking **Czechoslovakia** –
1964 plan for cultural cooperation

JMJP 5/29/64; SCMP 3229:31

64-77 **6/9/64** – Peking **Yemen** Joint Communiqué
Talks during President Abdullah Al Sallal's visit: international situation, PRC representation in UN, etc.

TYC 13:6(C); JMJP 6/15/64(C); JMST 1964, p. 465(C); PR 6/19/64, p. 11(E); SCMP 3241:35(E); CCD 125:59(E); AsR 5925(E, abbrev.)

64-78 **6/9/64** 6/9/64 Peking **Yemen** Treaty
Friendship

Replaces 1958 Treaty of Friendship [58-3].

TYC 13:5(C); YHTY 51(C,A); JMJP 6/15/64(C); JMST 1964, p. 341(C); PR 6/19/64, p. 10(E); SCMP 3241:38(E); ZD 1964:6:944(P,E); PI(H) 1964:7:286; AsR 5925

64-79 **6/9/64** – Peking **Yemen** Agreement
Economic and technical cooperation
JMJP 6/10/64; PR 6/19/64, p. 13; SCMP 3237:32; AsR 5925

64-80 **6/9/64** 9/10/64 Peking **Yemen** Agreement
Cultural cooperation
TYC 13:323(C); JMJP 6/10/64; PR 6/19/64, p. 13; SCMP 3237:32; AsR 5925

64-81 **6/10/64** – Pyongyang **Korea (N)** Protocol
Maritime transport
Signed by representatives of Ocean Transport Company of PRC and Foreign Transport Company of Korea (N).
JMJP 6/12/64; SCMP 3239:26

64-82 **6/11/64** 10/21/64 Belgrade **Yugoslavia** Protocol
Exchange of goods in 1964
TYC 13:308(C); YTS 1965:2:127(S-C,E); WGO 7:159

64-83 **6/14/64** – – **Mongolia** Minutes
Talks on boundary demarcation
Signed at third session of the Sino-Mongolian Joint Boundary Demarcation Committee.
JMJP 6/15/64; SCMP 3241:28; CCD 146:79

64-84 **6/15/64** – Colombo **Ceylon** Exchange of Letters
Conversion of PRC loan of 1958 into interest-free loan [58-83; 62-76]
JMJP 6/16/64; SCMP 3242:23

64-85 **6/16/64** – Peking **Tanganyika and Zanzibar (Tanzania)** Agreement
Economic and technical cooperation
JMJP 6/17/64; SCMP 3242:33; PI(H) 1964:7:286

64-86 **6/17/64** – Peking **Mongolia** –
1964 plan for cultural cooperation
JMJP 6/18/64; SCMP 3243:26

64-87 **6/18/64** 11/25/64 Warsaw **Poland** Protocol
Extension of 1954 Scientific and Technical Cooperation Agreement [54-47]
TYC 13:343(C); JMJP 6/22/64; SCMP 3245:39

64-88 **6/18/64** – Warsaw **Poland** Protocol
Scientific and technical cooperation
Signed at eleventh session of Sino-Polish Joint Standing Committee for Scientific and Technical Cooperation.
JMJP 6/22/64; SCMP 3245:39

64-89 **6/19/64** – Peking **Tanganyika and Zanzibar (Tanzania)** Joint Communiqué
Talks during Second Vice-President Rashidi Mfaume Kawawa's visit: anti-imperialism, Laos, etc.

Enumerates eight principles of PRC's foreign aid policy.

TYC 13:56(C); JMJP 6/22/64(C); JMST 1964, p. 474(C); PR 6/26/64, p. 12(E); SCMP 3246:32(E)

64-90 **6/30/64** 6/30/64 Ulan Bator **Mongolia** Protocol
Boundary demarcation

TYC 13:78(C); JMJP 7/3/64; CCD 146:79

64-91 **7/5/64** – Bucharest **Rumania** Protocol
Scientific and technical cooperation

Signed at ninth session of Sino-Rumanian Joint Committee for Scientific and Technical Cooperation.

JMJP 7/8/64; JMST 1965, p. 227; SCMP 3255:37

64-92 **7/7/64** – – **Ceylon** Agreement
PRC gift of passenger trains and trucks to Ceylon

JMST 1965, p. 229

64-93 **7/9/64** – Berlin **Germany (E)** Protocol
Scientific and technical cooperation

Signed at eighth meeting of Sino-German Standing Committee for Cooperation in Technology and Technical Sciences.

JMJP 7/12/64; SCMP 3258:28

64-94 **7/11/64** – Brazzaville **Congo (Brazzaville)** Agreement
Grant of interest-free loan by PRC to Congo (Br.)

JMST 1965, p. 230; SCMP 3261:26

64-95 **7/11/64** – Rangoon **Burma** Joint Communiqué
Talks during Premier Chou En-lai's visit: support for reconvening Geneva Conference on Laotian problem, Sino-Burmese relations, etc.

TYC 13:74(C); JMJP 7/13/64(C); JMST 1965, p. 307(C); SCMP 3259:25; AsR 5695(E)

64-96 **7/15/64** – Algiers **Algeria** Agreement
Cooperation between New China News Agency and Algerian Press Service

JMJP 7/17/64; PR 8/21/64, p. 6; SCMP 3262:26

64-97 **7/15/64** – Accra **Ghana** Protocol (supplementary)
Economic and technical cooperation

PRC grants new interest-free loan within period of Ghana's first seven-year development plan (1963-70) in addition to long-term interest-free loan stipulated in 1961 Agreement on Economic and Technical Cooperation [61-109].

JMJP 7/17/64; PR 8/21/64, p. 6; SCMP 3262:28

64-98 **7/17/64** – Accra **Ghana** –
1964-65 plan for cultural cooperation
JMJP 7/22/64; SCMP 3263:37

64-99 **7/17/64** – Peking **Pakistan** Communiqué
Economic and trade talks
JMST 1965, p. 228; SCMP 3263:38(E)

64-100 **7/23/64** 7/23/64 Brazzaville **Congo (Brazzaville)** Agreement
Trade and payments
TYC 13:281(C); JMJP 7/25/64; PR 8/21/64, p. 6; SCMP 3268:28; AfR 903

64-101 **7/23/64** – Karachi **Pakistan** Agreement
Friendship and cooperation between New China News Agency and Associated Press of Pakistan
Also referred to as "agreement on exchange of news." JMJP 8/11/64
JMST 1965, p. 228; SCMP 3268:38

64-102 **7/29/64** 10/1/64 Hanoi **Vietnam (N)** Agreement
Postal services
TYC 13:352(C); JMJP 7/31/64; SCMP 3272:29

64-103 **7/29/64** 10/1/64 Hanoi **Vietnam (N)** Agreement
Telecommunications
TYC 13:358(C); JMJP 7/31/64; SCMP 3272:29

64-104 **7/30/64** – Accra **Ghana** Agreement
News exchange between New China News Agency and Ghana News Agency
JMJP 8/5/64; SCMP 3272:18

64-105 **7/31/64** 7/31/64 Peking **Vietnam (N)** Agreement
Cooperation in public health work
TYC 13:347(C); JMST 1965, p. 226; SCMP 3273:39

64-106 **8/1/64** 1/1/64 Berlin **Germany (E)** Agreement
Exchange of goods and payments in 1964
TYC 13:319(C); JMJP 8/4/64; SCMP 3274:24; AGF p. 57; Dok 12:1150

64-107 **8/5/64** 8/5/64 Conakry **Guinea** Agreement
Cooperation in radio broadcasting

Signed by representatives of Broadcasting Administrative Bureau of PRC and National Radio Diffusion of Guinea.

TYC 13:322(C); JMJP 8/16/64; PR 8/21/64, p. 6; SCMP 3276:22

64-108 **8/11/64** – Havana **Cuba** Protocol
Economic cooperation

JMJP 8/16/64; PR 8/21/64, p. 6; SCMP 3280:21; JPRS 31276, p. 24 (Translations on Cuba, No. 285)(E)

64-109 **8/12/64** – Peking **Vietnam (N)** Protocol
Scientific and technical cooperation

Signed at fourth session of Sino-Vietnamese Executive Organ for Scientific and Technical Cooperation.

JMJP 8/13/64; SCMP 3280:25

64-110 **8/24/64** – Peking **UAR** Joint Communiqué
Scientific and technical cooperation

Issued by Science and Technology Committee of PRC and UAR Ministry of Scientific Research.

TYC 13:341(C); JMJP 8/25/64; SCMP 3288:40

64-111 **8/31/64** – Conakry **Guinea** Contract
Distribution of PRC films in Guinea

Signed by representatives of China Film Distribution and Exhibition Company and National Office of Cinematography of Guinean Ministry of Information and Tourism.

SCMP 3295:22

64-112 **8/31/64** – Conakry **Guinea** Contract
Exchange of newsreel materials

See note above.

SCMP 3295:22

64-113 **9/2/64** – Peking **Germany (E)** –
1964 plan for cultural cooperation

JMJP 9/4/64; SCMP 3295:22; AGF p. 57; Dok 12:1154

64-114 **9/10/64** – – **Multilateral** Protocol
Passenger train time schedule

Signed by delegates from Korea (N), Mongolia, and USSR.

JMJP 9/12/64; SCMP 3299:31

64-115 **9/12/64** – Kirin **Korea (N)** Protocol
Border railway

Signed at 1964 meeting of Sino-Korean Border Railway Joint Committee.

JMJP 9/13/64; SCMP 3299:30

64-116 **9/12/64** – Hanoi **Vietnam (N)** Protocol
Civil aviation
JMJP 9/14/64; SCMP 3300:33

64-117 **9/13/64** – Cotonou **Dahomey** Joint Communiqué
Talks during visit of PRC governament goodwill delegation: development of economic, technical, and cultural cooperation
JMST 1965, p. 230; PR 9/18/64, p. 29(E, sum.); SCMP 3301:20(E)

64-118 **9/19/64** 9/19/64 Peking **Algeria** Agreement
Trade
TYC 13:287(C); JMJP 9/20/64; PR 9/25/64, p. 3; SCMP 3304:21; AsR 6136

64-119 **9/19/64** 9/19/64 Peking **Algeria** Agreement
Payments
TYC 13:293(C); JMJP 9/20/64; PR 9/25/64, p. 3; SCMP 3304:21; AsR 6136

64-120 **9/19/64** – Peking **Algeria** Protocol
Economic and technical cooperation
JMJP 9/20/64; PR 9/25/64, p. 3; SCMP 3304:21; AsR 6136

64-121 **9/22/64** – Accra **Ghana** Contract
Exchange of short films
Signed by representatives of China Film Distribution and Exhibition Company and Ghana Film Industry Corporation.
JMST 1965, p. 230; SCMP 3306:27

64-122 **9/22/64** – Accra **Ghana** Contract
Exchange of newsreel materials
See note above.
JMST 1965, p. 230; SCMP 3306:27

64-123 **9/23/64** 12/20/64 Peking **Iraq** Agreement
Trade
TYC 13:277(C); JMJP 9/24/64; SCMP 3306:29

64-124 **9/24/64** – Yaounde **Cameroon** Joint Communiqué
Talks during visit of PRC government goodwill delegation: development of economic, technical, and cultural cooperation
JMST 1965, p. 230; SCMP 3308:32(E, abbrev.)

64-125 **9/24/64** – Sofia **Bulgaria** –
1964-65 plan for cooperation between Academies of Sciences
JMST 1965, p. 226; SCMP 3307:22

64-126 **9/24/64** 1/1/65 Peking **Korea (N)** Protocol
Mutual supply of goods in 1965

TYC 13:313(C); JMJP 9/25/64; SCMP 3307:33

64-127 **9/28/64** – Peking **Czechoslovakia** Protocol
Scientific and technical cooperation

Signed at eleventh session of Sino-Czechoslovak Joint Committee for Scientific and Technical Cooperation.

JMJP 9/29/64; SCMP 3310:27

64-128 **9/29/64** 9/29/64 Bangui **Central African Republic** Agreement
Economic and technical cooperation

Parties also issued Joint Communiqué 9/29/64, announcing establishment of diplomatic relations and joint subscription to five principles of peaceful coexistence in accordance with Notes exchanged 8/27/64. SCMP 3313:31(E)

TYC 13:260(C); SCMP 3381:25

64-129 **9/29/64** 4/1/65 Bangui **Central African Republic** Agreement
Cultural cooperation

See note above.

TYC 13:383(C); SCMP 3313:32

64-130 **9/29/64** 9/29/64 Bangui **Central African Republic** Agreement
Exchange of goods and payments

See note above.

TYC 13:262(C); SCMP 3313:32

64-131 **9/30/64** – Peking **Vietnam (N)** Protocol
Mutual supply of goods and payments in 1965

JMJP 10/1/64; SCMP 3313:53

64-132 **9/30/64** – Peking **Vietnam (N)** Exchange of Notes
Extension of 1955 Protocol on Small-Scale Trading in Border Areas [55-49]

TYC 13:310(C);

64-133 **9/30/64** – Peking **Vietnam (N)** Exchange of Notes
Extension of 1955 Protocol on Exchange of Goods between Local State Trading Companies in Border Areas [55-48]

TYC 13:312(C)

64-134 **10/2/64** – Peking **Kenya** Press Communiqué
Trade talks

JMST 1965, p. 231; SCMP 3313:45(E)

64-135 **10/2/64** 1/9/65 Peking **Congo (Brazzaville)** Treaty
Friendship

TYC 13:27(C); YHTY 65(C,Fr); JMJP 1/11/65(C); JMST 1965, p. 232(C); PR 1/15/65, p. 18(E); SCMP 3377:27(E); CCD 143:43(E); ADTJ 1636:1(Fr); WGO 7:277

64-136 **10/2/64** 10/2/64 Peking **Congo (Brazzaville)** Agreement
Maritime transport

TYC 13:366(C); JMJP 10/3/64; PR 10/9/64, p. 14; SCMP 3313:34; AfR 936

64-137 **10/2/64** – Peking **Congo (Brazzaville)** Agreement
Economic and technical cooperation

JMJP 10/3/64; PR 10/9/64, p. 14; SCMP 3313:34; AfR 936

64-138 **10/2/64** – Peking **Congo (Brazzaville)** Agreement
Cultural cooperation

JMJP 10/3/64; PR 10/9/64, p. 15; SCMP 3313:34; AfR 936

64-139 **10/3/64** – Peking **Congo (Brazzaville)** Joint Communiqué
Talks during President Massamba-Debat's visit: support for Second Conference of Non-Aligned Countries, Second Afro-Asian Conference, etc.

TYC 13:28(C); JMJP 10/4/64(C); JMST 1965, p. 366(C); PR 10/9/64, p. 14(E); SCMP 3314:20(E); ADTJ 1602:1(Fr); AfR 936

64-140 **10/3/64** 10/3/64 Peking **Rumania** Agreement
Cooperation in radio and television broadcasting

TYC 13:331(C); JMJP 10/4/64; SCMP 3314:36

64-141 **10/4/64** – Peking **Sudan** Contract
Distribution of films

Signed by representatives of China Film Distribution and Exhibition Company and Film Production Unit of Sudanese Ministry of Information and Labor.

JMJP 10/6/64; SCMP 3315:38

64-142 **10/4/64** – Peking **Nepal** Protocol
Canal construction for irrigation purposes

JMST 1965, p. 228; SCMP 3315:36

64-143 **10/5/64** – Peking **Cambodia** Joint Communiqué
Talks during Prince Norodom Sihanouk's visit: denunciation of alleged US violations of 1954 and 1962 Geneva Agreements on Indo-China

TYC 13:61(C); JMJP 10/6/64(C); JMST 1965, p. 304(C); PR 10/9/64, p. 11(E); SCMP 3315:24(E); CCD 136:7, 138:18; AsR 6123

64-144 **10/10/64** – Peking **Albania** Protocol
Exchange of goods and payments in 1965

JMJP 10/11/64; SCMP 3318:20; AsR 6246

64-145 **10/10/64** – Peking **Albania** Protocol
Albania's use of PRC's loans under 1961 Loan Agreement [61-18]
JMJP 10/11/64; SCMP 3318:20; AsR 6246

64-146 **10/10/64** – Peking **Albania** Agreement
Cooperation in customs services
JMJP 10/11/64; SCMP 3318:20; AsR 6246

64-147 **10/11/64** 10/11/64 Katmandu **Nepal** Agreement
Cultural cooperation
TYC 13:325(C); JMST 1965, p. 228; SCMP 3320:28

64-148 **10/22/64** 10/22/64 Bujumbura **Burundi** Agreement
Trade and payments
TYC 13:269(C); JMJP 10/24/64; SCMP 3326:24

64-149 **10/24/64** – Kabul **Afghanistan** Protocol
Exchange of goods in 1964-65
JMJP 10/30/64; SCMP 3327:23; AsR 6161

64-150 **10/24/64** 1/1/65 Colombo **Ceylon** Protocol
Exchange of commodities in 1965
TYC 13:317(C); JMJP 10/27/64; SCMP 3327:25; CTS 1965:2(S,E)

64-151 **10/24/64** – Colombo **Ceylon** Contracts (2)
Exchange of rice and rubber in 1965
JMJP 10/27/64; SCMP 3327:26

64-152 **10/24/64** – Colombo **Ceylon** Agreement
Grant of interest-free loan by PRC for period 1965-67
JMJP 10/27/64; SCMP 3327:26

64-153 **10/27/64** – – **Multilateral** Protocol
Cooperation in postal services and telecommunications
Signed at Conference of Ministers of Posts and Telecommunications of Socialist Countries.
JMST 1965, p. 232

64-154 **10/27/64** – Peking **Multilateral** Protocol
Through passenger railway service
Signed at meeting of Railway Cooperation Organization of Socialist Countries, attended by delegates from Bulgaria, Hungary, Vietnam (N), Germany (E), Korea (N), Mongolia, Poland, Rumania, and Czechoslovakia.
JMJP 11/6/64; JMST 1965, p. 232; SCMP 3336:32

64-155 **10/27/64** – Peking **Korea (N)** Protocol
Scientific and technical cooperation

Signed at seventh meeting of Sino-Korean Joint Committee for Scientific and Technical Cooperation.

JMJP 10/28/64; SCMP 3328:22

64-156 **11/3/64** – Peking **Mali** Joint Communiqué
Talks during President Keita's visit: Congo crisis, support for Second Afro-Asian Conference, PRC representation in UN, Taiwan, disarmament, etc.

TYC 13:15(C); JMJP 11/5/64(C); JMST 1965, p. 359(C); PR 11/13/64, p. 17(E); SCMP 3334:29(E); CCD 138:92(E)

64-157 **11/3/64** 4/20/65 Peking **Mali** Treaty
Friendship

TYC 13:381(C); YHTY 69(C,Fr); JMJP 4/23/65(C); JMST 1965, p. 232(C); PR 4/30/65, p. 25(E); SCMP 3445:31(E); CCD 151:63(E)

64-158 **11/3/64** – Peking **Mali** Agreement
Supply of equipment for industrial projects by PRC to Mali

JMJP 11/4/64; SCMP 3333:25

64-159 **11/4/64** – – **Mali** Protocol
Film cooperation in 1965

JMST 1965, p. 230

64-160 **11/6/64** – Peking **Multilateral** Protocol
Through freight railway service

Signed at meeting of Railway Cooperation Organization of Socialist Countries, attended by delegates from USSR, Bulgaria, Hungary, Vietnam (N), Germany (E), Korea (N), Mongolia, Poland, Rumania, and Czechoslovakia.

JMJP 11/7/64; JMST 1965, p. 232; SCMP 3336:32

64-161 **11/6/64** 11/6/64 Peking **Indonesia** Agreement
Air communications

TYC 13:368(C); JMJP 11/7/64; SCMP 3336:34

64-162 **11/6/64** 11/6/64 Peking **Indonesia** Protocol
Aviation agency business and reciprocal services

Signed by representatives of General Bureau of Civil Aviation of PRC and Garuda Indonesian Airways.

TYC 13:375(C); JMJP 11/7/64; SCMP 3336:34

64-163 **11/12/64** – Peking **Afghanistan** Joint Communiqué
Talks during King Mohammed Zahir Shah's visit: Sino-Afghan relations, support for Second Afro-Asian Conference, etc.

TYC 13:53(C); JMJP 11/15/64(C); JMST 1965, p. 338(C); PR 11/20/64, p. 17(E); SCMP 3339:22(E); CCD 138:90(E); AsR 6243(E)

64-164 **11/12/64** – Havana **Cuba** Protocol
Cooperation in radio and television broadcasting in 1964-65
JMJP 11/19/64; SCMP 3339:30

64-165 **11/25/64** – Colombo **Ceylon** Contracts (3)
Gift by PRC of machinery, equipment, and materials for construction of textile mill in Ceylon
Signed by Commercial Counsellor of PRC Embassy and representatives of Ceylon Treasury.
SCMP 3347:30

64-166 **11/26/64** – Peking **Germany (E)** –
1964 plan for cooperation between Academies of Sciences
JMJP 11/30/64; SCMP 3347:35; AGF p. 57

64-167 **11/27/64** - Peking **Multilateral** Protocol
Economics of postal services and telecommunications
Signed at Conference of Experts on Economics of Posts and Telecommunications of Socialist Countries, attended by delegates from USSR, Albania, Bulgaria, Hungary, Vietnam (N), Germany (E), Korea (N), Mongolia, Poland, Rumania, and Czechoslovakia.
JMJP 12/8/64; JMST 1965, p. 232; SCMP 3348:33

64-168 **11/28/64** – Tirana **Albania** Protocol
Scientific and technical cooperation
Signed at ninth meeting of Sino-Albanian Joint Committee for Cooperation in Technology and Technical Science.
JMJP 12/2/64; SCMP 3350:25

64-169 **11/30/64** – Rome **Italy** Agreement
Establishment of nongovernmental trade missions in Peking and Rome
Signed by representatives of Committee for Promotion of International Trade and Italian Foreign Trade Institute.
JMJP 12/9/64; JMST 1965, p. 231; PR 12/11/64, p. 25; SCMP 3355:25

64-170 **11/30/64** – Peking **Bulgaria** Protocol
Scientific and technical cooperation
Signed at eighth session of Sino-Bulgarian Joint Committee for Scientific and Technical Cooperation.
JMJP 12/2/64; SCMP 3350:28

64-171 **Dec.(?)** – – **Cambodia** –
Supply of military equipment by PRC
AsR 6279

64-172 **Dec.(?)** – – **Nepal** –
Extension of 1960 Economic Aid Agreement [60-48]
AsR 6264

64-173 **12/3/64** – Djakarta **Indonesia** Joint Press Communiqué
Talks during Foreign Minister Ch'en Yi's visit: PRC support for Indonesian policy of confrontation with Malaysia, joint support for Second Afro-Asian Conference, PRC representation in UN, etc.
TYC 13:33(C); JMJP 12/4/64(C); JMST 1965, p. 311(C); PR 12/11/64, p. 4(E); SCMP 3352:26(E); ZD 1964:11-12:1701(P,E)

64-174 **12/3/64** – Accra **Ghana** Protocol
Exchange of goods in 1965
TYC 13:268(C); SCMP 3353:25

64-175 **12/7/64** 12/7/64 Vienna **Austria** Agreement
Promotion of economic relations
Signed by representatives of China Committee for the Promotion of International Trade and Austrian Federal Chamber of Commerce. Also issued Memorandum listing goods to be exchanged. H12(3):70(G)
TYC 13:387(C); JMST 1965, p. 231; SCMP 3364:23; AsR 6255; H12(3):70(note)

64-176 **12/9/64** – Bucharest **Rumania** Agreement
Exchange of goods and payments in 1965
JMJP 12/11/64; PR 12/18/64, p. 11; SCMP 3357:23; AsR 6256

64-177 **12/10/64** – Nairobi **Kenya** Protocol
Economic and technical cooperation
JMJP 12/12/64; SCMP 3357:22

64-178 **12/10/64** – Nairobi **Kenya** Exchange of Letters
Dispatch of PRC technical experts to Kenya
SCMP 3357:23

64-179 **12/10/64** – Peking **Mongolia** Protocol
Scientific and technical cooperation
Signed at third session of Sino-Mongolian Executive Organ for Scientific and Technical Cooperation.
JMJP 12/12/64; SCMP 3357:23

64-180 **12/12/64** 1/1/65 Peking **Bulgaria** Agreement
Exchange of goods and payments in 1965
TYC 13:304(C); JMJP 12/13/64; SCMP 3358:24

64-181 **12/18/64** – Nairobi **Kenya** Agreement
Trade
JMJP 12/20/64; SCMP 3363:28

64-182 **11/20/64** – Peking **Mongolia** Exchange of Notes
12/19/64
Change of PRC executive organ under 1960 Agreement on Scientific and Technical Cooperation [60-74; 63-66]
TYC 13:344(C)

64-183 **12/19/64** – Peking **Pakistan** Minutes
Boundary demarcation talks

Signed at fourth session of Sino-Pakistani Joint Boundary Demarcation Committee.

SCMP 3363:30; AsR 6265

64-184 **12/21/64** – Peking **UAR** Agreement
Economic and technical cooperation

JMST 1965, p. 229; PR 12/25/64, p. 4; SCMP 3364:27; AsR 6255; AfR 1001

64-185 **12/21/64** 1/1/65 Peking **UAR** Exchange of Notes
Extension of Trade and Payments Agreements for three years [62-24,25]

TYC 13:299(C); JMST 1965, p. 229; PR 12/25/64, p. 4; SCMP 3364:27; AsR 6280; AfR 1001

64-186 **12/21/64** 1/1/65 Peking **UAR** Protocol
Trade in 1965

TYC 13:297(C); JMST 1965, p. 229; PR 12/25/64, p. 4; SCMP 3364:27; AsR 6280; AfR 1001; FIYB 1966:4:46(E)

64-187 **12/25/64** – Algiers **Algeria** Agreement
Scientific and technical cooperation

JMJP 12/27/64; SCMP 3366:27

64-188 **12/27/64** 12/27/64 Peking **Korea (N)** Agreement
Cooperation in radio and television broadcasting

TYC 13:335(C); JMST 1965, p. 227; SCMP 3368:29

64-189 **12/31/64** – Peking **Cuba** Agreement
Trade in period 1965-70

JMJP 1/1/65; SCMP 3371:30; JPRS 31189:38 (Translations on Cuba, No. 283)(E); AsR 6281

64-190 **12/31/64** – Peking **Cuba** Protocol
Trade in 1965

JMJP 1/1/65; SCMP 3371:30; JPRS 30643:22 (Translations on Cuba, No. 270)(E)

64-191 **12/31/64** – Peking **Cuba** Agreement
Payments in period 1965-70

JMJP 1/1/65; SCMP 3371:30; JPRS 31189:34 (Translations on Cuba, No. 283)(E)

64-192 **12/31/64** – Peking **Cuba** Protocol
General conditions for sale of crude sugar to PRC by Cuba

JMJP 1/1/65; SCMP 3371:30; JPRS 30643:37 (Translations on Cuba, No. 270)(E)

64-193 **12/31/64** – Peking **Cuba** Protocol
General conditions for delivery of goods between foreign trade organizations of two countries

JMJP 1/1/65; SCMP 3371:30; JPRS 31189:2 (Translations on Cuba, No. 283)(E)

1965

65-1 **1/4/65** – Peking **Cuba** Joint Communiqué
Trade talks

JMJP 1/5/65(C); SCMP 3373:29(E)

65-2 **1/5/65** – Dar es Salaam **Tanzania** Protocol
Economic and technical cooperation

JMJP 1/8/65; SCMP 3374:29; AfR 1019

65-3 **1/5/65** – Dar es Salaam **Tanzania** Exchange of Letters
Dispatch of PRC experts and technicians to Tanzania

SCMP 3374:29

65-4 **1/12/65** – Peking **Indonesia** Agreement
Tourist cooperation

Signed by representatives of China International Travel Service and National Indonesian Tourism.

JMJP 1/15/65; SCMP 3379:36

65-5 **1/13/65** – Cairo **UAR** Agreement
Scientific and technical cooperation

JMJP 1/15/65; SCMP 3380:30; AfR 1001; AsR 6270

65-6 **1/14/65** – Algiers **Algeria** Contract
Purchase of short-length films from PRC

SCMP 3381:23

65-7 **1/14/65** – Bangui **Central African Republic** Protocol
Economic and technical cooperation

JMJP 1/20/65; SCMP 3381:25

65-8 **1/21/65** – Katmandu **Nepal** Agreement (provisional)
Direct postal exchange

JMJP 1/23/65; SCMP 3386:33

65-9 **1/26/65** – Rangoon **Burma** Protocol
Sale of Burmese rice to PRC in 1965

Protocol also issued 1/26/55. SCMP 3388:25(E)

JMJP 1/26/65; SCMP 3388:25

65-10 **1/28/65** – Peking **Indonesia** Joint Statement
Talks during Foreign Minister Sübandrio's visit: anti-imperialism, reorganization of UN, crisis in Southeast Asia, Malaysia, etc.
JMJP 1/29/65(C); JMST 1965, p. 314(C); PR 2/5/65, p. 6(E); JPRS 29033:13 (Translations on South and East Asia, No. 79)(E); CCD 146:57(E); ZD 1965:1:76(P,E); ADTJ 1654:1(Fr); AsR 6370(E)

65-11 **1/28/65** – Peking **Indonesia** Agreement
Economic and technical cooperation
JMJP 1/29/65; PR 2/5/65, p. 8; SCMP 3390:19; AsR 6303

65-12 **1/28/65** – Peking **Indonesia** Agreement
Credit
JMJP 1/28/65; PR 2/5/65, p. 8; SCMP 3390:19; AsR 6303

65-13 **2/6/65** – Brazzaville **Congo (Brazzaville)** Protocol
Implementation of 1964 Loan Agreement [64-94]
JMJP 2/9/65; SCMP 3395:30

65-14 **2/6/65** – Brazzaville **Congo (Brazzaville)** Protocol
Economic and technical cooperation
JMJP 2/9/65; SCMP 3395:30

65-15 **2/10/65** – Peking **Tanzania** Agreement
Trade
JMJP 2/11/65; PR 2/12/65, p. 5; SCMP 3398:21

65-16 **2/10/65** – Peking **Tanzania** Protocol
Exchange of commodities for the period 1965-69
JMJP 2/11/65; SCMP 3398:21

65-17 **2/11/65** – Algiers **Algeria** Protocol
Implementation of earlier [unreported] agreement on PRC donation of military equipment to Algeria
SCMP 3399:20; CCD 151:49

65-18 **2/17/65** – Peking **Kuwait** Press Communiqué
Talks on economic cooperation and development of trade
JMJP 2/18/65(C); JMST 1965, p. 343(C); SCMP 3403:31(E)

65-19 **2/18/65** – Karachi **Pakistan** Agreement
Loan, and dispatch of experts and technicians by PRC
JMJP 2/20/65; SCMP 3403:33

65-20 **2/19/65** – Peking **Germany (E)** Agreement
Exchange of goods and payments in 1965
JMJP 2/19/65; PR 2/26/65, p. 27; SCMP 3404:24; AGF p. 57

65-21 **2/20/65** 11/9/65 Peking **Tanzania** Treaty
Friendship
YHTY 73(C,Swahili,E); JMJP 2/21/65(C); JMST 1965, p. 233(C); PR 2/26/65, p. 9(E); SCMP 3404:26(E); CCD 146:64(E); ILM 4:305(E)

65-22 **2/21/65** – Ulan Bator **Multilateral** Protocol
Through railway traffic plan for 1965
Signed by USSR, Mongolia, Vietnam (N), and Korea (N).
JMJP 2/27/65; SCMP 3405:32

65-23 **2/23/65** – Peking **Tanzania** Joint Communiqué
Talks during President Nyerere's visit: anti-imperialism, intervention in Congo (Leopoldville), Asian-African conference, etc.
JMJP 2/24/65(C); JMST 1965, p. 375(C); PR 2/26/65, p. 8(E); SCMP 3406:30(E); CCD 151:61(E)

65-24 **March (?)** – – **Tunisia** –
Renewal of 1960 Trade Agreement for one year [60-125]
AfR 1020

65-25 **3/7/65** – Peking **Pakistan** Joint Communiqué
Talks during President Ayub Khan's visit: Kashmir, PRC representation in UN, etc.
Issued by Foreign Ministers Chou En-lai and Bhutto.
JMJP 3/8/65(C); JMST 1965, p. 331(C); PR 3/12/65(E); SCMP 3414:31(E); CCD 146:61(E); PakDS 3:1:3 (June 1966)(E); AsR 6377(E)

65-26 **3/12/65** – Peking **Albania** –
1965-66 plan for cultural cooperation
JMJP 3/13/65; SCMP 3418:30

65-27 **3/15/65** – – **Ceylon** Exchange of Notes
PRC aid in construction of international conference building and other buildings in Ceylon
JMJP 3/15/65; SCMP 3419:30

65-28 **3/16/65** – Djakarta **Indonesia** Agreement
Scientific and technical cooperation
JMJP 3/18/65; SCMP 3421:28

65-29 **3/16/65** – Warsaw **Poland** Agreement
Turnover of goods and payments in 1965
JMJP 3/19/65; SCMP 3421:34

65-30 **3/17/65** – Bamako **Mali** Protocol
PRC aid in construction of Segou textile combine
JMJP 3/22/65; SCMP 3423:29

65-31 **3/18/65** – Peking **Syria** Agreement
Cultural cooperation
JMJP 3/19/65; PR 3/26/65, p. 5; SCMP 3422:37; STS 214:1(Fr)

65-32 **3/18/65** – Peking **Syria** –
1965 plan for cultural cooperation
SCMP 3422:37

65-33 **3/19/65** – Karachi **Pakistan** Press Communiqué
Boundary demarcation
Issued after fifth meeting of Sino-Pakistani Joint Boundary Demarcation Committee.
JMJP 3/21/65(C); SCMP 3423:31(E)

65-34 **3/22/65** – Peking **Albania** Protocol
Shipping
Signed at fourth meeting of Sino-Albanian Shipping Joint Stock Company.
JMJP 3/23/65; SCMP 3425:31

65-35 **3/22/65** – Phnom Penh **Cambodia** Agreement
Scientific and cultural cooperation
JMJP 3/23/65; SCMP 3425:31

65-36 **3/22/65** – Phnom Penh **Cambodia** –
1965 plan for scientific and cultural cooperation
JMJP 3/23/65; SCMP 3425:31

65-37 **3/23/65** – Sanaa **Yemen** Protocol
PRC aid in construction of Sanaa textile factory
JMJP 3/26/65; SCMP 3426:43

65-38 **3/24/65** – Ulan Bator **Mongolia** Protocol
Exchange of goods in 1965
JMST 1965, p. 227; SCMP 3426:31

65-39 **3/24/65** – Kabul **Afghanistan** Protocol
Boundary demarcation
JMJP 3/26/65; PR 4/2/65, p. 4; SCMP 3427:25; ILM 4:1059(E)

65-40 **3/24/65** – Kabul **Afghanistan** Agreement
Economic and technical cooperation
JMJP 3/26/65; PR 4/2/65, p. 4; SCMP 3427:25; ILM 4:1072(E)

65-41 **3/24/65** – Kabul **Afghanistan** Agreement
Cultural cooperation
JMJP 3/26/65; PR 4/2/65, p. 4; SCMP 3427:25; ILM 4:1070(E)

65-42 **3/24/65** – Prague **Czechoslovakia** –
1964-65 plan for cooperation between Academies of Sciences
SCMP 3427:31

65-43 **3/24/65** – Helsinki **Finland** Agreement
Trade in 1965
JMJP 3/29/65; SCMP 3427:32

65-44 **3/26/65** 3/26/65 Rawalpindi **Pakistan** Protocol
Demarcation of boundary between Sinkiang and contiguous areas under actual control of Pakistan
JMJP 3/26/65; PR 4/2/65, p. 5; SCMP 3428:38; AsR 6378

65-45 **3/26/65** – Rawalpindi **Pakistan** Agreement
Cultural cooperation
PR 4/2/65, p. 5; SCMP 3428:38

65-46 **3/26/65** – Budapest **Hungary** Agreement
Exchange of goods and payments in 1965
JMJP 3/29/65; SCMP 3429:33

65-47 **3/29/65** – Hanoi **Multilateral** Minutes
Railway administration

Signed at tenth Ministerial Conference of Railway Cooperation Organization of Socialist Countries, attended by delegates from Albania, Bulgaria, Hungary, Vietnam (N), Germany (E), Korea (N), Mongolia, Poland, Rumania, USSR, and Czechoslovakia, and by observers from Cuba and Comecon Secretariat.
SCMP 3431:42

65-48 **3/30/65** – Tirana **Albania** Press Communiqué
Talks during Premier Chou En-lai's visit: international situation, world communist movement, etc.
JMJP 3/31/65(C); JMST 1965, p. 267(C); SCMP 3430:38(E)

65-49 **3/30/65** – Djakarta **Indonesia** Minutes (with Appendixes)
Talks on implementation of 1961 Economic and Technical Cooperation Agreement [61-134]
JMJP 4/1/65; SCMP 3431:37

65-50 **4/1/65** – Algiers **Algeria** Joint Communiqué
Talks during Premier Chou En-lai's visit: anti-imperialism, intervention in Congo (L), Vietnam, Palestine Arabs, Second Afro-Asian Conference, etc.
JMJP 4/2/65(C); JMST 1965, p. 357(C); PR 4/9/65, p. 10(E); SCMP 3432:22(E); CCD 151:49(E); AsR 6436

65-51 **4/3/65** – Katmandu **Nepal** Press Communiqué
Talks during Foreign Minister Ch'en Yi's visit: economic and technical aid by PRC, international situation, five principles of peaceful coexistence, etc.

JMJP 4/4/65(C); JMST 1965, p. 335(C); SCMP 3433:37(E); CCD 151:41(E)

65-52 **4/3/65(?)** – Djakarta **Indonesia** Minutes (with Appendixes)
Talks on construction of paper factory by PRC in Indonesia

SCMP 3437:27; CCD 152:46

65-53 **4/8/65** – Prague **Czechoslovakia** Agreement
Exchange of goods and payments in 1965

JMJP 4/13/65; SCMP 3438:29

65-54 **4/17/65** – Bamako **Mali** –
1965 plan for cultural cooperation

JMJP 4/23/65; SCMP 3443:33

65-55 **4/21/65** – Peking **Uganda** Agreement
Economic and technical cooperation

JMJP 4/22/65; PR 4/30/65, p. 5; SCMP 3444:45

65-56 **4/26/65(?)** – Peking **Poland** Protocol
Scientific and technical cooperation

Signed at twelfth meeting of Sino-Polish Standing Committee for Scientific and Technical Cooperation.

JMJP 4/28/65; SCMP 3447:40

65-57 **4/29/65** – Moscow **USSR** Protocol
Exchange of goods in 1965

JMJP 5/1/65; SCMP 3450:41; Pr 4/30/65; Izv 5/1/65

65-58 **5/2/65** – Peking **UAR** Agreement
Air services

JMJP 5/3/65; SCMP 3451:37; AfR 1059

65-59 **5/3/65** – Peking **Germany (E)** –
1965 plan for cultural cooperations

JMJP 5/4/65; SCMP 3541:32; AGF p. 57

65-60 **5/3/65** – Peking **Yemen** –
1965 plan for cultural cooperation

JMJP 5/4/65; SCMP 3452:39

65-61 **5/3/65** – Peking **Ghana** Joint Press Communiqué
Talks during Foreign Minister Botsio's visit: international situation, etc.

JMJP 5/4/65(C); JMST 1965, p. 363(C); SCMP 3452:27(E); AfR 1060

65-62 **5/5/65** – Peking **Poland** –
1965 plan for cultural cooperation
JMJP 5/7/65; SCMP 3453:31

65-63 **5/11/65** 9/30/65(?) Peking **Yugoslavia** Protocol
Exchange of goods in 1965
JMJP 5/15/65; SCMP 3457:41; WGO 8:155

65-64 **5/12/65** – Brazzaville **Congo (Brazzaville)** Agreement
Exchange of news between New China News Agency and Congolese Information Agency
Signed by representatives of New China News Agency and Congolese Ministry of Information.
SCMP 3459:22

65-65 **5/13/65** – Peking **Bulgaria** –
1965 plan for cultural cooperation
JMJP 5/14/65; SCMP 3459:22

65-66 **5/15/65(?)** – Peking **Rumania** Protocol
Scientific and technical cooperation
Signed at tenth session of Sino-Rumanian Joint Committee for Scientific and Technical Cooperation.
JMJP 5/16/65; SCMP 3461:37

65-67 **5/19/65** – Accra **Ghana** Agreement
Cooperation between Academies of Sciences
JMJP 5/23/65; SCMP 3464:27

65-68 **5/21/65** – Peking **Cuba** Protocol
Scientific and technical cooperation in 1965
JMJP 5/23/65; SCMP 3465:35

65-69 **5/25/65** – Peking **USSR** –
1965 plan for cultural cooperation
JMJP 5/26/65; SCMP 3467:29; Pr, Izv 5/26/65

65-70 **5/27/65** 7/28/65 Bucharest **Rumania** Agreement
Cultural cooperation
JMJP 5/28/65; SCMP 3469:33; WGO 7:276

65-71 **5/28/65** – Peking **Hungary** Protocol
Scientific and technical cooperation
Signed at ninth meeting of Sino-Hungarian Committee for Scientific and Technical Cooperation.
JMJP 5/29/65; SCMP 3470:28

65-72 **6/3/65** – Algiers **Algeria** –
1965 plan for cultural cooperation
JMJP 6/8/65; SCMP 3474:20

65-73 **6/5/65** – Peking **Hungary** –
1965 plan for cultural cooperation
JMJP 6/8/65; SCMP 3474:22

65-74 **6/5/65** – Conakry **Guinea** –
1965 plan for cultural cooperation
JMJP 6/8/65; SCMP 3475:20

65-75 **6/8/65** – Peking **Albania** Agreement
PRC loan to Albania
JMJP 6/9/65; PR 6/11/65, p. 4; SCMP 3476:20

65-76 **6/8/65** – Peking **Albania** Agreement
Exchange of goods and payments in period 1966-70
JMJP 6/9/65; PR 6/11/65, p. 4; SCMP 3476:20

65-77 **6/8/65** – Peking **Albania** Protocols (2)
Economic cooperation
JMJP 6/8/65; PR 6/11/65, p. 4; SCMP 3476:20

65-78 **6/8/65** – Dar es Salaam **Tanzania** Joint Communiqué
Talks during Premier Chou En-lai's visit: anti-imperialism, intervention in Vietnam and Dominican Republic, Southern Rhodesia, Second Afro-Asian Conference, etc.
JMJP 6/9/65(C); JMST 1965, p. 381(C); PR 6/11/65, p. 7(E); SCMP 3476:30(E); CCD 153:83(E); AfR 118; AsR 6592(E)

65-79 **6/9/65** – Peking **Albania** Press Communiqué
Economic talks
JMJP 6/10/65(C); JMST 1965, p. 271(C); SCMP 3477:20(E, abbrev.)

65-80 **6/9/65** – Ulan Bator **Mongolia** –
1965 plan for cultural cooperation
JMJP 6/14/65; SCMP 3477:26

65-81 **6/10/65** – Kuwait **Kuwait** Joint Press Communiqué
Talks during visit of PRC goodwill delegation: development of trade and economic relations, five principles of peaceful coexistence
JMJP 6/12/65(C); JMST 1965, p. 343(C); SCMP 3478:24(E)

65-82 **6/12/65** – Moscow **USSR** Protocol
Scientific and technical cooperation
Signed at fourteenth meeting of Sino-Soviet Joint Committee for Scientific and Technical Cooperation.
JMJP 6/15/65; SCMP 3478:28; Pr 6/13/65

65-83 **6/13/65** – Brazzaville **Congo (Brazzaville)** Protocol
Economic and technical cooperation
JMJP 6/15/65; SCMP 3480:23

65-84 **6/18/65** – Prague **Czechoslovakia** –
1965 plan for cultural cooperation
JMJP 6/20/65; SCMP 3483:20

65-85 **6/18/65** – Pyongyang **Korea (N)** Contract
Mutual purchase of film distribution and exhibition rights
Signed by representatives of Korean Film Distribution Agency and China Film Distribution and Exhibition Company.
JMJP 6/21/65; SCMP 3483:28

65-86 **6/19/65** – Peking **Vietnam (N)** –
1965 plan for cultural cooperation
JMJP 6/20/65; SCMP 3483:34

65-87 **6/26/65** – Phnom Penh **Cambodia** Protocol
Revision of 1956 Trade Agreement [56-54]
JMJP 6/28/65; SCMP 3489:22

65-88 **6/26/65** – Phnom Penh **Cambodia** Protocol
Revision of 1956 Payments Agreement [56-55]
JMJP 6/28/65; SCMP 3489:22

65-89 **6/30/65** – Cairo **Multilateral** Press Communiqué
Talks among Premier Chou En-lai and Presidents Nasser, Sukarno, and Ayub Khan: postponement of Second Afro-Asian Conference
Issued also by UAR, Indonesia, and Pakistan.
JMJP 7/1/65(C); PR 7/9/65, p. 5(E, sum.); SCMP 3491:20(E)

65-90 **7/13/65** – Peking **Vietnam (N)** Agreement
Economic and technical assistance
JMJP 7/14/65; PR 7/16/65, p. 3; SCMP 3498:23

65-91 **7/13/65** – Colombo **Ceylon** Agreement
Supply of rolling stock to Ceylon
Signed by Commercial Counsellor of PRC Embassy to Ceylon on behalf of China National Machinery Import and Export and by representative of Ceylon Treasury.
SCMP 3499:17; CCD 158:97

65-92 **7/14/65** – Rangoon **Burma** Memorandum
Amendments to 1955 Air Transport Agreement [55-77]
JMJP 7/15/65; SCMP 3499:17

65-93 **7/15/65(?)** – Peking **Multilateral** Protocol
Postal services and telecommunications

Signed at sixth Conference of Ministers of Post and Telecommunications of Socialist Countries, attended by delegates from Albania, Bulgaria, Hungary, Vietnam (N), Germany (E), Korea (N), Cuba, Mongolia, Poland, Rumania, USSR, Czechoslovakia. Press Communiqué also issued. SCMP 3500:10(E)

JMJP 7/16/65; SCMP 3500:10

65-94 **7/15/65** – Peking **Germany (E)** Agreement
Exchange of university students and research workers

JMJP 7/18/65; SCMP 3500:12; AGF p. 57

65-95 **7/15/65(?)** – – **Mali** Contract
Construction of textile plant in Mali by PRC

CCD 158:96

65-96 **7/16/65** – Canton **Uganda** Joint Communiqué
Talks during President Obote's visit: anti-imperialism, US intervention in Vietnam, PRC representation in UN, Second Afro-Asian Conference, etc.

JMJP 7/17/65(C); PR 7/23/65, p. 18; SCMP 3501:25(E); CCD 157:98(E); AfR 1138(E, abbrev.); AsR 6603(E, abbrev.)

65-97 **7/17/65(?)** – Peking **Vietnam (N)** Press Communiqué
Talks during visit of governmental economic delegation from Vietnam (N): US intervention in Vietnam, economic aid, etc.

SCMP 3501:33(E)

65-98 **7/18/65** – Havana **Cuba** Protocol
Extension of 1960 Cultural Cooperation Agreement for five years [60-83]

JMJP 7/20/65; SCMP 3503:14

65-99 **7/20/65** – Peking **USSR** Protocol (supplementary)
Mutual supply of goods in 1965

JMJP 7/21/65; SCMP 3504:23; Pr 7/22/65; AsR 6628

65-100 **7/24/65** – Peking **Indonesia** Accord
Maritime transport

JMJP 7/25/65

65-101 **7/28/65** – Peking **Somalia** Joint Press Communiqué
Talks during President Osman's visit: national liberation fronts, technical cooperation, Second Afro-Asian Conference, etc.

JMJP 7/29/65(C); PR 8/6/65, p. 31(E); SCMP 3509:24(E); CCD 161:126(E)

65-102 **7/30/65** – Pyongyang **Korea (N)** –
1965 plan for cooperation between Academies of Sciences
JMJP 8/1/65; SCMP 3511:39

65-103 **8/1/65** – Peking **Burma** Joint Communiqué
Talks during General Ne Win's visit: anti-imperialism, peaceful coexistence, PRC representation in UN, etc.
JMJP 8/2/65(C); PR 8/6/65, p. 29(E); SCMP 3512:29(E); CCD 161:113(E)

65-104 **8/5/65** – Peking **Japan** Agreement
Agricultural technical exchange
Signed by representatives of Chinese Society of Agronomy, China-Japan Friendship Association of PRC, Chinese People's Institute of Foreign Affairs, and Japanese Association for Exchange of Technical Knowledge between Japan and China.
SCMP 3514:24

65-105 **8/5/65** 9/30/65 Accra **Ghana** Protocol
Dispatch of PRC military experts to Ghana
Ghana, Ministry of Information, *Nkrumah's Subversion in Africa* (1966), p. 56(E,C)

65-106 **8/13/65** – Brazzaville **Congo (Brazzaville)** –
1965 plan for cultural cooperation
JMJP 8/15/65; SCMP 3520:22

65-107 **8/17/65** – Mogadishu **Somalia** –
1965 plan for cultural cooperation
JMJP 8/19/65; SCMP 3523:38

65-108 **8/28/65** – Peking **Algeria** Joint Communiqué
Talks during visit of Minister of State Bitat: anti-imperialism, US intervention in Vietnam, Second Afro-Asian Conference, etc.
JMJP 8/29/65(C); PR 9/3/65, p. 7; SCMP 3530:24; AfR 1163

65-109 **8/29/65** – Peking **Nepal** Protocol
PRC aid in construction of east-west highway in Nepal
JMJP 9/8/65; PR 9/10/65, p. 3; SCMP 3531:39; AsR 6676

65-110 **9/2/65** – Bamako **Mali** Minutes
Talks on PRC aid for three construction projects in Mali
JMJP 9/7/65

65-111 **9/3/65** – Katmandu **Nepal** –
1965 plan for cultural cooperation
JMJP 9/5/65; SCMP 3534:42

65-112 **9/8/65** – Peking **Nepal** Press Communiqué
Talks during visit of Vice-Chairman Bista: economic aid, Vietnam, Second Afro-Asian Conference, etc.
JMJP 9/8/65(C); PR 9/10/65, p. 3(E, sum.); SCMP 3536:39(E); CCD 161:125(E)

65-113 **9/13/65** – Brazzaville **Congo (Brazzaville)** Minutes
Talks on PRC aid in construction of textile mill in Congo (Br.)
JMJP 9/16/65; SCMP 3540:26

65-114 **9/14/65** – Peking **Guinea** Agreement
Postal services
JMJP 9/15/65; SCMP 3540:26; CCD 162:74

65-115 **9/14/65** – Peking **Guinea** Agreement
Establishment of telecommunications
JMJP 9/15/65; SCMP 3540:26; CCD 162:74

65-116 **9/14/65** – Peking **Guinea** Minutes
Talks on economic and technical aid
SCMP 3540:26

65-117 **9/14/65** – Djakarta **Indonesia** Protocol
Cooperation in building hall for Conference of Newly Emerging Forces
JMJP 9/16/65; SCMP 3541:33

65-118 **9/16/65** – Hanoi **Vietnam (N)** –
1966 plan for cooperation in public health work
JMJP 9/17/65; SCMP 3541:39

65-119 **9/16/65** – Phnom Penh **Cambodia** Agreement
Exchange of press information between New China News Agency and Agence Khmere de Presse
Signed by representatives of New China News Agency and Agence Khmere de Presse.
SCMP 3542:21

65-120 **9/18/65** – Peking **Japan** Accord
Implementation of Liao-Takasaki Memorandum for trade in 1966 [62-103]
Signed by Liu Hsi-wen and Kaheita Okazaki.
JMJP 9/19/65; SCMP 3543:36

65-121 **9/23/65** – Peking **Multilateral** Official Communiqué
Games of Newly Emerging Forces (GANEFO)
Issued after second meeting of Council of GANEFO Federation, attended by delegates from twenty-nine countries and observers from thirteen more.
SCMP 3546:30(E)

65-122 **9/30/65** – Peking **Indonesia** Agreement
Economic and technical cooperation

JMJP 10/1/65; PR 10/8/65, p. 5; SCMP 3551:34

65-123 **9/30/65** – Peking **Indonesia** Agreement
Trade

JMJP 10/1/65; PR 10/8/65, p. 8; SCMP 3551:34

65-124 **9/30/65** – Peking **Indonesia** Agreement
Payments

JMJP 10/1/65, PR 10/8/65, p. 18; SCMP 3551:34

65-125 **9/30/65** – Peking **Indonesia** Unspecified (4)
Economic matters

SCMP 3551:34

65-126 **10/1/65** – Paris **France** –
1965-66 plan for cultural exchange

JMJP 10/5/65; SCMP 3553:30

65-127 **10/2/65** – Peking **Guinea** Contract
Distribution of PRC films and exchange of newsreel materials

Signed by representatives of China Film Distribution and Exhibition Company and National Cinema Service of Guinea (Sily-Cinema).

JMJP 10/13/65; SCMP 3553:31

65-128 **10/3/65** – Peking **Cambodia** Joint Statement
Talks during Prince Norodom Sihanouk's visit: anti-imperialism, Geneva Accords on French Indo-China, reorganization of UN, Taiwan, Vietnam, etc.

JMJP 10/4/65(C); PR 10/8/65, p. 16(E); SCMP 3533:22(E); CCD 161:119(E); AsR 6741(E, sum.)

65-129 **10/4/65** – Peking **Indonesia** Joint Statement
Talks during visit of delegation from People's Assembly of Indonesia: anti-imperialism, national liberation fronts, Malaysia, Second Afro-Asian Conference, etc.

Signed by representatives of Standing Committee of National People's Congress of PRC and People's Assembly of Indonesia.

JMJP 10/8/65(C); PR 10/15/65; SCMP 3556:25(E)

65-130 **10/6/65** – Damascus **Syria** Protocol
Cooperation in radio and television broadcasting

JMJP 10/9/65; SCMP 3556:32; STS 289:1

65-131 **10/6/65** – Peking **Albania** Protocol
Scientific and technical cooperation

Signed at tenth session of Sino-Albanian Joint Committee for Cooperation in Technology and Technical Science.

JMJP 10/9/65; SCMP 3557:22

65-132 **10/12/65** 1/1/66 Peking **Ceylon** Protocol
Exchange of commodities in 1966

JMJP 10/13/65; SCMP 3559:28; CTS 1965:11(S,E)

65-133 **10/26/65** – Prague **Czechoslovakia** Protocol
Scientific and technical cooperation

Signed at twelfth meeting of Sino-Czechoslovak Joint Committee for Scientific and Technical Cooperation.

JMJP 10/29/65; SCMP 3570:29

65-134 **November(?)** – – **Pakistan** Agreement
PRC economic aid in construction of plants, factories, and workshops in Pakistan

CCD 162:76

65-135 **11/1/65(?)** – Pyongyang **Korea (N)** Protocol
Scientific and technical cooperation

Signed at eighth session of Sino-Korean Committee for Scientific and Technical Cooperation.

JMJP 11/3/65; SCMP 3573:30

65-136 **11/6/65** – Peking **Afghanistan** Protocol
Exchange of goods during 1965-66

JMJP 11/7/65; SCMP 3577:23

65-137 **11/9/65** – Sofia **Bulgaria** Protocol
Scientific and technical cooperation

Signed at ninth session of Sino-Bulgarian Joint Committee for Scientific and Technical Cooperation.

JMJP 11/14/65; SCMP 3579:28

65-138 **11/9/65** – Pyongyang **Korea (N)** Agreement
Cooperation in public health work

JMJP 11/11/65; SCMP 3579:33

65-139 **11/9/65** – Pyongyang **Korea (N)** –
1965-66 plan for cooperation in public health

JMJP 11/11/65; SCMP 3579:33

65-140 **11/12/65** – Tirana **Albania** Protocol
Exchange of goods and payments in 1966

JMJP 11/22/65; SCMP 3581:21

65-141 **11/12/65** – Tirana **Albania** Protocol
Albania's use in 1966 of credits granted by PRC
SCMP 3581:21

65-142 **11/13/65** – Hanoi **Vietnam (N)** –
1965 plan for cooperation between PRC Academy of Sciences, and Vietnam (N) State Commission of Sciences and Technology and Academy of Social Science
JMJP 11/16/65; SCMP 3581:39

65-143 **11/18/65** – Moscow **USSR** –
1965-66 plan of cooperation between Academies of Sciences
Pr 11/19/65

65-144 **11/18/65** – Sinuiju **Korea (N)** Protocol
Border railway
Signed at meeting of Sino-Korean Border Railway Joint Committee.
JMJP 11/20/65; SCMP 3584:29

65-145 **11/23/65** – Peking **Finland** Agreement
Trade in 1966
JMJP 11/24/65; SCMP 3587:25

65-146 **11/22/65(?)** – Peking **Germany (E)** Protocol
Scientific and technical cooperation
Signed at ninth meeting of Sino-German Standing Committee for Cooperation in Technology and Technical Sciences.
JMJP 11/25/65; SCMP 3587:28

65-147 **Nov./Dec.** – – **Ceylon** Protocol
Exchange of PRC rice and Ceylon rubber
CCD 166:37

65-148 **Dec.(?)** – – **Morocco** Agreement
Renewal of 1963 Trade Agreement for one year [63-39]
AfR 1240

65-149 **12/1/65** – Bucharest **Rumania** –
1965-66 plan for cooperation between Academies of Sciences
JMJP 12/3/65; SCMP 3592:36

65-150 **12/2/65(?)** – Shenyang (Mukden) **Korea (N)** Accord
River navigation
Signed at fifth meeting of Joint Committee on Cooperation in Navigation on Yalu and Tumen Rivers.
JMJP 12/4/65; SCMP 3593:30

65-151 **12/3/65** – Hanoi **Vietnam (N)** Protocol
Scientific and technical cooperation

Signed at fifth meeting of Sino-Vietnamese Executive Organ for Scientific and Technical Cooperation.

JMJP 12/5/65; PR 12/10/65, p. 3; SCMP 3593:33

65-152 **12/5/65** – Peking **Vietnam (N)** Agreement
Loan by PRC

JMJP 12/6/65; PR 12/10/65, p. 3; SCMP 3594:27

65-153 **12/5/65** – Peking **Vietnam (N)** Protocol
Mutual supply of commodities and payments in 1966

JMJP 12/6/65; PR 12/10/65, p. 3; SCMP 3594:27

65-154 **12/14/65** – Pyongyang **Korea (N)** Protocol
Mutual supply of goods in 1966

JMJP 12/15/65; SCMP 3600:24

65-155 **12/15/65** – Warsaw **Poland** –
1965-66 plan for cooperation between Academies of Sciences

SCMP 3602:22

65-156 **12/17/65** – Peking **Japan** Agreement (with Appendixes)
Fishery regulation in Yellow and East China Seas during 1965-67

Signed by representatives of China Fishery Association and Japan-China Fishery Association of Japan. Joint Statement also signed 12/17/65.

JMJP 12/18/65(C); SCMP 3613:27(E); CCD 171:40(E)

65-157 **12/17/65** – Peking **Japan** Exchange of Letters
Exclusion of Japanese fishing vessels from PRC military security zones and conservation zone

See note above.

SCMP 3613:39(E) CCD 171:41(E)

65-158 **12/17/65** – Peking **Japan** Memorandum
Limitations on number of trawlers in designated areas

See note above.

SCMP 3613:41(E)

65-159 **12/21/65** – Peking **Rumania** Agreement
Barter and payments in 1966

JMJP 12/22/65(C); SCMP 3605:25

65-160 **12/23/65** – Prague **Czechoslovakia** –
1966-67 plan for cooperation between Academies of Sciences

JMJP 12/26/65; SCMP 3607:26

65-161 **12/29/65** – Peking **Cuba** Protocol
1966-67 plan for cultural cooperation
JMJP 12/30/65; SCMP 3609:29

1966

66-1 **1/22/66** – Peking **Japan** Joint Statement
Promotion of trade, technical exchanges, exhibitions, maritime, and other transport
Signed by representatives of China Committee for Promotion of International Trade and Japan-China Trade Promotion Association.
SCMP 3624:30(E)

66-2 **2/1/66** – Peking **Guinea** Protocol
Trade for 1966
JMJP 2/2/66; SCMP 3631:26

66-3 **2/4/66** – Peking **Czechoslovakia** Agreement
Exchange of goods and payments in 1966
JMJP 2/5/66; SCMP 3634:28

66-4 **2/11/66** – Peking **Rumania** –
1966-67 plan for cultural cooperation
JMJP 2/12/66; SCMP 3639:37

66-5 **2/20/66** – Peking **Hungary** Agreement
Exchange of goods and payments in 1966
JMJP 2/21/66; SCMP 3645:30

66-6 **2/25/66** – Pyongyang **Korea (N)** –
1966-67 plan for cultural cooperation
JMJP 2/27/66; SCMP 3648:30

66-7 **3/16/66** – Sofia **Bulgaria** Agreement
Exchange of goods and payments in 1966
JMJP 3/17/66; SCMP 3661:27

66-8 **3/21/66** – Hanoi **Vietnam (N)** Protocol
Border railway
Signed at ninth meeting of Sino-Vietnamese Joint Committee on Border Railways.
JMJP 3/23/66; SCMP 3665:41

66-9 **3/22/66** – Peking **Poland** Agreement
Exchange of goods and payments in 1966
JMJP 3/23/66; SCMP 3665:38

66-10 **3/25/66** – Berlin **Germany (E)** Agreement
Exchange of goods and payments in 1966
JMJP 3/29/66; SCMP 3668:25

66-11 **3/28/66** – Peking **Mongolia** Protocol
Mutual supply of goods in 1966
JMJP 3/29/66; SCMP 3670:34

66-12 **3/31/66** – Peking **Cambodia** –
1966 plan for cultural and scientific cooperation
JMJP 4/2/66; SCMP 3672:19

66-13 **3/31/66** – Rawalpindi **Pakistan** Joint Communiqué
Talks during visit of Chairman Liu Shao-ch'i and Vice-Premier Ch'en Yi: Kashmir, PRC representation in UN, etc.
JMJP 4/1/66(C); SCMP 3672:27(E); CCD 168:101(E); PakDS 3:1:3 (June 1966)(E); RI 1966:15:399(It)

66-14 **4/4/66** – Moscow **USSR** Agreement
Civil air transport
Supersedes 1954 Agreement [54-99].
JMJP 4/9/66; SCMP 3677:53; JPRS, Soviet Economic System: Current Developments 133:28; Izv 4/5/66

66-15 **4/8/66** – Kabul **Afghanistan** Joint Communiqué
Talks during visit of Chairman Liu Shao-ch'i and Vice-Premier Ch'en Yi: peaceful coexistence, PRC representation in UN, etc.
JMJP 4/9/66(C); SCMP 3677:34(E); CCD 168:102(E); RI 1966:17:452(It)

66-16 **4/14/66** – Brazzaville **Congo (Brazzaville)** –
1966 plan for cultural cooperation
JMJP 4/14/66; SCMP 3681:23

66-17 **4/19/66** – Rangoon **Burma** Joint Communiqué
Talks during visit of Chairman Liu Shao-ch'i and Vice-Premier Ch'en Yi: anticolonialism, PRC representation in UN, etc.
JMJP 4/20/66(C); SCMP 3683:27(E); CCD 171:61(E)

66-18 **4/19/66** – Peking **USSR** Protocol
Exchange of goods in 1966
JMJP 4/20/66; SCMP 3683:34; JPRS, Soviet Economic System: Current Developments 137:45; Pr 4/20/66

66-19 **4/20/66** – Damascus **Syria** –
1966-67 plan for cultural cooperation
JMJP 4/22/66; SCMP 3684:39

66-20 **4/22/66** – Peking **Vietnam (N)** Protocol
Scientific and technical cooperation

Signed at sixth meeting of Sino-Vietnamese Executive Organ for Scientific and Technical Cooperation.

JMJP 4/24/66; SCMP 3685:37

66-21 **4/22/66** – Dar es Salaam **Tanzania** Memorandum
Establishment of Sino-Tanzanian Maritime Transport Joint Stock Company

JMJP 7/9/66; SCMP 3736:31

66-22 **4/29/66** – Phnom Penh **Cambodia** Agreement
Economic and cultural cooperation

JMJP 5/1/66; PR 5/6/66, p. 5; SCMP 3690:26; CCD 171:59

66-23 **4/30/66** – Peking **Norway** –
1966-67 plan for cultural exchange

JMJP 5/2/66; SCMP 3690:39

66-24 **4/30/66** – Conakry **Guinea** –
1966 plan for cultural cooperation

JMJP 5/2/66; SCMP 3691:36

66-25 **May** – Sanaa **Yemen** Protocol
Extension of 1964 Agreement on Economic and Technical Cooperation [64-79]

AsR 7170

66-26 **5/2/66** – Peking **Nepal** Agreement
Trade, intercourse, and related questions between Nepal and the Tibet autonomous region of PRC

JMJP 5/3/66; SCMP 3691:37; CCD 171:64; AsR 7124

66-27 **5/4/66** – Tirana **Albania** Protocol
Shipping

Signed at fifth meeting of Administrative Council of Sino-Albanian Shipping Joint Stock Company.

JMJP 5/6/66; SCMP 3694:20

66-28 **5/4/66** – Cairo **UAR** Protocol
Trade in 1966

JMJP 5/10/66; SCMP 3694:35; AsR 7124

66-29 **5/7/66** – Peking **Tanzania** –
1966 plan for cultural cooperation

JMJP 5/8/66; SCMP 3695:50

66-30 **5/7/66** – Cairo **UAR** –
1966-67 plan for cultural cooperation

JMJP 5/10/66; SCMP 3696:44; AfD 2920

66-31 **5/11/66** – Peking **Albania** Joint Statement
Talks during Premier Shehu's visit: antirevisionism, national liberation movements, reorganization of UN, etc.
JMJP 5/15/66(C); SCMP 3698:24; CCD 171:48(E); ZD 1966:5:540(P,E); AsR 7160; CB 788:1(E)

66-32 **5/11/66** – Peking **Czechoslovakia** –
1966 plan for cultural cooperation
JMJP 5/12/66; SCMP 3698:28

66-33 **5/13/66** – Bamako **Mali** –
1966 plan for cultural cooperation
JMJP 5/16/66; SCMP 3700:30

56-34 **5/19/66** – Peking **Japan** Minutes
Trade talks on basis of Liao-Takasaki Memorandum [62-103]
JMJP 5/20/66(C); SCMP 3704:29(E)

66-35 **5/20/66** – Rabat **Morocco** Protocol (supplementary)
Trade
JMJP 5/22/66; SCMP 3705:27; AfR 1370

66-36 **5/23/66** – Sanaa **Yemen** –
1966-67 plan for cultural cooperation
JMJP 5/25/66; SCMP 3707:26

66-37 **5/24/66** – Kabul **Afghanistan** –
1966 plan for cultural cooperation
JMJP 5/28/66; SCMP 3708:19

66-38 **5/24/66** – Tirana **Albania** –
1966-67 plan for cooperation between PRC Academy of Sciences and State University of Tirana
JMJP 5/28/66; SCMP 3708:19

66-39 **5/26/66** – Havana **Cuba** Protocol
Trade in 1966
JMJP 6/2/66; SCMP 3712:25

66-40 **5/27/66** – Havana **Cuba** –
1965-66 plan for cooperation between Academies of Sciences
JMJP 6/2/66; SCMP 3712:26

66-41 **5/28/66** – Hanoi **Vietnam (N)** –
1966 plan for cultural cooperation
JMJP 5/29/66; SCMP 3710:35

66-42 **5/30/66** – Ulan Bator **Mongolia** Protocol
Scientific and technical cooperation

Signed at fourth session of Sino-Mongolian Executive Organ for Scientific and Technical Cooperation.

JMJP 6/2/66; SCMP 3711:34; CCD 175:50

66-43 **6/1/66** – Paris **France** Agreement
Air communications

Communiqué also issued 6/1/66. SCMP 3712:27(E)

JMJP 6/2/66; SCMP 3712:27; Journal Officiel de la République Française 1966:5324(Fr); AsR 7149

66-44 **6/1/66** – Pyongyang **Korea (N)** Agreement
Mutual assistance and cooperation in prevention and quarantine of animal diseases

JMJP 6/3/66; SCMP 3712:28

66-45 **6/1/66** – Rawalpindi **Pakistan** –
1966-67 plan for cultural cooperation

JMJP 6/3/66; SCMP 3713:31

66-46 **6/2/66** – Conakry **Guinea** Agreement
Exchange of news between New China News Agency and Guinean Press Agency

Signed by High Commissioner at Presidency in Charge of Information and Tourism of Guinea and PRC Ambassador to Guinea.

JMJP 6/5/66; SCMP 3714:36

66-47 **6/2/66** – Conakry **Guinea** Memorandum
Talks on PRC aid in construction of cinema in Guinea

See note above.

JMJP 6/5/66; SCMP 3714:36

66-48 **6/4/66** – Baghdad **Iraq** –
1966-67 plan for cultural cooperation

JMJP 6/9/66; SCMP 3714:38

66-49 **6/4/66** – Baghdad **Iraq** Protocol
Cooperation in radio and television broadcasting

JMJP 6/9/66; SCMP 3714:38

66-50 **6/8/66** – Peking **Tanzania** Agreement
Economic cooperation

JMJP 6/9/66; SCMP 3717:29; AfR 1420

66-51 **6/9/66** – Peking **Mali** Agreement
Granting of loans by PRC to Mali

JMJP 6/10/66; SCMP 3718:31

66-52 **6/10/66** 8/31/66 Belgrade **Yugoslavia** Protocol
Exchange of goods in 1966
JMJP 6/13/66; SCMP 3719:38; WGO 9:20

66-53 **6/11/66** – Mogadishu **Somalia** –
1966 plan for cultural cooperation
JMJP 6/13/66; SCMP 3720:36

66-54 **6/20/66** – Warsaw **Poland** Protocol
Scientific and technical cooperation
Signed at thirteenth session of Sino-Polish Standing Committee for Scientific and Technical Cooperation.
JMJP 6/22/66; SCMP 3725:34

66-55 **6/20/66** – Algiers **Algeria** Memorandum
Talks on PRC aid in construction of exhibition hall in Algeria
JMJP 6/25/66; SCMP 3726:31

66-56 **6/23/66** – Rawalpindi **Pakistan** Protocol
PRC aid in construction of heavy machinery complex in West Pakistan
JMJP 6/26/66; SCMP 3729:42; AsR 7215

66-57 **6/24/66** – Warsaw **Poland** –
1966 plan for cultural cooperation
JMJP 6/26/66; SCMP 3728:29

66-58 **6/24/66** – Bucharest **Rumania** Joint Communiqué
Talks during Premier Chou En-lai's visit: Sino-Rumanian relations
ZD 1966:6:639(P, Rumanian); SCMP 3728:31(E)

66-59 **6/27/66** – Moscow **USSR** –
1966 plan for cultural cooperation
JMJP 6/27/66; SCMP 3730:46; CDSP 18:26:9; Pr 6/28/66; Izv 6/29/66

66-60 **6/28/66** – Tirana **Albania** Communiqué
Talks during visit of Chinese Communist Party and PRC government delegation: reaffirmation of Joint Statement of 5/11/66 [66-31]
JMJP 6/29/66(C); SCMP 3730:33(E); CCD 175:53(E)

66-61 **6/30/66** – Katmandu **Nepal** Agreement (supplementary)
Maintenance of Katmandu-Kodari highway
AsR 7214

66-62 **7/1/66** – Sofia **Bulgaria** –
1966 plan for cultural cooperation
SCMP 3733:34

66-63 **7/2/66** – Peking **Vietnam (N)** Agreement
Agricultural aid by PRC to Vietnam (N)

JMJP 7/2/66; SCMP 3733:37

66-64 **7/4/66** – Rawalpindi **Pakistan** Agreement
Barter

AsR 7225

66-65 **7/4/66** – Berlin **Germany (E)** Protocol
Scientific and technical cooperation

Signed at tenth meeting of Sino-German Standing Committee for Cooperation in Technology and Technical Sciences.

JMJP 7/23/66; SCMP 3735:22

66-66 **7/5/66** – Peking **Korea (N)** Protocol
Scientific and technical cooperation

Signed at ninth session of Sino-Korean Committee for Scientific and Technical Cooperation.

JMJP 7/6/66; SCMP 3735:25

66-67 **7/6/66** – Havana **Cuba** Agreement
Scientific and technical cooperation

JMJP 7/9/66; SCMP 3737:32

66-68 **7/7/66** – – **Tanzania** Accord
Establishment of Sino-Tanzanian Maritime Transport Joint Stock Company

Implements agreement in Memorandum of 4/22/66 [66-21].

JMJP 7/9/66; SCMP 3736:31; AfR 1432, 1582

66-69 **7/20/66** – Budapest **Hungary** –
1966 plan for cultural cooperation

JMJP 7/23/66; SCMP 3746:32

66-70 **7/22/66** – Berlin **Germany (E)** –
1966 plan for cultural cooperation

JMJP 7/28/66; SCMP 3748:24

66-71 **7/25/66** – Peking **France** Protocol
Reciprocal grant of technical services in civil aviation

JMJP 7/28/66; SCMP 3749:22

66-72 **7/27/66** – Peking **Sudan** Protocol
Trade in 1967

JMJP 7/28/66; SCMP 3750:41

66-73 **7/29/66** – Peking **Afghanistan** Protocol
Economic and technical cooperation

JMJP 7/29/66; SCMP 3752:26

66-74 **7/30/66** – Peking **Korea (N)** –
1966-67 plan for cooperation between Academies of Sciences
JMJP 7/31/66; SCMP 3753:33

66-75 **7/31/66** – Bucharest **Rumania** Protocol
Scientific and technical cooperation
Signed at eleventh meeting of Sino-Rumanian Joint Committee for Scientific and Technical Cooperation.
JMJP 8/1/66; SCMP 3753:34

66-76 **8/9/66(?)** – Budapest **Hungary** Protocol
Scientific and technical cooperation
Signed at tenth meeting of Sino-Hungarian Committee for Scientific and Technical Cooperation.
JMJP 8/13/66; SCMP 3760:17

66-77 **8/13/66(?)** – Tananarive **Malagasy** –
Technical aid by PRC
JPRS 37434:21 (Translations on Africa No. 428)

66-78 **8/21/66** – Peking **Vietnam (N)** –
1966-67 plan for cooperation between PRC Academy of Sciences, and Vietnamese State Commission of Sciences and Technology and Academy of Social Science
JMJP 8/24/66; SCMP 3768:21

66-79 **8/22/66** – Peking **Zambia** Joint Press Communiqué
Talks during visit of Vice-President Kamanga: Southern Rhodesia, international situation, etc.
JMJP 8/23/66(C); PR 8/26/66, p. 13(E);
SCMP 3768:22(E)

66-80 **8/22/66** – Peking **Zambia** Agreement
Cultural cooperation
JMJP 8/23/66; PR 8/26/66, p. 13; SCMP 3768:21

66-81 **8/29/66** – Peking **Vietnam (N)** Agreement
Economic and technical assistance to Vietnam (N)
JMJP 8/30/66; PR 9/2/66, p. 3; SCMP 3773:31

66-82 **9/29/66** – Peking **Mongolia** –
1966 plan for cultural cooperation
JMJP 9/30/66; SCMP 3793:45

66-83 **10/10/66** – Dar es Salaam **Tanzania** Contracts (3)
Supply of PRC equipment and technical aid in construction of textile mill in Tanzania
AfR 1510

66-84 **10/12/66** – Peking **Vietnam (N)** –
1967 plan for cooperation in public health work
JMJP 10/13/66; SCMP 3802:29

66-85 **10/18/66** – Katmandu **Nepal** Exchange of Notes (?)
PRC economic aid to Nepal
PRC agrees to convert total sum of aid due under 1956 and 1960 agreements from Indian rupees to pounds sterling at gold standard value of two currencies prior to devaluation of Indian rupee [56-111;60-48].
JMJP 10/20/66; SCMP 3806:35(E, sum.)

66-86 **10/20/66** – Peking **Albania** Agreement
PRC loan to Albania for petroleum industry
JMJP 10/21/66; SCMP 3807:29

66-87 **10/21/66** – Rawalpindi **Pakistan** Agreement
Maritime transport
JMJP 10/22/66; SCMP 3808:36

66-88 **10/23/66** – Mogadishu **Somalia** Exchange of Letters
Working conditions for PRC experts in Somalia
JMJP 10/28/66; SCMP 3812:29; Africa Diary 3207

66-89 **10/23/66** – Peking **Vietnam (N)** Minutes
Talks on scientific and technical cooperation
JMJP 10/28/66; SCMP 3812:29

66-90 **10/28/66** – – **Czechoslovakia** Protocol
Scientific and technical cooperation
Signed at thirteenth meeting of Sino-Czechoslovak Joint Committee for Scientific and Technical Cooperation.
JMJP 11/2/66; SCMP 3813:32

66-91 **11/6/66** – Peking **USSR** Protocol
Scientific and technical cooperation
Signed at fifteenth session of Sino-Soviet Joint Committee for Scientific and Technical Cooperation.
JMJP 11/7/66; SCMP 3819:41; AsR 7410; NYT 11/7/66, p. 79

66-92 **11/16/66** – Peking **Guinea** Agreement
Economic and technical cooperation
JMJP 11/17/66; PR 11/25/66, p. 5; SCMP 3824:42

66-93 **11/16/66** – Peking **Guinea** Protocol
Economic and technical aid
SCMP 3824:42

66-94 **11/16/66** – Peking **Guinea** Agreement
PRC grant of commercial loan to Guinea
JMJP 11/17/66; PR 11/25/66, p. 5; SCMP 3824:42

66-95 **11/16/66** – Peking **Guinea** Protocol
Trade in 1967
JMJP 11/17/66; PR 11/25/66, p. 5; SCMP 3824:42

66-96 **11/21/66** – Peking **Albania** Protocol
Exchange of goods and payments in 1967
JMJP 11/22/66; SCMP 3827:26

66-97 **11/21/66** – Peking **Albania** Protocol
Albania's use of PRC loans in 1967
JMJP 11/22/66; SCMP 3827:26

66-98 **11/21/66** – Peking **Japan** –
Trade in 1967 in accordance with Liao-Takasaki Memorandum [62-103]
JMJP 11/22/66; SCMP 3827:30; AsR 7468

66-99 **11/23/66** – Peking **Vietnam (N)** Agreement
Mutual supply of goods and payments in 1967
JMJP 11/24/66; SCMP 3828:34

66-100 **11/29/66** – Colombo **Ceylon** Protocol
Exchange of goods in 1967
JMJP 11/30/66; SCMP 3832:31

66-101 **11/29/66** – Colombo **Ceylon** Contracts (2)
Exchange of rice and rubber in 1967
SCMP 3832:31

66-102 **11/30/66** – Tirana **Albania** Protocol
Scientific and technical cooperation
Signed at eleventh session of Sino-Albanian Joint Committee for Cooperation in Technology and Technical Science.
JMJP 12/2/66; SCMP 3834:13

66-103 **12/3/66** – Peking **Korea (N)** Protocol
Mutual supply of goods in 1967
JMJP 12/4/66; SCMP 3835:28

66-104 **12/21/66** – Katmandu **Nepal** Agreement
Economic and technical cooperation
JMJP 12/27/66; SCMP 3849:37; AsR 7513

66-105 **12/28/66** – Kabul **Afghanistan** Protocol
Exchange of goods in 1966-67
JMJP 12/31/66; SCMP 3852:38

66-106 **12/30/66** – Peking **Korea (N)** Agreement
Cooperation in radio and television broadcasting
JMJP 12/31/66; SCMP 3852:45

1967

67-1 **1/17/67** – Rawalpindi **Pakistan** –
PRC supply of grain
JMJP 1/19/67; AsR 7577

67-2 **1/26/67** – Peking **Finland** Exchange of Notes
Trademark registration
FTS(SAS) 1967:22:329(F,E)

67-3 **1/31/67** – Peking **Bulgaria** Agreement
Exchange of goods and payments in 1967
JMJP 2/5/67; SCMP 3875:27

67-4 **2/14/67** – Bucharest **Rumania** Agreement
Exchange of goods and payments in 1967
SCMP 3883:29; Bucharest Domestic Broadcasting 2/14/67. (reprinted in FBIS, Daily Report, 1967:32:JJ. 1); AsR 7584

67-5 **2/16/67** – Peking **Mauritania** Agreement
Trade
Ratified by PRC State Council 3/14/67. JMJP 3/19/67, quoting New China News Agency 3/18/67 news release, reports that Agreement has formally entered into force.
JMJP 2/17/67; PR 2/24/67, p. 15; SCMP 3883:27

67-6 **2/16/67** – Peking **Mauritania** Agreement
Economic and technical cooperation
See note above.
JMJP 2/17/67; PR 2/24/67, p. 15; SCMP 3883:27

67-7 **2/16/67** – Peking **Mauritania** Agreement
Cultural cooperation
See note above.
JMJP 2/17/67; PR 2/24/67, p. 15; SCMP 3883:27

67-8 **2/17/67** – Peking **Mauritania** Joint Press Communiqué
Talks during visit of Foreign Minister Birane Mamadou Wane: Vietnam, Palestine Arabs, Rhodesia, PRC representation in UN, Cultural Revolution, etc.
PR 2/24/67, p. 14(E); SCMP 3884:?

67-9 **2/27/67** – Peking **Bulgaria** Protocol
Scientific and technical cooperation

Signed at tenth session of Sino-Bulgarian Joint Committee for Scientific and Technical Cooperation.

JMJP 3/1/67; SCMP 3890:27

67-10 **3/14/67** – Katmandu **Nepal** Contract
PRC supply of rice to Nepal

JMJP 3/20/67

67-11 **3/21/67** – Peking **Cuba** Protocol
Trade in 1967

JMJP 3/23/67; SCMP 3906:26

67-12 **4/13/67** – Damascus **Syria** Exchange of Letters
PRC technical aid in construction of cotton spinning mill in Syria

JMJP 4/20/67; SCMP 3923:32; AsR 7764

67-13 **4/14/67** – Peking **Germany (E)** Agreement
Exchange of goods and payments in 1967

SCMP 3921:32

67-14 **4/24/67** – Tirana **Albania** –
1967-68 plan for cultural cooperation

JMJP 4/27/67; SCMP 3927:37

67-15 **4/25/67** – Peking **Vietnam (N)** –
1967 plan for cultural cooperation

JMJP 4/27/67; SCMP 3927:40

67-16 **4/25/67** – Helsinki **Finland** Agreement
Trade in 1967

JMJP 4/27/67; SCMP 3928:30

67-17 **4/25/67** – Helsinki **Finland** Exchange of Letters
Revision of 1953 Payments Agreement to convert clearing currency from ruble to Finnish mark [53-32]

FTS(SAS) 1967:46:575(F,E)

67-18 **4/28/67** – Peking **Zambia** Agreement
Trade

JMJP 4/29/67; SCMP 3931:35

67-19 **5/25/67** – Peking **UAR** Protocol
Trade in 1967

SCMP 3949:29

67-20 5/25/67 – Katmandu **Nepal** Protocol
PRC aid in construction of power station and transmission line in Nepal

Nepalese government Press Communique also issued 5/25/67.

JMJP 5/29/67; SCMP 3950:48; AsR 7792

67-21 5/28/67 – Katmandu **Nepal** Agreement (?)
PRC aid in extension of Kodari highway to Katmandu

AsR 7792

67-22 5/28/67 – Peking **Albania** Protocol
Shipping

Signed at sixth meeting of Administrative Council of Sino-Albanian Shipping Joint Stock Company.

JMJP 5/29/67; SCMP 3950:31

67-23 6/23/67 – Peking **Zambia** Agreement
Economic and technical cooperation

JMJP 6/24/67; SCMP 3969:40; Africa Diary 3500

67-24 6/25/67 – Peking **Zambia** Joint Communiqué
Talks during President Kaunda's visit: Rhodesia, PRC representation in UN, national liberation movements, Vietnam, etc.

JMJP 6/27/67(C); PR 6/30/67, p. 12(E); SCMP 3970:45(E)

67-25 6/22/67 – Budapest **Hungary** Agreement
Exchange of goods and payments in 1967

JMJP 7/2/67; SCMP 3973:42

67-26 6/30/67 – Warsaw **Poland** Agreement
Exchange of goods and payments in 1967

JMJP 7/2/67; SCMP 3973:43

67-27 7/27/67 – Moscow **USSR** Protocol
Exchange of goods in 1967

Pr, Izv 7/28/67

67-28 8/3/67 – Peking **Vietnam (N)** Protocol
Scientific and technical cooperation

Signed at seventh meeting of Sino-Vietnamese Executive Organ for Scientific and Technical Cooperation.

JMJP 8/4/67; SCMP 3997:48

67-29 8/5/67 – Peking **Vietnam (N)** Agreement
PRC economic and technical aid

JMJP 8/6/67; PR 8/11/67, p. 28; SCMP 3997:48; NYT 8/6/67, p. 2

67-30 **8/14/67** – Peking **Mali** Agreement(s)
PRC economic aid to Mali
JMJP 8/15/67; PR 8/25/67, p. 25

67-31 **8/16/67** – Mogadishu **Somalia** Minutes
Talks on rice and tobacco experiment station built by PRC experts
JMJP 8/19/67; SCMP 4007:36

67-32 **8/19/67** – Mogadishu **Somalia** –
1967-68 plan for cultural cooperation
JMJP 8/20/67; SCMP 4007:37

67-33 **9/5/67** – Peking **Tanzania** **Zambia** Agreement
PRC economic and technical aid in construction of Tanzania-Zambia railway
JMJP 9/6/67; SCMP 4017:32; AsR 7976

67-34 **9/14/67** – Peking **Pakistan** –
1967-68 plan for cultural cooperation
JMJP 9/15/67; SCMP 4024:42

Addenda

Additional entries

The first six entries below are unreported agreements referred to recently in the PRC press after alleged violations. The remaining four entries are reported agreements discovered after completion of the calendar.

1955 – – **India** Exchange of letters
Exchange of mail between China's Tibet region and India

Mentioned in a statement issued by the Chinese Ministry of Posts and Telecommunication dated August 15, 1963.

JMJP 8/16/63; SCMP 3043:19

1956 – – **Soviet Union** Agreement
Abolition of visas

Mentioned in a verbal statement from a representative of the Chinese Foreign Ministry to the Soviet Embassy in Peking dated February 10, 1967. The statement indicated that several such agreements were concluded since 1956.

JMJP 2/11/67; SCMP 3880:49

10/15/57 – – **Soviet Union** Agreement
New technology for national defense. The Soviet Union agreed to provide China with a sample of an atomic bomb and technical data concerning its manufacture.

Mentioned in a statement by the spokesman of the Chinese Government dated August 15, 1963.

JMJP 8/15/63; PR 8/16/63, p. 7; SCMP 3043:27

19 ? – – **India** Agreement
Establishment of consulates-general at Calcutta, Bombay, Shanghai, and Lhasa

Mentioned in Chinese note to Indian Embassy in Peking dated December 8, 1962.

WCC 9:200; JMJP 12/10/62; SCMP 2879:31

1960 – – **India** Agreement
Change of location for the exchange of mail

Mentioned in a statement issued by the Chinese Ministry of Posts and Telecommunication dated August 15, 1963.

JMJP 8/16/63; SCMP 3043:19

1960 – – **Soviet Union** Agreement
Abolition of certificates of vaccination against small-pox

Mentioned in a statement issued by the Chinese Ministry of Public Health dated June 29, 1967.

JMJP 6/30/67

5/31/60 – Ulan Bator **Mongolia** Protocol
Economic and technical aid by PRC

SCMP 2273:39

5/31/60 – Ulan Bator **Mongolia** Agreement
Technical aid by PRC

Applies balance of funds under 1956 Economic and Technical Aid Agreement [56-96].

SCMP 2273:39

Aug./Sept. 1964 – – **Congo (Brazzaville)** Agreement
Credit (interest-free loan)

AfD 1929

9/15/66 – Peking **France** Exchange of Notes
9/22/66
Amendment of Article 12 of Air Communications Agreement of 6/1/66 [66-43]

Journal Officiel de la République Française, 1968:1020(Fr)

Additional references

These references to *Africa Diary* supplement those already listed for the following calendar entries:

61-107	Ghana: Top-level talks, AfD 99
61-108	Ghana: Friendship, AfD 99
61-109	Ghana: Economic and technical aid, AfD 99
61-110	Ghana: Trade and payments, AfD 99
61-111	Ghana: Cultural cooperation, AfD 99
61-122	Guinea: Economic and technical aid, AfD 166
61-125	Mali: Economic and technical aid, AfD 167
61-145	Morocco: Payments, AfD 243
61-147	Ghana: Trade and payments, AfD 242
61-148	Ghana: Cultural cooperation, AfD 242
61-149	Ghana: Trade, AfD 242
61-150	Ghana: Economic and technical aid, AfD 242
61-151	Ghana: Banking (aid), AfD 242
61-152	Ghana: Banking (trade), AfD 242
62-24	UAR: Trade, AfD 466
62-25	UAR: Payments, AfD 466
62-26	UAR: Trade, AfD 466
62-49	Sudan: Trade, AfD 584
62-97	Ghana: Economic and technical aid, AfD 835
62-104	Mali: Economic and technical aid, AfD 869
63-88	UAR: Trade, AfD 1287
63-96	Somalia: Top-level talks, AfD 1322
63-103	Mali: Radio, AfD 1352
63-116	Algeria: Loan, AfD 1431

64-45	UAR: Cultural cooperation, AfD 1771
64-72	Sudan: Top-level talks, AfD 1800
64-85	Tanganyika and Zanzibar (Tanzania): Economic and technical aid, AfD 1972
64-97	Ghana: Economic and technical aid, AfD 1897
64-100	Congo (Br): Trade and payments, AfD 1922
64-118	Algeria: Trade, AfD 1991
64-119	Algeria: Payments, AfD 1991
64-120	Algeria: Economic and technical aid, AfD 1991
64-124	Cameroon: Lower-level talks, AfD 2036
64-128	Central African Republic: Economic and technical aid, AfD 2036
64-129	Central African Republic: Trade and payments, AfD 2036
64-130	Central African Republic: Trade and payments, AfD 2036
64-135	Congo (Br): Friendship, AfD 2014
64-136	Congo (Br): Maritime transport, AfD 2014
64-137	Congo (Br): Economic and technical aid, AfD 2014
64-138	Congo (Br): Cultural cooperation, AfD 2014
64-156	Mali: Top-level talks, AfD 2071
64-157	Mali: Friendship, AfD 2071
64-184	UAR: Economic and technical aid, AfD 2136
65-2	Tanzania: Economic and technical aid, AfD 2168
65-23	Tanzania: Top-level talks, AfD 2245
65-50	Algeria: Top-level talks, AfD 2303
65-55	Uganda: Economic and technical aid, AfD 2374
65-78	Tanzania: Top-level talks, AfD 2404
65-96	Uganda: Top-level talks, AfD 2469
65-110	Mali: Technical aid talks, AfD 2550
66-30	UAR: Cultural cooperation, AfD 2920
66-50	Tanzania: Economic aid, AfD 2951
66-68	Tanzania: Sino-Tanzanian Maritime Transport Joint Stock Company, AfD 2989
66-83	Tanzania: Technical aid, AfD 3145
67-34	Tanzania/Zambia: Economic and technical aid, AfD 3610

Appendix • Glossary • Indexes

Table 1. Topical distribution of PRC agreements: 1949-67
(The period is broken down by revolutionary years, i.e., from 1st October to 30th September)

Year	Trade	Culture	Science and technology	Economic and technical aid	Friendship and foreign policy alignment	Finance	Postal services and telecommunications	Railway	Boundary	Aviation	Navigation	Fishery	Military	Joint stock companies	Diplomatic and consular	Nationality	Trademark	Customs	Repatriation	Miscellaneous	Total
1949-50	7	–	–	M 3	M 1	–	8	M 2	–	–	–	–	2	3	–	–	–	–	–	5	31
1950-51	11	2	–	2	1	–	3	2	–	1	2	–	0	2	–	–	–	–	–	0	26
1951-52	32	7	1	2	0	–	5	M 2	–	1	0	–	M 7	0	–	–	–	–	–	1	58
1952-53	35	M 8	3	M 4	0	3	5	3	–	0	0	–	4	0	–	–	–	–	2	2	69
1953-54	M 29	M 17	6	M 1	M 6	6	M 2	2	–	0	0	–	M 0	0	–	–	–	–	0	3	72
1954-55	M 41	18	M 15	M 8	M 7	0	7	M 4	–	1	M 0	4	M 2	M 5	1	3	–	–	1	2	119
1955-56	M 55	M 22	17	M 9	M 5	11	5	M 6	–	6	M 2	5	0	0	M 1	M 1	1	M –	M 0	7	153
1956-57	M 46	14	M 15	M 10	20	M 5	M 5	1	–	M 0	1	5	0	0	0	0	2	1	0	7	132
1957-58	M 45	16	24	9	8	M 5	5	2	–	4	M 3	0	1	0	0	0	1	M 0	0	3	126

Table 1 (cont.)

Year	Trade	Culture	Science and technology	Economic and technical aid	Friendship and foreign policy alignment	Finance	Postal services and telecommunications	Railway	Boundary	Aviation	Navigation	Fishery	Military	Joint stock companies	Diplomatic and consular	Nationality	Trademark	Customs	Repatriation	Miscellaneous	Total
1958-59	M 35	24	18	17	7	M 7	0	2	–	6	M 1	1	1	0	2	0	M 0	0	0	2	123
1959-60	M 33	17	18	M 9	19	M 4	1	3	6	1	M 1	1	0	0	1	1	0	1	0	2	118
1960-61	M 44	M 21	M 22	M 26	15	8	0	M 2	M 8	1	M 1	1	0	0	1	1	0	0	0	12	163
1961-62	M 41	19	23	M 14	5	5	2	2	M 3	1	4	1	M 0	2	M 1	M 0	0	0	0	3	126
1962-63	M 40	27	18	M 10	14	5	3	1	10	3	M 3	2	0	1	0	0	0	0	0	5	142
1963-64	43	M 34	27	M 18	24	2	3	6	7	5	3	3	0	0	0	0	0	0	0	1	176
1964-65	M 37	M 36	M 19	M 40	24	3	6	4	4	4	3	0	3	0	0	0	0	1	0	8	192
1965-66	M 24	M 29	M 27	M 13	9	0	0	2	0	3	M 2	3	0	2	0	0	0	0	0	4	118
1966-67	22	6	7	20	2	1	0	0	0	0	2	0	0	0	0	0	1	0	0	0	61
Total	620	317	260	215	167	65	60	46	38	37	28	26	20	15	7	6	5	3	3	67	2005

M: Category also represented in one or more agreements listed in "Miscellaneous" column.

Table 2. National treaty contacts with PRC: 1949-67

(This table includes both single contacts, in bilateral agreements, and plural contacts, in trilateral and other multilateral agreements)

PARTNER (in order of total volume)	1949 -50	1950 -51	1951 -52	1952 -53	1953 -54	1954 -55	1955 -56	1956 -57	1957 -58	1958 -59	1959 -60	1960 -61	1961 -62	1962 -63	1963 -64	1964 -65	1965 -66	1966 -67	Total
USSR	22	7	11	9	7	22	22	16	17	12	12	17	14	7	7	10	4	2	218
Vietnam (N)	–	–	1	2	5	15	15	13	7	14	11	14	10	12	17	11	10	6	163
Korea (N)	6	0	1	7	10	6	13	8	13	17	8	10	8	10	11	11	10	2	151
Poland	2	8	3	5	6	5	11	8	13	8	7	7	9	4	5	10	4	1	116
Albania	–	–	–	2	1	9	4	8	5	9	5	15	9	7	10	16	7	6	113
Germany (E)	–	2	5	7	10	6	11	9	8	13	9	4	5	4	5	10	4	1	113
Mongolia	–	–	1	10	4	3	11	5	9	7	13	9	6	6	7	11	3	0	105
Czechoslovakia	1	2	7	8	5	3	8	10	7	9	7	3	10	5	4	10	4	1	104
Hungary	–	3	3	7	6	5	7	9	10	10	8	5	4	5	4	9	3	1	99
Rumania	–	–	3	6	8	5	7	7	6	8	6	8	5	8	4	10	5	1	97
Bulgaria	–	–	3	5	6	6	8	5	5	9	5	4	5	4	4	9	3	2	83
Ceylon	–	–	1	8	0	3	5	11	1	7	2	4	7	8	7	9	2	3	78
Burma	–	–	–	–	3	7	7	2	4	0	8	14	8	5	3	3	1	0	65
Indonesia	–	–	1	0	3	5	0	5	1	2	2	6	1	3	6	20	1	0	56
Cuba	–	–	–	–	–	–	–	–	–	–	4	11	8	8	5	10	4	1	51
Cambodia	–	–	–	–	1	1	7	3	3	1	3	7	4	3	3	6	3	0	45
Nepal	–	–	–	–	–	1	4	5	0	0	5	5	4	2	4	8	2	5	45
Pakistan	–	–	1	2	0	1	2	3	1	1	0	0	1	10	7	7	5	3	44
Egypt (UAR)	–	–	–	–	–	8	3	5	4	3	2	1	3	3	3	6	2	1	44
Japan	–	–	1	1	1	6	9	5	2	0	1	0	0	4	6	2	5	1	44
Guinea	–	–	–	–	–	–	–	–	–	–	7	2	3	2	7	4	5	4	34
Finland	–	–	2	3	2	2	2	2	2	1	2	2	1	2	1	1	1	3	29
Afghanistan	–	–	–	–	–	1	0	2	1	1	4	1	1	2	6	5	4	1	29
Yugoslavia	–	–	–	–	–	–	10	6	4	1	1	1	1	0	2	1	1	0	28
Ghana	–	–	–	–	–	1	0	0	0	0	0	5	7	3	8	4	0	0	28

Table 2. (cont.)

PARTNER (in order of total volume)	1949 -50	1950 -51	1951 -52	1952 -53	1953 -54	1954 -55	1955 -56	1956 -57	1957 -58	1958 -59	1959 -60	1960 -61	1961 -62	1962 -63	1963 -64	1964 -65	1965 -66	1966 -67	Total
India	–	2	1	1	4	7	1	3	1	1	1	0	2	0	1	0	0	0	25
Syria	–	–	–	–	–	1	4	1	1	4	2	1	0	4	2	2	2	1	25
Mali	–	–	–	–	–	–	–	–	–	–	–	5	2	7	4	3	2	1	24
Algeria	–	–	–	–	–	–	–	–	–	1	1	1	0	1	10	6	1	0	21
Iraq	–	–	–	–	–	1	0	0	0	4	4	0	4	1	3	0	2	0	19
Tanzania	–	–	–	–	–	–	–	–	–	–	–	–	–	1	3	7	4	4	19
Yemen	–	–	–	–	–	1	0	0	4	2	0	0	1	0	4	2	2	0	16
Congo (Br)	–	–	–	–	–	–	–	–	–	–	–	–	–	–	2	11	1	0	14
Laos	–	–	–	–	1	1	1	0	0	0	0	2	4	3	1	0	0	0	13
Sudan	–	–	–	–	–	1	2	0	1	0	0	0	1	2	3	1	1	0	12
France	–	–	2	1	1	0	3	0	0	0	0	0	2	0	0	0	3	0	12
Somalia	–	–	–	–	–	–	–	–	–	–	–	–	–	4	1	2	1	3	11
Morocco	–	–	–	–	–	–	–	–	1	2	0	1	1	1	2	0	2	0	10
U.K.	–	–	1	2	1	0	1	0	0	0	0	1	2	0	1	0	0	0	9
Tunisia	–	–	–	–	–	–	–	–	1	0	0	2	0	0	2	1	0	0	6
Zambia	–	–	–	–	–	–	–	–	–	–	–	–	–	–	–	–	2	4	6
Norway	–	–	–	–	–	–	–	–	2	0	0	1	0	1	0	0	1	0	5
Kenya	–	–	–	–	–	–	–	–	–	–	–	–	–	–	1	4	0	0	5
Germany (W)	–	–	2	0	0	0	0	3	0	0	0	0	0	0	0	0	0	0	5
Denmark	–	–	–	–	–	–	–	–	3	0	0	1	0	0	0	0	0	0	4
Mauritania	–	–	–	–	–	–	–	–	–	–	–	–	–	–	–	–	–	4	4
Central African Republic	–	–	–	–	–	–	–	–	–	–	–	–	–	–	3	1	0	0	4
Ethiopia	–	–	–	–	–	1	0	0	0	0	0	1	0	0	2	0	0	0	4
Lebanon	–	–	–	–	–	1	3	0	0	0	0	0	0	0	0	0	0	0	4
USA	–	–	–	–	*	1	0	0	0	0	0	0	2	0	0	0	0	0	3
Sweden	–	–	–	–	–	1	0	1	1	0	0	0	0	0	0	0	0	0	3

Table 2. (cont.)

PARTNER (in order of total volume)	1949 -50	1950 -51	1951 -52	1952 -53	1953 -54	1954 -55	1955 -56	1956 -57	1957 -58	1958 -59	1959 -60	1960 -61	1961 -62	1962 -63	1963 -64	1964 -65	1965 -66	1966 -67	Total
Switzerland	–	–	1	0	0	0	0	1	0	0	0	0	0	0	0	0	0	0	2
Uganda	–	–	–	–	–	–	–	–	–	–	–	–	–	–	–	2	0	0	2
Netherlands	–	–	1	0	0	0	0	0	0	0	0	0	0	0	1	0	0	0	2
Cameroon	–	–	–	–	–	–	–	–	–	–	–	–	–	–	2	0	0	0	2
Austria	–	–	–	–	–	–	1	0	0	0	0	0	0	0	0	1	0	0	2
Italy	–	–	1	0	0	0	0	0	0	0	0	0	0	0	0	1	0	0	2
Kuwait	–	–	–	–	–	–	–	–	–	–	–	–	–	–	–	2	0	0	2
Burundi	–	–	–	–	–	–	–	–	–	–	–	–	–	–	–	1	0	0	1
Dahomey	–	–	–	–	–	–	–	–	–	–	–	–	–	–	1	0	0	0	1
Malagasy	–	–	–	–	–	–	–	–	–	–	–	–	–	–	–	–	1	0	1
Nigeria	–	–	–	–	–	–	–	–	–	–	–	1	0	0	0	0	0	0	1
Belgium	–	–	1	0	0	0	0	0	0	0	0	0	0	0	0	0	0	0	1
Brazil	–	–	–	–	–	–	–	–	–	–	–	1	0	0	0	0	0	0	1
Chile	–	–	–	1	0	0	0	0	0	0	0	0	0	0	0	0	0	0	1
Malaya	–	–	–	–	–	–	–	1	0	0	0	0	0	0	0	0	0	0	1
Singapore	–	–	–	–	–	–	–	1	0	0	0	0	0	0	0	0	0	0	1
Mexico	–	–	–	–	–	–	–	–	–	–	–	–	–	–	1	0	0	0	1
Uruguay	–	–	–	–	–	–	1	0	0	0	0	0	0	0	0	0	0	0	1
Hong Kong	–	–	–	–	–	–	–	–	–	–	–	1	0	0	0	0	0	0	1
Tibet	–	1	0	0	0	0	0	0	0	0	0	0	0	0	0	0	0	0	1
Total	31	25	55	91	81	137	184	158	138	147	140	174	153	152	196	250	118	62	2292

*The USA issued a separate Declaration at the end of the Geneva Conference on Indo-China in July, 1954. Though unilateral, this document associates itself in large part with the Final Declaration of the Conference signed by the USSR, UK, France, Cambodia, North Vietnam, Laos, and the PRC.

Note: Of the multilateral agreements contained in the Calendar, the only one deliberately excluded from the count of national treaty contacts in this table is the communiqué issued after the second meeting of the Federation of the Games of the Newly Emerging Forces on 23rd September 1965. It should be noted, however, that in addition to those included in the table the PRC established "peripheral" treaty contacts at the Bandung Conference in April, 1955, with Iran, Jordan, Liberia, Libya, the Phillipines, Saudi Arabia, Thailand, Turkey, and South Vietnam; at the Geneva Conference on Laos in July, 1962, with Canada, Thailand, and South Vietnam; and at the Djakarta Preparatory Meeting of the Second Afro-Asian Conference in April, 1964, with Iran, Liberia, and the Phillipines.

Table 3. Topical distribution of agreements listed in PRC's official compilation (TYC): 1949-64

(The following classification is the same as the classification used in the compilation)

Political	
(1) Friendship	15
(2) Joint announcement, communiqué, or declaration	102
(3) Others	15
Legal	
(1) Consular relations	3
(2) Nationality	3
Boundary	17
Boundary problems (use of boundary river, etc.)	4
Economic	
(1) Commerce and navigation	11
(2) Economic aid, loan, and technical cooperation	20
(3) Trade and payment	249; 19*
(4) General conditions for delivery of goods	85; 2*
(5) Registration of trade mark	4
(6) Others	15; 2*
Cultural	
(1) Cultural cooperation	30
(2) Broadcasting and TV cooperation	30
(3) Exchange of students	3
(4) Others	1; 1*
Science and technology	37
Agriculture and forest	9
Fishery	3; 12*
Health and sanitation	5
Post and telecommunication	44
Communication and transportation	
(1) Railways	10
(2) Air transportation	12
(3) Water transportation	12
(4) Highway	1
Law of war	5
Military	1*

*Described as "semiofficial" agreements.
Source: Am. J. Int'l. L. 61:1096 (1967).

Table 4. National distribution of agreements listed in PRC's official compilation (TYC): 1949-64

Afghanistan	11	Germany (W)	4*	Rumania	36
Albania	22	Ghana	11	Singapore and Malaya	1*
Algeria	8	Guinea	8	Somalia	4
Austria	2*	Hungary	40	Soviet Union	40
Bulgaria	30	India	10	Sudan	6
Burma	31	Indonesia	21	Sweden	2
Burundi	1	Iraq	6	Switzerland	1
Cambodia	25	Japan	24*	Syria	4
Central African Republic	3	Korea (N)	39	Tanzania	2
		Laos	7	Tunisia	2
Ceylon	20	Lebanon	1	United Arab Republic	23
Congo (Br)	4	Mali	2	United Kingdom	1; 1*
Cuba	11	Mongolia	32	United Nations	1*
Czechoslovakia	37	Morocco	1	United States	1
Denmark	4	Nepal	18	Vietnam (N)	47
Ethiopia	2	Nigeria	1	Yemen	7
Finland	19;2*	Norway	2	Yugoslavia	15
France	3*	Pakistan	9		
Germany (E)	23	Poland	35		

*Described as "semiofficial" agreements.
Source: Am. J. Int'l. L. 61:1097 (1967).

GLOSSARY

Publications

Collection of friendship treaties concluded by the People's Republic of China; Chung-hua jen-min kung-ho-kuo yu-hao t'iao-yüeh hui-pien 中华人民共和国友好条約汇編

Collection of laws and decrees of the Central People's Government; Chung-yang jen-min cheng-fu fa-ling hui-pien 中央人民政府法令彙編

Collection of laws and regulations of the People's Republic of China; Chung-hua jen-min kung-ho-kuo fa-kuei hui-pien 中華人民共和國法規彙編

Compilation of foreign relations documents of the People's Republic of China; Chung-hua jen-min kung-ho-kuo tui-wai kuan-hsi wen-chien chi 中华人民共和国对外关系文件集

Compilation of treaties of the People's Republic of China; Chung-hua jen-min kung-ho-kuo t'iao-yüeh-chi 中华人民共和国条約集

People's daily; Jen-min jih-pao 人民日报

People's handbook; Jen-min shou-ts'e 人民手册

Terms

Academy of Sciences; k'o-hsüeh yüan 科学院

accord; hsieh-i 协議

administrative committee; kuan-li wei-yüan-hui
管理委員会

agreement; hsieh-ting 协定

air transport; hang-k'ung yün-shu 航空运輸

alliance; t'ung-meng 同盟

barter; i-huo 易貨

boundary; pien-chieh 边界

boundary demarcation; piao-chieh; k'an-chieh
標界；勘界

broadcasting and television; kuang-po ho tien-shih
广播和电視

commerce; t'ung-shang 通商

commodity; shang-p'in 商品

company; kung-szu 公司

consular treaty; ling-shih t'iao-yüeh 領事条約

contract; ho-t'ung 合同

cooperation in public health; wei-sheng ho-tso
卫生合作

corporation; kung-szu 公司

cultural cooperation; wen-hua ho-tso 文化合作

declaration; hsüan-yen 宣言

economic aid; ching-chi yüan-chu 經済援助

economic and technical cooperation; ching-chi chi-shu ho-tso 經済技术合作

exchange of goods; chiao-huan huo-wu; huan-huo; huo-wu chiao-huan 交換貨物；換貨；貨物交換

exchange of notes; huan-wen 換文

executive organ; chih-hsing chi-kou 执行机构

friendship; yu-hao 友好

general conditions for delivery of goods; chiao-huo kung-t'ung t'iao-chien 交貨共同条件

goods; huo-wu 貨物

joint arrangement; kung-t'ung pan-fa 共同办法

joint committee; lien-ho wei-yüan-hui 联合委員会

joint communiqué; lien-ho kung-pao 联合公报

joint statement; lien-ho sheng-ming; kung-t'ung sheng-ming 联合声明；共同声明

loan; tai-k'uan 貸款

maritime transport; hai-yün; hai-shang yün-shu 海运；海上运輸

memorandum; pei-wang-lu 备忘录

minute; chi-lu-shu; chi-yao 記录书；紀要

most-favored nation; tsui-hui-kuo 最惠国

mutual assistance; hu-chu 互助

mutual non-aggression; hu pu ch'in-fan 互不侵犯

mutual supply of goods; hu-hsiang kung-ying huo-wu 互相供应貨物

nationality; kuo-chi 国籍

navigation; hang-hai 航海

parcel; pao-kuo 包裹

payment; chih-fu; fu-k'uan 支付；付款

plan; chi-hua 計划

post; yu-cheng 邮政

press communiqué; hsin-wen kung-pao 新聞公报

protocol; i-ting-shu 議定书

scientific and technical cooperation; k'o-hsüeh ho chi-shu ho-tso 科学和技术合作

shipping company; lun-ch'uan kung-szu 輪船公司

small-scale trade; hsiao-o mao-i 小額貿易

standing committee; ch'ang-jen wei-yüan-hui 常任委员会

state trading company; kuo-ying mao-i kung-szu 国营貿易公司

talk; hui-t'an 会談

technical science; chi-shu k'o-hsüeh 技术科学

technology; chi-shu 技术

telecommunication; tien-hsin 电信

telephone; tien-hua 电話

trade; mao-i 貿易

trade mark registration; shang-piao chu-ts'e 商標註册

treaty; t'iao-yüeh 条約

turnover; chou-chuan 周轉

Bilateral and Trilateral Agreements by Partners

Note: A dash indicates that the type of document is not reported.

Partners:

Afghanistan
Albania
Algeria
Austria
Belgium
Brazil
Bulgaria
Burma
Burundi
Cambodia
Cameroon
Central African Republic
Ceylon
Chile
Congo (Brazzaville)
Cuba
Czechoslovakia
Dahomey
Denmark
Egypt (UAR)
Ethiopia
Finland
France
Germany (E)
Germany (W)
Ghana
Guinea
Hong Kong
Hungary
India
Indonesia
Iraq
Italy
Japan
Kenya
Korea (N)
Kuwait
Laos
Lebanon
Malagasy
Malaya
Mali
Mauritania
Mexico
Mongolia
Morocco
Nepal
Netherlands
Nigeria
Norway
Pakistan
Poland
Portugal
Rumania
Singapore
Somalia
Sudan
Sweden
Switzerland
Syria
Tanzania
Tibet
Tunisia
Uganda
United Kingdom
United Nations Organization
Uruguay
United States of America
Union of Socialist Soviet Republics
Vietnam (N)
Yemen
Yugoslavia
Zambia

Afghanistan

1/22/57	Joint Communiqué: Talks (top level)
7/28/57	Agreement: Exchange of goods and payments (1957-59)
10/26/57	Joint Communiqué: Talks (top level)
9/9/59	Joint Communiqué: Talks (top level)
8/26/60	Joint Communiqué: Talks (top level)
8/26/60	Treaty: Friendship
8/26/60	Exchange of Notes: Friendship
8/26/60	Agreement: Exchange of goods and payments
9/21/61	Protocol: Exchange of goods and payments (1961)
7/18/62	Protocol: Exchange of goods and payments (1962)
3/2/63	Press Communiqué: Boundary
8/3/63	Joint Press Communiqué: Boundary
10/9/63	Agreement: Exchange of goods and payments
10/9/63	Protocol: Exchange of goods (1963-64)
11/22/63	Treaty: Boundary
11/24/63	Press Communiqué: Boundary
12/11/63	Press Communiqué: Aviation
10/24/64	Protocol: Exchange of goods (1964-65)
11/12/64	Joint Communiqué: Talks (top level)
3/24/65	Protocol: Boundary
3/24/65	Agreement: Economic and technical aid
3/24/65	Agreement: Cultural cooperation
11/6/65	Protocol: Exchange of goods (1965-66)
4/8/66	Joint Communiqué: Talks (top level)
5/24/66	– Plan for cultural cooperation
7/29/66	Protocol: Economic and technical aid
12/28/66	Protocol: Exchange of goods (1966-67)

Albania

10/10/54(?)	– Economic aid
10/14/54	Agreement: Scientific and technical cooperation
10/14/54	Agreement: Cultural cooperation
12/3/54	Agreement: Exchange of goods and payments (1955)
12/3/54	Agreement: Credit
12/3/54	Protocol: Plan for scientific and technical cooperation
3/2/55	– Plan for cultural cooperation
9/28/55	Agreement: Radio cooperation
9/28/55	– Plan for cultural cooperation
3/13/56	Protocol: Exchange of goods and payments (1956)
10/22/56	Protocol: Scientific and technical cooperation
12/19/56	Exchange of Notes: Economic aid
3/8/57	Protocol: Exchange of goods and payments (1957)
3/8/57	Protocol: Economic aid
3/8/57	Protocol: Delivery of goods
5/31/57	Agreement: Postal service and telecommunications
3/12/58	Protocol: Exchange of goods and payments (1958)
3/12/58	Exchange of Notes: Delivery of goods

4/29/58	— Plan for cultural cooperation
6/4/58	Protocol: Scientific and technical cooperation
1/16/59	Agreement: Trade (1961-65)
1/16/59	Agreement: Loan
1/16/59	Protocol: Exchange of goods and payments (1959)
1/16/59	Protocol: Economic aid
1/16/59	Protocol: Clearance of account (economic aid)
4/20/59	Agreement: Payments (noncommercial)
7/11/59	Agreement: Radio cooperation
3/4/60	— Plan for cultural cooperation
3/15/60	Protocol: Exchange of goods and payments (1960)
3/15/60	Protocol: Economic aid
3/15/60	Exchange of Notes: Delivery of goods
10/18/60	Protocol: Scientific and technical cooperation
10/24/60	— Plan for cultural cooperation
1/31/61	Exchange of Notes: Delivery of goods
2/2/61	Press Communiqué: Economic and trade talks
2/2/61	Treaty: Commerce and navigation
2/2/61	Protocol: Exchange of goods and payments (1961)
2/2/61	Agreement: Loan
2/2/61	Protocol: Loan
2/2/61	Protocol: Loan (1961)
2/2/61	Protocol: Clearance of accounts (loan)
4/23/61	Protocol: Economic and technical aid
4/23/61	Protocol: Technical aid
4/23/61	Protocol: Loan
4/23/61	Exchange of Notes: Supply of grains and foodstuffs to Albania
4/25/61	Press Communiqué: Economic talks
12/26/61	Agreement: Establishment of Sino-Albanian Shipping Joint Stock Company
1/13/62	Agreement: Loan
1/13/62	Exchange of Notes: Economic and technical aid
1/13/62	Protocol: Exchange of goods and payments (1962)
1/13/62	Protocol: Credit
1/13/62	Protocol: Scientific and technical cooperation
1/15/62	Press Communiqué: Economic talks
4/11/62	Agreement: News agencies
5/7/62	Protocol: Shipping
12/11/62	— Plan for cultural cooperation
12/12/62	Protocol: Scientific and technical cooperation
1/17/63	Protocol: Exchange of goods and payments (1963)
1/17/63	Protocol: Loans
2/18/63	Agreement: Insect pests and plant diseases
5/2/63	Protocol: Management of Sino-Albanian Shipping Joint Stock Company
10/15/63	Protocol: Scientific and technical cooperation
12/6/63	Protocol: Exchange of goods and payments (1964)
12/6/63	Protocol: Loan
12/6/63	Joint Communiqué: Trade talks
1/2/64	Agreement: Cooperation in public health

1/8/64	Joint Statement: Talks (top level)
3/5/64	Agreement: Agricultural cooperation
3/25/64	Accord: Cooperation between Academies of Sciences
3/25/64	– Plan for cooperation between Academies of Sciences
5/23/64	Protocol: Shipping
10/10/64	Protocol: Exchange of goods and payments (1965)
10/10/64	Protocol: Loan
10/10/64	Agreement: Customs
11/28/64	Protocol: Scientific and technical cooperation
3/12/65	– Plan for cultural cooperation
3/22/65	Protocol: Shipping
3/30/65	Press Communiqué: Talks (top level)
6/8/65	Agreement: Loan
6/8/65	Agreement: Exchange of goods and payments (1966-70)
6/8/65	Protocols (2): Economic aid
6/9/65	Press Communiqué: Economic talks
10/6/65	Protocol: Scientific and technical cooperation
11/12/65	Protocol: Exchange of goods and payments (1966)
11/12/65	Protocol: Credit
5/4/66	Protocol: Shipping
5/11/66	Joint Statement: Talks (top level)
5/24/66	– Plan for cooperation between Academies of Sciences
6/28/66	Communiqué: Talks (lower level)
10/20/66	Agreement: Loan
11/21/66	Protocol: Exchange of goods and payments (1967)
11/21/66	Protocol: Loans
11/30/66	Protocol: Scientific and technical cooperation
4/24/67	– Plan for cultural cooperation
5/28/67	Protocol: Shipping

Algeria

12/20/58	Joint Communiqué: Talks (top level)
5/19/60	Joint Communiqué: Talks (top level)
10/5/60	Joint Communiqué: Talks (top level)
9/11/63	Agreement: Cultural cooperation
10/11/63	Communiqué: Loan
10/28/63	Agreement: Economic and technical aid
12/27/63	Joint Communiqué: Talks (top level)
4/14/64	– Plan for cultural cooperation
4/14/64	Agreement: Radio and television cooperation
7/15/64	Agreement: News agencies
9/19/64	Agreement: Trade
9/19/64	Agreement: Payments
9/19/64	Protocol: Economic and technical aid
12/25/64	Agreement: Scientific and technical cooperation
1/14/65	Contract: Films
2/11/65	Protocol: Military aid
4/1/65	Joint Communiqué: Talks (top level)

6/3/65	– Plan for cultural cooperation
8/28/65	Joint Communiqué: Talks (top level)
6/20/66	Memorandum: Talks on technical aid (specific project)

Austria

9/13/56	Protocol: Promotion of trade
12/7/64	Agreement: Promotion of trade, etc.

Belgium

4/12/52(?)	Agreement: Trade

Brazil

8/21/61	Agreement: Trade and payments

Bulgaria

7/14/52	Agreement: Cultural cooperation
7/21/52	Agreement: Exchange of goods and payments (1952)
7/21/52	Protocol: Delivery of goods
12/3/52	Agreement: Exchange of goods and payments (1953)
12/3/52	Protocol: Delivery of goods
5/22/53	Exchange of Notes: Plan for cultural cooperation
10/15/53	Agreement: Radio cooperation
3/25/54	Agreement: Exchange of goods and payments (1954)
3/25/54	Protocol: Delivery of goods
3/25/54	Protocol: Clearance of trade
5/4/54	– Plan for cultural cooperation
1/27/55	Agreement: Exchange of goods and payments (1955)
1/27/55	Protocol: Delivery of goods
2/17/55	– Plan for cultural cooperation
3/23/55	Agreement: Scientific and technical cooperation
7/11/55	Agreement: Insect pests and plant diseases
9/14/55	Agreement: Postal services and telecommunications
11/11/55(?)	Protocol: Scientific and technical cooperation
1/19/56	– Plan for cultural cooperation
1/21/56	Agreement: Exchange of goods and payments (1956)
1/21/56	Protocol: Delivery of goods
3/27/56	Exchange of Notes: Delivery of goods
9/16/56	Protocol: Scientific and technical cooperation
1/28/57	Agreement: Exchange of goods and payments (1957)
1/28/57	Protocol: Delivery of goods
2/20/57	– Plan for cultural cooperation
10/11/57	Joint Statement: Talks (top level)
10/11/57	Agreement: Exchange of goods and payments (1958-60)

3/13/58	Protocol: Exchange of goods and payments (1958)
3/19/58	– Plan for cultural cooperation
11/13/58	Protocol: Scientific and technical cooperation
11/27/58	– Plan for cultural cooperation
12/18/58	Protocol: Exchange of goods and payments (1959)
12/18/58	Protocol: Trade (1958-60)
4/23/59	Agreement: Cooperation between Academies of Sciences
8/6/59	Agreement: Radio and television cooperation
8/28/59	Protocol: Scientific and technical cooperation
12/5/59	– Plan for cultural cooperation
3/15/60	– Plan for cooperation between Academies of Sciences
3/15/60	Protocol: Exchange of goods (1960)
11/5/60	Protocol: Scientific and technical cooperation
3/8/61	Protocol: Exchange of goods and payments (1961)
4/20/61	– Plan for cooperation between Academies of Sciences
5/25/61	– Plan for cultural cooperation
3/30/62	Protocol: Exchange of goods and payments (1962)
3/30/62	Protocol: Delivery of goods
4/18/62	– Plan for cultural cooperation
9/13/62	Protocol: Scientific and technical cooperation
3/5/63	Agreement: Exchange of goods and payments (1963)
3/20/63	– Plan for cultural cooperation
6/19/63	– Plan for cooperation between Academies of Sciences
11/26/63	Protocol: Scientific and technical cooperation
3/21/64	– Plan for cultural cooperation
4/14/64	Agreement: Exchange of goods and payments (1964)
9/24/64	– Plan for cooperation between Academies of Sciences
11/30/64	Protocol: Scientific and technical cooperation
12/12/64	Agreement: Exchange of goods and payments (1965)
5/13/65	– Plan for cultural cooperation
11/9/65	Protocol: Scientific and technical cooperation
3/16/65	Agreement: Exchange of goods and payments (1966)
7/1/66	– Plan for cultural cooperation
1/31/67	Agreement: Exchange of goods and payments (1967)
2/27/67	Protocol: Scientific and technical cooperation

Burma

4/22/54	Agreement: Trade (1954-57)
4/22/54	Exchange of Notes: Trade balance
6/29/54	Joint Statement: Talks (top level)
11/3/54	Protocol: Rice and other commodities (1954-55)
11/3/54	Contract: Rice
12/12/54	Communiqué: Talks (top level)
3/29/55	Contracts (3): Trade
10/8/55	Agreement: Aviation
10/8/55	Protocol: Aviation

10/8/55	Exchange of Notes: Nationality of pilots
11/11/55(?)	Protocol: Aviation
12/29/55	Protocol: Rice and other commodities (1955-56)
1/10/56	Exchange of Notes: Trade
1/19/56	Contract: Rice
11/9/56	Joint Press Communiqué: Talks (top level)
12/20/56	Joint Statement: Talks (top level)
11/1/57	Agreement: Postal
11/1/57	Agreement: Postal (parcels)
1/31/58	Agreement: Telecommunications
2/21/58	Agreement: Trade (1958-60)
1/28/60	Joint Communiqué: Talks (top level)
1/28/60	Treaty: Friendship
1/28/60	Agreement: Boundary
4/19/60	Joint Communiqué: Talks (top level)
7/6/60	Communiqué: Boundary
8/2/60	Communiqué: Boundary
9/15/60	Communiqué: Boundary
9/24/60	Joint Press Communiqué: Boundary, gifts, etc.
10/1/60	Treaty: Boundary
10/1/60	Exchange of Notes: Boundary, nationality, etc.
10/4/60	Joint Communiqué: Talks (top level)
10/6/60	Communiqué: Boundary
10/24/60	Communiqué: Trade talks
10/24/60	Accord (with Exchange of Letters): Rice
12/24/60	Communiqué: Boundary
1/9/61	Joint Communiqué: Talks (top level)
1/9/61	Agreement: Economic and technical aid
1/9/61	Agreement: Payments
1/27/61	Agreement: Trade (1961-66)
4/16/61	Joint Communiqué: Talks (top level)
5/9/61	Communiqué: Boundary
6/4/61	Joint Press Communiqué: Boundary
10/13/61	Protocol: Boundary
10/14/61	Joint Communiqué: Talks (top level)
12/13/61	Protocol: Economic and technical aid
12/13/61	Protocol: Rice
12/21/61	Exchange of Letters: Economic and technical aid
12/21/61	Exchange of Letters: Technical aid
12/31/62	Joint Communiqué: Trade talks
12/31/62	Protocol: Trade (1963)
4/25/63	Joint Communiqué: Talks (top level)
8/1/63	Agreement: News agencies
8/28/63	Exchange of Notes: Ship's papers
10/23/63	Protocol: Rice
2/18/64	Joint Communiqué: Talks (top level)
7/11/64	Joint Communiqué: Talks (top level)
1/26/65	Protocol: Rice (1965)
7/14/65	Memorandum: Aviation
8/1/65	Joint Communiqué: Talks (top level)
4/19/66	Joint Communiqué: Talks (top level)

Burundi

10/22/64	Agreement: Trade and payments

Cambodia

2/18/56	Joint Communiqué: Talks (top level)
4/24/56	Agreement: Trade
4/24/56	Agreement: Payments
4/29/56	Joint Communiqué: Trade talks
6/21/56	Joint Communiqué: Economic aid talks
6/21/56	Agreement: Economic aid
6/21/56	Protocol: Economic aid
11/27/56	Joint Communiqué: Talks (top level)
6/7/57	Exchange of Notes: Trade and payments (1957-58)
6/22/57	Contract: Trade (1957-58)
3/26/58	Exchange of Notes: Economic aid
6/28/58	Exchange of Notes: Trade and Payments (1958-59)
8/24/58	Joint Statement: Talks (top level)
6/1/59	Exchange of Notes: Trade and payments
11/21/59	Exchange of Notes: Tariffs
5/8/60	Joint Statement: Talks (top level)
7/6/60	Exchange of Notes: Trade payments and economic aid
12/19/60	Joint Statement: Talks (top level)
12/19/60	Treaty: Friendship
12/19/60	Protocol: Economic and technical aid
12/19/60	Protocol: Economic aid
12/19/60	Agreement: Navigation
12/19/60	Exchange of Letters: Technical aid (railway and agriculture)
8/3/61	Exchange of Notes: Trade and payments
5/23/62	Exchange of Notes: Ship's papers
7/5/62	Exchange of Notes: Trade and payments
2/27/63	Joint Communiqué: Talks (top level)
5/5/63	Joint Statement: Talks (top level)
6/15/63	Exchange of Notes: Trade and payments
11/25/63	Agreement: Aviation
11/26/63	Protocol: Aviation
10/5/64	Joint Communiqué: Talks (top level)
Dec.(?)/64	– Supply of military equipment
3/22/65	– Plan for scientific and cultural cooperation
6/26/65	Protocol: Trade
6/26/65	Protocol: Payments
9/16/65	Agreement: News agencies
10/3/65	Joint Statement: Talks (top level)
3/31/66	– Plan for cultural and scientific cooperation
4/29/66	Agreement: Economic and cultural cooperation

Cameroon

9/24/64	Joint Communiqué: Talks (lower level)

Central African Republic

9/29/64	Agreement: Economic and technical aid
9/29/64	Agreement: Cultural cooperation
9/29/64	Agreement: Exchange of goods and payments
1/14/65	Protocol: Economic and technical aid

Ceylon

4/14/52(?)	Agreement: Trade
10/4/52	Agreement: Trade
10/4/52	Contract: Rice
12/18/52	Agreement: Rubber and rice (1953-57)
12/18/52	Contracts (2): Rubber and rice (1953)
9/21/53	– Trade (1954-55)
9/21/53	Contracts (2): Rubber and rice (1954)
10/8/54	Contracts (2): Rubber and rice (1955)
10/12/55(?)	Agreement: Rubber (1955)
10/14/55	Contracts (2): Rubber and rice (1956)
10/16/55(?)	Agreement: Rice
9/14/56	Joint Communiqué: Promotion of trade, cultural cooperation, etc.
12/29/56	Joint Communiqué: Trade talks
12/29/56	Exchange of Notes: Trade
12/29/56	Contracts (2): Rubber and rice (1957)
2/5/57	Joint Statement: Talks (top level)
9/19/57	Agreement: Trade and payments (1958-62)
9/19/57	Exchange of Letters: Import control
9/19/57	Exchange of Letters: Trade involving third countries
9/19/57	Protocol: Exchange of goods (1958)
9/19/57	Agreement: Economic aid
9/20/57	Communiqué: Economic talks
9/17/58	Exchange of Notes: Loan
3/26/59	Agreement: Aviation
3/26/59	Protocol: Aviation
3/26/59	Exchange of Notes: Nationality of pilots
6/13/59	Joint Communiqué: Trade talks
6/13/59	Protocol: Exchange of goods (1959)
6/13/59	Contracts (2): Rubber and rice
1/3/60	Agreement(?): Rubber and rice
2/8/60	Protocol: Exchange of goods (1960)
4/4/61	Joint Communiqué: Trade talks
4/4/61	Protocol: Exchange of goods (1961)
5/4/61	Minutes: Aviation talks
8/7/61	Exchange of Letters: Technical aid (specific project)
10/7/61	Protocol: Exchange of goods (1962)

10/8/61	Joint Communiqué: Trade talks
Dec. 1961(?)	Agreement(?): Rubber and rice
2/7/62	Exchange of Notes: Ship's papers
5/28/62	Exchange of Notes: Economic aid
8/1/62	Exchange of Letters: Loan
9/15/62	Press Communiqué: Trade talks
10/3/62	Joint Communiqué: Conference on trade and economic and technical aid
10/3/62	Agreement: Trade and payments (1962-67)
10/3/62	Agreement: Economic and technical aid
10/3/62	Protocol: Exchange of goods (1963)
10/3/62	Contracts (2): Rubber and rice (1963)
1/8/63	Joint Communiqué: Talks (top level)
7/25/63	Agreement: Maritime transport
10/10/63	Protocol: Exchange of goods (1964)
2/28/64	Contract: Cotton
2/28/64	Exchange of Notes: Economic aid, development of trade
2/29/64	Joint Communiqué: Talks (top level)
6/15/64	Exchange of Letters: Loan
7/7/64	Agreement: Gift
10/24/64	Protocol: Exchange of goods (1965)
10/24/64	Contracts (2): Rubber and rice (1965)
10/24/64	Agreement: Loan
11/25/64	Contracts (3): Gift
3/15/65	Exchange of Notes: Aid (specific project)
7/13/65	Agreement: Railway
10/12/65	Protocol: Exchange of goods (1966)
Nov.-Dec./65	Protocol: Rubber and rice
11/29/66	Protocol: Exchange of goods (1967)
11/29/66	Contracts (2): Rubber and rice (1967)

Chile

10/23/52	Agreement: Trade

Congo (Brazzaville)

7/11/64	Agreement: Loan
7/23/64	Agreement: Trade and payments
10/2/64	Treaty: Friendship
10/2/64	Agreement: Maritime transport
10/2/64	Agreement: Economic and technical aid
10/2/64	Agreement: Cultural cooperation
10/3/64	Joint Communiqué: Talks (top level)
2/6/65	Protocol: Loan
2/6/65	Protocol: Economic and technical aid
5/12/65	Agreement: News agencies
6/13/65	Protocol: Economic and technical aid

8/13/65	— Plan for cultural cooperation
9/13/65	Minutes: Talks on technical aid (specific project)
4/14/66	— Plan for cultural cooperation

Cuba

12/31/59	Contract: Sugar
7/23/60	Agreement: Trade and payments
7/23/60	Agreement: Scientific and technical cooperation
7/23/60	Agreement: Cultural cooperation
11/30/60	Joint Communiqué: Trade talks
11/30/60	Agreement: Economic aid
11/30/60	Protocol: Trade (1960)
11/30/60	Protocol: Scientific and technical cooperation
1/21/61	Contract: Sugar
1/21/61	Contract: Copper ore
2/15/61	Agreement: Television exchange
3/8/61	Exchange of Letters: Payments (noncommercial)
4/20/61	— Plan for cultural cooperation
9/11/61	Agreement: Films (features)
9/11/61	Agreement: Films (newsreels and documentaries)
10/2/61	Joint Communiqué: Talks (top level)
10/21/61	Agreement: Telecommunications
10/21/61	Agreement: Postal services
1/27/62	Agreement: Radio and television cooperation
1/27/62	Protocol: Radio and television cooperation
4/25/62	Protocol: Trade (1962)
7/20/62	— Plan for cultural cooperation
8/23/62	Protocol: Scientific and technical cooperation
2/22/63	Protocol: Trade and payments (1963)
2/22/63	Protocol: Delivery of goods
2/22/63	Agreement: Loan
2/26/63	Joint Communiqué: Economic talks
2/28/63	Agreement: Films
6/25/63	Agreement: Cooperation between Academies of Sciences
6/25/63	— Plan for cooperation between Academies of Sciences
7/24/63	— Plan for cultural cooperation
11/14/63	Memorandum: Import and export trade (1964)
11/15/63	Protocol: Scientific and technical cooperation
1/14/64	Protocol: Plan for cultural cooperation
1/15/64	Protocol: Exchange of goods and payments
8/11/64	Protocol: Economic aid
11/12/64	Protocol: Radio and television cooperation
12/31/64	Agreement: Trade (1965-70)
12/31/64	Protocol: Trade (1965)
12/31/64	Agreement: Payments
12/31/64	Protocol: Delivery of sugar
12/31/64	Protocol: Delivery of goods
1/4/65	Joint Communiqué: Trade talks
5/21/65	Protocol: Scientific and technical cooperation

7/18/65	Protocol: Cultural cooperation
12/29/65	Protocol: Plan for cultural cooperation
5/26/66	Protocol: Trade (1966)
5/27/66	– Plan for cooperation between Academies of Sciences
7/6/66	Agreement: Scientific and technical cooperation
3/21/67	Protocol: Trade (1967)

Czechoslovakia

6/14/50	Agreement: Trade (1950)
6/21/51	Agreement: Exchange of goods and payments (1951)
6/21/51	– Delivery of goods
5/6/52	Agreement: Postal services
5/6/52	Agreement: Telecommunications
5/6/52	Agreement: Scientific and technical cooperation
5/6/52	Agreement: Cultural cooperation
5/24/52	Agreement: Aviation
7/15/52	Protocol: Exchange of goods and payments (1952)
7/15/52	Protocol: Delivery of goods
5/7/53	Agreement: Exchange of goods and payments (1953)
5/7/53	Protocol: Delivery of goods
5/7/53	Agreement: Radio cooperation
6/24/53	Protocol: Scientific and technical cooperation
6/27/53	Exchange of Notes: Plan for cultural cooperation
8/18/53	Agreement: Insect pests and plant diseases
4/27/54	Agreement: Exchange of goods and payments (1954)
4/27/54	Protocol: Delivery of goods
7/17/54	– Plan for cultural cooperation
9/2/54	Protocol: Scientific and technical cooperation
3/1/55	Exchange of Notes: Plan for cultural cooperation
4/6/55	Agreement: Exchange of goods and payments (1955)
4/6/55	Protocol: Delivery of goods
11/11/55	Agreement: Exchange of goods and payments (1956)
12/3/55	Protocol: Scientific and technical cooperation
1/3/56	– Plan for cultural cooperation
7/4/56	Protocol: Exchange of goods (1958-62)
9/5/56	Protocol: Scientific and technical cooperation
11/7/56	Agreement: Cooperation between Academies of Sciences
12/8/56	– Plan for cultural cooperation
3/6/57	Agreement: Exchange of goods and payments (1957)
3/27/57	Joint Communiqué: Talks (top level)
3/27/57	Treaty: Friendship
3/27/57	Agreement: Cultural cooperation
3/27/57	Agreement: Cooperation in public health
9/12/57	Protocol: Scientific and technical cooperation
2/16/58	– Plan for cultural cooperation
4/16/58	Agreement: Exchange of goods and payments (1958)
4/16/58	– Delivery of goods
5/7/58	Protocol: Exchange of goods
8/15/58(?)	Protocol: Scientific and technical cooperation

Jan./59	–	Plan for cultural cooperation
3/3/59	Agreement:	Scientific cooperation
3/3/59	–	Plan for cooperation between Academies of Sciences
3/12/59	Agreement:	Exchange of goods and payments (1959)
4/13/59(?)	Agreement:	Trade (1960-62)
4/30/59	Agreement:	Radio and television cooperation
5/20/59	Protocol:	Scientific and technical cooperation
12/10/59	Agreement:	Cooperation between Academies of Sciences
2/2/60	Protocol:	Exchange of goods and payments (1960)
2/18/60	–	Plan for cooperation between Academies of Sciences
2/19/60	–	Plan for cultural cooperation
5/7/60	Treaty:	Consular
2/24/61	Protocol:	Scientific and technical cooperation
4/4/61	–	Plan for cultural cooperation
4/10/61	–	Plan for cooperation between Academies of Sciences
10/20/61	Protocol:	Exchange of goods and payments (1961-62)
10/20/61	Protocol:	Delivery of goods
3/7/62	Agreement:	Currency
4/3/62	–	Plan for cultural cooperation
7/1/62	Protocol:	Scientific and technical cooperation
7/17/62	Protocol:	Exchange of goods and payments (1962)
7/20/62	Exchange of Notes:	Scientific and technical cooperation
9/30/62	Agreement:	Cooperation between Academies of Sciences (1962-66)
9/30/62	–	Plan for cooperation between Academies of Sciences
4/19/63	Agreement:	Exchange of goods and payments (1963)
5/15/63	–	Plan for cultural cooperation
7/15/63	Protocol:	Scientific and technical cooperation
8/17/63	Exchange of Notes:	Insect pests and plant diseases
11/20/63	Agreement:	Currency
4/24/64	Agreement:	Exchange of goods and payments (1964)
5/27/64	–	Plan for cultural cooperation
9/28/64	Protocol:	Scientific and technical cooperation
3/24/65	–	Plan for cooperation between Academies of Sciences
4/8/65	Agreement:	Exchange of goods and payments (1965)
6/18/65	–	Plan for cultural cooperation
10/26/65	Protocol:	Scientific and technical cooperation
12/23/65	–	Plan for cooperation between Academies of Sciences
2/4/66	Agreement:	Exchange of goods and payments (1966)
5/11/66	–	Plan for cultural cooperation
10/28/66	Protocol:	Scientific and technical cooperation

Dahomey

9/13/64	Joint Communiqué:	Talks (lower level)

Denmark

12/1/57	Agreement:	Trade and payments
12/1/57	Exchange of Notes:	Most-favored-nation treatment (customs and navigation)

4/12/58	Exchange of Notes: Trademark registration
9/7/61	Exchange of Notes: Tax exemptions to students, etc.

Egypt (UAR)

5/31/55	Minutes: Talks (lower level)
8/10/55	Contract: Cotton
8/22/55	Agreement: Trade (1955-58)
8/22/55	Protocol: Trade (1955-56)
8/23/55	Contract: Cotton
8/23/55	Contract: Steel
8/26/55	Joint Communiqué: Trade talks
4/15/56	Agreement: Cultural cooperation
4/16/56	Communiqué: Trade talks
5/20/56	– Plan for cultural cooperation
10/22/56	Joint Communiqué: Trade talks
10/22/56	Protocol: Trade (1956-57)
10/22/56	Agreement: Payments
10/22/56	Exchange of Letters: Trade
lst Week, Nov./56	– Gift
12/21/57	Communiqué: Trade talks
12/21/57	Protocol: Trade (1958)
12/21/57	Exchange of Letters: Payments
8/25/58	Agreement: Postal
12/15/58	Agreement: Trade (1959-61)
12/15/58	Agreement: Payments
12/15/58	Protocol: Trade (1959)
2/24/60	Joint Communiqué: Trade talks
2/24/60	Protocol: Trade (1960)
2/5/61	Protocol: Trade (1961)
3/17/62	Agreement: Trade
3/17/62	Agreement: Payments
3/17/62	Protocol: Trade (1962)
1/5/63	Agreement: Telecommunications
4/25/63	Joint Communiqué: Talks (top level)
7/14/63	Protocol: Trade (1963-64)
12/21/63	Joint Communiqué: Talks (top level)
4/11/64	– Plan for cultural cooperation
8/24/64	Joint Communiqué: Scientific and technical cooperation
12/21/64	Agreement: Economic and technical aid
12/21/64	Exchange of Notes: Trade and payments
12/21/64	Protocol: Trade (1965)
1/13/65	Agreement: Scientific and technical cooperation
5/2/65	Agreement: Aviation
5/4/66	Protocol: Trade (1966)
5/7/66	– Plan for cultural cooperation
5/25/67	Protocol: Trade (1967)

Ethiopia

9/5/61	Communiqué: Promotion of trade, cultural cooperation, etc.
2/1/64	Joint Communiqué: Talks (top level)

Finland

4/12/52(?)	Agreement: Trade (1952-53)
9/21/52	Agreement (with USSR): Exchange of goods and payments in 1952
6/5/53	Agreement: Trade (1953-54)
6/5/53	– Delivery of goods
6/5/53	Agreement: Payments
6/17/54	– Delivery of goods
6/21/54	Agreement: Trade (1954-55)
12/13/54	Protocol: Trade (1954-55)
8/8/55	Agreement: Trade (1955-56)
3/31/56	Exchange of Notes: Most-favored-nation treatment (customs and navigation)
7/31/56	Agreement: Trade (1956-57)
8/7/57	Exchange of Notes: Trade (1957)
8/7/57	Exchange of Notes: Payments (interpretation)
12/18/57	Agreement: Trade (1957-58)
2/15/58	Exchange of Letters: Payments
5/15/59	Agreement: Trade (1958-59)
12/16/59	Agreement: Trade (1959-60)
2/29/60	– Telecommunications
4/11/61	Agreement: Trade (1961)
4/11/61	Exchange of Notes: Payments
3/29/62	Agreement: Trade (1961-62)
5/29/63	Agreement: Trade (1963)
5/29/63	Exchange of Notes: Payments
10/28/63	Agreement: Trade (1964)
3/24/65	Agreement: Trade (1965)
11/23/65	Agreement: Trade (1966)
1/26/67	Exchange of Notes: Trademark registration
4/25/67	Agreement: Trade (1967)
4/25/67	Exchange of Letters: Payments (currency)

France

4/4/52	Agreement: Trade
8/9/52	Contract: Barter
6/5/53	Agreement: Barter
2/19/56	Joint Statement: Trade talks
2/19/56	Protocol: Payments (banking)
2/19/56	Protocol: Payments
10/1/65	– Plan for cultural exchange
6/1/66	Agreement: Aviation
7/25/66	Protocol: Aviation

Germany (E)

10/10/50	Agreement: Exchange of goods and payments (1951)
11/4/50	Exchange of Notes: Delivery of goods
10/9/51	Agreement: Cultural cooperation
10/12/51	Agreement: Postal services
10/12/51	Agreement: Telecommunications
5/28/52	Agreement: Exchange of goods and payments (1952)
5/28/52	Protocol: Delivery of goods
2/9/53	– Plan for cultural cooperation
4/30/53	Agreement: Exchange of goods and payments (1953)
4/30/53	Protocol: Delivery of goods
7/3/53	Agreement: Press
8/8/53	Protocol (supplementary): Exchange of goods and payments (1953)
10/30/53	Agreement: Scientific and technical cooperation
11/28/53	– Plan for cultural cooperation
12/10/53	– Noncommercial payments (banking)
3/30/54	Agreement: Exchange of goods and payments (1954)
3/30/54	Protocol: Delivery of goods
6/10/54	Agreement: Radio cooperation
6/23/54	Protocol: Scientific and technical cooperation
7/25/54	Joint Communiqué: Talks (top level)
8/31/54	Protocol (supplementary): Exchange of goods (1954)
12/27/54	– Plan for cultural cooperation
12/27/54	Protocol: Exchange of students
4/24/55	Agreement: Exchange of goods and payments (1955)
4/24/55	Protocol: Delivery of goods
8/20/55	Protocol: Scientific and technical cooperation
9/16/55	– Delivery of goods
11/20/55	Agreement: Exchange of goods and payments (1956)
11/20/55	Protocol: Delivery of goods
12/25/55	Joint Statement: Talks (top level)
12/25/55	Treaty: Friendship
12/25/55	Agreement: Cultural cooperation
12/25/55	Agreement: Insect pests and plant diseases
2/2/56	– Plan for cultural cooperation
5/22/56	Protocol: Delivery of goods
10/24/56	Agreement: Cooperation between Academies of Sciences
1/8/57	Press Communiqué: Talks (top level)
March/57	Protocol: Scientific and technical cooperation
4/5/57	Agreement: Exchange of goods and payments (1957)
4/5/57	Protocol: Delivery of goods
6/15/57	– Plan for cultural cooperation
9/26/57	Protocol: Economic aid
12/16/57	Agreement: Cooperation in public health work
3/22/58	– Plan for cultural cooperation
3/27/58	Agreement: Noncommercial payments
4/23/58	Agreement: Exchange of goods and payments (1958)
5/22/58	Protocol: Delivery of goods
7/31/58	Protocol: Scientific and technical cooperation
10/9/58	Agreement: Films
1/27/59	Joint Statement: Talks (top level)

1/27/59	Treaty: Consular
2/5/59	Agreement: Exchange of goods and payments (1959)
2/5/59	Protocol: Delivery of goods
3/9/59	Contract: Economic and technical aid (specific project)
3/9/59	Protocol: Economic and technical aid (specific project)
3/17/59	– Plan for cooperation between Academies of Sciences
3/17/59	Agreement: Cooperation between Academies of Sciences
4/25/59	Agreement: Radio and television cooperation
4/25/59	Protocol: Television cooperation
1/18/60	Treaty: Commerce and navigation
1/18/60	Agreement: Exchange of goods (1960-62)
1/19/60	Communiqué: Talks (lower level)
3/23/60	Protocol: Exchange of goods and payments (1960)
3/23/60	Protocol: Delivery of goods
3/25/60	– Plan for cultural cooperation
4/13/60	Protocol: Scientific and technical cooperation
5/10/61	– Plan for cultural cooperation
5/15/61	Protocol: Exchange of goods and payments (1961)
5/15/61	Protocol: Delivery of goods
6/15/61	Agreement: Currency
7/20/62	Protocol: Scientific and technical cooperation
8/4/62	Protocol: Exchange of goods and payments (1962)
8/4/62	Protocol: Delivery of goods
8/14/62	– Plan for cultural cooperation
6/7/63	– Plan for cultural cooperation
6/22/63	Agreement: Exchange of goods and payments (1963)
6/22/63	Protocol: Delivery of goods
10/15/63	Protocol: Scientific and technical cooperation
1/16/64	Protocol: Scientific and technical cooperation
7/9/64	Protocol: Scientific and technical cooperation
8/1/64	Agreement: Exchange of goods and payments (1964)
9/2/64	– Plan for cultural cooperation
11/26/64	– Plan for cooperation between Academies of Sciences
2/19/65	Agreement: Exchange of goods and payments (1965)
5/3/65	– Plan for cultural cooperation
7/15/65	Agreement: Exchange of students
11/22/65(?)	Protocol: Scientific and technical cooperation
3/25/66	Agreement: Exchange of goods and payments (1966)
7/4/66	Protocol: Scientific and technical cooperation
7/22/67	– Plan for cultural cooperation
4/14/67	Agreement: Exchange of goods and payments (1967)

Germany (W)

4/10/52	Agreement: Trade
6/25/52	Agreement: Trade
9/27/57	Agreement: Trade
9/27/57	Exchange of Notes: Trade
9/27/57	Exchange of Notes: Arbitration (trade)

Ghana

8/18/61	Joint Communiqué: Talks (top level)
8/18/61	Treaty: Friendship
8/18/61	Agreement: Economic and technical aid
8/18/61	Agreement: Trade and payments
8/18/61	Agreement: Cultural cooperation
11/1/61	Protocol: Trade and payments (1961-62)
11/1/61	Exchange of Letters: Plan for cultural cooperation
11/1/61	Exchange of Letters: Trade
11/1/61	Exchange of Letters: Economic and technical aid
11/1/61	"Undertaking": Banking (economic and technical aid)
11/1/61	"Undertaking": Banking (trade and payments)
11/2/61	Joint Communiqué: Trade talks
10/18/62	Protocol: Economic and technical aid
1/23/63	Joint Press Communiqué: Talks (lower level)
3/26/63	Agreement: Maritime transport
1/16/64	Joint Communiqué: Talks (top level)
2/5/64	Protocol: Exchange of goods (1964)
7/15/64	Protocol: Economic and technical aid
7/17/64	– Plan for cultural cooperation
7/30/64	Agreement: News agencies
9/22/64	Contract: Films
9/22/64	Contract: Films (newsreel materials)
12/3/64	Protocol: Exchange of goods (1965)
5/3/65	Joint Press Communiqué: Talks (top level)
5/19/65	Agreement: Cooperation between Academies of Sciences
8/5/65	Protocol: Military aid

Guinea

10/7/59	Agreement: Cultural cooperation
10/7/59	– Plan for cultural cooperation
6/3/60	– Plan for cultural cooperation
9/13/60	Joint Communiqué: Talks (top level)
9/13/60	Treaty: Friendship
9/13/60	Agreement: Economic and technical aid
9/13/60	Agreement: Trade and payments
7/4/61	Contract: Films
9/18/61	Protocol: Economic and technical aid
7/9/62	Protocol: Trade (1962)
Sept./62	Contract: Films
Sept./62	Contract: Films (newsreel material)
5/2/63	Protocol: Trade (1963)
5/2/63	Protocol: Economic and technical aid
1/7/64	Protocol: Trade (1964)
1/26/64	Joint Communiqué: Talks (top level)
5/12/64	– Plan for cultural cooperation
8/5/64	Agreement: Radio cooperation
8/31/64	Contract: Films
8/31/64	Contract: Films (newreel materials)
6/5/65	– Plan for cultural cooperation
9/14/65	Agreement: Postal services
9/14/65	Agreement: Telecommunications
9/14/65	Minutes: Talks on economic and technical aid

10/2/65	Contract: Films
2/1/66	Protocol: Trade (1966)
4/30/66	– Plan for cultural cooperation
6/2/66	Agreement: News agencies
6/2/66	Memorandum: Talks on technical aid (specific project)
11/16/66	Agreement: Economic and technical aid
11/16/66	Protocol: Economic and technical aid
11/16/66	Agreement: Loan
11/16/66	Protocol: Trade (1967)

Hong Kong

11/15/60	Agreement(?): Water supply

Hungary

1/22/51	Agreement: Exchange of goods and payments (1951)
2/19/51	– Delivery of goods
7/12/51	Agreement: Cultural cooperation
7/21/52	Protocol: Exchange of goods and payments
7/21/52	Protocol: Delivery of goods
8/20/52(?)	Exchange of Notes: Plan for cultural cooperation
3/30/53	Agreement: Exchange of goods and payments (1953)
3/30/53	Protocol: Delivery of goods
5/19/53	Exchange of Notes: Plan for cultural cooperation
7/16/53	Agreement: Postal services
7/16/53	Agreement: Telecommunications
10/3/53	Agreement: Scientific and technical cooperation
10/15/53	Agreement: Radio cooperation
4/30/54	Protocol: Exchange of goods and payments
4/30/54	Protocol: Delivery of goods
8/31/54	Exchange of Notes: Plan for cultural cooperation
12/28/54	Agreement: Insect pests and plant diseases
1/10/55	Protocol: Scientific and technical cooperation
1/20/55	Protocol: Plan for cultural cooperation
4/26/55	Agreement: Exchange of goods and payments (1955)
4/26/55	Protocol: Delivery of goods
1/27/56	Agreement: Exchange of goods and payments (1956)
1/27/56	Protocol: Delivery of goods
1/27/56	– Plan for cultural cooperation
2/29/56	Protocol: Scientific and technical cooperation
4/29/56	Exchange of Notes: Delivery of goods
1/11/57	Joint Communiqué (with USSR): Talks (lower level)
1/17/57	Joint Statement: Talks (top level)
5/13/57	Agreement: Credit
6/8/57	Agreement: Exchange of goods and payments (1957)
6/8/57	Protocol: Delivery of goods
7/18/57	– Plan for cultural cooperation
8/3/57	Protocol: Scientific and technical cooperation

10/4/57	Joint Statement: Talks (top level)
3/21/58	Agreement: Exchange of goods and payments (1958)
4/3/58	– Plan for cultural cooperation
4/21/58	Agreement: Trade (1959-62)
5/17/58	Agreement: Cooperation between Academies of Sciences
6/12/58	Protocol: Trade
8/8/58	Agreement: Films
8/22/58	Protocol: Scientific and technical cooperation
10/5/58	Agreement: Tourism
1/9/59	– Plan for cultural cooperation
3/17/59	Agreement: Exchange of goods and payments (1959)
3/17/59	Protocol: Delivery of goods
4/3/59	– Plan for cooperation between Academies of Sciences
4/6/59	Agreement: Radio cooperation
5/6/59	Joint Communiqué: Talks (top level)
5/6/59	Treaty: Friendship
11/10/59	– Plan for cooperation between Academies of Sciences
11/17/59	Protocol: Scientific and technical cooperation
12/11/59	Agreement: Aviation
2/16/60	– Plan for cultural cooperation
2/28/60	Agreement: Exchange of goods and payments (1960)
2/28/60	Protocol: Delivery of goods
10/20/60	Protocol: Scientific and technical cooperation
3/8/61	– Plan for cultural cooperation
3/27/61	– Plan for cooperation between Academies of Sciences
7/15/61	Agreement: Currency
7/15/61	Protocol: Exchange of goods and payments (1961)
2/2/62	– Plan for cultural cooperation
3/30/62	Agreement: Exchange of goods and payments (1962)
3/30/62	Protocol: Delivery of goods
12/14/62	Protocol: Scientific and technical cooperation
4/10/63	Agreement: Exchange of goods and payments (1963)
4/10/63	Protocol: Delivery of goods
5/25/63	– Plan for cultural cooperation
12/11/63	Protocol: Scientific and technical cooperation
1/31/64	Agreement: Radio and television cooperation
3/24/64	– Plan for cultural cooperation
3/28/64	Agreement: Exchange of goods and payments (1964)
3/26/65	Agreement: Exchange of goods and payments (1965)
5/28/65	Protocol: Scientific and technical cooperation
6/5/65	– Plan for cultural cooperation
2/20/66	Agreement: Exchange of goods and payments (1966)
7/20/66	– Plan for cultural cooperation
8/9/66(?)	Protocol: Scientific and technical cooperation
6/22/67	Agreement: Exchange of goods and payments (1967)

India

4/25/51	Contract: Rice
5/23/51	Contract: Grain

5/26/52	Contract: Rice
10/13/52	Contract: Rice
4/29/54	Agreement: Trade and intercourse with Tibet
4/29/54	Exchange of Notes: Tibet (military, postal services, telecommunications, etc.)
6/28/54	Joint Statement: Talks (top level)
7/21/54	Agreement: Tobacco
10/14/54	Agreement: Trade (1954-56)
10/14/54	Exchange of Notes: Transit of goods to Tibet
10/14/54	Exchange of Notes: Trade, navigation, insurance, etc.
10/19/54	Accord: Tobacco and silk
12/15/54	Contract: Silk
4/1/55	Protocol: Tibet (postal services and telecommunications)
8/28/56	Agreement: Rice
5/25/57	Exchange of Letters: Trade
5/25/57	Exchange of Letters: Promotion of trade
6/7/57	Exchange of Notes: Real estate in Yatung
May/58	Agreement: Trade (1958-59)
5/25/59	Exchange of Letters: Trade
4/25/60	Joint Communiqué: Talks (top level)

Indonesia

4/12/52(?)	Agreement: Trade
11/30/53	Agreement: Trade (1953-54)
9/1/54	Protocol: Trade (1955-56)
9/1/54	Agreement: Payments
12/29/54	Joint Communiqué: Dual nationality
4/22/55	Treaty: Dual nationality
4/28/55	Joint Statement: Talks (top level)
6/3/55	Exchange of Notes: Dual nationality
10/14/56	Joint Press Communiqué: Talks (top level)
11/3/56	Agreement: Trade (1956-57)
11/3/56	Exchange of Notes: Payments
11/3/56	Exchange of Notes: Trade balance
11/3/56	Exchange of Notes: Economic and technical aid
4/17/58	Exchange of Notes: Loan
10/13/58	Contract: Rice
Nov./58	– Trade
10/11/59	Joint Communiqué: Talks (top level)
1/20/60	Joint Press Communiqué: Dual nationality
12/15/60	"Arrangement": Dual nationality
4/1/61	Joint Communiqué: Talks (top level)
4/1/61	Treaty: Friendship
4/1/61	Agreement: Cultural cooperation
4/18/61	Exchange of Notes: Economic and technical aid
6/15/61	Joint Press Communiqué: Talks (top level)
10/11/61	Agreement: Economic and technical aid
11/1/62	Agreement: Radio and television cooperation
1/8/63	Joint Communiqué: Talks (top level)

4/20/63	Joint Statement: Talks (top level)
10/16/63	Exchange of Notes: Economic and technical aid
11/28/63	Accord: Film (sports)
1/28/64	Contract: Economic and technical aid
5/9/64	Joint Communiqué: Olympic Games
5/13/64	Joint Communiqué: Scientific and technical cooperation
11/6/64	Agreement: Aviation
11/6/64	Protocol: Aviation
12/3/64	Joint Press Communiqué: Talks (top level)
1/12/65	Agreement: Tourism
1/28/65	Joint Statement: Talks (top level)
1/28/65	Agreement: Economic and technical aid
1/28/65	Agreement: Credit
3/16/65	Agreement: Scientific and technical cooperation
3/30/65	Minutes: Talks on economic and technical aid
4/3/65(?)	Minutes: Talks on technical aid (specific project)
7/24/65	Accord: Maritime transport
9/14/65	Protocol: Economic and technical aid (specific project)
9/30/65	Agreement: Economic and technical aid
9/30/65	Agreement: Trade
9/30/65	Agreement: Payments
9/30/65	(Unspecified)(4): Economic matters
10/4/65	Joint Statement: Talks (top level)

Iraq

1/3/59	Agreement: Trade and payments
1/3/59	Exchange of Letters: Trade involving third countries
4/4/59	Agreement: Cultural cooperation
4/8/59	– Plan for cultural cooperation
5/15/60	– Plan for cultural cooperation
5/25/60	Joint Communiqué: Trade talks
5/25/60	Agreement: Trade (1960-61)
5/25/60	Agreement: Payments
10/18/61	Joint Communiqué: Trade talks
10/18/61	Agreement: Trade
11/25/61	– Plan for cultural cooperation
3/11/62	Contract: Dates
1/10/63	Accord: Trade
5/25/64	– Plan for cultural cooperation
9/23/64	Agreement: Trade
6/4/66	– Plan for cultural cooperation
6/4/66	Protocol: Radio and television cooperation

Italy

4/12/52(?)	Agreement: Trade
11/30/64	Agreement: Establishment of trade mission

Japan

6/1/52	Accord: Trade in 1952
12/31/52	Protocol: Trade (first half of 1953)
10/29/53	Accord: Trade (1953-54)
4/15/55	Joint Communiqué: Fishery talks
4/15/55	Agreement: Fisheries (1955-56)
4/15/55	Exchange of Letters: Fisheries (1955-56)
4/15/55	Exchange of Memoranda: Fisheries (1955-56)
5/4/55	Agreement: Trade (1955)
10/15/55	Protocol: Trade (1955)
10/17/55	Joint Communiqué: Talks (lower level)
11/16/55	Joint Communiqué: Talks (lower level)
11/27/55	Agreement: Cultural exchanges
5/8/56	Joint Communiqué: Fishery talks
5/8/56	Protocol: Fisheries (1956-57)
5/8/56	Exchange of Notes: Fisheries (1956-57)
5/8/56	Exchange of Notes: Fisheries (1956-57)
6/28/56	Joint Communique: Repatriation, etc.
10/15/56	Joint Statement: Trade talks
11/29/56	Joint Communiqué: Fishery talks
5/30/57	Exchange of Notes: Fisheries (1957-58)
5/30/57	Exchange of Notes: Fisheries (1957-58)
5/30/57	Exchange of Notes: Fisheries (1957-58)
11/1/57	Joint Statement: Trade talks
3/5/58	Agreement: Trade
Oct./59	Agreement: Fisheries
11/9/62	Memorandum: Trade (1963-67)
12/27/62	Protocol: Trade
1/22/63	Memorandum: Fisheries
9/23/63	Agreement: Trade (1963-64)
11/9/63	Agreement: Fisheries
11/9/63	Exchange of Letters: Fisheries
11/9/63	Exchange of Memoranda: Fisheries
4/19/64	Minutes: Trade talks
4/19/64	Minutes: Talks on exchange of correspondents
4/19/64	Minutes: Talks on exchange of representatives and establishment of liaison offices
8/5/65	Agreement: Agricultural technical exchange
9/18/65	Accord: Trade (1966)
12/17/65	Agreement: Fisheries
12/17/65	Exchange of Letters: Fisheries
12/17/65	Memorandum: Fisheries
1/22/66	Joint Statement: Promotion of trade, maritime transport, etc.
5/19/66	Minutes: Trade talks
11/21/66	– Trade (1967)

Kenya

5/10/64	Agreement: Economic and technical aid
10/2/64	Press Communiqué: Trade talks

12/10/64	Protocol: Economic and technical aid
12/10/64	Exchange of Letters: Technical aid
12/18/64	Agreement: Trade

Korea (N)

12/25/49	Agreement: Postal services
12/25/49	Protocol: Postal services
12/25/49	Agreement: Telecommunications
12/25/49	Agreement: Telephone services
12/25/49	Protocol: Telecommunications and telephone services
8/18/50	Agreement: Barter
5/31/52	Protocol: Postal and telephone services and telecommunications
4/11/53	Agreement (with UN): Repatriation of sick and injured POW's
6/8/53	Agreement (with UN): Repatriation of POW's
7/27/53	Agreement (with UN): Armistice in Korea
7/27/53	Agreement (supplementary)(with UN): Armistice in Korea
11/23/53	Communiqué: Talks (top level)
11/23/53	Agreement: Economic and cultural cooperation (1954-64)
1/25/54	Agreement: Railway
3/30/54	Agreement: Postal services
5/20/54	Agreement: Currency
5/20/54	Protocol: Currency exchange in border areas
5/20/54	Protocol: Noncommercial remittances
6/30/54	Protocol: Delivery of goods
9/4/54	Protocol: Exchange of goods (1954)
12/31/54	Protocol: Economic aid
12/31/54	Protocol: Exchange of goods (1955)
12/31/54	Protocol: Delivery of goods
4/21/55	Contract: Films
6/22/55	– Plan for cultural cooperation
7/12/55	Exchange of Notes: Plan for cultural cooperation
12/21/55	Agreement: Currency
12/21/55	Protocol: Noncommercial remittances
1/12/56	Protocol: Exchange of goods (1956)
1/12/56	Protocol: Economic and technical aid
1/14/56	Protocol: River transport
5/30/56	– Plan for cultural cooperation
7/3/56	Agreement (with USSR): Rescue at sea
8/13/56	Agreement: Radio cooperation
9/2/56	Protocol: Water conservation on Tumen River
1/24/57	Protocol: Exchange of goods (1957)
1/24/57	Protocol: Economic aid
4/10/57	Agreement: Insect pests and plant diseases
6/7/57	Agreement: Postal services
6/7/57	Agreement: Telecommunications
10/8/57	Protocol: Tumen River project
12/30/57	– Plan for cultural cooperation
12/31/57	Agreement: Scientific and technical cooperation
12/31/57	Agreement: Cooperation in hydrological work

1/21/58	Protocol: Exchange of goods (1958)
1/21/58	Protocol: Delivery of goods
2/19/58	Joint Statement: Military withdrawal from Korea (N)
4/6/58	Accord: Flood control on Tumen River
9/27/58	Agreement: Exchange of goods (1959-62)
9/27/58	Agreement: Loan
9/27/58	Agreement: Loan (other projects)
9/27/58	Protocol: Economic and technical aid (specific project)
10/17/58	Joint Communiqué: Military withdrawal from Korea (N)
10/18/58	Protocol: Scientific and technical cooperation
11/19/58	Protocol: Exchange of goods (1959)
12/8/58	Joint Statement: Talks (top level)
12/16/58(?)	Protocol: Barter in border areas
12/27/58	Agreement: Currency (and noncommercial payments)
12/27/58	Protocol: Currency exchange in border areas
12/27/58	Protocol: Noncommercial remittances
12/29/58	Protocol: Clearance of accounts (economic aid)
2/18/59	Agreement: Aviation
2/18/59	Protocol: Air services
2/18/59	Protocol: Technical aid (aviation)
2/21/59	Agreement: Cultural cooperation
5/21/59	Protocol: Scientific and technical cooperation
8/25/59	Agreement: Fisheries
2/5/60	– Plan for cultural cooperation
2/29/60	Protocol: Exchange of goods (1960)
5/23/60	Agreement: Border river navigation
7/4/60	Agreement: Cooperation between Academies of Sciences
7/4/60	– Plan for cooperation between Academies of Sciences
10/13/60	Agreement: Loan
10/13/60	Agreement: Economic and technical aid
10/18/60	Protocol: Scientific and technical cooperation
3/18/61	Protocol: Exchange of goods (1961)
3/18/61	Protocol: Economic and technical aid
3/28/61	Protocol: Technical aid
3/31/61	– Plan for cultural cooperation
7/11/61	Treaty: Friendship
7/15/61	Joint Communiqué: Talks (top level)
10/30/61	Protocol: Scientific and technical cooperation
11/24/61	Protocol: River transport
1/8/62	– Protocol: Exchange of goods (1962)
4/30/62	– Plan for cultural cooperation
6/15/62	– Plan for cooperation between Academies of Sciences
9/22/62(?)	Protocol: Scientific and technical cooperation
11/5/62	Communiqué: Trade talks
11/5/62	Treaty: Commerce and navigation
11/5/62	Agreement: Exchange of goods (1963-67)
11/5/62	Protocol: Exchange of goods (1963)
3/27/63	– Plan for cultural cooperation
6/10/63	– Plan for cooperation between Academies of Sciences
6/21/63	Protocol: Scientific and technical cooperation
6/23/63	Joint Statement: Talks (top level)

9/27/63	Press Communiqué: Talks (top level)
10/14/63	Protocol: Exchange of goods (1964)
11/15/63	Protocol: Railway
11/25/63	Protocol: River navigation
4/18/64	– Plan for cultural cooperation
4/29/64	– Plan for cooperation between Academies of Sciences
5/9/64	Agreement: Technical aid
6/10/64	Protocol: Maritime transport
9/12/64	Protocol: Railway
9/24/64	Protocol: Exchange of goods (1965)
10/27/64	Protocol: Scientific and technical cooperation
12/27/64	Agreement: Radio and television
6/18/65	Contract: Films
7/30/65	– Plan for cooperation between Academies of Sciences
11/1/65(?)	Protocol: Scientific and technical cooperation
11/9/65	Agreement: Cooperation in public health work
11/9/65	– Plan for cooperation in public health work
11/18/65	Protocol: Railway
12/2/65(?)	Accord: River navigation
12/14/65	Protocol: Exchange of goods (1966)
2/25/66	– Plan for cultural cooperation
6/1/66	Agreement: Animal diseases
7/5/66	Protocol: Scientific and technical cooperation
7/30/66	– Plan for cooperation between Academies of Sciences
12/3/66	Protocol: Exchange of goods (1967)
12/30/66	Agreement: Radio and television cooperation

Kuwait

2/17/65	Press Communiqué: Talks on economic aid and development of trade
6/10/65	Joint Press Communiqué: Talks (lower level)

Laos

8/25/56	Joint Statement: Talks (top level)
3/8/61	Exchange of Notes: Exchange of cultural and economic delegations
4/25/61	Joint Statement: Talks (top level)
10/7/61	Agreement(?): Establishment of consulates
1/13/62	Agreement: Technical aid (specific project)
1/13/62	Agreement: Aviation
12/4/62	Joint Press Communiqué: Talks (top level)
3/10/63	Joint Communiqué: Talks (top level)
3/11/63	Agreement: News agencies
4/8/64	Joint Communiqué: Talks (top level)

Lebanon

12/31/55	Agreement: Trade
12/31/55	Exchange of Letters: Establishment of trade mission
12/31/55	Exchange of Letters: Trade involving third countries

Malagasy

8/13/66(?)	– Technical aid

Malaya

10/3/56	Joint Communiqué (with Singapore): Trade talks

Mali

2/28/61	Agreement: Trade and payments
2/28/61	Exchange of Letters: Credit
3/4/61	Joint Communiqué: Trade talks
7/12/61	Contract: Films
9/22/61	Agreement: Economic and technical aid
7/30/62	Contract: Films
7/30/62	Contract: Films (newsreel materials)
11/9/62	Protocol: Economic and technical aid
5/15/63	Agreement: Cultural cooperation
5/15/63	Contract: Films (documentary)
5/15/63	Contract: Films
5/17/63	Protocol: Films (technical aid)
8/31/63	Agreement: Radio cooperation
9/27/63	– Plan for cultural cooperation
12/30/63	Protocol (supplementary): Economic and technical aid
1/21/64	Joint Communiqué: Talks (top level)
4/26/64	– Plan for cultural cooperation
5/12/64	Protocol (supplementary): Exchange of goods and payments
3/17/65	Protocol: Technical aid (specific project)
4/17/65	– Plan for cultural cooperation
7/15/65(?)	Contract: Technical aid (specific project)
5/13/66	– Plan for cultural cooperation
6/9/66	Agreement: Loans
8/14/67	Agreement(s): Economic aid

Mauritania

2/16/67	Agreement: Trade
2/16/67	Agreement: Economic and technical aid
2/16/67	Agreement: Cultural cooperation
2/17/67	Joint Press Communiqué: Talks (top level)

Mexico

Jan./64	Contract: Films

Mongolia

9/15/52	Agreement (with USSR): Railway
10/4/52	Agreement: Economic and cultural cooperation (1952-62)
1/16/53	Agreement: Postal services
1/16/53	Agreement: Telecommunications
2/24/53	Protocol(?): Exchange of goods and payments
2/24/53	Agreement: Credit
2/24/53	Protocol: Credit (banking procedure)
8/20/53	Protocol (supplementary): Exchange of goods and payments (1953)
8/20/53	Protocol: Clearance of trade
4/7/54	Protocol: Exchange of goods and payments (1954)
4/7/54	Protocol: Delivery of goods
5/19/54	Exchange of Notes: Plan for cultural cooperation
10/12/54	Joint Communiqué (with USSR): Railway
12/16/54	Protocol: Exchange of goods (1955)
3/14/55	Exchange of Notes: Plan for cultural cooperation
10/17/55	Protocol (with USSR): Railway
10/17/55	Agreement: Railway
10/17/55	Protocol: Railway
12/21/55	Agreement: Radio cooperation
1/4/56	Joint Communiqué (with USSR): Railway
2/7/56	Protocol: Exchange of goods (1956)
2/7/56	Protocol: Delivery of goods
2/25/56	Agreement: Postal Services
8/29/56	Agreement: Economic and technical aid
12/22/56	Protocol: Exchange of goods (1957)
3/8/57	– Plan for cultural cooperation
10/3/57	Protocol: Railway
10/3/57	Protocol (with USSR): Railway
1/17/58	Agreement: Aviation
1/24/58	Agreement: Technical aid (aviation)
1/24/58	Protocol: Aviation
1/28/58	Protocol: Exchange of goods (1958)
2/21/58	Agreement: Cultural cooperation
2/21/58	– Plan for cultural cooperation
12/29/58	Agreement: Economic and technical aid agreement
12/29/58	Protocol: Economic and technical aid
1/5/59	– Plan for cultural cooperation
1/30/59	Protocol: Exchange of goods (1959)
12/22/59	Agreement: Noncommercial payments
2/23/60	Protocol: Exchange of goods (1960)
2/23/60	Exchange of Notes: Delivery of goods
2/23/60	– Plan for cultural cooperation
5/6/60	Agreement: Radio cooperation
5/23/60	Protocol: Clearance of accounts (economic and technical aid)
5/31/60	Joint Statement: Talks (top level)
5/31/60	Treaty: Friendship
5/31/60	Agreement: Economic and technical aid
5/31/60	Agreement: Scientific and technical cooperation
9/20/60	Agreement: Technical aid

4/7/61	– Plan for cultural cooperation
4/26/61	Communiqué: Trade talks
4/26/61	Treaty: Commerce
4/26/61	Protocol: Exchange of goods (1961)
6/26/61	Protocol: Technical aid
8/31/61	Protocol (with USSR): Railway
8/31/61	Protocol: Railway
1/13/62	– Plan for cultural cooperation
2/25/62	Protocol: Exchange of goods (1962)
5/31/62	Joint Arrangement: Scientific and technical cooperation
6/4/62	Protocol: Plan for scientific and technical cooperation
12/26/62	Treaty: Boundary
3/18/63	Protocol: Exchange of goods (1963)
3/30/63	– Plan for cultural cooperation
5/20/63	Minutes: Boundary talks
5/25/63	Exchange of Notes: Scientific and technical cooperation
1/17/64	Protocol: Scientific and technical cooperation
1/20/64	Protocol: Exchange of goods (1964)
6/14/64	Minutes: Boundary talks
6/17/64	– Plan for cultural cooperation
6/30/64	Protocol: Boundary
12/10/64	Protocol: Scientific and technical cooperation
12/19/64	Exchange of Notes: Scientific and technical cooperation
3/24/65	Protocol: Exchange of goods (1965)
6/9/65	– Plan for cultural cooperation
3/28/66	Protocol: Exchange of goods (1966)
5/30/66	Protocol: Scientific and technical cooperation
9/29/66	– Plan for cultural cooperation

Morocco

10/13/57(?)	Agreement: Exchange of goods (1958)
10/27/58	Agreement: Trade
9/30/59	Agreement: Trade (1959-60)
11/10/60	Agreement: Trade (1960-61)
10/27/61	Agreement: Payments
3/30/63	Agreement: Trade
12/31/63	Joint Communiqué: Talks (top level)
Dec.(?)/65	Agreement: Trade (1966)
5/20/66	Protocol (supplementary): Trade

Nepal

9/20/56	Joint Communiqué: (Miscellaneous)
9/20/56	Agreement: Friendship, trade, and intercourse between Tibet and Nepal
9/20/56	Exchange of Notes: Consular, military withdrawal from Tibet, nationality, trade, etc.
9/20/56	Exchange of Notes: Exchange of diplomatic agents

10/7/56	Joint Statement: Talks (top level)
10/7/56	Agreement: Economic aid
10/7/56	Exchange of Notes: Payments
10/7/56	Exchange of Notes: Currency
1/29/57	Joint Communiqué: Talks (top level)
3/21/60	Joint Communiqué: Talks (top level)
3/21/60	Agreement: Boundary
3/21/60	Agreement: Economic aid
4/28/60	Treaty: Friendship
4/29/60	Joint Communiqué: Talks (top level)
10/26/60	Communiqué: Boundary
2/15/61	Communiqué: Boundary
8/24/61	Communiqué: Boundary
9/5/61	Protocol: Economic aid
9/5/61	Exchange of Letters: Technical aid
10/5/61	Treaty: Boundary
10/15/61	Joint Communiqué: Talks (top level)
10/15/61	Agreement: Economic and technical aid (specific project)
8/14/62	Exchange of Notes: Nationality, boundary question, etc.
1/13/63	Protocol: Technical aid (specific project)
1/20/63	Protocol: Boundary
4/27/64	Protocol (supplementary): Economic aid
5/15/64	Exchange of Letters: Boundary
5/19/64	Agreement: Trade
10/4/64	Protocol: Technical aid (specific project)
10/11/64	Agreement: Cultural cooperation
Dec.(?)/64	– Economic aid
1/21/65	Agreement (provisional): Postal services
4/3/65	Press Communiqué: Talks (top level)
8/29/65	Protocol: Technical aid (specific project)
9/3/65	– Plan for cultural cooperation
9/8/65	Press Communiqué: Talks (top level)
5/2/66	Agreement: Trade and intercourse between Tibet and Nepal
6/30/66	Agreement (supplementary): Technical aid (specific project)
10/18/66	Exchange of Notes(?): Economic aid (currency)
12/21/66	Agreement: Economic and technical aid
3/14/67	Contract: Rice
5/25/67	Protocol: Technical aid (specific project)
5/28/67	Agreement(?): Technical aid (specific project)

Netherlands

4/14/52	Agreement: Trade
5/6/64	Exchange of Letters: Promotion of trade

Nigeria

6/18/61	Communiqué: Economic talks

Norway

6/4/58	Agreement: Trade and payments (most-favored-nation treatment)
6/16/58	Exchange of Letters: Trade and payments
4/4/61	Exchange of Notes: Exemption of visa fees
6/18/63	Agreement: Cultural cooperation
4/30/66	– Plan for cultural exchange

Pakistan

4/12/52(?)	Agreement: Trade
3/14/53	Agreement: Cotton
3/14/53	Contract: Coal
3/19/56	Contract: Coal
5/10/56	Contract: Coal
10/23/56	Joint Statement: Talks (top level)
12/24/56	Joint Statement: Talks (top level)
6/3/56	Contract: Barter of coal for cotton
8/8/58	Agreement: Barter of rice for cotton and jute
10/4/58	Exchange of Letters: Most-favored-nation treatment
5/3/62	Press Communiqué: Boundary
12/28/62	Joint Communiqué: Boundary
1/5/63	Agreement: Trade
3/2/63	Agreement: Boundary
3/4/63	Joint Communiqué: Talks (top level)
6/13/63	Press Communiqué: Boundary
8/29/63	Agreement: Aviation
8/30/63	Agreement: Aviation services
9/5/63	Press Communiqué: Boundary
9/16/63	Accord: Telecommunications
9/30/63	Contract: Exchange of cement for jute
2/17/64	Joint Communiqué: Boundary
2/23/64	Joint Communiqué: Talks (top level)
3/8/64	Protocol: Aviation services
3/15/64	Press Communiqué: Boundary
7/17/64	Communiqué: Economic and trade talks
7/23/64	Agreement: News agencies
12/19/64	Minutes: Boundary talks
2/18/65	Agreement: Loan and technical aid
3/7/65	Joint Communiqué: Talks (top level)
3/19/65	Press Communiqué: Boundary
3/26/65	Protocol: Boundary
3/26/65	Agreement: Cultural cooperation
Nov.(?)/65	Agreement: Economic aid
3/31/66	Joint Communiqué: Talks (top level)
6/1/66	– Plan for cultural cooperation
6/23/66	Protocol: Technical aid (specific project)
7/4/66	Agreement: Barter
10/21/66	Agreement: Maritime transport
1/17/67	– Supply of grain
9/14/67	– Plan for cultural cooperation

Poland

3/1/50	Agreement: Exchange of goods (1950)
3/1/50	Protocol: Exchange of goods (1950)
1/29/51	Agreement: Exchange of goods and payments (1951)
1/29/51	Agreement: Telecommunications
1/29/51	Agreement: Postal services
1/29/51	Agreement: Shipping and navigation
1/29/51	Agreement: Aviation
2/1/51	Protocol: Delivery of goods
4/3/51	Agreement: Cultural cooperation
June/51	Agreement: Establishment of Sino-Polish Shipping Joint Stock Company
2/8/52	– Plan for cultural cooperation
7/11/52	Protocol: Exchange of goods and payments (1952)
7/11/52	Protocol: Delivery of goods
1/26/53	– Plan for cultural cooperation
5/25/53	Agreement: Exchange of goods and payments (1953)
5/25/53	Protocol: Delivery of goods
10/15/53	Agreement: Radio cooperation
2/19/54	Agreement: Exchange of goods and payments (1954)
2/19/54	Protocol: Delivery of goods
2/23/54	– Plan for cultural cooperation
7/20/54	Agreement: Scientific and technical cooperation
2/11/55	– Plan for cultural cooperation
3/21/55	Agreement: Exchange of goods and payments (1955)
3/21/55	Protocol: Delivery of goods
6/8/55	Minutes: Talks between Academies of Sciences
6/11/55(?)	Protocol: Scientific and technical cooperation
12/21/55	Agreement: Exchange of goods and payments (1956)
12/21/55	Protocol: Delivery of goods
1/28/56	– Plan for cultural cooperation
2/24/56	Exchange of Notes: Postal and telegraph services
2/25/56	Protocol: Postal services and telecommunications
4/23/56	Protocol: Scientific and technical cooperation
6/21/56	Agreement: Trade
7/14/56	Agreement: Exchange of students
10/29/56	Protocol: Cooperation between Academies of Sciences
12/20/56	– Plan for cultural cooperation
1/16/57	Joint Statement: Talks (top level)
4/1/57	Agreement: Exchange of goods and payments (1957)
4/1/57	Protocol: Delivery of goods
4/11/57	Joint Statement: Talks (top level)
10/29/57	Protocol: Cooperation in public health work
11/4/57	Protocol: Scientific and technical cooperation
11/27/57	– Plan for educational cooperation
12/2/57	– Plan for cultural cooperation
12/30/57	– Plan for cooperation between Academies of Sciences
2/22/58	Agreement: Noncommercial payments

4/5/58	Protocol: Delivery of goods
4/5/58	Communiqué: Trade talks
4/7/58	Agreement: Trade (1959-62)
4/7/58	Agreement: Exchange of goods and payments (1958)
9/15/58	Protocol: Scientific and technical cooperation
1/30/59	– Plan for cultural cooperation
2/14/59	Protocol: Delivery of goods
2/20/59	– Plan for cooperation between Academies of Sciences
3/6/59	Agreement: Exchange of goods and payments (1959)
4/15/59	Agreement: Radio and television cooperation
4/15/59	Protocol (supplementary): Radio and television cooperation
11/1/59	Protocol: Scientific and technical cooperation
2/11/60	Protocol: Exchange of goods (1960-61)
2/11/60	– Plan for cultural cooperation
2/22/60	Agreement: Exchange of goods and payments (1960)
2/22/60	Protocol: Delivery of goods
10/9/60	Agreement: Cooperation between Academies of Sciences
10/9/60	– Plan for cooperation between Academies of Sciences
11/30/60	Protocol: Scientific and technical cooperation
5/15/61	Agreement: Currency
7/10/61	Protocol: Delivery of goods
7/13/61	Agreement: Exchange of goods and payments (1961)
9/20/61	Protocol: Scientific and technical cooperation
2/28/62	– Plan for cultural cooperation
3/27/62	Protocol: Delivery of goods
3/28/62	Agreement: Exchange of goods and payments (1962)
5/22/62	– Plan for cooperation between Academies of Sciences
6/25/62	Protocol: Scientific and technical cooperation
9/8/62	Minutes: Trade talks
4/20/63	– Plan for cultural cooperation
4/30/63	Agreement: Exchange of goods and payments (1963)
5/4/63	Protocol: Scientific and technical cooperation
2/5/64	Agreement: Exchange of goods and payments (1964)
3/30/64	– Plan for cooperation between Academies of Sciences
5/18/64	– Plan for cultural cooperation
6/18/64	Protocol: Scientific and technical cooperation
6/18/64	Protocol: Scientific and technical cooperation
3/16/65	Agreement: Exchange of goods and payments (1965)
4/26/65(?)	Protocol: Scientific and technical cooperation
5/5/65	– Plan for cultural cooperation
12/15/65	– Plan for cooperation between Academies of Sciences
3/22/66	Agreement: Exchange of goods and payments (1966)
6/20/66	Protocol: Scientific and technical cooperation
6/24/66	– Plan for cultural cooperation
6/30/67	Agreement: Exchange of goods and payments (1967)

Portugal

8/23/52	Agreement: Settlement of military disputes on PRC-Macao border

Rumania

12/12/51	Agreement: Cultural cooperation
6/23/52	Agreement: Cultural cooperation
7/30/52	Agreement: Exchange of goods and payments (1952)
7/30/52	Protocol: Delivery of goods
1/9/53	Agreement: Scientific and technical cooperation
1/19/53	Agreement: Exchange of goods and payments
1/19/53	Protocol: Delivery of goods
6/9/53	– Plan for cultural cooperation
10/15/53	Agreement: Radio cooperation
10/15/53	Protocol: Scientific and technical cooperation
4/19/54	Agreement: Exchange of goods and payments (1954)
4/19/54	Protocol: Delivery of goods
5/17/54	Contract: Films
5/17/54	Contract: Films (newsreel)
5/28/54	– Plan for cultural cooperation
10/15/54	Protocol: Scientific and technical cooperation
1/20/55	Agreement: Exchange of goods and payments (1955)
1/20/55	Protocol: Delivery of goods
3/10/55	– Plan for cultural cooperation
7/30/55	Agreement: Postal services and telecommunications
10/27/55	Protocol: Scientific and technical cooperation
1/3/56	Agreement: Exchange of goods and payments (1956)
1/3/56	Protocol: Delivery of goods
2/13/56	– Plan for cultural cooperation
4/28/56	Exchange of Notes: Delivery of goods
12/12/56	Protocol: Scientific and technical cooperation
2/21/57	– Plan for cultural cooperation
4/19/57	Agreement: Exchange of goods and payments (1957)
4/19/57	Protocol: Delivery of goods
9/10/57	Communiqué: Scientific and technical cooperation
3/30/58	Agreement: Exchange of goods and payments (1958)
3/30/58	Protocol: Delivery of goods
4/7/58	Joint Statement: Talks (top level)
4/12/58	– Plan for cultural cooperation
7/21/58	Agreement: Trade (1958-62)
10/10/58	Agreement: Radio and television cooperation
2/13/59	Agreement: Currency (noncommercial payments)
3/10/59	– Plan for cultural cooperation
3/22/59	Protocol: Exchange of goods and payments (1959)
3/22/59	Protocol: Delivery of goods
4/13/59	Agreement: Cooperation between Academies of Sciences
10/12/59	Protocol: Scientific and technical cooperation
2/16/60	– Plan for cultural cooperation

2/29/60	– Plan for cooperation between Academies of Sciences
3/15/60	Protocol: Exchange of goods and payments (1960)
3/15/60	Protocol: Delivery of goods
3/17/61	– Plan for cultural cooperation
4/28/61	– Plan for cooperation between Academies of Sciences
7/7/61	Protocol: Exchange of goods and payments (1961)
7/7/61	Protocol: Delivery of goods
2/17/62	– Plan for cultural cooperation
5/29/62	Protocol: Exchange of goods and payments (1962)
5/29/62	Protocol: Delivery of goods
7/17/62(?)	Protocol: Scientific and technical cooperation
4/8/63	Agreement: Exchange of goods and payments (1963)
4/8/63	Protocol: Delivery of goods
6/8/63	Agreement: Scientific and technical cooperation
6/8/63	Protocol: Scientific and technical cooperation
7/5/63	– Plan for cultural cooperation
7/6/63	Agreement: Cooperation between Academies of Sciences
7/6/63	– Plan for cooperation between Academies of Sciences
12/27/63	Agreement: Exchange of goods and payments (1964)
12/27/63	Protocol: Delivery of goods
1/23/64	– Plan for cultural cooperation
7/5/64	Protocol: Scientific and technical cooperation
10/3/64	Agreement: Radio and television cooperation
12/9/64	Agreement: Exchange of goods and payments (1965)
5/15/65(?)	Protocol: Scientific and technical cooperation
5/27/65	Agreement: Cultural cooperation
12/1/65	– Plan for cooperation between Academies of Sciences
12/21/65	Agreement: Barter and payments (1966)
2/11/66	– Plan for cultural cooperation
6/24/66	Joint Communiqué: Talks (top level)
7/31/66	Protocol: Scientific and technical cooperation
2/14/67	Agreement: Exchange of goods and payments (1967)

Singapore

10/3/56	Joint Communiqué (with Malaya): Trade talks

Somalia

1/10/63	Agreement: Cultural cooperation
5/15/63	Agreement: Trade and payments
8/9/63	Agreement: Economic and technical aid
8/9/63	Joint Communiqué: Talks (top level)
2/4/64	Joint Communiqué: Talks (top level)

7/28/65	Joint Press Communiqué: Talks (top level)
8/17/65	– Plan for cultural cooperation
6/11/66	– Plan for cultural cooperation
10/23/66	Exchange of Letters: Technical aid
8/16/67	Minutes: Talks on technical aid (specific project)
8/19/67	– Plan for cultural cooperation

Sudan

4/12/56	Communiqué: Trade talks
4/12/56	Exchange of Letters: Development of trade
1/9/58	Communiqué: Trade talks
5/23/62	Agreement: Trade
3/3/63	Contract: Films
9/1/63	Accord: Telecommunications
1/30/64	Joint Communiqué: Talks (top level)
5/9/64	Exchange of Notes: Trade
5/19/64	Joint Communiqué: Talks (top level)
10/4/64	Contract: Films
7/27/66	Protocol: Trade (1967)

Sweden

6/24/55	Exchange of Notes: Establishment of consular relations
4/8/57	Exchange of Notes: Trademark registration
11/8/57	Agreement: Trade

Switzerland

4/15/52(?)	Agreement: Trade
3/8/57	Exchange of Notes: Trademark registration

Syria

11/30/55	Agreement: Trade
11/30/55	Agreement: Payments
6/12/56	Agreement: Cultural cooperation
6/12/56	– Plan for cultural cooperation
7/3/57	Agreement: Trade and payments
2/23/59	Agreement: Films
2/21/63	Agreement: Trade
2/21/63	Agreement: Payments
2/21/63	Agreement: Economic and technical aid
2/24/63	Exchange of Notes: Loan (currency)
Jan./64	Accord: Telecommunications
3/18/65	Agreement: Cultural cooperation
3/18/65	– Plan for cultural cooperation

10/6/65	Protocol: Radio and television cooperation
4/20/66	– Plan for cultural cooperation
4/13/67	Exchange of Letters: Technical aid (specific project)

Tanganyika: See Tanzania

Tanzania (Tanganyika and Zanzibar)

12/13/62	Agreement: Cultural cooperation
6/16/64	Agreement: Economic and technical aid
6/19/64	Joint Communiqué: Talks (top level)
1/5/65	Protocol: Economic and technical aid
1/5/65	Exchange of Letters: Technical aid
2/10/65	Agreement: Trade
2/10/65	Protocol: Exchange of goods (1965-69)
2/20/65	Treaty: Friendship
2/23/65	Joint Communiqué: Talks (top level)
6/8/65	Joint Communiqué: Talks (top level)
4/22/66	Memorandum: Establishment of Sino-Tanzanian Maritime Transport Joint Stock Company
5/7/66	– Plan for cultural cooperation
6/8/66	Agreement: Economic aid
7/7/66	Accord: Establishment of Sino-Tanzanian Maritime Transport Joint Stock Company
10/10/66	Contracts (3): Economic and technical aid (specific project)
9/5/67	Agreement (with Zambia): Economic and technical aid

Tibet

5/23/51	Agreement: "Peaceful liberation" of Tibet

Tunisia

9/25/58	Agreement: Exchange of goods (1959)
11/30/60	Agreement: Trade (1960-61)
7/14/61	Accord: Films
1/10/64,	Joint Communiqué: Talks (top level)
March(?)/65	– Trade (1965)

UAR: See Egypt

Uganda

4/21/65	Agreement: Economic and technical aid
7/16/65	Joint Communiqué: Talks (top level)

United Kingdom

4/12/52	Agreement: Trade
7/6/53	Accord: Trade
9/29/53	Exchange of Letters: Military incident in Pearl River Delta
6/1/56	Exchange of Notes: Trademark registration
10/11/63	Accord: Exchange of television films

United Nations

4/11/53	Agreement (with Korea [N]): Repatriation of sick and injured prisoners of war in Korea
6/8/53	Agreement (with Korea [N]): Repatriation of prisoners of war in Korea
7/27/53	Agreement: Armistice in Korea
7/27/53	Agreement (supplementary): Armistice in Korea
1/10/55	Joint Communiqué: Talks (top level)

Uruguay

12/17/55	Joint Statement: Promotion of trade

USA

9/10/55	Agreed Announcement: Repatriation

USSR

2/7/50	Agreement: Telecommunications
2/7/50	Agreement: Postal services
2/14/50	Joint Communiqué: Miscellaneous
2/14/50	Treaty: Friendship
2/14/50	Agreement: Chinese Changchun Railway, Port Arthur, and Dairen
2/14/50	Agreement: Credit
2/14/50	Exchange of Notes: Friendship, Chinese Changchun Railway, Port Arthur, Dairen, recognition of Mongolian People's Republic
2/14/50	Exchange of Notes: Transfer of Manchurian property
2/14/50	Exchange of Notes: Transfer of Soviet military compound in Peking
2/15/50	Protocol: Postal services
3/27/50	Agreement: Establishment of Sino-Soviet Non-Ferrous and Rare Metals Joint Stock Company
3/27/50	Agreement: Establishment of Sino-Soviet Petroleum Joint Stock Company
3/27/50	Agreement: Establishment of Sino-Soviet Civil Aviation Joint Stock Company
3/27/50	Agreement: Technical aid
4/19/50	Agreement: Trade

4/19/50	Protocol: Exchange of goods (1950)
4/19/50	Protocol: Delivery of goods
4/19/50	Protocol: Economic and technical aid (1950-52)
4/25/50	Protocol: Organization of Chinese Changchun Railway
7/20/50	Protocol: Completion of transfer of Soviet military compound in Peking
8/7/50	Protocol: Measures for transfer of Manchurian property
8/28/50	Agreement: Completion of transfer of Manchurian property
10/25/50	Protocol: Technical aid
1/2/51	Agreement: Navigation in boundary waters
1/16/51	Agreement: Railway
3/14/51	Agreement: Railway
6/15/51	Protocol: Exchange of goods (1951)
6/15/51	Protocol: Economic and technical aid (1951)
7/28/51	Agreement: Establishment of Sino-Soviet Joint Stock Company for Shipbuilding and Repair
12/6/51	Agreement: Technical aid
3/29/52	Protocol: Delivery of goods
4/12/52	Protocol: Exchange of goods (1952)
4/12/52	Protocol: Economic and technical aid (1952)
8/9/52	Agreement: Exchange of students, etc.
9/15/52	Joint Communiqué: Miscellaneous
9/15/52	Exchange of Notes: Port Arthur naval base
9/15/52	Joint Communiqué: Chinese Changchun Railway
9/15/52	Agreement (with Mongolia): Railway
9/21/52	Agreement (with Finland): Exchange of goods and payments (1952)
9/21/52	Agreement: Trade
12/31/52	Final Protocol: Chinese Changchun Railway
12/31/52	Miscellaneous: Transfer of insurance assets and operations in Manchuria
3/21/53	Protocol: Exchange of goods (1953)
3/21/53	Agreement: Loan
3/21/53	Protocol: Economic and technical aid (1953)
3/21/53	Agreement: Technical aid
Summer/53	Agreement: Economic and technical aid
10/31/53	Exchange of Notes: Postal services
1/23/54	Protocol: Exchange of goods (1954)
1/23/54	Protocol: Economic and technical aid (1954)
5/29/54	Contract: Films
8/21/54	Agreement: Radio cooperation
10/12/54	Communiqué: Miscellaneous
10/12/54	Joint Declaration: International situation
10/12/54	Joint Declaration: Policy towards Japan, peaceful coexistence, etc.
10/12/54	Joint Communiqué: Port Arthur naval base
10/12/54	Joint Communiqué: Transfer of Soviet shares in Joint Stock Companies
10/12/54	Agreement: Scientific and technical cooperation
10/12/54	Joint Communiqué: Railway construction
10/12/54	Joint Communiqué (with Mongolia): Railway construction
10/12/54	Agreement: Credit
10/12/54	Protocol: Economic and technical aid

12/28/54	Protocol: Scientific and technical cooperation
12/30/54	Agreement: Aviation
12/30/54	Protocol: Transfer of Soviet shares in Sino-Soviet Civil Aviation Joint Stock Company
12/30/54	Protocol: Transfer of Soviet shares in Sino-Soviet Non-Ferrous and Rare Metals Joint Stock Company
12/30/54	Protocol: Transfer of Soviet shares in Sino-Soviet Petroleum Joint Stock Company
12/30/54	Protocol: Transfer of Soviet shares in Sino-Soviet Joint Stock Company for Shipbuilding and Repair
2/11/55	Protocol: Exchange of goods (1955)
2/12/55	Protocol: Delivery of goods
4/27/55	Agreement: Technical aid in peaceful use of nuclear energy
5/24/55	Final Protocol: Port Arthur naval base
6/13/55(?)	Protocol: Scientific and technical cooperation
8/16/55	Agreement: Insect pests and plant diseases
10/17/55	Protocol (with Mongolia): Railway
11/29/55	"Arrangement": Films (copyright)
12/27/55	Protocol: Exchange of goods (1956)
12/27/55	Exchange of Notes: Delivery of goods
1/4/56	Joint Communiqué (with Mongolia): Railway
1/4/56	Agreement: Technical aid (aviation)
1/4/56	Communiqué: Scientific and technical cooperation
4/7/56	Joint Communiqué: Miscellaneous
4/7/56	Agreement: Technical aid
4/7/56	Agreement: Railway
6/14/56	Exchange of Notes: Delivery of goods
6/23/56	Protocol: Scientific and technical cooperation
7/3/56	Agreement (with Korea [N]): Rescue at sea
7/5/56	Agreement: Cultural cooperation
7/13/56	– Plan for cultural cooperation
7/25/56	Protocol (supplementary): Exchange of goods (1956)
8/18/56	Agreement: Investigation of Heilungkiang River Valley
9/18/56	– Transfer of Manchurian archives
12/24/56	Protocol: Scientific and technical cooperation
1/11/57	Joint Communiqué (with Hungary): Talks (lower level)
1/18/57	Joint Statement: Talks (top level)
1/18/57	– Plan for cultural cooperation
2/15/57	Protocol: Postal services and telecommunications
2/15/57	Protocol: Technical aid (post and telecommunications)
3/27/57	Protocol: Transfer of Red Cross hospital
4/10/57	Protocol: Delivery of goods
4/11/57	Protocol: Exchange of goods (1957)
4/11/57	Exchange of Notes: Trade
4/12/57	– Plan for radio cooperation
5/26/57	Communiqué: Talks (top level)
7/17/57	Protocol: Scientific and technical cooperation
10/3/57	Protocol (with Mongolia): Railway
11/21/57	– Plan for cultural cooperation
12/11/57	Protocol: Cooperation between Academies of Sciences

12/11/57	Protocol: Plan for cooperation between Academies of Sciences
12/21/57	Agreement: Commercial navigation in boundary waters
12/30/57	Protocol: Payments (noncommercial)
1/18/58	Agreement: Scientific and technical cooperation and technical aid
1/18/58	Protocol: Cooperation between Academies of Agricultural Sciences
1/18/58	Protocol: Scientific and technical cooperation between Ministries of Higher Education
4/23/58	Joint Communiqué: Trade talks
4/23/58	Protocol: Exchange of goods (1958)
4/23/58	Treaty: Commerce and navigation
7/4/58	Protocol: Scientific and technical cooperation
8/3/58	Joint Communiqué: Talks (top level)
8/8/58	Agreement: Technical aid
1/17/59	Protocol: Scientific and technical cooperation
1/17/59	Protocol: Technical aid
2/7/59	Agreement: Economic and technical aid (1959-67)
2/26/59	Protocol: Exchange of goods (1959)
3/11/59	– Joint use of Amur River
3/18/59	– Plan for cultural cooperation
6/1/59	– Plan for cooperation between Academies of Sciences
6/23/59	Treaty: Consular
7/4/59	Protocol: Scientific and technical cooperation
10/12/59	Protocol: Scientific and technical cooperation
12/12/59	Agreement: Currency
12/31/59	– Plan for cultural cooperation
1/29/60	Agreement: Forestry
2/20/60	– Plan for cooperation between Academies of Sciences
2/24/60	– Plan for scientific and technical cooperation
3/29/60	Protocol: Exchange of goods (1960)
6/10//60	Agreement: Cooperation between Academies of Medical Sciences
7/25/60	Protocol: Railway
2/4/61	– Plan for cultural cooperation
3/2/61	Press Communiqué: Economic and trade talks
3/20/61	Agreement: Currency
4/7/61	Protocol: Exchange of goods (1961)
4/7/61	Agreement: Postponed repayment of trade debts to USSR
4/7/61	Protocol: Delivery of sugar
4/8/61	Joint Communiqué: Trade talks
5/25/61	Agreement: Radio and television cooperation
5/25/61	Agreement: Cooperation between Academies of Sciences
6/19/61	Agreement: Economic cooperation
6/19/61	Agreement: Scientific and technical cooperation
6/21/61	Protocol: Cooperation between Academies of Sciences
6/21/61	– Plan for cooperation between Academies of Sciences
6/22/61	Communiqué: Talks on scientific, technical, and economic cooperation
8/26/61	Communiqué: Trade talks

8/31/61	Protocol (with Mongolia): Railway
10/6/61	Protocol: Scientific and technical cooperation
10/6/61	– Plan for cooperation between Academies of Sciences
1/23/62	– Plan for cultural cooperation
4/17/62	Joint Resolutions: Survey of Heilungkiang River Valley
4/20/62	Protocol: Exchange of goods (1962)
5/7/62	Accord: Registration of shipping
5/13/62	Protocol: Economic cooperation
6/23/62	Protocol: Plan for scientific and technical cooperation
7/21/62	– Plan for cooperation between Academies of Sciences
8/28/62	Protocol: Delivery of goods
12/1/62	Protocol: Aviation
2/23/63	– Plan for cultural cooperation
4/20/63	Protocol: Exchange of goods (1963)
4/20/63	Protocol: Preterm payment of trade debts to USSR
4/21/63	Communiqué: Trade talks
6/19/63	Protocol: Plan for scientific and technical cooperation
10/13/63(?)	Protocol: Railway
11/29/63	– Plan for cooperation between Academies of Sciences
2/29/64	– Plan for cultural cooperation
5/13/64	Protocol: Exchange of goods (1964)
5/13/64(?)	Protocol: Trade payments
4/29/65	Protocol: Exchange of goods (1965)
5/25/65	– Plan for cultural cooperation
6/12/65	Protocol: Scientific and technical cooperation
7/20/65	Protocol (supplementary): Exchange of goods (1965)
11/18/65	– Plan for cooperation between Academies of Sciences
4/4/66	Agreement: Aviation
4/19/66	Protocol: Exchange of goods (1966)
6/27/66	– Plan for cultural cooperation
11/6/66	Protocol: Scientific and technical cooperation
7/27/67	Protocol: Exchange of goods (1967)

Vietnam (N)

4/7/52	– Delivery of goods
11/6/52	Agreement: Postal services
8/25/53	Protocol: Small-scale trading in border areas
7/5/54	Communiqué: Geneva Conference on Indo-China
7/7/54	Protocol: Exchange of goods (1954)
7/7/54	Protocol: Small-scale trading in border areas
7/7/54	Protocol: Currency exchange in border areas
12/24/54	Agreement: Postal services
12/24/54	Protocol (supplementary): Postal services
12/24/54	Agreement: Telecommunications
12/24/54	Protocol: Technical aid (postal services and telecommunications)

12/24/54	Protocol: Technical aid (railway)
12/24/54	Protocol: Technical aid (aviation and meteorology)
12/24/54	Protocol: Technical aid (highways)
12/24/54	Protocol: Technical aid (water conservation)
5/25/55	Agreement: Railway
7/7/55	Joint Communiqué: Talks (top level)
7/7/55	Protocol: Cultural cooperation
7/7/55	Protocol: Exchange of goods by local state trading companies in border areas
7/7/55	Protocol: Small-scale trading in border areas
7/16/55	Contract: Films
11/25/55	Agreement: Currency
11/25/55	Protocol: Currency exchange in border areas
11/25/55	Protocol: Noncommercial remittances
11/25/55	Protocol: Clearance of trade
12/30/55	Contract: Purchase of airplanes
12/30/55	Contract: Technical aid (aviation)
4/5/56	Agreement: Aviation
6/18/56	Protocol: Delivery of goods
7/26/56	Agreement: Exchange of goods and payments (1956)
7/26/56	Protocol: Economic Aid
7/26/56	Protocol: Technical Aid
11/22/56	Joint Communiqué: Talks (top level)
12/20/56	Agreement: Maritime transport
3/30/57	– Plan for cultural cooperation
4/12/57	Agreement: Transit of cargoes
4/25/57	Joint Communiqué: Fisheries
5/15/57	Contract: Publications
7/31/57	Agreement: Exchange of goods and payments (1957)
7/31/57	Protocol: Economic and technical aid
7/31/57	Protocol: Exchange of goods by local state trading companies in border areas
7/31/57	Protocol: Small-scale trading in border areas
12/11/57	– Plan for cultural cooperation
3/15/58	Agreement: Radio cooperation
3/31/58	Agreement: Exchange of goods and payments (1958)
3/31/58	Exchange of Notes: Delivery of goods
3/31/58	Agreement: Technical aid
3/31/58	Protocol: Economic and technical aid
12/8/58	Protocol: Railway
1/16/59	Agreement: Cultural cooperation (1959-64)
1/16/59	– Plan for cultural cooperation
2/18/59	Agreement: Exchange of goods and payments (1959)
2/18/59	Agreement: Economic and technical aid
2/18/59	Exchange of Notes: Economic aid
2/18/59	Protocol: Economic and technical aid
2/18/59	Protocol: Technical aid
2/18/59	Protocol: Economic and technical aid
2/18/59	Protocol: Economic and technical aid
2/18/59	Agreement: Trade (1960-62)
6/20/59	Agreement: Currency (and noncommercial payments)

6/27/59	Protocol: Scientific survey of Gulf of Tonkin
12/31/59	Protocol: Technical aid
2/16/60	– Plan for cultural cooperation
3/7/60	Agreement: Exchange of goods and payments
3/7/60	Protocol: Exchange of goods and payments (1960)
3/7/60	Protocol: Economic and technical aid
3/7/60	– Trade in border areas
3/28/60	Protocol: Technical aid (specific project)
5/14/60	Joint Communiqué: Talks (top level)
11/28/60	Agreement: Scientific and technical cooperation
11/28/60	– Implementation of scientific and technical cooperation
11/28/60	Protocol: Plan for scientific and technical cooperation
1/31/61	Press Communiqué: Economic and trade talks
1/31/61	Agreement: Loans
1/31/61	Protocol: Economic and technical aid
1/31/61	Protocol: Exchange of goods (1961)
1/31/61	Protocol: Transit of cargo
1/31/61	Exchange of Notes: Small-scale trading in border areas
1/31/61	Exchange of Notes: Exchange of goods between local state trading companies in border areas
4/18/61	– Plan for cultural cooperation
6/15/61	Joint Communiqué: Talks (top level)
7/20/61	Protocol: Plan for scientific and technical cooperation
1/20/62	Protocol: Exchange of goods and payments (1962)
1/20/62	Exchange of Notes: Small-scale trading in border areas
1/20/62	Exchange of Notes: Exchange of goods between local state trading companies in border areas
5/5/62	– Plan for cultural cooperation
7/31/62	Protocol: Scientific and technical cooperation
8/22/62	Protocol: Fisheries
12/5/62	Communiqué: Trade talks
12/5/62	Treaty: Commerce and navigation
12/5/62	Protocol: Exchange of goods and payments (1963)
12/5/62	Exchange of Notes: Small-scale trading in border areas
12/5/62	Exchange of Notes: Exchange of goods between local state trading companies in border areas
12/24/62	– Plan for cultural cooperation
2/23/63	Protocol: Railway
5/16/63	Joint Statement: Talks (top level)
7/18/63	Protocol: Scientific and technical cooperation
8/10/63	Exchange of Notes: Scientific and technical cooperation
8/27/63	Agreement: Fisheries
10/24/63	Protocol: Exchange of goods and payments (1964)
10/24/63	Exchange of Notes: Small-scale trading in border areas
10/24/63	Exchange of Notes: Exchange of goods between local state trading companies in border areas
2/6/64	Agreement: Cooperation between Academies of Sciences
2/6/64	– Plan for cooperation between Academies of Sciences
3/9/64	Protocol: Railway
4/27/64	Contract: Publications

4/29/64	Accord (supplementary): Cultural cooperation
7/29/64	Agreement: Postal services
7/29/64	Agreement: Telecommunications
7/31/64	Agreement: Cooperation in public health work
8/12/64	Protocol: Scientific and technical cooperation
9/12/64	Protocol: Aviation
9/30/64	Protocol: Exchange of goods and payments (1965)
9/30/64	Exchange of Notes: Small-scale trading in border areas
9/30/64	Exchange of Notes: Exchange of goods between local state trading companies in border areas
6/19/65	– Plan for cultural cooperation
7/13/65	Agreement: Economic and technical aid
7/17/65(?)	Press Communiqué: Talks (lower level)
9/16/65	– Plan for cooperation in public health work
11/13/65	– Plan for cooperation between Academies of Sciences
12/3/65	Protocol: Scientific and technical cooperation
12/5/65	Agreement: Loan
12/5/65	Protocol: Exchange of goods and payments (1966)
3/21/66	Protocol: Railway
4/22/66	Protocol: Scientific and technical cooperation
5/28/66	– Plan for cultural cooperation
7/2/66	Agreement: Agricultural aid
8/21/66	– Plan for cooperation between Academies of Sciences
8/29/66	Agreement: Economic and technical aid
10/12/66	– Plan for cooperation in public health work
10/23/66	Minutes: Talks on scientific and technical cooperation
11/23/66	Agreement: Exchange of goods and payments (1967)
4/25/67	– Plan for cultural cooperation
8/3/67	Protocol: Scientific and technical cooperation
8/5/67	Agreement: Economic and technical aid

Yemen

1/12/58	Joint Communiqué: Talks (top level)
1/12/58	Treaty: Friendship
1/12/58	Treaty: Commerce
1/12/58	Agreement: Scientific and cultural cooperation
1/23/59	Protocol: Technical aid (specific project)
1/23/59	Protocol: Technical aid (specific project)
3/18/62	Protocol: Technical aid (specific project)
6/9/64	Joint Communiqué: Talks (top level)
6/9/64	Treaty: Friendship
6/9/64	Agreement: Economic and technical aid
6/9/64	Agreement: Cultural cooperation
3/23/65	Protocol: Technical aid (specific project)
5/3/65	– Plan for cultural cooperation
May/66	Protocol: Economic and technical aid
5/23/66	– Plan for cultural cooperation

Yugoslavia

2/14/56	Agreement: Postal services
2/14/56	Agreement: Telecommunications
2/17/56	Agreement: Trade (1956)
2/17/56	Exchange of Letters: Settlement of interpretation dispute (Trade Agreement)
2/17/56	Agreement: Payments
2/17/56	Exchange of Letters: Settlement of interpretation dispute (Payments Agreement)
2/17/56	Agreement: Scientific and technical cooperation
2/17/56	Exchange of Letters: Settlement of interpretation dispute (Scientific and Technical Cooperation Agreement)
4/27/56	Contract: Films
4/27/56	Contract: Films (newsreels)
1/4/57	Protocol: Exchange of goods (1957)
1/4/57	Exchange of Notes: Cooperation in aviation and marine insurance
1/4/57	Statute: Committee for Scientific and Technical Cooperation
6/7/57	Agreement: Cultural cooperation
6/7/57	– Plan for cultural cooperation
8/26/57	Exchange of Notes: Interpretation of 1956 Trade Agreement
11/1/57	– Scientific and technical cooperation
12/27/57	Protocol: Scientific and technical cooperation
2/28/58	Protocol: Exchange of goods (1958)
3/29/58	– Plan for cultural cooperation
3/18/59	Protocol: Exchange of goods (1959)
3/25/60	Protocol: Exchange of goods (1960)
7/15/61	Protocol: Exchange of goods (1961)
6/28/62	Protocol: Exchange of goods (1962)
11/5/63	Protocol: Exchange of goods (1963-64)
6/11/64	Protocol: Exchange of goods (1964)
5/11/65	Protocol: Exchange of goods (1965)
6/10/66	Protocol: Exchange of goods (1966)

Zambia

8/22/66	Agreement: Cultural cooperation
8/22/66	Joint Press Communiqué: Talks (top level)
4/28/67	Agreement: Trade
6/23/67	Agreement: Economic and technical aid
6/25/67	Joint Communiqué: Talks (top level)
9/5/67	Agreement (with Tanzania): Economic and technical aid (specific project)

Zanzibar: See **Tanzania**

Multilateral Agreements (four or more parties)

(Trilateral agreements, like bilateral, are listed in the preceding index, by non-Chinese parties)

12/5/50	"Acceptance" of 1947 Universal Postal Convention
7/13/52	"Recognition" of 1925 Protocol for Prohibition of Use in War of Asphyxiating, Poisonous, or Other Gases and of Bacteriological Methods of Warfare
7/13/52	"Recognition" of 1949 Convention for Amelioration of Condition of Wounded and Sick in Armed Forces in Field
7/13/52	"Recognition" of 1949 Convention for Amelioration of Condition of Wounded, Sick, and Shipwrecked Members of Armed Forces at Sea
7/13/52	"Recognition" of 1949 Convention relative to treatment of prisoners of war
7/13/52	"Recognition" of 1949 Convention relative to Protection of Civilian Persons in Time of War
7/31/53	Agreement: Railway (freight)
7/31/53	Agreement: Railway (passenger)
8/3/53	Agreement: Red Cross teams in Korea
10/2/53	Communiqué: Radio cooperation
1/1/54	Agreement: Railway
7/24/54	Final Declaration: Indo-China
4/24/55	Final Communique: Bandung Conference
3/26/56	Agreement: Nuclear research
6/12/56	Agreement: Fishery research, etc.
6/28/56	Regulations: Railway
9/23/56	Statute: Nuclear research
10/5/56	Agreement: Cooperation between institutes of agricultural research
10/31/56	Minutes: Conference on postal services, telecommunications, hydrography, and meteorology
6/7/57	Regulations: Railway
10/23/57	"Acceptance" of 1930 International Load Line Convention for Shipping
12/16/57	Agreement: Postal services and telecommunications
12/23/57	"Acceptance" of 1948 International Regulations for Preventing Collisions at Sea
3/24/58	Agreement: Scientific cooperation (specific project)
6/5/58	"Adherence" to 1929 Warsaw Convention for Unification of Certain Rules relating to International Carriage by Air
12/9/58	Protocol: Railway
1/21/59	Protocol: Nuclear research
4/28/59	Communiqué: Forthcoming summit conference on Germany and West Berlin
12/5/59	Protocols: Railway
12/11/59	Agreement: Currency (banking)
8/26/60	Protocol: Railway
11/28/60	Press Communiqué: Fisheries
4/27/62(?)	Protocol: Railway
6/22/62	(Miscellaneous): Railway
7/23/62	Declaration: Neutrality of Laos
7/23/62	Protocol: Military withdrawal from Laos

2/8/63	Agreement: Payments (noncommercial)
1/24/64	Protocol: Railway
4/15/64	Final Communiqué: Preparatory meeting of Second Afro-Asian Conference
9/10/64	Protocol: Railway
10/27/64	Protocol: Railway (passenger)
10/27/64	Protocol: Postal services and telecommunications
11/6/64	Protocol: Railway (freight)
11/27/64	Protocol: Postal services and telecommunications
2/21/65	Protocol: Railway
3/29/65	Minutes: Railway talks
6/30/65	Press Communiqué: Talks (top level)
7/15/65(?)	Protocol: Postal services and telecommunications
9/23/65	Communiqué: Games of Newly Emerging Forces (GANEFO)

Agreements by Subject Matter

This index is based on the general description of subject matter for the entries in the Calendar. Limited mostly to title categories, the headings and subheadings below do not constitute an exhaustive reference to the contents of the PRC agreements. This index should not, therefore, be used as a complete research tool, only as a reference to the contents of the Calendar.

Reference here is to entry number only. Descriptive references are supplied in the two preceding indexes.

In most cases in this index, we have adhered to the official title of the agreement, but some minor modifications have been made to clarify the exact nature of the contents. General aid agreements, for example, are often described officially as cooperation agreements, in accordance with diplomatic euphemism. Where they are economic or technical in nature, the euphemism is discarded and they are indexed here as aid agreements. Agreements officially described as providing for cooperation in science and technology are indexed under **Scientific and technical cooperation.**

Bei Fragen zur Produktsicherheit wenden Sie sich bitte an:
If you have any questions regarding product safety,
please contact:

Walter de Gruyter GmbH
Genthiner Straße 13
10785 Berlin
productsafety@degruyterbrill.com